Agehananda Bharati

THE TANTRIC TRADITION

SAMUEL WEISER INC.
New York

SAMUEL WEISER, INC.
734 Broadway
New York, N. Y. 10003

First Published by Rider & Co. 1965
Third Impression 1970
This Revised American Paperback Edition 1975

ISBN 0-87728-253-6

या देवी मम हृदये
शक्तिरूपेण संस्थिता ।
कमलायै सुकोमलायै
तदर्पितं प्रोत्साहित्रे ॥

To
LILLIAN Y. NAKAI

CONTENTS

Preface 9

1 The Philosophical Content of Tantra 13

2 Tantric Terminology 41

3 India and Tibet in Tantric Literature 58

4 Pilgrimage 85

5 On Mantra 101

6 On Intentional Language (Sandhābhāṣā) 164

7 On Initiation 185

8 Polarity Symbolism in Tantric Doctrine and Practice 199

9 *Sādhaka* and *Sādhanā*: the Aspirant and the Observance 228

10 The Tradition and the Target 279

Bibliographical Selection 303

Index 337

PREFACE

IT IS very difficult, and perhaps unnecessary, to be humble about a work of objective importance. Whether this book will evoke praise or censure from professional and lay audiences, there is no doubt that a study of the tantric tradition was overdue. Reams upon reams have been published, and are being published, on Indian religion and philosophy, and the Indian lore has long reached the paperback stage. Anyone reading an occidental language can obtain translations and interpretations of the Upaniṣads, the Bhagavadgītā, the Dhammapāda, Bardo Thodöl, Zen, and even some tougher material such as Buddhist Logic, or philosophy of grammar. Tantric literature, however, and the tantric forms of religion have been neglected or ignored on purpose and this is known to all oriental scholars, whatever their cultural and ethnical provenance. Arthur Avalon (Sir John Woodroffe's *nom-de-plume*) was an enthusiastic promoter of tantric studies at the beginning of this century. Although his work can hardly stand scholarly scrutiny, it was nevertheless instrumental in making tantrism and tantric studies respectable. In spite of it, hushed silence and mystery has kept surrounding tantric texts and the tantric lore, intensified perhaps rather than lessened subsequent to Sir John's valiant efforts.

In the vast bulk of indological and other orientalistic writing on indocentric religious thought, practice, and literature, serious work on the tantras has remained so limited and so specialized, that they have not come to form a genre within oriental studies, though they are as qualified as, say, the Upaniṣads and the Pāḷi Canon. For this omission, there is positively no excuse, unless prudishness, fear of social and scientific opprobrium, and other items of the puritanical calculus were held to be valid excuses. No doubt, tantrism is a delicate theme because of its intensive and extensive erotic ramifications. But then, the *Kāmasūtra* and a great amount of marginally erotic literature from the East have been published and are easily accessible to the western world; erotic sculpture and painting, whose existence had been systematically ignored or even denied by Indian and occidental authors until well after the Second World War, is now being reproduced, photographed, and published with serious commentary, and this has fed back into India whose cultural leaders and scholars are now accepting, albeit reluctantly, the great importance of this aspect of Indian culture. I suspect that this feed-back follows a pattern: Indian scholars during the past one hundred years have often resuscitated interest in Indian topics in direct emulation of their western colleagues. The concupiscent fringe of Indian culture has been so well documented and brought to light that all scholars in India except the popularizers of the Vivekananda and 'modern-Swami' oriented Hinduism acknowledge it, with a shrug as it were. Though this may seem to be a bizarre conclusion, it does appear that sex, when viewed as an element in secular Indian culture, is no longer tabu; it remains tabu when shown to be part of Indian religion and philosophy, or of that cultural pattern which Indians call 'spiritual' in their discourse with occidentals, contrasting it with the 'materialism' of the West.

The exquisite work done by a few scholars who braved potential and actual criticism, and who dealt with tantric material—I am thinking mainly of Professors Mircea Eliade (Paris–Chicago), H. V. Guenther (Banaras–Saskatoon), D. L. Snellgrove (London), G. Tucci (Rome)—appears like a drop in the ocean; an ocean that contains much redundant water, let it be said: outstanding scholars still produce translations and treatises on the Ṛgveda, the Bhagavadgītā and other overdone texts, when their energy could be profitably directed towards fields that have barely been entered upon—tantrism among the foremost.

Indian authors who study tantrism, the two Bhattacharyas, S. B. Dasgupta, Chintaharan Chakravarti and some few others do so with a persistent apologetic note which, to our feeling, jeopardizes the advancement of tantric studies in the area most germane to them. I have yet to meet an Indian-born scholar who stands squarely by the tantric tradition. They seem to feel that tantrism may be studied and written about provided their own identification is Vedāntic or otherwise orthodox, either in the classical or in the modern sense; in other words, if they conform to the official culture of India, which is decidedly non- and anti-tantric. The official Indian culture, formulated by Vivekananda and his numerous admitted or unadmitted followers, by Gandhi and Radhakrishnan, keep tantrism well outside the ken of permissible interests.

The motivation and the genesis of this study are as eclectic as tantrism itself: although the author feels committed to certain features of the tantric tradition, both as member of a monastic order which has stood in a precarious, overtly hostile, but psychologically and culturally loaded relationship to tantrism, and as a cultural anthropologist with a strong linguistic predilection, he had to proceed with caution and with firmness. Where a spade is a spade, it has to be called a spade. Fortunately, spades are not always spades in tantrism, and this fact should make the study more palatable to the propounders of India's official culture.

This book was written with the financial support of the Inner Asia Project of the Far Eastern Institute of the University of Washington, in the lovely north-western Pacific city of Seattle. As a research associate in that institute, my Indic interests were marginal to the main direction of Inner Asian research, and I regarded my contribution to the Inner Asia Project as a series of feeder services. One of the advantages of affluent academia lies in the fact that a scholar may study and publish things for which he is not really paid. The employing powers that be, not only connive at this institutionalized deviation from a declared purpose, but encourage their pursuit, and this I believe very largely accounts for the incredible advancement of North American research.

I am deeply indebted to a fairly wide, but strictly defined, number of people for this accomplishment. Dr. Hellmut Wilhelm, Professor of Chinese Studies, Associate Director of the

Far Eastern Institute and doyen of Sinological research in that area, the most profound and versatile and, let me add, the interpersonally warmest of all my friends and advisers, has been a constant source of help and inspiration. Professor Herbert W. Passin, now at Columbia University, Prof. Leon N. Hurvitz, University of British Columbia, Lama Kunga Labrang, Senior Abbot of the Jekundo Monastery in Central Tibet, now with the Inner Asia Project at the University of Washington, have helped, in equally important though contextually very different ways, to create the climate in which this sort of investigation could be accomplished. The leisure and munificence which enabled me to complete this study is due to Dr. George E. Taylor, Chairman of the Far Eastern & Russian Institute at the University of Washington. Had it not been for his venturesome attitude in inviting and harbouring scholars with unconventional and sometimes weird interests, this book might not have been written. I am deeply grateful to Professor Mircea Eliade (Sorbonne-Paris, and University of Chicago) for his kind and paternal criticism in the initial stages of my research, and for his constant encouragement and the ideal of scholarship which he has been setting for a younger generation of scholars. To him, and to Professor Chintaharan Chakravarti of the University of Calcutta I am also grateful for permitting me to use bibliographical material they had previously published. Further, to the publishers of *History of Religions* (Chicago) and of the *Journal of the American Oriental Society,* for allowing me to use some of my own material already published in these learned periodicals.

Most importantly, however, my gratitude goes to Mahãmahopãdhyaya Gopinath Kaviraj of Sigra, Varanasi, one time librarian at the Government Sanskrit College in that holy city; that most knowledgeable Hindu tantric and scholar, who by blessings given and letters sent helped me to persist and continue, prodding me when the going was rough.

AGEHANANDA BHARATI

Nairobi, Kenya
1964

I

THE PHILOSOPHICAL CONTENT OF TANTRA

THROUGHOUT this book I shall keep cautioning readers about the use of 'philosophy' and 'philosophical' in our context. Historians of western philosophy—beginning with Erdmann and Überweg in the last century, and continuing with virtually all academical philosophers of the western world up to date—have denied Indian thought the title 'philosophy'. Indologists and oriental scholars, however, have been using the term for Hindu, Buddhist, and Jain thought quite indiscriminately—and this did not matter too much because there was and there is the assumption that the twain, professional orientalists and professional philosophers, do not meet. I think this is wrong. It is extremely difficult to make them meet, because a lot of cross-disciplinary studies are needed for both—the philosophers will have to read some original tracts of Indian thought and its paraphrase in other Asian languages; and the orientalists will have to acquire some knowledge of contemporary philosophy, especially on the terminological side. This has not been done: scholars who wrote and write on Indian 'philosophy'—Stcherbatsky, Raju, Glasenapp, Edgerton, Radhakrishnan, to mention but a few—did not seriously attempt to read modern philosophy and use its accurate terminology. All of them somehow assume that western philosophy had reached its climax with Kant, Hegel, or Bradley, and hence they do not feel the need to improve on their archaic terminology. I think they are mistaken. Terminologies previous to that of the analytical schools of twentieth-century philosophy are deficient.[1] It could be objected that contemporary occidental philosophy may be unequal to the task of providing adequate terminology for Indian thought patterns; this may be so, but pre-twentieth-century occidental philosophy is even less adequate; modern philosophy uses all the tools of the classical philosophical tradition, plus the considerably sharper and more sophisticated tools of multi-value-logic, logical empiricism, and linguistic analysis.

However, with some very few exceptions, authors on Indian thought, both western and Indian, have not tried to acquire and use these better tools—they have so far been satisfied to carry on with the philosophically outdated tools of the European traditions of the last two centuries, especially of the Fichte-Kant-Hegel tradition, widened in size, but not in quality, by additions of such British philosophers as Bradley and Bosanquet. Exceptions so far have been few: Professor Ingalls at Harvard, and his student Professor K. Potter, are known to this author to avail themselves of contemporary philosophical terminology when dealing with Indian material; and Professor H. V. Guenther, formerly at Banaras, who consciously and determinedly capitalizes on the work of such thinkers as C. D. Broad, Ayer, Russell, Wisdom, Veatch, Strawson, Ullmann, and a large number of less known British and American teachers of philosophy.

If I may venture a guess as to why writers on Indian philosophy refused to acquire and use more up-to-date tools, I believe the main reason is not so much inertia but the idea that Kant, Hegel, and Bradley, etc., were spirits more kindred to the Indians; that their idealistic or at least metaphysical predilections qualified them better for the providing of interpretative concepts than the twentieth-century anti-metaphysical, anti-systematic, anti-'idealistic' philosophers ('idealistic' in the popular, non-philosophical sense, and emotive equivalent of 'truth-seeking' as opposed to 'fact-seeking'). Here again they err; in the first place, the great philosophers of the European eighteenth and nineteenth centuries were no more favourably inclined towards Indian philosophy than are modern analytical thinkers; but more importantly, the fact of a system of thought being closer in emotive tone to another system of thought does not guarantee that the former is a competent arbiter of the latter. This wrong assumption goes back to an even older historical phenomenon—the great attraction, largely sentimental, which nineteenth-century German classical scholars and poets felt for things Indian in the belief of a 'kindred soul'; this is being echoed in India by the majority of pandits and holy men: it is very hard to convince pandits and monks in India that Sanskrit is *not* taught and spoken in high schools in Germany, and that Germans are *not* the only Sanskrit scholars outside India.

I therefore submit that students of Indian philosophy should learn to use the more precise terminology of contemporary western philosophy when they attempt to translate and define Indian philosophical texts. From this standpoint it might have been wise to substitute 'philosophy' by some such word as 'ideology' or 'speculative patterns' for the bulk of Indian (and hence Tibetan) scholastic lore; in fact, short of logic (*nyāya, tarka*), Indian philosophy has been ideology. Yielding to the majority, however, we shall continue to refer to these patterns—including tantric patterns—as 'philosophy', bearing the said strictures in mind. Indian thought does not contain much of what modern philosophers would call 'philosophy'—but they would not object to tantric thought being added as a new branch of investigation: as 'psycho-experimental-speculation'; I recommend this lengthy phrase, because it summarizes tantric 'philosophy'; but I shall not use it unless it proves acceptable to scholars at some later date; I shall use 'philosophy' in this book, but whenever I speak about tantric 'philosophy' it is to be understood as shorthand for 'psycho-experimental-speculation'.

If the old philosophical terminology is used the contents of most Indian systems can indeed be told in very few words, but I am convinced that this succinctness is as deceptive and vague as the terminology of classical philosophy. It is this deceptiveness to which an Indian scholar like S. B. Dasgupta succumbed when he wrote about tantric literature, that it was:

'. . . an independent religious literature, which utilized relevant philosophical doctrines, but whose origin may not be traced to any system or systems of philosophy; it consists essentially of religious methods and practices which have been current in India from a very old time. The subject matter of the tantras may include esoteric yoga, hymns, rites, rituals, doctrines and even law, medicine, magic and so forth . . .'[2]

The same scholar quotes a Buddhist tantric definition of tantrism, '*tanyate vistrīyate jñānamanena iti tantram*'.[3] Now the indologist who uses classical occidental terminology would render this' that by which knowledge (or wisdom, intuition, etc.) is extended or elaborated, is tantra'. The vagueness of this translation —unnoticed by indologists because they are so used to it—rests on an inadequate rendition of '*jñāna*'; without going into an elaborate analysis of '*jñāna*', let me say that 'wisdom' or 'intuitive wisdom' are too vague, and for Buddhist tantra incorrect. Professor Guenther translates *jñāna* (*ye śes*) 'analytical appreciative understanding', and this is borne out by the Sanskrit definition; for if *jñāna* were the immutable wisdom, say, of the Vedāntic variety, it could neither be extended nor elaborated. The Brahmanical—or at least the Vedānta monist's '*jñāna*' is a state of being, not one of knowing; the root *jñā*, in its Vedāntic sense, does not connote cognition, but the irrefutable intuition of a single, all-including entity, other than which nothing persists; yet, even the term 'intuition' is not really adequate here, because it still implies an intuiting subject and an intuited object, whereas the Vedāntic *jñāna* does not tolerate any such dichotomy.

We must now show what philosophy is common to all Indian schools of religious thought; and then, what philosophy is common between Hinduism and Mahāyāna Buddhism of the tantric variety; we can omit Theravāda Buddhism and Jainism from the survey, because their axiomatic differences are too great on all levels from the subject-matter of this study. It is not advisable to try to list here the differences between tantric and non-tantric forms of Hinduism and Buddhism, simply because they are not of a philosophical order. In other words, there is nothing in Buddhist and Hindu tantric philosophy which is not wholly contained in some non-tantric school of either. Or to put it differently, tantrism has not added any *philosophical* novelty to Hinduism and Buddhism; I do not even think that it emphasizes certain aspects of Mahāyāna or Hindu philosophy more than do the respective non-tantric doctrines preceding it. To give an illustration: The Mādhyamikas teach and emphasize the complete identity of *nirvāṇa* and *saṃsāra*, i.e. of the absolute and the phenomenal modes of existence; the Vajrayāṇa Buddhists take this notion for granted—it is on the ritualistic or contemplatively methodical side that differences arise, and these are indeed fundamental. In a similar fashion the non-tantric monists or Śivites (Śaṃkarācārya and his school, or the Southern Śiva-Āgama teachers), pronounce and emphasize the oneness of Śiva and Śakti, and so do the Hindu tantrics of the Śākta schools—they do not add any philosophical or speculative innovation to their non-tantric antecedents—but they do different things and practise different *sādhanā* (contemplative exercises). There is thus no difference between tantric and non-tantric philosophy, as speculative eclecticism is pervasive; there is all the difference in the practical, the *sādhanā*-part of tantrism.

There are perhaps just two elements common to all Indian philosophy: first, the axiom of inevitable metempsychosis (this is shared with *all* religious systems indigenous in India) and the notion of possible emancipation connected with the former as the apodosis of a single proposition, the axiom of metempsychosis being its protasis.[4]

The second common element is the notion of some absolute which underlies the phenomenal universe. Indian scholars and other votaries of the oneness of all religions have postulated that the Vedāntic *brahman* and the Mahāyānist *śūnya* are the same concept, the difference being merely terminological. I shall withhold my judgment on this point at present. If *śūnya* and the *brahman* are concepts which lean on the same proclivity to absolutize the permanent as experienced or inferred beneath or alongside with the ephemeral, this would not suffice to establish the identity of *śūnyatā* and the *brahman*. The Mahāyāna Buddhist would certainly reject this identification, and the possible rejoinder that he does so because he has to insist on being fundamentally different from the Brahmin tradition is not justified until there is a precise analytical formulation of *brahman* and *śūnyatā* juxtaposed. No such formulation has come forth so far.[5]

The element common to Hindu and Mahāyāna philosophy is what Indian scholastic methodology calls *samanvaya*, i.e. the institutionalized attitude of reconciling discursively contrary notions by raising them to a level of discourse where these contradictions are thought to have no validity. It is due to *samanvaya* that the gap between the phenomenal (*saṃvṛti*, *vyavahāra*) and the absolute (*paramārtha*) truths spares the Hindu or Mahāyāna thinker the philosophical embarrassment the outsider feels when he views *paramārtha* and *vyavahāra* philosophy side by side, in Indian religious literature.

What distinguishes tantric from other Hindu and Buddhist teaching is its systematic emphasis on the identity of the absolute (*paramārtha*) and the phenomenal (*vyavahāra*) world when filtered through the experience of *sādhanā*. Tantric literature is not of the philosophical genre; the stress is on *sādhanā*. But it seems to me that one philosophical doctrine inherent in esoteric Hinduism and Mahāyāna Buddhism—especially of the Mādhyamika school—the identity of the phenomenal and the absolute world—was singled out by all tantric teachers as the nucleus around which all their speculation was to revolve; I also believe that the doctrinary discrepancies between the various schools of speculative thought are *really* resolved in tantric *sādhanā*: all scholastic teachers in India declare that there is *samanvaya*, but the tantric actually experiences it; I have tried to elaborate a model of this phenomenon, which had been suggested to me by my own preceptor, the late Víśvānanda Bhāratī.[6]

The other philosophical doctrine common to Hindu and Buddhist tantra is probably due to some sort of doctrinary diffusion. It is of the type of a universe-model: reality is one, but it is to be grasped through a process of conceptual and intuitive polarization.[7] The poles are activity and passivity, and the universe 'works' through their interaction. The universe ceases to 'work'—i.e. its state of absolute oneness and quiescence is realized—when these two poles merge. They are merged doctrinarily by the repeated declaration of their fundamental oneness, and are experienced by the tantric's reliving of this merger through his integrating *sādhanā* or spiritual disciplines.

Only this much is really common between Hindu and Buddhist tantric doctrines, for their respective ascriptions to the two poles are obverse to each other. The Hindu assigned the male symbol apparatus to the passive, the female totheactive pole; the Buddhist did the opposite; the Hindu assigned the knowledge principle to the passive male pole, and the dynamic principle to the active female pole; the Vajrayāṇa Buddhist did it the other way round.

All tantric philosophy sets forth the power of a conceptual decision, not withstanding the fact that the execution of ritualistic contemplation is carried out in minute detail. It appears that conceptual decision leading to permanent enstasis (*jñāna, bodhi*) has higher prestige than other procedures. Thus we find this statement in the account of a Tibetan teacher:

'by a doctrine which is similar to the application of fat to a wound when an arrow piece remains inside, nothing can be reached; by a doctrine which is similar to tracing the footsteps of a thief to a monastery when he had escaped to the forest and mountain, nothing can be gained, so also *having declared one's own mind to be non-substantial* (by its nature), the fetters of the outside world will fall off by themselves, because all is *śūnyatā*.'[8]

I have no scriptural evidence for this surmise, but I feel that the tendency to supersede the necessity of minute exertion by a basically intellectual act is a typical tantric element of speculation. We find an important analogy in orthodox Brahmanical thought: Śaṃkarācārya declared that the cognitive understanding of the meaning of the four great Upaniṣadic dicta, 'this *ātma* is *brahma*', 'I am *brahma*', 'thou art that', and 'the conscious self is *brahma*', results in immediate liberation. Most of his contemporaries and particularly his later opponents (especially Rāmānuja in the eleventh century, and his school) opposed this notion vehemently, insisting on prolonged observance and discipline. Śaṃkarācārya's attitude towards tantra is ambivalent, but there is reason to believe that he was profoundly influenced by tantric notions.[9]

Romanticizing German indology was highly enthusiastic about Indian thought, and this is one of the reasons why Hindu pandits are full of praise for German indology.[10] Thus, H. V. Glasenapp wrote:

'. . . the notion that the whole universe with the totality of its phenomena forms one single whole, in which even the smallest element has an effect upon the largest, because secret threads connect the smallest item with the eternal ground of the world, this is the proper foundation of all tantric philosophy.'[11]

There is decidedly such a thing as a common Hindu and Buddhist tantric ideology, and I believe that the real difference between tantric and non-tantric traditions is methodological: tantra is the psycho-experimental interpretation of non-tantric lore. As such, it is more value-free than non-tantric traditions; moralizing, and other be-good clichés are set aside to a far greater extent in tantrism than in other doctrine. By 'psycho-experimental' I mean 'given to experimenting with one's own mind', not in the manner of the speculative philosopher or the poet, but rather in the fashion of a would-be psychoanalyst who is himself being analysed by some senior man in the trade. This, I think, is the most appropriate analogue in the modern world: the junior psychoanalyst would be the disciple, the senior one the guru. The tantric adept cares for liberation, like all other practising Hindus or Buddhists; but his method is different, because it is purely experimental—in other words, it does not confer ontological or existential status upon the objects of his meditations. This is the reason why tantrics are not in the least perturbed by the proliferation of gods and goddesses, minor demons and demonesses, and other creatures of various density and efficacity—they do not attempt to reduce their number, for these are necessary anthropomorphic ways of finding out 'what is inside the mind'. The tantric entertains one or two axioms, no doubt—the absolutistic and the phenomenal-noumenal-identity axioms, but they are not really important except as speculative constructs. Similarly, the psychologist entertains a few axioms, as for instance the one identifying sanity with adjustment to the cultural milieu of his environment which he shares with the anthropologists interested in 'culture and personality', or the axiom that there is such a thing as mental illness;[12] but the practising analyst is not really interested in these axioms as he carries on his work—in fact, these axiomatic notions are quite irrelevant to the execution of his work. They are 'at the back of his mind', but he can leave them there when he works.

To sum up the rambling question whether or not we should make a distinction between what is specifically tantric and what is not. On the theological and speculative level the answer is decidedly yes. All tantrics flout traditional, exoteric orthodoxy, all put experiment above conventional morality denying ultimate importance to moralistic considerations which is not contradicted by the fact that most tantric texts pay initial homage to conventional conceptions of morality; and all agree that their specific method is dangerous, and radical, and all claim that it is a shortcut to liberation.

I do not believe that either the Hindus or the Buddhists were consciously working out a similar psycho-experimental pattern, and I do not think that they were making a conscious effort to unite Hindus and Buddhists, even though they may well have been aware of great similarities between their practices. But B. Bhattacharya's statement

'. . . the *kālacakra* or Circle of Time[13] as the highest god was set up by a particular section which wanted that the Hindus should unite with the Buddhists under the common nonsectarian banner of the Time-God Kālacakra in order to present a united front against the cultural penetration of Semitic peoples which had already invaded Central Asia and Iran.'[14]

hardly deserves attention except as a statement *à la mode*.

Hindu scholars, with no exception to my knowledge, believe in a virtual doctrinary identity of Advaita monism and Mādhyamika absolutism, and this is detrimental to the study of Indian absolutistic philosophy, and irrelevant to any tantric study. B. Bhattacharya describes *śūnya* and the contemplation of it exactly like the *brahman* of the Advaita monist; he refers to the meditative process of the Mādhyamikas as 'securing oneness with the *śūnya* or *Infinite Spirit*!'[15] I think the similarity of diction and style is a trap into which Indian scholars readily fall because there is no tradition of textual criticism in India. Advayavajra, a famous Buddhist tantric teacher, says: '*Pratibhāsa* (i.e. apparent reality) is (like) the bridegroom, the beloved one, conditioned only (i.e. subject to the chain of dependent origination, *pratītya samutpāda*, Tibetan *brel*), and Śūnyatā, if She were corpse-like, would not be (likened to) the bride.'[16] Now one of India's authorities on Buddhist tantrism, the late Pandit Haraprasad Sastri, misunderstood this singularly important passage, when he paraphrased it:[17]

'here *śūnyatā* is the bride and its reflection is the bridegroom. Without the bridegroom the bride is dead. If the bride is separated, the bridegroom is in bondage . . .'

H. P. Sastri was probably aware of the fact that the main doctrine of Vajrayāṇa theology is essencelessness in the true Buddhist sense. Yet he was misled by the powerful modern Indian scholastic trend to see *advaita*-monistic doctrine in Mahāyāna Buddhism.[18] 'Without the bridegroom the bride is dead'—this is the exact inverse analogy of the Hindu tantric dictum 'Śiva is a corpse without Śakti' (*śivaḥ śaktivihīnaḥ śavaḥ*), which provides an important rule for Hindu tantric iconography.[19] H. P. Sastri was obviously under the spell of this pervasive tantric proposition, else it is hard to see why one of the most eminent old-time Bengali Sanskritists should have misinterpreted this important passage.

There is also a subtler reason for the tendency to identify Buddhist and Hindu tantric doctrine. Buddhist tantrism has borrowed many of its lesser deities from Hinduism, or at least from the large stock of deities present in areas which nurtured Hindu, Buddhist, and aboriginal Indian mythology.[20] With the Indian love for enumeration and classification, mythological groups of 3, 4, 5, etc., items abound just as they do in doctrinary groups—and it is quite irrelevant which came first, Hindu or Buddhist tantrics, in the application of these charismatic group numbers; thus, for example, an old Hindu tantric text[21] explains the five faces of Śiva as representing his five aspects as Vāmadeva, Tatpuruṣa, Aghora, Sadyojāta, and Īśana, each of which is a frequent epithet of Śiva, with slightly varying modes of meditation prescribed for each of them in Śivite literature. To these aspects, different colours, different directional controls, etc., are ascribed. The five *dhyāni* Buddhas also have different colours, directions, etc., ascribed to them, control over which being the domain of each of the Buddhas.[22] These arrangements in numerically identical groups prompt many scholars to equate the two mythologies. This is a perfectly permissible procedure if we study diffusion of concepts as anthropologists; but the moment we extend diffusion patterns from mythology to philosophy we are tempted to reason fallaciously, according to the invalid model 'in mythology, Buddhist and Hindu, 3 (4, 5, 7, etc.) tokens within one theme, *therefore* in philosophy, Buddhist and Hindu, 3 (4, 5, 7, etc.) tokens within one theme'. We tend to forget that philosophical concepts, even when they are *numbered* according to a traditional pattern, develop and change much more independently than do mythological concepts, for the simple reason that Indian mythological icons, once created, are hardly ever modified, because there is no impetus to modify them—on the contrary, the contemplatives feel more successful if they succeed in visualizing the object in accordance with the prescribed icon.* There is a lot of impetus, however, to amplify philosophical doctrines—the teaching or the commentary of a revered preceptor is never as unambiguous a thing as an icon: in the mind of the pious scholar, an icon cannot be improved upon, a commentary must be constantly clarified and amended, due to its inevitable complexity. This dichotomy in the Hindu and Buddhist scholar's attitude—no

* I am using 'icon' in the modern analytical sense, as any fixed sensuous concept, regardless of whether it is conceptual or materialized in artistic representation.

modification of icons, but constant elaboration of philosophical concepts—is not shared, say, by the Roman or Greek Catholic scholar: there are no canons about how Christ's body or face should be modelled or painted. Hindu and Buddhist iconography prescribes pictorial icons in exact detail, and there is very little scope for modification.

The Hindu scholastic's effort to explain Mahāyāna doctrine in terms of Vedāntic notions is of course much older than the nineteenth century, but its western echo or counterpart reinforced the trend. Deussen's generation was not familiar with medieval Hindu tantric texts which assimilated Vajrayāṇa doctrine into a Hindu frame. European indology perhaps arrived at this notion independently, prompted by the inherent romanticism of early indology. In a text which I would date between the twelfth and fourteenth centuries, a Kashmiri scholar discusses the word *makārā* as a name of the Universal Goddess (Devī); he there describes her as 'beholding her own body as both *śūnya* and non-*śūnya*'[23] which he then glosses in Vedāntic fashion: '*śūnya* means of the form of pure mind, but not non-existent by nature, and non-*śūnya* means polluted by māyā'.[24]

It is quite possible that Makārā was a Hindu tantric goddess, if the name is really a personification of the '5-m-s' *pañcamakāra*[25] as it does seem to be. She is not listed in Bhattacharya's *Buddhist Iconography*, nor in the fairly exhaustive *Sādhanāmālā*. However, it is impossible to say which deity was Hindu and which Buddhist in medieval tantric Kashmir. By that time, Hindu scholars had come to avoid terms like *śūnya* together with other terms of a specifically Buddhist flavour, and Sitikaṇṭha's apology for its use in the prescribed meditation on that goddess would indicate that her *dhyāna* was originally Buddhist.

Modern Brahmin scholars who remain unfamilar and hence unaffected by occidental literature on Indian thought, continue to antagonize the Buddhist doctrines about as vehemently as their classical forbears. Thus, Pdt. Lakṣmīnātha Jhā, former Head of the Department of Indian Philosophy at the Sanskrit Mahāvidyālaya, Banaras, says: 'If the root of phenomenal existence be manifest to intuition, then what is the foundation of phenomenal existence whereof it is a manifestation, since everything (according to *Mādhyamikas*) is *śūnya*? Hence, the doctrine that everything is *śūnya* conflicts with everything, and because it denies a foundation for anything, it has to be rejected.'[26]

It is as yet impossible for a Hindu or a Buddhist unfamiliar with occidental methods of philosophical analysis to state the basic difference of Hindu and Buddhist tantric philosophy without a slant and with objectively valid precision. There is a lot of precise terminology within the scholastic traditions of India, and *a fortiori* of Tibet, but neither the Hindu nor the Buddhist has developed a terminology sufficient to step out from the *ātma* and no-*ātma* complex. This we can do at present perhaps only by aid of non-Sanskritic analytical language. This is the situation: the Hindu insists on the notion of a Self, or a transcendent-immanent personality principle, or an *ātman* or *brahman*. The Buddhist, in theory at least, denies any self or any super-self. However, in practice the Vajrayāṇa and to a certain extent all Mahāyāna Buddhist doctrines have a sort of *Ersatz*-self or super-self, something which defies any treatment in terms of the Hindu 'entity-postulating' languages, yet it has some sort of subsistence. Now I believe that the crux of the matter lies in the fact, not hitherto mentioned by any scholar known to me, that the principle, or quasi-entity which Mahāyāna and Vajrayāṇa accepts (*śūnyatā*, Buddhahood, and all the complexes which tantric Buddhism personifies in its deities, populating the universe with psycho-experimentally necessary and highly ingenuous anthropomorphic hypostases of philosophical 'non-entities', for example, the Goddess *Nairātmyā*—Tibetan *bdag med ma*) is not a principle accepted *in lieu of* the Hindu entity, but it is a principle accepted *in spite of* the Hindu principle, and arrived at by totally different speculative processes. The Buddhist teachers must have been aware of the danger of postulating anything that might smack of the teachings which the Buddha had rejected; I am not persuaded by the rather facile assumption, shared by many Indian and occidental scholars, that the later Buddhists had forgotten that the mainstay of Buddhism had been dismantling the notion of Being and of Self; nor by the oft-propounded idea that an ideological group which keeps up its distinct identity chiefly by refuting another ideological group gradually assumes the latter's terms and ideas. This may be so among political groups (the Nazis developed a system and a language which was very similar, in many points, to communism which they fought), but it is hardly believable about scholars who are critically aware of their doctrinary differences from the ideology which they oppose. In other words, I cannot bring myself to believe that Asaṅga or Advayavajra or any other tantric Buddhist teacher should have been unaware of the possible charge of 'your *śūnyatā* or your *nairātmya* are so thoroughly rarefied that there is no difference left between them and Brahmin notions of Being'. *Śaṃkarācārya* was called a crypto-Buddhist (*prachanna-bauddha*) by his Brahmin opponents, because his *brahman* was so utterly rarefied and depersonalized that it reminded the less informed of the assumed Buddhist nihil, the *śūnya*.[27] Had any of the famous Buddhist teachers been charged with being a crypto-Hindu, such a charge would have probably been recorded. As it is, scholastic Hindus feel a strong doctrinary resentment against Buddhist doctrine, and it is only the occidentalized, 'all-religions-are-basically-one' Hindus who declare the Buddhist teachings as a form of Hinduism or vice versa. The Buddhist dialectician proceeds from the denial of any entity, from the axiom of momentariness, and arrives at the notion of *śūnyā*; the Hindu dialectician has a built-in deity as the basis for his speculations on a self, on a static entity. To the outsider, however, the rarefied *brahman* of the Vedānta monists and the Buddhist *śūnya* may look similar or 'virtually' identical as intellectual constructs. But they are not. Buddhism has no ontology, no metaphysics; Hinduism has a powerful ontology—this is the one unbridgeable difference between all of its forms and Buddhism of all schools.

That the psycho-experimentalist, the tantric, or anyone who takes *sādhanā* seriously (and taking *sādhanā* seriously means regarding it as more important, though not necessarily more interesting, than philosophy), may come to feel that there is some sort of identity between *śūnyatā* and *brahman*, is a different matter: it does not conflict with what is said above, and there is no gainsaying the fact that reports on the 'feeling' in Vedānta-trained enstasis and in tantric enstasis is very similar indeed. Yet, even if two authentic reports on enstatic experience should coincide, it does not follow from this that the schools from which these reports derive teach a similar philosophy. The notion upheld among religious teachers in India today that a specific *sādhanā* yields a specific philosophy or vice versa, I believe to be wrong; it hails from an understandable pious wish that the corpus of doctrine, embodied in one tradition, should be autonomous, and should encompass both *sādhanā* and philosophy.[28] To put this point succinctly: no specific *sādhanā* follows from any one philosophy, nor does any specific philosophy follow from any particular *sādhanā*. Our own tantric tradition provides the best illustration: tantric *sādhanā* follows a single pattern, Vajrayāṇa Buddhist and Hindu tantric *sādhanā* is indistinguishable, in spite of the immense disparity between the two philosophies.

I admit, however, that the language of Vajrayāṇa suggests ontology to a degree where a scholar, who did not know Hindu or Buddhist philosophy, but did know Sanskrit and modern occidental philosophy, would be at a loss to realize that Buddhist philosophy was non-ontological as opposed to Hindu philosophy. To quote a typical passage from a Vajrayāṇa text: 'of firm essence, unfragmented, unbreakable, indivisible in character, incombustible, indestructible, *śūnyatā* is *vajra* (i.e. the Buddhist Void is the Buddhist Adamantine, the *Vajra*).'[29] Word for word, this description of *sūnyatā* and *vajra* could apply to the *brahman* of the Vedāntin, and for that of all Hindus, and I do not think there is any adjective in this passage which has not been applied to the *brahman*, with the exception perhaps of *asauśīryam* (lit. 'unperforated'), which I have not seen in a Hindu text; 'unbreakable, indivisible, incombustible', almost in this order, is the description of the infinite *brahman* in the Bhagavadgītā.[30] It is futile to speculate why the tantric writers availed themselves of terms which were excessively popular with their Brahmin opponents, in describing the ultimate. I think the main reason is simply that these terms are ready theological superlatives, abstract enough for the statement of principles. On the other hand, these adjectives would be less suggestive of ontology had they not been constantly used by Hindu, i.e. ontological, thinkers. Without the Hindu reference, these terms can be used as epithets to non-ontological notions just as much as they can for ontological ones. They may be semantically more suggestive of ontological background, because 'things' are 'breakable' and 'divisible', etc.; yet such consideration is somewhat jejune, for after all the ontological notions of Hinduism, or of any ontological philosophy, as the '*on*' of the Eleadic philosophers, or the '*ens*' of Thomism, or 'Being' (*das Sein*, as opposed to *das Seiende*) of Heidegger are not really any of the 'things' which are breakable or combustible. This is just an illustration of the fact that languages use object-language terms to qualify non-object-language concepts.

The specific case of extension of ontological vocabulary to non-ontological thought may have another, somewhat more technical cause: the tantric Buddhist commentators had to vindicate their preceptors' facile use of 'surrounding' terminology: by this I mean that the first tantric teachers, such as the eighty-four *siddhas*, who were mostly rustic folk without much liking for and no pretence to learning, were constantly exposed to Hindu village parlance around them, and popular Hinduism was hardly distinguishable from popular Buddhism in early medieval Bengal. Their more learned commentators in turn used learned non-Buddhist vocabulary to denote Buddhist concepts, in conscious analogy, perhaps, to their unsophisticated preceptors' use of unsophisticated non-Buddhist vocabulary. It is a pattern frequently observed elsewhere: the words of Christ, often indiscriminately reminiscent of Hellenic pantheistic ideology ('I and the Father are one'), had to be exegetically 'atoned for' by the learned Fathers and scholastics in later days. St. Augustine's work was one great effort to eradicate any trace of Hellenic and Alexandrinian pantheism and to put dualistic monotheism on a firm basis. Christ had been exposed to 'surrounding' non-Judaeic terminology, the Province of Galilea being suffused by popular Hellenic doctrines largely pantheistic ('What good can come of Nazareth?' John i, 46). In later centuries, we have an exact analogue in the teachings of Mohammed. The main difficulty for all learned commentators who write as apologists for their naive preceptors consists in the attempt to make the learned believe that the preceptors had entertained sophisticated theological ideas which they chose to put into naive language for the benefit of the crowd—yet no exegete who does not also happen to be an anthropologist would state the facts as they are: that the founders or the first saintly preceptors of most religious traditions were naive, and did not teach discursive theology, not because they did not want to, but because they knew nothing about it.[31]

Thus, Bhusukapāda, a *siddha* listed in all Tibetan histories of Buddhism, seemed to put a blend of Vijñānavāda, Mādhyamika and Vedānta teachings in his saying: 'the great tree of *sahaja*[32] is shining in the three worlds; everything being of the nature of *śūnya*, what will bind what? As water mixing with water makes no difference, so also, the jewel of the mind enters the sky in the oneness of emotion. Where there is no self, how can there be any non-self? What is increate from the beginning can have neither birth, nor death, nor any kind of existence. Bhusuka says: this is the nature of all—nothing goes or comes, there is neither existence nor non-existence in *sahaja*.'[33] It is quite evident that once this sort of poetry, vague in doctrinary content but rich in potential theological terminology, is accepted as canonical, commentators of any of the philosophical schools can use it for their specific exegeses. I think an analogy in modern times is permissible, because village religion has not changed very much in India. Thus, the unsophisticated *sādhū* and his village audience use and understand terms like *ātman*, *brahman*, *māyā*; for them, these terms are less loaded than for the specialist, but they are used all the same. Similarly, I think Bhusuka, Kāṇha, and Sarāha, etc., used '*śūnya*' and '*sahaja*' in this untechnical, but to their rustic audiences perfectly intelligible, sense; not, again, because of pedagogical prowess and 'to make it easy', but because those preceptors did not have any scholastic training—for them, these terms were as un-loaded as for their audience, at least on the discursive level. This is not to deny the possibility that the spiritual experience related to their *sādhanā* did enhance the charisma of these terms for the adepts.

Now of all Indian ideologies, tantrism is the most radically absolutistic, and the 'two truths' coalesce completely; the intuition of this coalescence indeed constitutes the highest 'philosophical' achievement of the tantric—(here I am using 'philosophical' in the way H. V. Guenther does—he translates *'rnal byor'-yogi*, by 'philosopher'). Any Tibetan teacher, such as Kham lung pa, 'admitted the theory of the two truths, according to which the 'All was either conventional or transcendental'.[34] There is a constant merger of the phenomenal *saṃvṛti* into the absolute *paramārtha*, logically because the former has the 'void' *śūnya* as its basis, and in the experience of the adept, because he dissolves the phenomenal in *śūnya*, this being the proper aim of all sādhanās; and the frame of reference wherein the tantric conducts all his sādhanā is the complete identity of the two. Thus the *Guhyasamāja*, one of the most important and oldest Buddhist tantric texts, says (the Buddha Vairocana speaking), 'my "mind" (*citta, sems*) is such that it is bereft of all phenomenal existence, "elements" (*dhātus*) and "bases" (*āyatanas*) and of such thought categories as subject and object, it is without beginning and has the nature of *śūnya*'.[35]

There are very few concepts which Hindu and Buddhist tantrism do not share. The 'three bodies' (*trikāya, sku gsum*) doctrine, however, is uniquely Buddhist and has no parallel in Hindu tantrism. This, I think, is the only case where there was a real separation of terminological spheres: there is nothing like a '*trikāya*' doctrine in Hinduism, although the Kashmiri '*Trika*' School of Śaivism has traces of a threefold division of 'body'-principles, possibly similar to the Vaiṣṇava notion of the deity in its threefold aspect as 'attraction' (*Saṃkarṣaṇa*), 'Unrestrainability' (*Aniruddha*), and 'the purely mythological' (*Dāmodara*). In the *Mahāyāna* classification of the three 'bodies', definitional certainty is by no means equally strong. Thus, *dharma-kāya* and *nirmāṇakāya* (*chos kyi sku* and *sprul sku*), it seems to me, are relatively uncomplicated notions, but there is a lot of uncertainty about *sambhoga-kāya*.[36] On the Hindu tantric side, I think that, apart from those mythological proper names which the Buddhist tantric pantheon does not share, the only term Buddhist tantric literature avoids is '*śakti*' in its technical sense, i.e. as the dynamic principle symbolized as the female counterpart to the static wisdom principle.

Summing up on tantric philosophy, these are the points that can be made: Hindu tantrism and Buddhist tantrism take their entire speculative apparatus from non-tantric absolutist Hindu and Buddhist thought, and although systematized tantrism is even more eclectic than pretantric ideologies, there is a pretty clear distinction between Hindu and Buddhist tantric ideas. Common to both is their fundamental absolutism; their emphasis on a psycho-experimental rather than a speculative approach; and their claim that they provide a shortcut to redemption. The main speculative difference between Hindu and Buddhist tantrism is the Buddhist ascription of dynamicity to the male and of 'wisdom' to the female pole in the central tantric symbolism, as opposed to the Hindu ascription of dynamicity to the female and (static) wisdom to the male pole; and lastly, the difference is terminological inasmuch as certain technical terms—very few though—are used by either the Buddhist or the Hindu tantric tradition only.

This book presupposes familiarity with the basic doctrines of Hinduism and Buddhism—it is for this reason that the chapter on tantric philosophy is short and emendatory rather than a survey. There is really no tantric philosophy apart from Hindu or Buddhist philosophy, or, to be more specific, from Vedāntic and Mahāyāna thought.

The diagram which now follows should provide a model for the interrelation of doctrine and target in the tantric tradition.

The late Swami Viśvānanda Bhāratī suggested to me that the problem of variant doctrine and common target can be likened to a 'children's top' (*bhramarakrīḍanakam*). I found this a helpful model:

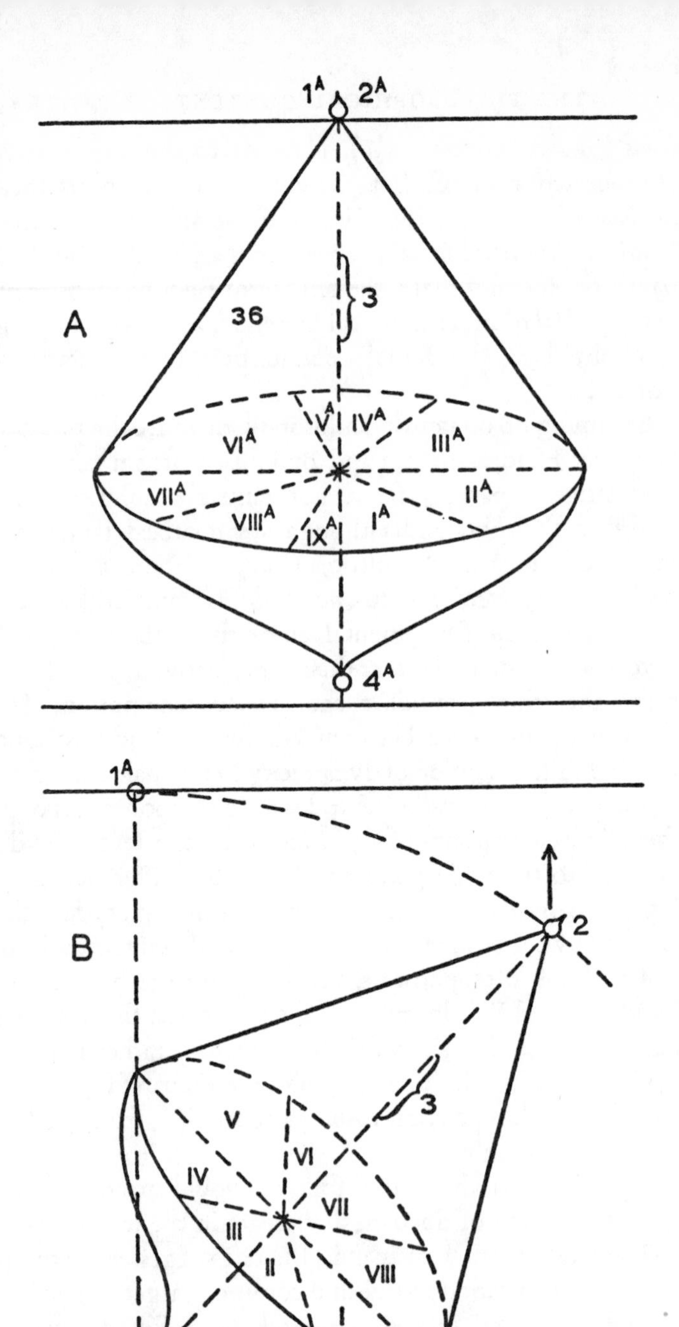

1A 2A
A
36
3
VA IVA
VIA IIIA
VIIA IIA
VIIIA IXA IA
4A
1A
2
B
3
V
VI
IV
VII
III
II VIII
I
4
5

LEGEND

The upper diagram A is the model for the enstatic process 'in practice' when *sādhanā* is being performed;
the lower diagram B is the model for the doctrinary process, where *sādhanā* is not performed, though postulated.

1, 1A . . . the stipulated target of religious life, common to all Indian indigenous systematized traditions (*kaivalya*, *nirvāṇa*, etc.).
2, 2A . . . the actual achievement of the individual adept.
3, 3A . . . the axis represents the individual adept's progress towards (1).
4, 4A . . . the starting point of actual *sādhanā* and the starting point (doctrinal) of all Indian indigenous systematized traditions.
I, IA, II, IIA, III, IIIA, etc. the various schools of thought and religious discipline, etc. The whole circle represents the totality of all Indian, etc. systems, and there would have to be exactly as many sectors as there are systems, etc. Schools with opposing tendencies would be inscribed at opposite ends (f.i. Buddhist tantrism and Theravada would be III and VII, etc.).
5 . . . the dead point where the top rests when not in motion—it does not raise the adept (and the system) beyond the starting point (4, 4A).

INTERPRETATION

In B, each system claims its own superiority, because the entire scholastic-redemptive tradition indeed seems to 'rest' on any specific tradition (on point 5). Also, '*sādhanā*' (4) seems to be special to each system—which is an error, because the base of the top is a point equally supporting all 'systems'. This fact, however, becomes evident only in A, i.e. when *sādhanā* is actually done, not just postulated.
When in motion, ideologies get 'blurred'; *sādhanā* is therefore not 'specific' to any one system, *sādhanās* vary much less than ideological systems (as peripheral points and segments move fast, whereas the base (4A) shows only small amplitudinal divergence).
In A, the actual and the stipulated achievement coincide, IA and 2A coalesce. In B, the actual achievement (2) can never reach (1), for the accepted formula is 'no *sādhanā*, no *mukti* (*nirvāṇa*, *kaivalya*, etc.)'.
The periphery of the largest circle in the top structures represents the propounders and adherents of the various systems, but this delimitation must not be too rigid: each sector represents the systems as well as their

founders and their adherents and texts, etc.—in other words, what is called the '*pārampara*' in Sanskrit terms which I would render 'total scholastic-redemptive tradition'.

In B, the whole doctrinal structure is intact, but dysfunctional—as nothing short of *nirvāṇa* (*kaivalya*, *mukti*, etc.) is the aim of all *pāramparās*, the target cannot be reached by *any* school unless there is actual *sādhanā*, but if there is *sādhanā*, it can be reached by *any* one school.

By aid of this model, some further facets of the problem can be represented:

a) the *more* widely ramified the component systems are, i.e. the more complex, the higher are the chances of reaching the common target: the wider ramification would be represented by a longer diameter; the longer the diameter, the closer 2 (2) gets to (1) even in B; lesser ramification, 'simpler' religious teachings and fewer sects (*sāmpradāyas*) being represented through a top with a proportionately smaller diameter, rest more askew than tops with larger diameter, the section between the largest circle and the base (4) remaining identical in length.
b) there is some variation not only in *sādhanā* in A—4A, A does not rest in one spot, but moves slightly (this amplitude indicating the divergence between opposed *sādhanās* tantric and non-tantric), but also in the target, as (2A) does move slightly in A—there is some difference in the experience of Buddhist *nirvāṇa* and, say, of Vedāntic *kaivalya*, though they can all be subsumed under 'emancipation' (*mukti*).

Prof. K. H. Potter has given a different, equally helpful model in his 'progress' and 'leap' philosophy nomenclature.[37] All tantric thought would be of the 'leap' variety.

NOTES*

[1] Wittgenstein and the Vienna school, Russell, Wisdom, Logico-empiricism, the philosophers of linguistic analysis, the type of philosophy which MIND deals with in England, and most American philosophical trade journals and American chairs take seriously.

* For abbreviations of bibliographical material, see Bibliography.

[2] S. B. Dasgupta, *An Introduction to Tantric Buddhism,* Calcutta University Press, Calcutta 1950, p. 1.

[3] *Ibid.*

[4] Classical philosophy uses these terms only for conditional sentences; modern linguistically oriented philosophy, however, permits the use of protasis and apodosis also for more general propositions; our specific proposition would be 'as there is rebirth, there is also the possibility of escape from it'.

[5] In a letter to me, dated Banaras, October 5, 1958, Dr. Guenther deals with the *śunya*-pattern, and here I quote what seems to me relevant for our discussion: 'No, we can never identify *śūnyatā* with subsistence. I translate it by "nothingness" but I add the following explanation: "*śūnyatā* is neither existence nor non-existence; thus, several schools like the *Sautrāntikas* took to be an *ens.* Their explanation of *nirvāṇa* was one by analogy, i.e. that it was like the extinction of a flame, as the *kleśas* (negative adhering impressions) lose their power. This explanation is really quite good (*eigentlich sehr gut*), for it shows the dynamic aspect of *nirvāṇa,* for which the Vaibhāṣikas' assumption of existence (*bhāva*) is rather naive ("for which" refers to the dynamic aspect—"*fuer welchen die Annahme der Existenz eigentlich recht naiv ist*"). Unfortunately, however, the Sautrāntikas chose the term *abhāva* "non-existence" for this extinction, i.e. non-existence of the *kleśas* (negative adhering impressions). But I can imagine a thing which has been negated; which fact gave rise to the notion, that even non-existence is a mode of existing, i.e. what Meinong and Broad call "subsisting". . . . The Sautrāntikas, who introduced the concept *śūnya* . . . had a glimpse of what was to be essential, but they as yet lacked the power of profound analysis which the Mādhyamikas evolved. Usually, *śūnya* is translated by "void, empty". But there are many reasons against this rendition. "Empty", for us, has a conceptual flavour of hollowness, something predominantly negative. But *śūnya* means the very contrary, one could only describe it as neither capable of being made fuller nor capable of decrease (. . . *weder zusaetzlich anfuellbar noch abnehmbar*). It is thus a plenum—in the philological Latin sense, not in the philosophical sense. As *śūnya* is thus a positive concept, which, however, does not yield to any of our current positive or negative descriptions, it is for us "nothing by all ordinary standards" (the quotes are Guenther's). Now for Heidegger the "nothing" has very often the characteristic of fear. He has seen this correctly, because in the very moment where everything vanishes for us, we are faced by a "nothing", but he did not work this out too clearly, for his "nothing" is a created nothing, created in the judgment of fear (*ein geschaffenes Nichts im Urteil der Angst*). It (i.e. Heidegger's "nothing") is, so to speak, a reservation of the ego, but not yet an unconditioned experience of freedom (*mukti*) as a road (*mārga*) toward the realization of our latent possibilities. Now, *śūnya* is also at times being used in this Heideggerian sense. Here is this specific usage, in *Sarāha, ka khasya dohā-ṭippaṇī, ka kha'i do ha'i bshad pa bris pa, bstan*

'gyur (Derge ed.), rgyud, vol. zhi, fol. 58 b- (Guenther gives his translation only, not the original): "The nature of pure transcendence—*gnyug ma'i sems kyi rang bzhin-nijacittasya svabhāva*—is intuited by pure sensation to be nothing, but it is not something declared to be empty (lit. made empty) by the reasoning intellect." And, continuing the passage, Sarāha says further "since the world of appearance (appearance is not to be understood in Kant's or Bradley's sense, it is symbolific transformation in the sense of Susan K. Langer) does not exist here, there is nihilism, a state of misery (despair), but when this state of misery (despair) has disappeared, the world of appearance as it exists for the philosopher (Guenther consistently renders *rnal 'byor pa, yogin*, as "philosopher"—and does not use the Sanskrit yogin as other Buddhologists would do) turns into radiance and nothingness." According to a manuscript of the "oral tradition", "radiance" (*gsal, prabhāsvara*) refers to the *rnam pa*, Skr. *ākāra*, which could be translated as "causal characteristic", and which essentially signifies the dynamics of symbolific transformation. But this dynamics is not anything concrete, it is again *śūnya*, and in this passage belief in its "existence" is rejected in a manner similar to Whitehead's treatment of the "fallacy of misplaced concreteness".'

[6] Vd. appendix to this chapter.

[7] Vd. Chapter, 'Polarity Symbolisms'.

[8] *Blue Annals*, I/290, G. N. Roerich, Calcutta 1949–53.

[9] Although the *Saundaryalaharī*, ascribed to Śaṃkarācārya by orthodox Brahmin tradition, is probably not his work (vd. N. D. Brown, *The Saundaryalaharī*, H.O.S. 1959), the fact that it has been persistently ascribed to him is in itself an important indication: he was constantly exposed to tantric environments. The *Śaṃkaradigvijaya*, his biography ascribed to his disciple Padmapādācarya, recounts his conversion from a monism which excluded the female principle is polar as in all tantrism. That particular episode tells how Śaṃkarācārya, when walking along the Ganges at Benaras after having taken his bath, encountered a wailing woman holding her dead husband's body over her knees. When the *ācārya* demanded that she remove the polluting corpse from his presence, she said to him something like 'why don't you, an omnipotent *ācārya*, command the corpse to remove itself?' Irritated, Śaṃkarācārya exclaimed 'how could it, there is no *śakti* in it'—whereupon the lady, manifesting her real form as the Goddess, the magna mater, instructed the *ācārya* about his error: nothing can move without *śakti*, dynamis. It is on the basis of this incident that Śaṃkarācārya is said to have compiled the *Saundaryalaharī*. This story is well known far beyond the narrow circle of scholars who read the "*Digvijaya*". The best account of Śaṃkarācārya's "conversion" from nonpolar monism to polar monism of the Śākta variety is found in a Bengali work *Ācārya-Śaṃkar-o-Rāmānuj* by S. Bhattacharya, who also published an excellent study of Hindu tantrism in Bengal "*Tantra Paricaya*". We should also remember that Śaṃkarācārya's opponents called him a "*prachanna bauddha*", a crypto-

Buddhist, with possible reference to tantric Buddhism which was then very much in vogue in India. It is also interesting to note that some of the most important Hindu tantras, like the *Mahāṇirvana* and the *Kula-cūdāmaṇi*, refer to him as the "*ādigura*", the first preceptor (of tantrism); tantric commentators frequently refer to him as *Dramiḍācārya*, i.e. the Dravidian Master, though this identification with the actual Dramiḍācārya is pure fantasy.'

[10] The notion prevails that Sanskrit is compulsory in German high schools; vd. my *Ochre Robe*, Ch. VIII, Allen & Unwin, London 1961.

[11] Glasenapp, 'Tantrismus und Schaktismus', *Ostasiatische Zeitschrift*, VI. 22, 1936, 120, 'die Vorstellung, dass die ganze Welt mit der Fuelle ihrer Erscheinungen ein ganzes bildet, bei dem auch das kleinste auf das groesste eine Wirkung ausueben kann, weil geheimnisvolle Faeden auch das geringste mit dem ewigen Weltgrunde verknuepfe, ist die eigentliche Grundlage aller tantrischen Philosophie'. 'Geheimnisvolle Faeden' etc. sounds very nice, and Indian pandits are fond of such colourful simile; but this style is not really helpful for the study of Indian thought. The less edifying, but more precise, terminology of analytical modern philosophy is not popular in India, mainly, I think, because it lacks 'inspiration' and is hence thought to be less close to the spirit of Indian philosophy. This is wrong. Indian commentarial literature is at least as dull and unedifying as modern analytical terminology.

[12] There is a growing school of psychiatrists which denies that there is such a thing as mental disease; its spokesman is Prof. Thomas S. Szasz, of the New York Upstate Medical College, vd. *The Myth of Mental Illness*, Harper Bros., New York 1961.

[13] An important tantric doctrine with much literature, it figures importantly in the Tibetan *rgyud* tradition as the *kālacakra-dus kyi khor lo*: Prof. Hoffmann in Munich is working at a history of the *kālacakra* system, whose origins are mythical, or at least very obscure.

[14] A confusion very frequent among pandits in India; Islam—it is to this religion that the line refers—originated among Semitic peoples; it spread into parts of Asia through Arab missionaries no doubt, but it was the Turks, Afghans, and the Mongols who carried Islam into India; there had been some Arab settlements in Sind as early as the eighth century, barely a hundred years after the *Hijra*, but they did not make converts, being merely merchants and obviously not interested in spreading the Faith. This confusion is due to the influence of nineteenth-century German indologists, which was the first learned group to spell out the Aryan myth; a myth which has been immensely popular with Indian pandits ever since.

[15] *Niṣpannayogāvali*, intd. p. 15, G.O.S. CIX., Baroda.

[16] Advayavajrasaṃgraha, G.O.S. 40, *pratibhāso varaṃ kāntaḥ pratītyotpādamātrakaḥ/na syād yadi mṛtaiva syāt śūnyatā kāminī matā.*

[17] G.O.S. 40, introduction, xiii.

[18] The trend has been quite contagious and several western scholars have come to hold the same view; vd. J. G. Jennings *Vedantic Buddhism*, published in 1949, which is subtitled 'a collection of historical texts translated from the original Pali' [*sic*]; I suspect, however, that European scholarship may well be co-responsible for the inauguration of this trend, which has gained official approbation in India, where well-meaning politicians are keen to point out the essential oneness of Buddhism and Hinduism. European, particularly German, scholars had propounded the doctrine of a basic oneness of Indian religions long before it became politically interesting in India. Thus, the late Prof. W. Koppers said in a lecture at the University of Vienna, in March 1948: 'Whatever doctrinary differences, you will be amazed at the oneness in essentials, of Buddhism and Hinduism. Mahāyāna Buddhism and Vedānta Hinduism are one and the same anyway, but you will see that even Hīnayāna Buddhism bears the same marks (*die gleichen Kennzeichen traegt*). And there is small wonder about that: for after all, truth can only be one, and religions are great when they approach this oneness. . . .'

[19] On this point, see my Chapter on 'Polarity Symbolism'.

[20] Hindu tantrism may well have borrowed some deities from Vajrayāṇa mythology, f.i. the Goddess Ekajaṭā, who seems to be a Tibetan import, or re-import; she is called 'preserved in Tibet' or 'rescued in Tibet' *bhoṭeṣu rakṣitā*; see Chapter 3 for an elaborate account. Other deities possibly borrowed by Hindu tantrics from Vajrayāṇa are Mahācīnatārā, Kurukullā, Jāṅgulī, vd. also '*Buddhist Iconography*', B. Bhattacharya.

[21] *The Niśvāsatattvasaṃhitā*, of which P. C. Bagchi found a manuscript in the Nepal Darbar Library, vd. Bagchi, *Studies in Tantra.*

[22] Vairocana, centre, white; Akṣobhya, east, blue; Ratnasaṃbhava, south, yellow; Amitābha, west, red; Amoghasiddhi, north, green.

[23] *Darśayanti śūnyāśunyaṃ nijaṃ vapuḥ*; Sitikantha's *Mahānaya Prakāśa*, ed. Pdt. Mukund Rama Shastri, Kashmere Series Vol. XXI, 1918, 1st Udaya, p. 21.

[24] *Śūnyaṃ śūnyācidrūpaṃ na tu abhāvasvabhāvam aśūnyaṃ māyākaluṣitam:* ibd. For my definition of *māyā* see my *Ochre Robe*, Glossary p. 281, which I borrow for this note: 'a key-word of Brahmin and Vedāntic thought. It is inaccurately rendered "illusion"; correctly, it means the totality of phenomenal experience and of relative existence, it denotes the qualified universe as opposed to the absolute, the *brahman*. The classical analogy showing the relation of *brahman* and *māyā*: a man sees a rope and thinks it is a snake, and he is affected as though it were a snake, unless he realizes its real character: the "snake" is *māyā*, the "rope" is *brahman*. The scriptural qualification of *māyā* is "ineffable" or "indescribable" *anirvacanīya*. No proposition about its nature can ever stand unchallenged.'

[25] See Chapter 9 for elaboration.

[26] The original reads: *Sarvaśūnyatve kaḥ saṃvṛterāśrayaḥ yasyaivamavabhāsaḥ-tataḥ sarvaśūnyavādaḥ sarvaviruddha eva ityevam adhiṣṭhānābhāvādevāpākṛtam*

'*Prakāśa*'. See also my article 'Modern Hindu Exegesis of Mahāyāna Doctrine', *Philosophy: East and West*, Vol. XII/7, Univ. of Hawaii Press, 1962, and '*Vikāsa*' to Śaṃkarabhāṣyam, Catuḥsūtrī, publ. Banaras 1951.

[27] On this point, vd. my paper 'Was Śaṃkarācārya a Crypto-Buddhist?' publ. in *Thought*, New Delhi 1954.

[28] I think the two models preceding the notes support my denial of this claim.

[29] *Advayavajrasaṃgraha*, G.O.S. XL, 15: *dṛḍhaṃ sāram asauśīryam acchedyābhedyalakṣaṇam, adahyāvināśi* [*sic*] *ca śūnyata vajramucyate.*

[30] 2nd canto, '*abhedyo'yam acchedyo'yam . . . adahyo'yam.*

[31] The Buddhist tantric, and to a certain degree the Hindu tradition, offers an interesting exception, in a way. The Buddha may not have been counted among the learned of his day, but he was certainly a sophisticated speaker and a good exegate of his own doctrine. The eighty-four siddhas, however, were naive in this sense—and it was only their commentators who caught up with exegetical discursiveness. Similarly, the seers of the Upaniṣads certainly used more sophisticated terminology than the medieval Hindu saints (Kabīr, Nānak, Tulsīdās etc.) who accepted the Upaniṣad as *śruti*. The Hindu medieval saints, however, did not find learned commentators in their turn as the Buddhist tantric saints had found, for the Sanskrit pandits ignored the Hindu medieval saints, reverting to *śruti* and to earlier learned commentary.

[32] The key-term of medieval Indian tantric Buddhism, to which Indian authors like S. B. Dasgupta refer as Vajrayāṇa or Sahajayāna; *sahaja* lt. means 'congenital'; i.e. the method is natural, and 'easy' in this sense, easy being the derived meaning of '*sahaja*'; in a more technical sense, '*sahaja*' is synonymous with '*śūnya*', i.e. that which is the lasting aspect of the universe.

[33] *Bauddhagān o Dohā* No. 43, '*sahaja maha taru pharia tiloe, khasama sabhave re nanate ka Koe, Jima jale paṇia taliya bheda no jaa, tima mana....* (I am using S. B. Dasgupta's translation in *Obscure Cults as Background to Bengali Literature*, Calcutta 1946, p. 48).

[34] *Blue Annals*, I/285—thus Roerich's rendition of the terms; I don't think it is useful; *kun rdzob* is *saṃvṛti* or *vyavahāra*, i.e. existence or cognition on the phenomenal, discursive level; *don dam* (pa) is *paramārtha* or absolute—'transcendental' is too Kantian a term; I suggest, as always, to leave *paramārtha* after studying its meaning; Murti gives a precise definition of *paramārtha* and *vyavahara* in *The Central Philosophy of Buddhism*; vd. index to that work.

[35] *Guhyasamāja Tantra*, G.O.S. LIII, p. 12 *sarva-bhāva-vigataṃ skandhadhātvāyatano-grahya-grāhaka-varjitaṃ dharma-nairātmya-samatayā svacittam-ādi-anutpannaṃ śūnyatā-bhāvam.*

[36] H. V. Guenther, in a hitherto unpublished manuscript *The Jewel Garland of Philosophical Faiths* (which is a translation and critical study of the *Grub pa'i mtha 'i rnam par bzhag pa rin po che'i phreng ba* by Dkon mchog 'jigs med dbang po), explains the three '*kaya-s*' thus;

'"activities of Buddha" is a term for the Buddhahood of man as it unfolds itself through the existential norms known by their Indian names: *dharmakāya, saṃbhogakāya,* and *nirmāṇakāya.* The first of the three is the transcending awareness at the root of man's being, as it works in rejecting all sham reality and intuitively cognizing reality as it is. *Sambhogakāya* is unlimited communication or the uninterruptedness of the Mahāyānic teaching; and *Nirmāṇakaya* is man's authentic being-in-the world as exemplified by the twelve episodes in a Buddha's life and by the establishment of the teaching being both a guidance and an awareness.'

[37] K. H. Potter, *Presuppositions of Indian Philosophy,* Prentice Hall, Englewood-Cliffs, New Jersey 1963.

2

TANTRIC TERMINOLOGY

I DO NOT think that a whole chapter on terminology in the early portions of this book rather than as an appendix requires any justification; nor is it due to the author's linguistic-analytical slant in his philosophical interests. A book attempting to survey the tantric tradition in its essentials must give very special attention to terminology and definition. In a wider or more general sense, this has been done in the preceding chapter. However, reference to established Hindu and Buddhist philosophical terminology is neither sufficient nor warrantable, because a considerable portion of non-tantric Hindu and Buddhist philosophical nomenclature was subjected to semantic change, sometimes subtle, sometimes very radical indeed. A term frequently and innocuously used, say, in the Mādhyamika-kārikās, and translated by one constant term into Tibetan, does not necessarily have the same meaning in Tibetan or Indian tantric texts. The fact that the student sees the terms consistently used in the Indian original and in the Tibetan translation might tempt him to assume that they mean the same when they appear in a Sanskrit tantric text and its Tibetan translation. This is dangerous even when the term occurs in Sanskrit Hindu and Buddhist texts alone, where no Tibetan translation is available—hardly any Hindu Śākta text appears in the Tibetan tantras (*rgyud*). The best example is Sanskrit *mudrā*, which means 'the female adept' in the Buddhist tantric lore, and 'parched kidney beans' and other spiced grains in the Hindu Śākta tradition; quite apart from the many tantric and non-tantric passages, Hindu and Buddhist, where *mudrā* means a ritualistic or iconographic gesture.

The purpose of this chapter, then, is to analyse some crucial Sanskrit and Tibetan Buddhist tantric terms and to establish their exact connotation. This has so far not been done, largely due to a lack of communication between philosophers and cultural anthropologists on the one side, and philologically oriented Buddhologists on the other. The fault seems to be that of the Buddhologists, who did not care, up to this day, to brush up their occidental vocabulary and to provide precise renditions of Buddhist, and *a fortiori*, tantric philosophical terminology. The reason for this neglect seems to lie in the notion that occidental philosophy works on totally different lines and that it can therefore not provide terminological equivalents. This was true with the traditional western philosophers who excluded Indian thought from their study as below philosophical dignity[1] and whose attitude was reciprocated by the orientalist brand of counter-arrogance: that western philosophy was lacking the spiritual insight which could help it tackle the esoteric problems of Asian thought. Traditional philosophy—say, up to Russell and Ayer—was really not interested in creating a precise vocabulary that could suggest operational equivalents for Indian and Tibetan scholastic terminology. The analytical schools of Britain and America, however, have worked out a vocabulary which could be highly useful in rendering the former intelligible. To my knowledge, however, no indologist with the exception of H. V. Guenther in India and Europe and Karl H. Potter in North America have cared to avail themselves of the work that has been done by occidental philosophers who regard language analysis as the main function of philosophy.[2]

I shall start with a simple example: Tibetan *sems*, Sanskrit *citta*, is translated by such vague terms as 'mind' or even 'soul'—the latter being a downright atrocious translation so far as Buddhism is concerned. At best, the inadequacy of such renditions is admitted with a shrug—as a bequest of last-century indology. However, I feel convinced that modern philosophy does give us an instrument to work out these vexing problems. With the growth of Tibetan Buddhist studies arose the habit of giving the Sanskrit term for the Tibetan in lieu of a translation, thus shelving the real issue; for while it is true that, for example, '*nirmāṇakāya*' is the Sanskrit equivalent of '*sprul sku*', it is not very helpful to just write '*nirmāṇakāya*' in Roman characters, although the realization of the inadequacy of a term like 'phantom-body' is laudable. For what, then, is the '*nirmāṇakāya*'?

It goes without saying that we cannot impugn the Tibetan translations of the original Sanskrit terms, and that for logical reasons: the Tibetans had no concepts matching the learned terminology of their Indian preceptors. We must assume that Buddhism was planted on a conceptual vacuum in Tibet. Any term chosen once, and used without modification, had come to stay. It is quite unlike trying to find an occidental term for a Sanskrit or Tibetan scholastic idiom, because occidental languages have a backlog of viable, even though risky, Graeco-Roman-Judaeo-Christian concepts. This shows itself in the translation of such innocuous words as *lha* (*deva*) as 'god'—or *dṅos pa* (*vastu*) as 'substance' or 'nature'. 'Substance' cannot get rid of its Thomistic or Aristotelian flavour, and there is nothing of the kind in the Buddhist '*vastu*'. We shall see, however, that contemporary, non-Aristotelian philosophy might provide a useful term for the Buddhist concept. H. V. Guenther suggests 'reality',[3] which would be acceptable if, as he does, the word is used as shorthand for 'all objects'; in other words if the Aristotelian flavour hovering around nouns suffixed by *-ty* can be kept out. I would recommend 'totality of sense-data' or even just 'all objects'; and never omitting the article—for *deva* (*lha*), 'a god'.

To say that Tibetan renditions of Sanskrit terminology are 'more exact'[4] than any western rendition is a sort of wrongly formulated tautology: the Tibetan term had to create the new concept, not to translate it. Translation is possible where both languages have words for a concept; if we call the work of the *Lo tsa ba* 'translation', it is either incorrect or a courtesy: for he had to concoct Tibetan words for the Sanskrit original. Linguists might call this a one-zero relational process.[5]

I believe that the cumbersome but accurate terminology of contemporary analytic philosophy has to be used to outgrow terminological nonchalance, even at the risk of having to adopt tools which so far belonged to another discipline. It seems to me that the philosophical analyst's apparatus may at times tempt us to ascribe too much sophistication to the Indian and Tibetan pundits. I think Guenther often yields to this temptation—his translation of sGam.po.pa sometimes reads like a psychologist's manual. The danger can be avoided if we consistently use the modern terminology under a special rubric;[6] the Indian and Tibetan philosophers' categories are intuitive ones, those of western philosophy are discursive postulates, from the crude Aristotelian 'Laws of Thought' to today's logical calculi. Hence if we translate, for instance, '*sems*' by 'causal characteristic of mind',[7] our rubric—which we may call an 'intuition-rubric'—would read somewhat like: 'given that the word is used not as connoting a discursive or cognitive category but as corroborating an intuitive (i.e. non-discursive) experience'—*sems* (*citta*) means 'causal characteristic of mind'; '*bdag med* (*anātman*)' means 'non-individuality', etc.

I now proceed with some typical paradigms. I shall concentrate, in this chapter, on terms of the 'mind' class—which in a special sense is almost coextensive with Buddhist terminology in general, 'mind' in its widest sense being all that exists—particularly with the Yogācāra School which provided Tantric Buddhism with its theological superstructure, sharing a hard core with the older Mādhyamika teachings.

sems (*citta*)

Jaeschke was ignorant of the doctrinal meaning of this term in theology. In the first place, he equated it with Sanskrit *sattva* ('being'). S. C. Das placed it last in his enumeration of three Sanskrit equivalents; and rightly so, because in theological parlance '*sems*' translates '*sattva*' only in terms like '*mahāsattva*' (*sems dpa cen po*). It is hardly astonishing that not one of Jaeschke's

English renditions was determined by a passage of theological significance—he adduces only instances of trivial use, like '*sem khon du chud pa*', 'one very much grieved', '*sem chun ba*', 'a timid mind', etc. As English equivalents he lists the vague 'spirit'-'mind'-'soul'. But these are inapplicable in any Tibetan or Indian Buddhist context; I suspect he used '*sems*' to render the Christian 'soul' for the benefit of his flock. None of these English terms are useful in Buddhist terminology.

S. C. Das does not fare much better. He was right about his Sanskrit equivalents, *citta, manas, sattva,* if his arrangement does imply descending semantical frequency.[8] He lists 'soul' (qualifying it 'as power of moral volition'), 'spirit'; 'the heart where the soul resides'; 'mind'.

There are two ways to produce a correct translation of this and other equally fundamental terms; we either look for a phrase which can serve as a common denominator whenever the word occurs. Thus, Guenther wrote in a different context:[9] 'In the case of *sems*, we might use "spirituality" as a common denominator term'. The alternative would be to use an adequate paraphrase culled from analytical terminology each time the term occurs, putting the original in parentheses; the term *is* used as an operational counter by the pandit and the Tibetan translator, and he knows its particular import from the context—which can, of course, not be known through any occidental translation using vague generic terms. For example, we might say: 'mental events (*sems*) . . .'; 'recurrent associative event (*sems*) . . .', etc. Personally, I would incline towards the second method. There is the possibility of a combination of the two methods, if we agree that a particular occidental term be used as an 'operational counter' each time the Tibetan 'operational counter' appears in the text, provided the former is never used to translate any other original term. Thus, if we choose 'spirituality' for '*sems*', we must not use 'spirituality' to render any other term, like '*thugs*'; at least not as long as we do not know for certain that '*thugs*' and '*sems*' are not complete synonyms in scholastic literature.

The most frequent amplification of *sems* is *sems pa,* which is the equivalent of Sanskrit *caitta*. This is a term which can be rendered most precisely by 'motivation'. The '*chos mṅon pa kun las btus pa*' (*Abhidarmasamuccaya*) identifies '*karma*' with it.[10] '*Motivation*' in analytical philosophy includes both the urge to perform an action and the goal of the action in a teleological sense.[11]

In an important article, Guenther elucidates some of these terms.[12] He says, 'it has been customary to translate the terms "*sems* (*citta*)" and "*sems las byung ba* (*caitta*)" by "mind" and "mental event" respectively.[13] But this translation, however philologically correct, does not tell us much until we know what is meant by these terms in relation to each other. At first sight, the relation is comparable with that which common sense assumes to exist between "thing" and the "states of the thing". In this particular (i.e. the Buddhist tantric notion-A.B.) case, mind (*sems, citta*) would be the "thing" and mental event (*sems las byung ba, caitta*) the "state of the thing" . . .'

This is borne out by an important tantric text, which says 'this mind under consideration, when it has been changed by conditions such as trances and dispositions, should be known as only a state of mind'.[14]

Hence, whenever '*sems* (*citta*) occurs together with '*sems las byung ba*' (*caitta*), we might translate it as 'conditioned mind' and 'state of mind' respectively.

The necessity of separate renderings of '*sems*' becomes evident from these two examples. In one case, when it translates '*citta*' we use 'conditioned mind'; and in the other, when it translates '*cetanā*' we use 'motivation'; now compare these different renditions for meaningfulness, with the common rendering of '*sems*' as 'mind', regardless of its context, The Tibetan translators had something more specific in mind than just 'mind'. This example is important for any future study of the development of ideas in Buddhism. '*Citta*' in Pālī is best rendered as 'attitude'.[15] It goes without saying that Rhys Davis, Oldenberg, and the other old-timers in Pālī Buddhism constantly used 'mind' and its other occidental synonyms.

I suggest that the development of Pālī '*citta*' into tantric '*citta*' (*sems*), i.e. from 'attitude' to a 'conditioned mind', is sound psychology. 'Mind'—generally used as sGam.po.pa's 'operational counter'—is conditioned by constantly recurring attitudes; in strict Yogācāra argument it is actually but the nominalistically conceived sum-total of attitudes.

I have come to regard terminological susceptibilities as an important tool for tracing religious axioms. To use this example—'*citta*' when used by a Brahmin scholar always means something like 'mindstuff'—Swami Vivekananda constantly translated '*citta*' this way; no Buddhist of any school would ever think of any sort of 'stuff' when he hears '*citta*'.

yid (*manas*)

Jaeschke again has soul, mind; Das adds 'intellect' and both explain 'especially the powers of perception and imagination'. 'Soul' is impossible anyway; but whereas '*sems*' might be translated 'mind' as an operational counter, 'mind' should never be used to render '*yid*' (*manas*). The 'powers of perception and imagination' are subsumed under all Buddhist terms of the epistemological order, the description is too wide to be of use. The precise role of '*yid*' (*manas*) in Buddhist tantra and in Yogācāra is that of conceptualization. Guenther puts it this way, 'it is that function-event which is particularly concerned with conceptualization'.[16] The Vajrayāṇa phrase '*amanasikāra*' (Tibetan *yid la mi byed pa*) implies the important meditation-hint 'not to conceptualize' the various forms that arise in the course of the contemplative's training.

In early scholastic literature, the epistemological term *sems* (*citta*), *yid* (*manas*) and *rnam par śes pa* (*vijñāna*) are as yet used synonymously (*Abhidharmakośa* II, 34). In tantric times, this is no longer the case; as in all scholastic philosophy, progress involved subtler terminological distinction. *Yid* (*manas*), in tantric Buddhism, transmits sensations to its centre for their interpretation. Once this interpreting function subsides as a result of the prescribed meditative processes, the individual's notions about external objects vanish and the *yid* (*manas*) is harmonized with its origin; there is no conception whatever left. This basis is not a substratum in the Brahmanical sense (which later incidentally converges with the Thomistic notion of a 'substratum'), but a sort of pool into which things merge and from which they arise again. I think it could be likened to a 'flying start' in a horse-race: the 'flying-start' is not really a location but a function located on a particular line. The Yogācāra call this the '*ālayavijñāna* (*kun ghi rnam par śes pa*), the 'consciousness-receptacle' (Frauwallner translates it '*Schatzkammerbewusstsein*'—which sounds very nice but does not seem too helpful).

Guenther does use 'mind' for '*yid*' once in a while against his own knowledge of the specific use of '*yid*', but in the same book he paraphrases it as 'workings of the mind'. Considering the above, I would render '*yid*' (*manas*) 'interpreting function' or 'conceptualizing function'.

Rnam par śes pa (*vijñāna*)

The non-scholastic meaning of '*vijñāna*' in Sanskrit and the derived languages is simply 'consciousness' or, sometimes, 'intellect'. In Buddhist theology, however, it is a key term, being the quintessence of the radical idealist school (Vijñānavāda or Yogācāra); in their world view, which at times seems to me to be dangerously close to solipsism, the term covers the entire natural realm, somewhat in a Berkeleyan fashion—except that *esse* is a *totaliter percipi*, there being no divine mind as a separate ontological *ens*. Popular literature on Buddhism (Humphreys, Glasenapp) uses 'subjective-objective' and tries to explain how the objective merges in the subjective; which is an outsider's diction, there being no 'objective' of any kind in Vijñānavāda—nor, for that matter, in any important school of Buddhism.

Jaeschke lists 'perfect knowledge, consciousness'; 'perceptions, cognitions' (i.e. as one of the five *skandhas* or aggregates *phun po*); and the inevitable 'soul', even though only that of the departed. Then, however, Jaeschke adds something very wise in parentheses: 'the significations . . . I presume, should be distinguished, as is done here, according to the different spheres in which they are used and not to be explained out of the other'.

Das adds, 'by other authorities, it is stated *rnam par śes pa* is of two kinds, phenomenal consciousness or *snan pa'i rnam par śes pa* and *dnos po so ser rnam par rtog pa'i rnam par śes pa* "consciousness of external things", or that which distinguishes one from another'. This is all right but very vague, as other epistemological terms connote the same functions, too.

Tantric Buddhism is a bit more specific: the tantric term *rnam par śes pa* (*vijñāna*) means something else than 'consciousness'. Guenther suggests it might be rendered by 'energy'.[17] This is not a quantitative concept only.[18] Advayavajra says: 'The five *skandhas* (*phun po*) are the five Tathāgatas. How then, have the first four been marked Akṣobhya in order to show that they are congealed *vijñāna*? *Vijñāna* is both quantity and quality—it is known through symbols (i.e. the identification with the Buddha Akṣobhya, he being the personification of *vijñāna*), it is free from such distinctions as subject and object . . . This *vijñāna*, which may be likened to the clear sky at noon in the autumn, is spoken of as void of attribute, as primary.'[19] In this definition, 'energy' will certainly be an adequate rendering of '*vijñāna*'.

In a different context in tantric literature, however, *rnam par śes pa* (*vijñāna*) does not mean 'energy'. When juxtaposed with *sems* (*citta*) and *yid* (*manas*), the term implies 'discrimination', viz. selecting one or the other characteristic from the welter of sensible data and making it the sole content of its operation; it thus participates in sensation *and* perception. This supports my plea for an individual treatment of each instance where a technical term occurs. 'Discrimination' and 'Energy' are totally different things, hence neither of the two would do for a constant rendering of '*rnam par śes pa* (*vijñāna*). Only when used in its widest sense may we choose the common-denominator-term 'consciousness'. This common denominator usually coincides with the oldest use of the term, i.e. the Pālī use: *viññāna* in the Pālī canon can always be translated 'consciousness'; and it is clear that the Tibetan or Indian Buddhist tantric pandits used the term as an 'operational counter' quite frequently. To illustrate this suggested procedure '*rnam par śes pa*' (*vijñāna*) can be translated 'consciousness', 'energy', 'discrimination'.

The doctrine of the 'bodies' (*sku, kāya*) of the Buddha is one of the greatest troublemakers. There has not been, so far, any adequate description of this intricate and possibly bizarre teaching, and I suspect that the main reason for this is the lack of occidental terminology; here we cannot hope to find much help from contemporary analytical writers, for they are hardly concerned with mystical matters; some terms will just have to be coined. *Chos kyi sku* (*dharmakāya*), *loṅs spyod rdzogs pa'i sku* (*sambhogakāya*), and *sprul sku* (*nirmāṇakāya*) have been translated in annoyingly disparate ways—the blame is usually put on the originators of the terms suggesting that this particular doctrine was some sort of supra-mystical docetism; yet I do not believe that the ideas behind these terms are any more vague than other esoteric terms used in tantric Buddhism. Das interprets the terms 'spiritual existence', 'celestial existence', and 'bodily existence' respectively; these are too vague even to be called false; and Jaeschke's well-meant explanations (pp. 22, 336) are just wrong. 'Emanation-body', 'Manifestation Body' are certainly better than the atrocious 'phantom-body' some scholars have been using for *sprul sku* (*nirmāṇakāya*), but they, too, miss the point, because they share a fundamental error: '*sku*' (*kāya*) in the technical sense is not 'body' of any sort, because 'body' is an ontological term—it denotes an entity like 'chair' or 'Śakyamuni'. It is profitable to avoid all ontological terms when we deal with Buddhist philosophy, because there is no ontology in it; Buddhism is *bdag med gyi bstan pa* (*anātmavāda*), the doctrine of no-self: ontology is the doctrine of self, however conceived. Against this, it might be contended that the Buddhist iconographer draws images of the *chos kyi sku*, knowing perfectly well that it is an abstraction; he draws images of the Void embraced by the 'means' (*stoṅ pa ñid, thabs—śūnyatā, upāya*), and for that he draws an image of the Goddess 'No-Self' (*Bdag med ma, Nairātmyā*)—neither the artist nor the worshipper (the two are mutually dependent in mystical religions) impugn any philosophical concept through such anthropomorphisms. According to Guenther[20] sGam.po.pa says quite unambiguously that the three *kāyas* are 'existential modes or norms'. Thus, *sprul sku* (*nirmāṇakāya*) is 'but a name for the exercise of function or compassion, *sñin rje* (*karuṇa*) and of love, *byams pa* (*maitrī*) and the effort to achieve illumination (*byan cub, bodhi*)'. For any but a purely iconological context, I would then suggest 'totality principle' for *dharmakāya*; 'ecstatic principle' for *sambhogakāya*;[21] and 'principle of redemptive function' for *nirmāṇakāya*. Between the last and a 'phantom body' there is a wide gap, no doubt; 'phantom body' and, for that matter, any other '. . .-body' sounds more interesting, but it is less correct than 'principle'. I do not suggest that 'principle' be final for *sku* (*kāya*)—the word has an ontological flavour that might be avoided by using 'function', but 'function' had better be reserved for phrases pertaining to non-speculative terminology.

This takes us into the most delicate terminological field. I said earlier that ontological terms should be ostracized in the translation of Buddhist texts. There are, however, Sanskrit and Tibetan terms which have ontological significance as dictionary terms; but though the scholastics were aware of this, it did not interfere with non-ontological use of these terms. There is an excellent analogy in the western world: the term 'idealism' has a popular, non-philosophical meaning, viz. given to non-pragmatical, normative ways of life and thought, opposed to materialistic, worldly, etc. As a philosophical term, 'idealism' designates the view that objects have no existence apart from the perceiving mind, i.e. in opposition to realism. Now, although a philosopher knows and probably uses the word in its popular, dictionary sense when he talks to the loquacious newspaperman, or to the janitor, he will use it in its technical sense in the classroom. The two usages do not in any way conflict with each other.[22] The three terms which I would adduce here are *ṅo bo* (*vastu*), *raṅ bžin* (*svabhāva*), and *mtshan ñid* (*lakṣaṇa*).

Ṅo bo (*vastu*)

Jaeschke has 'entity, nature, essence, substance'; Das lists 'essence, substance, intrinsic nature'; he lists it as the Tibetan equivalent of '*svabhāva*'; but this is correct only in non-tantric terminology—

for '*vastu*' and '*svabhāva*' were used synonymously in pre-tantric Indian Mahāyāna Buddhism.

Guenther recently wrote[23] 'a heavy error brought into Buddhist discussion is our concept of substance. Hence, the translation of "*vastu*" is always wrong. sGam.po.pa distinguishes between *ṅo bo*, *raṅ bžin* and *mtshan ñid*. The last is simply "causal characteristic", but for the other two I do not have any adequate terms as yet.' I suggested 'substratum-postulate', 'substance-postulate', 'accident model-postulate', and for '*raṅ bžin* (*svabhāva*) 'total intellectual content'. He replied that these suggestions were the right things, but he did not write which of them he was going to choose in his present research on the *phyag rgyas chen po* (*mahāmudrā*).[24] He did not, however, agree to my suggestion for *raṅ bžin* (*svabhāva*), and suggested[25] that the term has to be dealt with individually in each case, which is grist on my own mill.

According to the definition of the word '*tantra*' (*rgyud*) in the *Guhyasamāja-Tantra*,[26] *svabhāva* (*raṅ bžin*) is identical with *hetu* (*rgyu*), not with *vastu* (*ṅo bo*) as it had been in pre-tantric literature. '*Hetu*' (*rgyu*) always represents an immanent associative nexus (we must avoid the word 'causality' or 'causal nexus' in Buddhism), there being no external nexus; that is to say, the term *hetu* (*rgyu*) refers, in tantric scholastic literature, to the meditative realm, not to that of falling apples, etc. Apart from it, *hetu* (*rgyu*) as identified with *svabhāva* (*raṅ bžin*) is a particular individuality which just 'is what it is', and could be described almost as a being in itself, provided we do not identify it in any manner with the Kantian Thing-in-Itself, forgetful of our 'rubric'. Therefore, we might interpret '*svabhāva*' (*raṅ bžin*) as 'actuality'; it is manifest in the human being as a congeries of a concrete and autonomous causal situation; this is incidentally the most cautious definition of a 'human being' in Buddhistic terms; we avoid 'soul', 'being', and similar ontological terms. This notion has a certain similarity with Whitehead's 'eternal object'—a phrase which sounds worse than it is. Every actual occasion (such as the 'human being') is defined as to its character by the specific manner of actualization. The *raṅ bžin* (*svabhāva*) of the series called 'human being', for instance, is that facet of dependent origination *rten 'brel* (*pratītya samutpāda*) which stresses the aspect of *sems* (*citta*) and its derivates. 'Actuality' is thus far less vague and misleading than the usual indological translation of '*svabhāva*' as 'nature', 'existence', etc. The older translators' vocabulary has given rise to a notion which has gained currency among many students of Buddhist literature as literature rather than as philosophy. Professor Glasenapp once said, 'In tantric Buddhism, and in tantra in general, everything seems to mean everything at some time or the other.'

If we ask whether terms of occidental philosophical usage have equivalents in tantric Buddhism, the question always has at least heuristic value. Take this very word 'existence', which has been used, among other terms, to render '*svabhāva*'. A reference given to me by Guenther will come in handy here. He writes:[27] 'The causal situation (sc. in Buddhist tantric literature) is rather fluid and within it new patterns of performance are possible at any moment. Padma dkar po treats this problem in connection with what the texts call '*dṅos po'i gnas lugs*', which I interpret either as 'factuality' or simply as 'existence'. I compare this to the principle of a guided missile, where the target determines the present action even though the target is still a future event. Padma dkar po says: 'Existence (*dṅos po'i gnas lugs*) is termed continuity of the being-itself "*raṅ bžin gyi rgyud, svabhāvatantra*", because it continues to exist like the serene sky (whether clouds may appear or not), encompassing everything from sentient beings and ending with the Buddhas. Since this being-itself is not tainted by latent experiences (*bag chags, vāsanā*)[28] and exists as an ultimate inner light (which again is only an "operational term", not any "thing"), it is referred to by many such names as "suchness" (*de bžin ñid, tathatā*), etc . . . (still Padma dkar po)' although never parting from its being-itself, it is infinitely open to new possibilities as the appearance of things animate and inert which have traits and characteristics of many kinds). Thus it becomes the causal situation (this is how *raṅ bžin* would have to be rendered here, if we are to be consistent) for the psycho-physical constituents (which I suggest for *phuṅ po, skandha*), materiality-producing-forces (*khams gsum,* (*tri-*) *dhātu*), inter-actional fields (which Guenther suggests for *skye mched, ṣaḍāyatana*. Das has the impossible 'sense-organs'—and other phenomena belonging to the relative existence (*khor ba, saṃsāra*).

dṅos po, bhāva

Guenther writes:[29] 'This term has a wider range of meaning than our "existence". It also denotes "materiality", "substantiality".' It has to be borne in mind, however, that these terms, as well as 'existence', are no predicates (see our rubric!); the Buddhists would probably have rejoiced at Russell's famous dictum, 'It is a shame on the face of thinking humanity that for over two thousand years thinkers did not know that there was a difference between the copula "is" (in "Socrates is wise") and the existential "is" in ("God is" or is not).' sGam.po.pa makes a very important distinction between *gnas lugs* and *yin lugs*; the former could be rendered as 'factuality', 'plain there-ness', or to use an existentialist philosopher's term for a change, '*das Dasein*' (K. Jaspers); *yin lugs* is purely descriptive—the Tibetan '*yin*' never means 'to be' in the sense of 'exist'—it is always a copula, i.e. to be this or that. I would suggest 'modal existence' following A. N. Prior,[30] better than Guenther's suggested 'determinative mode'.[31] Here we have to realize a very important point: the Sanskrit '*bhāva*' has meant so many things to the Indian philosopher, but only one section of its semiotic development was taken count of by the Tibetans—the purely Buddhist section, that is. In theological Sanskrit, however, apart from Buddhist usage, '*bhāva*' really meant the very opposite of *dṅos po*, namely ontological existence, solid spiritual being as the substratum of everything; in the Upaniṣads, it is often synonymous with '*sat*'; and *sat* is one of the appellations of Being *par excellence*, i.e. the Brahman. Hence, a translation of *dṅos po* as 'modality' or 'modal existence' would be helpful not only to philosophers in the West, but essential to the great number of Hindu scholars who read most of their secondary literature in English. For if they read 'thing, natural body, matter, subject' (Jaeschke, Das) for *dṅos po*, whether they are aware that '*dṅos po*' translates '*bhāva*' or not, they will g t quite a misleading notion:

if they know that '*dṅos po*' is '*bhāva*', they will identify it with the ontological '*bhāva*' of Brahmin canonical usage, unless they are taught to understand all these terms under the Buddhist 'rubric'; and if they do not know it, reading an English translation which does not mention the Tibetan or Sanskrit original, then it is completely impossible for them to glean the correct meaning from such terms as Jaeschke and Das listed for *dṅos po*.

I shall exemplify, in conclusion, the basic difference between the Brahmin and the Buddhist standpoint, quoting internal authority:

The notion of an immutable ontological 'Being' is canonified in the words chanted by every Brahmin monk daily up to this date, '*pūrṇamidaṃ pūrṇāt pūrṇamudacyate, pūrṇasya pūrṇamādāya pūrṇam evāvaśiṣyate*'[32]—'this whole existence arises from that which is whole, and if the whole be removed from the whole, yet the whole remains'. The '*pūrṇam*' simply could not be expressed in Tibetan Buddhistic Equivalent, unless indeed its use as an heretical erroneous notion (*hla ba'i zag pa, dṛṣti*) is pointed out. 'Existence' is perfectly all right without further adumbration, because the ontological totum has been a pervasive concept in western philosophy from Parmenides to Berkeley. A diametrically opposed notion is documented in Sthiramati's *Vṛtti* on Vasubandhus's *Triṃśikā*, that most important scholium of Sanskrit Buddhist doctrine,[33] '*na ca saṃcitam avayavasaṃhitamātrād anyad vidyate tadavayavam apohya saṃcitakaravijñānabhāvāt*'—'the whole is not something different from its parts in their operation together, because we do not perceive a whole after having subtracted its parts'. Should the reason why this important work has not been adequately translated into any western language so far be sought in the implicit acceptance of an ontological world-view by occidental Buddhologists?[34]

NOTES

[1] See, Erdmann, Johann Eduard, *History of Philosophy*, 3 vols. Harcourt, Brace & Co., New York 1925, Introduction to the first volume.

[2] In a rather more specialized field, i.e. *Navya Nyāya* logic, Professor D. H. Ingalls and his former student, Professor K. H. Potter, have been leaning heavily on contemporary American logicians, for their work—see, Ingalls' *Materials for the Study of Navya Nyāya*, Harvard University Press, and Potter '*Raghunātha Śiromaṇi's Padārthatattvanirūpana*, ibid. Potter studies modern logic under W. O. Quine.

[3] Guenther translated *Sekoddeśa*, p. 49, 'the outer world is no reality *per se*, it is apprehended in exactly the same way as a veil or a dream'—*nir-vastuka* corresponding to 'no reality *per se*!' *Yuganaddha*, Varanasi 1963, p. 60.

[4] Professor J. Ensink, 'The Sanskrit equivalent of a Tibetan term is a much more exact datum than a rendering in any other language.' From the fact that this statement introduces the Preface of Lokesh Chandra's first volume *Tibetan-Sanskrit-Dictionary*, Delhi, 1959–63, we learn that even Indian scholars zealous for the originality and dominance of things Indian *vis-à-vis* other Asian cultures do not realize that this is an understatement.

[5] The first phrase is due to St. Ullman, *Principles of Semantics*; the one-zero relational process' is my own analogy; Ullman did not encounter any such pattern.

[6] I use 'rubric' in the sense R. G. Collingwood used it in his *Metaphysics*—i.e. as a categorical clause tactily understood to precede every proposition.

[7] This term is C. D. Broad's, *Mind and Its Place in Nature*, MacMillan & Co. New York 1891–2, p. 432.

[8] This does not become clear from the relevant passage in the introduction; in fact, the statement 'Sanskrit scholars will perhaps consider these equivalents rather unsystematically arranged', p. xiv, would seem to deny the implication of an order of descending importance. The only extensive Tibetan-English Dictionary, first published in 1902, it was reprinted without change by the Government of West Bengal Press in 1960.

[9] A personal letter, dated August 16, 1959, that sGam.po.pa uses '*sems*' almost as one does the general term 'spirituality', and he calls it an 'operational counter', following A. Rapaport.

[10] In Guenther's translation: 'What is *karma*? It is motivation and motivatedness'—see *sGam.po.pa*, Rider & Co., London 1959, p. 74.

[11] This is a particularly opportune place to remind ourselves of the 'rubric': for in western philosophy the 'goal' of an action, if not known, is postulated—all 'progressive' ideologies are eventually based on a postulate, even when they claim that they intuit a goal (for which see K. Popper's *Open Society* in his chapter on Marxism); in Indian thought, the 'goal' (e.g. *nirvaṇa, mahāsukha*, etc.) is intuited—the notion of a postulate being alien to all Indian thought except perhaps to some logical schools of recent times.

[12] 'The Concept of Mind in Buddhist Tantrism', *Journal of Oriental Studies*, Hong Kong, July 1956.

[13] I am sure no Buddhologist has used 'mental event'—I think Guenther confuses this with his own earlier use of the phrase in his *Philosophy and Psychology of Abhidhamma*; the term is loaded with 'Gestalt'-psychology, to which he seemed strongly attracted until a few years ago.

[14] *Doha mdzod kyi snying po son gyi glu'i grel ba, Dohakośa hṛdaya-arthāgītiṭīkā, by Gynis med avadhūtī, bstan'gyur, rgyud, vol. zi fol. 74b Derge ed., trl. in op. cit., p. 263.*

[15] See Guenther, *Philosophy of Abhidhamma, passim*, and my review of it in J.A.S. XVIII/2, p. 306.

[16] 'Concept of Mind in Buddh. Tantr.', footnote 46, Hong Kong, July 1956.

[17] Cf. *sGam.po.pa*, p. 188.

[18] *Yuganaddha*, p. 175.

[19] Advayavajra's *Pañcākāra*, p. 43.

[20] In a letter dated August 16, 1959, Banaras.

[21] See Lama Anagarika Govinda, *Foundations of Tibetan Mysticism*, Rider & Co., London, 1959, p. 213: 'that which constitutes the spiritual or ideal character of a Buddha, the creative expression of formulation of this universal principle in the realm of inner vision: the Saṃbhogakāya, the "Body of Bliss" (rapture or a spiritual enjoyment), from which all true inspiration is born'.

[22] This analogy does not lose its usefulness even if we know that the popular term 'idealism' derives from 'ideal', the philosophical term from 'idea', i.e. in the Platonic sense of *eidola*; the analogy is semantical, not etymological. A philosopher who is not aware of the different etymological derivations would use the term in its two different applications just as I do even though I happen to know the different etymologies 'ideal-ism' and 'idea-lism'.

[23] Letter to me August 8, 1959, Banaras.

[24] Letter dated October 10, 1959, Banaras.

[25] October 17, 1959, Banaras.

[26] I am here putting the Sanskrit word first, as we have the *Guhyasamāja-Tantra* in the Sanskrit original.

[27] Letter October 17, 1958, Banaras.

[28] C. D. Broad would equate them with his 'experientially initiated possibilities of experience'.

[29] *sGam.po.pa*, p. 276.

[30] A. N. Prior, *Time and Modality*, London 1959.

[31] Letter August 16, 1959, Banaras.

[32] *Bṛhadāranyaka Up.*, V/1.

[33] Sthiramati's *Vṛtti*, p. 16; see also Guenther, *Philosophy and Psychology in the Abhidharma*, p. 288, Buddha Vihara, Lucknow 1957.

[34] Contemporary analysis and common sense would here unite with Buddhism, against the static Aristotelian-Christian ontology; see, F. H. Allport, *Theories of Perception and the Concept of Structure*, pp. 141 ff.

3

INDIA AND TIBET IN TANTRIC LITERATURE

ONCE the terminological problem has been pointed out, and some important illustrations have been made, we can now proceed to a survey which presupposes some acquaintance with the Tibetan Sanskrit lexical situation and at the same time provides a transition to the diffuse patterns of the tantric tradition.

In most of the academies in the western world where Tibetan is taught it is handled as a subject ancillary to Buddhist studies, as a sort of fill-in for research in Buddhist Sanskrit texts which have not, or only partially, been preserved in the original language. Tibetan studies, and especially Tibetan linguistics *per se*—without reference to Buddhism or to Buddhist texts—are as yet exceedingly rare, and the few scholars who are interested in Tibet, not as a feeder service to Indian and Buddhist studies, but as a culture area in itself, are few and far between. Scholars like Rolf Stein at Paris, Petech at Rome, Hugh Richardson in Britain, and the Seattle group, rightly resent the fact that Tibetan is being treated as nothing but a stopgap for unavailable Sanskrit material.

With the research of Professor G. Tucci at Rome and the Tibetologists at the University of Washington, in Seattle, there is a good chance that this state of affairs will be remedied. In addition to this, the physical presence of Tibetan scholars in India and in other parts of the world, including the United States, Britain, and several European countries, should be conducive to the study of

Tibetan culture *per se*. However, ironically perhaps and certainly understandably, scholars from among the Tibetan immigration in India are themselves not overly keen on divulging secular knowledge about their country. Occidental scholars, orientalists, and cultural anthropologists alike, don't seem to realize—or realize with reluctance only—that their zeal, their 'scientific' interests, are not necessarily shared by their informants. For the Tibetans at least, it is the Sanskrit-cum-Buddhist tradition which gives them the only lasting satisfaction and all the prestige they think worth while. The Tibetan scholars at Seattle, Washington—one of them being among the three most learned in the Tibetan emigration—smiled, at first, at the anthropologists' and sociologists' interest in Tibet for its own sake, that is without reference to Buddhism and its scholastic tradition. In the minds of many learned Tibetan scholars or monks, Sanskrit is and remains the *phags skad* (*āryabhāṣā*), the 'Noble Language', and Lama Kunga Labrang wanted to learn the *Nāgarī* alphabet from me in order to be able to transcribe Tibetan Buddhist texts into the original script, or into what he thought was the original script, of the Buddhist tradition.

Although it is perfectly justifiable for the cultural anthropologist to be interested in a cultural milieu, in a tradition without reference to its literary background, in the case of Tibet he is not likely to get much co-operation from his informants, unless they have been confronted with occidental scholars and exposed to western learning for a long time. In this manner the Tibetan attitude is accidental grist for the occidental Buddhologist mill: just as Tibetan *per se* is no object of linguistic study except as a feeder-service to the missing Sanskrit originals, to the western Buddhologist, the Tibetan monk-scholar feels exactly the same way and hardly regards Tibetan as an important object of study apart from Buddhist interest.

It goes without saying that references to India and to Indian mythological or ritualistic matters abound in Tibetan literature. Compared with these references, those to Tibet are negligible, in number and importance, in Indian texts. The reasons for this scarcity of references to the northern neighbour are sundry: first, there has never been much interest in non-Indian regions, throughout the religious and philosophical literature of India—after all, India is the most important and the only spiritually significant part of Jambudvīpa[1] (i.e. the generic name for the regions adjacent to India in the north, north-east, east, and south-east, with India at the centre; the etymology of the word and its exact connotation is not clear). There is a Jaina work called *Jambudvīpaprajñāpti*, the 'introduction to the knowledge of Jambudvīpa'; it is the sixth 'Upāṅga' of the eight Canonical Texts of the Jainas; Jacobi assigned this work to the third century A.D., which would place it at least two centuries previous to the beginnings of Buddhist proselytization in Tibet. The work enumerates Naipāla, Mahācīna, and Cīnadeśa—the term 'Bhoṭa' does not appear in it (vd. ed. *Jainagranthamālā*, Banaras 1899).

Secondly, Tibet as a geographical referend might well be included—or at least, not excluded—in the numerous Purānic accounts of India and Jambudvīpa; the orthodox northern demarcation of India is, of course, the Himālaya, but it is never quite clear what region is precisely denoted by such terms as *uttare pārvataḥ*, 'the mountains in the North', *auttarīyah* (i.e. *-deśah*, 'the northern regions'), both of which occur scores of times in Purānic and Epic literature; these terms definitely include Nepal, Sikkim, and Bhutan, but possibly also parts of Tibet. Thus, the Hindu *Pheṭkārinī Tantra* (ed. Moradabad 1920, p. 5)—a late work, probably of the thirteenth century—mentions the Goddess Ugratārā as *auttarīyair ārādhitā* 'worshipped by those in the North'; this Goddess is not worshipped in Kashmir, nor, to my knowledge, by Nepalese Hindus—on the other hand, the *sgrol-ma* (Tārā) of various forms is extremely popular in the Tibetan pantheon. B. Bhattacharya thinks she is a purely Buddhist goddess who was subsequently Hinduized (*Buddhist Iconography*, 77 f). Ugratārā in Buddhist tantric literature is synonymous with Mahācīnatārā (vd. Bhattacharya, ibid.). There is an image of Ugratārā in the Vajrayoginī Temple at Saṅku in Nepal, but Hindu visitors at this shrine call her Śamkarī, Spouse of Śiva, prompted possibly by the similarity of the place name, i.e. Saṅku (the Nepalese hardly distinguish the palatal and the dental sibilant). Whenever Hindus worship Tārā, she is simply the wife of Śiva, as in Bengal, where the male first name Tārāpati, Lord of Tārā, is extremely frequent. I do not know whether Bhattacharya really meant to say that Tārā was a purely Buddhist goddess, albeit Hinduized; I believe the Hindu Tārā is simply an entirely different deity; the name is a common epithet of all the great Hindu goddesses, and we find it in the *Sahasranāma*, in the 'Invocation of the thousand Names', of Lalitā (Śiva's spouse proper), of Sarasvatī, and of Lakṣmī; neither of them bears any relation to a Tibetan or Vajrayāṇa Buddhist goddess.

In this connection, it must also be said that the division into three *krāntas* or 'circles' of worship, and ritualistic tradition, is common to all Tantric texts, Hindu, Buddhist, and Jaina. Bagchi writes:[2] 'There is ample evidence to prove that the zone of heterodox Tantras went far beyond the natural limits of India. Some of the Tantras divide the Tantric world into three *krāntas* or regions, Viṣṇukrānta, Aśvakrānta, and Rathakrānta. Aśvakrānta comprises the region from the Vindhya mountains (in Central India) to Mahācīna including Nepal, and Rathakrānta from the Vindhya to the great ocean including Cambodia and Java. . . .'

This division into three vaguely circumscribed regions is rather typical of what I would call 'religious geography' in India; it is sufficiently broad so as to include whatever region was not really accessible to the compilers, or what they knew from pious hearsay. I am not even quite sure if Mahācīna ever meant Tibet: the late Dr. Raghuvira told me he thought it was Mongolia, and this is what Bagchi appears to have held.[3] Most scholars in India seem to agree that Mahācīna and Bhoṭa are synonyms; I would, however, suggest that the term should not really be equated with an actual geographical name—I think 'Mahācīna' to Hindu tantric authors suggested the entire region to the north of the Himālayas, Tibet, and at least parts of Mongolia and western China. There is no text in tantric literature which would indicate a serious attempt to demarcate any regions lying outside India; we have a parallel in the most-read sacred literature of the Hindus, the Purāṇas—'Suvarṇadvīpa', i.e. the 'Golden Continent' is mentioned in all of them, but the referends differ—the *Bhāgavatapurāṇa*[4] calls it *pālebhyo pūrve sthita*, 'located eastward from the Pālas, i.e. Bengal', which might mean Burma or perhaps Siam; the more recent *Skandapurāṇa*[5] refers to Suvarṇadvīpa as *agneyeṣu vistṛtaḥ* 'stretched out in the south-east', which would point to the usually accepted identification of Suvarṇadvīpa with Indonesia.[6]

The third reason for the lack of geographical detail in Indian texts seems to me the unbelievable credulousness of the Indian religious with regard to reports on places of worship outside his own ken—this has not changed through the ages. I have heard two Hindu priests at Ernakulam (Kerala) saying that Śakti herself dispenses drugs against gout and other diseases: She, in the form of a virgin, lived in a cave at a shrine in a far-off western land called 'Rudradeśa', i.e. 'Region of Śiva'. I found out that this news was inspired by the fame of the Lady of Lourdes in France; the history of this modification was easy to trace, and exemplifies the said credulousness: the area around Ernakulam has a substantial population of Syrian Christians, and many women of that community have been given the name 'Lourdhammal'[7] since the beginning of this century. 'Lourdes' sounds very similar to 'Rudra-deś' when pronounced by speakers of Malayalam and Tulu—most Syrian Christians unfamiliar with occidental languages and spellings would pronounce the last syllable of 'Lourdes' not knowing that it is mute in French.

More possible reasons for the scarcity of topographical reference or for the lack of geographical accuracy in such references can be readily adduced and subsumed in the above three headings. Caste-Hindus lose their caste when they cross the northern mountains just as when they cross the ocean; places that cannot be inspected are not described with any claim to precision; escorts of Buddhist missionaries who returned from Tibet told wild tales about that inaccessible country, with impunity; Tibetans who came to study at Nālandā or Vikramaśilā might have done the same.

We can hardly trust Tibetan sources when they tell us about the conquest of large parts of India by Tibetan rulers, with which Tārānātha's *History* is replete; chiefly because no Indian sources whatever corroborate these reports. It is thinkable that Tārānātha did not really mean a region beyond Nepal or beyond Bengal when he speaks of 'Central India'.[8] Tibetan warrior chiefs seem to have made inroads into Magadha, Bengal, and perhaps the regions adjacent to Western Napal, i.e. the districts of Almora and Gorakhpur in Uttar Pradesh. Nothing comprehensive has yet been written about these Tibetan conquests on Indian territory; there are scattered references in volumes 3, 4, and 5 of the encyclopaedic *History and Culture of the Indian People.*[9] One of the very few reliable sources of Indian historiography is the famous *Rājātaraṅgiṇī* by the Kashmiri court scholar Kalhāṇa, who flourished in the twelfth century A.D.[10] In this enthusiastic treatment of King Lalitāditya, who ascended the throne of Kashmir about A.D. 724, Kalhāṇa reports the king was 'eager for conquests and passed his life chiefly on expeditions'. He sent a diplomatic mission to the Chinese Emperor in A.D. 733 to induce him to make common cause against the Tibetans.[11] In his enumeration of countries and kings whom Lalitāditya defeated, Kalhāṇa writes,[12] 'he conquered the Kambojas,[13] the Tukharas, Bhauṭṭas (i.e. Tibetans), Dāradas (i.e. the Dardic groups of which the actual Kashmiris are a part), and vanquished a king named Mammuni.'

In the first half of the eighth century, Tibet wielded enormous influence over Nepal. In a grant of the Licchavi King Śivadeva, dated A.D. 714, there is a reference to '*Bhoṭṭa-Viṣṭi*' or a corvee payable to Tibet.[14] That Nepal was a vassal to Tibet during this era is not documented by any Indian or Tibetan source, except for this casual reference to the corvee; there is only a Chinese source which throws light on this phase.[15]

King Yaśovarman of the Central Indian Chandella Dynasty ascended the throne after his father King Harśa's death around A.D. 925. An inscription at Khajuraho in Vindhya Pradesh, Central India, mentions that he received an image of the God Viṣṇu from Devapāla (i.e. of the Bengali Pāla Dynasty which was one of the foremost champions of Buddhism), which had been given to

Devapāla's father Herambāpāla by King Sahi who had obtained the image from the King of Bhoṭa (Tibet).[16]

There seems to be no mention of Tibet in any secular Indian document between the two periods referred to above.

That Tibetans may have held portions of Bengal for a short time seems to be supported by the fact that the early Arab travellers Ibn Haukal and Iṣṭakhrī who wrote in the tenth century, refer to the Bay of Bengal as the 'Tibetan Sea'.[17] As to the exact extent of their actual conquests in India, we have to rely on Tibetan sources, due to the complete lack of Indian material.[18]

Zia Barni, an officer at the court of Muhammad-bin-Tughlag, who ascended the throne of Delhi in 1325, wrote a sort of political record of his time in Persian, *Ta'rīkh-i-Firuz-Shāhī*, and the famous Arab traveller Ibn Batutah mentions Muhammed-bin-Tughlag's plans to 'capture the mountain of Kara-jal . . . which lies between the territories of Hind and those of China'.[19]

A thirteenth-century work in Old Bengali, the *Prākṛta-paiṅgalam*,[20] says that 'the King of Kāśī fought successfully with the kings of Gauḍa, Vaṅga, Kaliṅgā, Telaṅgaṇā, Mahārāṣṭra, Saurāṣṭra, Champaraṇa, Nepāla, Bhoṭa, Cīnā, Lahovara (Lahore), Oḍrā, and Mālavā.' D. C. Ganguly[21] thinks that the 'King of Kāśī' (i.e. Banaras) is Govindacandra of the Gahaḍāvala Dynasty, of Rājput provenance; Govindacandra ruled approximately from A.D. 1114 to 1154. The enumeration of Bhoṭa and Cīnā as separate, as also the juxtaposition with much less distant and much less important, small regions like Lahore and Champaraṇa, seems to imply that some border regions are meant in this passage also, rather than Tibet or China. If contemporary vernacular usage may be used for analogy, the custom of the Kumaoni-Hindi speaking people in the District of Almora is to refer to the northern neighbour by a sort of directional metonymy—'Bhoṭa' for them means the district adjacent to their own in the North, and they would probably think of just two small areas, Garbiang on the Indian and Taghlakot on the Tibetan side of the Indo-Nepalese-Tibetan corner of the Almora District. They do not, however, mean just the area inhabited by the Bhūṭiyas, a Hindu group with a Tibetan ethnical and a mixed linguistic background (Bhūṭiya is structurally Tibetan with a very large percentage of Indian words), for the Bhūṭiyas live in settlements between Kumaon villages, and not beyond Garbiang.[22]

I now proceed to Sanskrit texts, most of which are straight tantric literature. Here our search is bound to yield, at least quantitatively, better results. In tantric literature and practice, the direction of influence is almost entirely a one-way affair—it seems reasonable to assume that the tantric elements were imported into Tibet along with the Buddhist precepts, though this does not preclude the possibility that certain features of tantric practice could have had some analogues in pre-Buddhist Tibet; Hoffmann and Nebesky-Wojkowitz think that the tantric practices among the '*Ka' rgywd pa* monks are largely of Bon provenance; Tucci does not commit himself, to my knowledge. Be that as it may, I do not think there is any portion of the *rgyud* section of the Tibetan canon which could not be traced to some Indian model so far as practice and doctrine are concerned. From this conjecture —it cannot be anything more at this point—it in no way follows that there could not have been similar procedures, or even apparently identical items, in pre-Buddhist Bon: similar efforts yield independent inventions and parallel procedures in religious and mystical matters in areas that have had no mutual contact of any sort.[23]

I think that the numerous references to Tibetan deities and Tibetan *ācāras*, i.e. ritualistic and meditative methods, have no geographical significance whatever, so far as the authors were concerned; I would venture to say that *ācāras* which would seem either very strange or repulsive to the Indian aspirant, were particularly eligible for the epithets 'of Mahācīna' or 'of Bhoṭa'. This trend has continuity in modern Hindu scholarship; P. C. Bagchi,[24] B. Bhattacharya in his short prefaces to Vajrayāṇa texts published in the Gaekwad Series, and all the less illustrious pandits known to me, tend to claim rather peremptorily that the left-handed rites, and the deities propitiated by such and other uncanny ritual, are of non-Indian origin.

The *Kubjikā Tantra*, a late work probably related to the Gorakhnāth tradition, says:[25] 'Go to India to establish yourself in the whole country and make manifold creations in the sacred places of primary and secondary importance.' The goddess Kubjikā is the tutelary deity of the low-caste potters, who are therefore said to belong to the *kubjikāmnaya* or the Kubjikā tradition; the goddess is also worshipped by the Bhūṭiyas of Almora and has many small shrines in the Nepalese and Indian *terai*. It being Śiva who gives the order to the goddess in the stanza quoted above, the idea seems to be that she should proceed from their home, Mount Kailāsa in Tibet, and establish her own worship in India.

The terms '*Cīnācāra*' and '*Mahācīna*' are used as synonyms in the *Tārātantra* which has been adopted by Hindu and Buddhist tantrics.[26] The age of this text is unknown, and no one seems to have tried to date it even approximately.[27] The Tantra says that the cult of Cīna-Tārā came from the country of Mahācīna. The great Brahmin seer Vasiṣṭha went to Mahācīna to meet the Buddha and obtain instruction from him. This episode is only mentioned in the *Tārātantra*; the text, however, which presents it in detail, is the *Rudrayāmala*, a text whose age cannot be determined yet; its popularity in Bengal and Assam might indicate that it is of Bengali origin; it is certainly later than the *Mahānirvāṇa*, as it quotes several passages from the latter which is usually ascribed to the eleventh century A.D. By that time, organized Buddhism had virtually disappeared from India, and the Vajrayāṇa tradition had been effectively disparaged by the Hindu pandits. It is all the more astonishing that this account of Vasiṣṭha, a patron sage of the orthodox Brahmins, is related here in such detail, though the rest of the work teaches orthodox Brahmanical views. The account is found in the eighteenth chapter of the *Rudrayāmala*:[28] Vasiṣṭha the self-controlled, the son of Brahmā, practised austerities for many ages in a lonely place. He did spiritual exercises (*sādhanā*) for six thousand years, but still the daughter of the Mountain (i.e. the goddess Pārvatī, Śiva's Śakti) did not appear to him. Getting angry, he went to his father and told him the method of his *sādhanā*. He then requested Brahmā: 'Give me another *mantra*, O Lord, since this one does not grant me *siddhi* (i.e. the desired success, vision of the goddess), else I shall utter a terrible curse in your presence.' Brahmā dissuaded him and said: 'O son, who art learned in the path of yoga, do not act like this. Worship her again with full devotion, then she will appear and grant you boons. She is the supreme Śakti . . . [here follows an enumeration of the various qualities and epithets of the goddess]. . . . She is attached to the pure Cīnacāra (*śuddha-cīnācāra-ratā*; i.e. the ritualistic method of *Cīna*). She is the initiator of the Śakti-cakra (*śakti-cakra-pravartikā*; i.e. the circle of worshippers of the goddess). . . . She is Buddheśvarī, i.e. the Preceptress of Buddha[29]. . . .' Having heard (these admonitions of Brahmā) . . . he (Vasiṣṭha) betook himself to the shores of the sea. For a thousand years he did *japa* (repetition) of her *mantra*; still he received no instructions from her. Thereupon the sage grew extremely angry, and being perturbed in his mind he began to curse the Mahāvidyā (i.e. the goddess). Having sipped water (i.e. having done *ācamana*—the ritualistic sipping of water which precedes any religious and many profane actions of the Brahmins) he uttered a great, terrible curse. Thereupon the Lady of the tantrics (Kuleśvarī) appeared before the sage. She who dispels the yogis' apprehensions said: 'How now, Brahmin, why hast thou uttered a terrible curse without any reason? Thou dost not understand my tantric precepts (*kulāgamā*), nor knowest thou how to worship me. How can a god or a man ever obtain the sight of my lotus-feet by mere yoga practice (*yogābhyāsamātra*)? Meditation on me is without austerity and without pain. To him who desires my tantric precepts (*kulāgamā*), who is successful (*siddha*) in my *mantra*, and who has known my Vedic precepts (already), my *sādhanā* (exercise for final vision) is meritorious and inaccessible even to the Vedas (*vedānāmapyago-cara*). Roam in Mahācīna, the country of the Buddhists, and always follow the Atharvaveda (*bauddhadeśe 'tharvavede mahācīne sadā vraja*).[30] Having gone there and seen my lotus-feet which are *mahābhāva* (i.e. the total bliss experience which is my essence) thou shalt, O great seer, become versed in my *kula* (i.e. the tantric "family") and a great *siddha* (adept).' Having thus spoken, she became formless and vanished into the ether and then passed through the ethereal region. The great seer having heard this from the Mahāvidyā Sarasvati went to the land of Cīna where Buddha is established (*buddhapratiṣṭhita*). Having (there) repeatedly bowed to the ground, Vasiṣṭha said: 'Protect me, O Mahādeva who art imperishable in the form of Buddha (*buddharūpe Mahādeva*).[31] I am the very humble Vasiṣṭha, son of Brahmā. My mind is ever perturbed. I have come here to Cīna for the *Sādhanā* of the great goddess. I do not know the path leading to *siddhi* (occult success). Thou knowest the path of the *devas*. Yet, seeing the type of discipline (viz. the left-handed rituals involved), doubts assail my mind. Destroy them and my wicked mind bent on the Vedic ritual (only). O Lord, in thy abode there are rites which have been ostracized from the Veda (*vedabahiṣkṛtāh*). How is it that wine, meat, woman are drunk, eaten, and enjoyed by heaven-clad (i.e. nude, *digambara*) *siddhas* (adepts) who are excellent (*varāḥ*) and trained in the drinking of blood?[32] They drink constantly and enjoy beautiful women (*muhurmuhuḥ prapibanti ramayanti varāṅganām*). With red eyes they are always exhilarated and replete with flesh and wine (*sadā māṃṣāsavaiḥ pūrṇāḥ*). They have power to give favours and to punish. They are beyond the Vedas (*vedasyāgocarāh*). They enjoy wine and women (*madyastrīsevane ratāh*).' Thus spoke the great yogi, having seen the rites which are banned from the Veda. Then bowing low with folded palms he humbly said, 'How can inclinations such as these be purifying to the mind? How can there be *siddhi* (occult success) without the Vedic rites?'

The Buddha then proceeds to explain the *Cīnacāra* (the discipline of *Cīna*) at length to the Brahmin sage, and the explanation boils down to a hierarchy of spiritual disciplines, the lowest of them being that for '*paśus*' (lowly type of aspirants), tantamount to the Vedic ritual, the highest and most efficient being *Cīnacāra* involving the use of wine, meat, women, etc. The text then concludes thus: 'Having said this, he whose form is Buddha made him (i.e. Vasiṣṭha) practise *sādhanā* (spiritual exercises). He said, "O Brahmin, do thou serve Mahāśakti. Do thou now practise *sādhanā* with wine and thus shalt thou get the sight of the lotus-feet of Mahāvidyā (i.e. the goddess—all the terms used here are synonyms for the goddess, i.e. Mahāsakti, Mahāvidyā, "the great power", "the great knowledge" Sarasvatī, etc.).' Vasiṣṭha then did as he was told and obtained *siddhi* through *Cīnacāra*.

The *Brahmāyāmala* is a similar text, though it does not seem to be quite so popular in Bengal as the *Rudrayāmala*. P. C. Bagchi thought it was composed in the eighth century.[33] The *Brahmāyāmala* gives a similar account of this key episode, a difference being that Vasiṣṭha starts off at Kāmakhyā, the famous *pīṭha* (shrine) of the goddess in Assam, not far from the Tibetan and the Chinese border. Here, Vasiṣṭha complains of his failure and is told to go to the Blue Mountains (*Nīlācalā*) and worship the supreme goddess at *Kāmakhyā* (Kamrup, Assam). He was told that Viṣṇu in the form of the Buddha alone knew the ritual according to the indispensable *Cīnacāra*. Vasiṣṭha therefore went to the country of Mahācīna, which is situated on the slope of the Himālaya[34] and which is inhabited by great adepts and thousands of beautiful young damsels whose hearts were gladdened with wine, and whose minds were blissful due to erotic sport (*vilāsa*). They were adorned with clothes which kindle the mood for dalliance (*sṛṅgārāveśa*) and the movement of their hips made their girdles tinkle with their little bells. Free of fear and prudishness, they enchanted the world. They surrounded Īśvara in the form of Buddha. . . . When Vasiṣṭha saw Him in the form of Buddha (*buddharūpī*) with eyes drooping from wine, he exclaimed: 'What, is Viṣṇu doing these things in his Buddha-form? This *ācāra* (method) is certainly opposed to the teaching of the Veda (*vedavādaviruddha*). I do not approve of it.' When he thus spoke to himself he heard a voice coming from the ether saying: 'O thou who art devoted to good acts, do not entertain such ideas. This *ācāra* (method) yields excellent results in the worship of Tārinī (i.e. Tārā). She is not pleased with anything which is contrary to this (*ācāra*). If thou dost wish to gain Her grace speedily, then worship her according to *Cīnacāra* (the method of *Cīna*). . . .' Buddha, who had taken wine . . . spoke to him: 'The five *makāras* (i.e. the ingredients of left-handed tantric ritual, *mada* wine, *matsya* fish, *māṃsa* meat, *mudrā* parched kidney bean and other aphrodisiacs, and *maithuna* or ritualistic copulation) are (constituents of) *Cīnacāra* . . . and they must not be disclosed (to the non-initiate).'

The Buddhist goddess Tārā and the goddess Nīlasarasvatī (i.e. the blue goddess Sarasvatī) are probably identical.[35] She is called '*akṣobhya-devīmūrdhanyā*' (having Akṣobhya on her head')—and she is said to dwell 'on the west side of Mount Meru', implying Mahācīna, Bhoṭa, etc. The text is the fifth chapter of the *Sammoha Tantra*[36] which is a rather late Hindu or Buddhist work current in Nepal—it was composed approximately in the thirteenth century according to Sastri's introduction. The text is a good specimen of Professor Edgerton's Buddhist Hybrid Sanskrit.[37] Bagchi renders it thus:[38] Maheśvara said to Brahmā: 'Hear from me with attention about Mahānīlasarasvatī. It is through her favour that you will narrate the four Vedas. There is the lake called Cola on the western side of Mount Meru. The Mother Goddess Nilogratārā herself was born there. . . . The light issuing from my upper eye fell into the lake Cola and took on a blue colour. There was a sage called Akṣobhya, who was Śiva himself in the form of a *muni* (seer), on the northern side of Mount Meru. It was he who meditated first on the goddess, who was Pārvatī herself reincarnated in Cīnadeśa (the country Cīna) at the time of the great deluge. . . .'

Bagchi adds, 'It is idle to try to find out a precise geographical information here, but it may be suggested that Cola is probably to be connected with the common word for lake *kul*, *kol*, which is found with names of so many lakes to the west and north of T'ien shan, i.e. in the pure Mongolian zone.'[39]

The third chapter of our *Sammoha Tantra* enumerates a number of *pīṭhas* (centres of worship of a female deity),[40] and divides them into regions according to their use of the *kādi* and the *hādi* methods, respectively.[41] 'Bhoṭa', 'Mahācinā', and 'Cīna' are enumerated only with *kādi pīthas*. The commonly accepted, though by no means undisputed, orthodox idea is that *kādi* mantras and their use as part of a ritualistic method are aimed at securing worldly or magical success; *hādi* mantras on the other hand are said to help towards the supreme achievement of *nirvāṇa* or its Hindu equivalents. I think that something like this accounts for the fact that Bhoṭa, Cīna, Mahācīna are listed in *kādi* areas, and not in the *hādi* area enumeration. The regions beyond the mountain stand for magic and *siddhi* whose pursuits are always viewed to an extent as heretical. Some of the *hādi* regions listed in the text (vol. 7a) 'cannot be identified' so Bagchi avers;[42] some of them, however, seem to be adjacent to Tibetan soil but are still cis-Himālayan—thus 'Bālhika' which must be Balkh, 'Dyorjalā' which might well be a predecessor of 'Darjeeling', which name is derived either from Tibetan *rDorje-gliṅ 'thunderbolt (vajra-) region'*, or from Sanskrit *durjayaliṅga*, 'the invincible Śiva'.

The same text also lists the number of tantras current in different regions, and claims 'in Cīna there are a hundred principal and seven subsidiary ones'. I do not know if this number correlates with any listing of the *Rgyud*-sections in the Tibetan canon or with any other non-Indian enumeration.[43]

The *Kālīvilāsa Tantra*[44] is a late Hindu text, whose age has not been determined; from its style I would think we might safely place it between the thirteenth and the seventeenth centuries. It is very popular among non-tantric Brahmins in Bengal, and it sounds a note hostile to left-handed rites which were equally popular with the non-Brahmin tantric groups of Bengal. The text condemns the ritualistic use of women, wine, etc., and says that the tantras enjoining left-handed ritual are 'prohibited in our era' (*kalau varjitāni*). The *Kālīvilāsa*, quoting the *Mahāsiddhasarasvatī Tantra*,[45] says that the tantras of the Aśvakrānta region, i.e. the region from the Vindhya mountains northward including Nepal, Tibet, etc., were promulgated to confuse the hypocrites (*pāṣaṇḍa*) and the heretics. Quoting the *Kulārṇava Tantra*, the text says Mahādeva (Śiva) spoke of the *kaula*-rites (the left-handed rites of the Aśvakrānta region) 'lest all men should get liberated (i.e. prematurely)'—which is a rather insidious statement against left-handed forms of tantric practice, in a tantric text of the right-handed tradition.

The next quotation is from the famous *Karpurādistotram*, a

Hindu tantric work which has given much pain to non-tantric Hindus. The work is fairly old; though Avalon[46] did not try to establish any date, I would place it between the ninth and eleventh centuries; its style bears marked similarity to that of the *Saundaryalaharī* traditionally ascribed to, but certainly not much more recent than Śaṃkarācārya (eighth century); the latter inspired a lot of poetical piety among tantrics and non-tantrics in the following two or three centuries, and I think this work can be safely classed as belonging to this category. It has been extremely popular in Bengal and Assam up to this day. Of all the major Hindu Śākta tantras, this one is the most radically 'left-handed'. Verse 16 says:[47] 'Whosoever on Tuesday midnight . . . makes offering but once with devotion of a hair of his Śakti in the cremation ground, becomes a great poet, a Lord of the earth, and goes forth mounted on an elephant.' Now the commentator explains this passage as '(he who) offers a pubic hair of his Śakti with its root'—*ritualem post copulationem semine suo unctam.*[48] In a subcommentary[49] called *Rahasyārthasādhikā* (i.e., aid to the hidden meaning [of the *Karpurādistotra*]), Vimalānanda Svāmī says that this refers to '*Mahācīna—sādhanā*' and to the *sādhanā* (mode of worship) of the Goddess Mahānīlā who is worshipped in that region. This note—which is not called for by the text—would corroborate my previous suggestion: a text which expatiates left-handed rites will usually be given a metaphorical ('afferent' in my terminology) interpretation by an orthodox Hindu commentator; but if the text is so overtly left-handed that no such interpretation is possible, the doctrine is made to lie outside India—and Mahācīna is a sort of scapegoat. Once this is done, there are no scruples about putting it thickly, i.e. *yoni-śiśna-galitabīja-yuktaṃ samūlaṃ cikuram*, ibid., '*radice extirpatem capillam cum semine membro virile pudendoque muliebre ablata*, sc. *qui offert.*'

The *Kaulāvalinirṇaya*[50] must be a late text (about sixteenth century), as it quotes from almost all the well-known Hindu tantras including the *Karpurādistotram*. The text identifies Tārā with the somewhat uncanny Hindu-Buddhist goddess Chinnamastā, 'Split-Head', the goddess who holds her own chopped-off heads (two of them) in her hands, blood gushing forth from her decapitated trunk, which she catches with her mouths thus supported by her hands. Verse 54 says 'he who is desirous of wealth should meditate through *japa*-repetition of the mantra on the Vidyā (i.e. Tāra, Chinnamastā) through the ritualistic union with the supreme woman (*parayoṣit*—either the consecrated Śakti, or, literally, a woman married to another man; the latter interpretation being the one given by the opponents of the tantric tradition), emitting his semen in the 'creeper-mood' (*latābhāva*-compounds with *latā*-'creeper', as first constituent always indicate left-handed rites, the derived meaning being the (consecrated) woman who embraces the adept like a creeper, 'he, the best of the adepts; let him ceaselessly do *japa* of his mantra for the sake of obtaining *dharma, artha,* and *kāma,* thus Tārā grants quick success in the Cīna-method.'[51]

This is a typical instance of what I have come to regard as a pervasive convention: the methods of '*Cīna*', *Mahācīna*' and 'Bhoṭa'—the terms seem to be used interchangeably in these texts —are conducive to all kinds of success *except* that of total liberation; in this verse there is the most perfect statement of the convention: *kāma*—creature comforts; *artha*—secular success; *dharma*—religious merit leading to better rebirth, but not '*mokṣa*', the supreme human goal—are granted by the votary of the '*Cīna*', etc., methods.

Verse 59 repeats the proposition expressly for Chinnamastā: 'in the method of Mahācīna, the goddess Chinnamastā bestows success'.[52]

The most outstanding purely Buddhist text relevant to our topic is the *Sādhanāmālā*, a Buddhist Hybrid Sanskrit classic. The oldest manuscript is of the year A.D. 1167 as the colophon shows.[53] The *Sādhanāmālā* has two *sādhanās* (ritualistic procedures) dedicated to the goddess Mahācīnatārā, and two *dhyānas* (meditations), one in prose and one in verse, describing the goddess in identical form.[54] *Sādhanāmālā* No. 127 describes her thus: 'she stands in the *pratyālīḍha* posture (i.e. with one leg straight, the other one slightly bent), is awe-inspiring, has a garland of heads hanging from her neck, is short and has a protruding belly; of terrible looks, her complexion is like that of the blue lotus; she is three-eyed, one-faced, celestial, and laughs terribly; in a pleasantly excited mood (*suprahṛṣṭā*—in the mood of erotic excitement), she stands on a corpse, is decked with an eightfold snake-ornament, has red, round eyes, wears garments of tigerskin around her loins, is in youthful bloom, is endowed with the five auspicious *mudrās* (here postures, i.e. counting her four hand gestures, and her bodily posture as the fifth), and has a lolling tongue; she is most terrible, appearing fierce with her bare fangs, carries the sword and the *kartrī* (in the classical idiom *kartarī*—a knife) in her two right hands, and the lotus and skull in her two left hands; whose crown consisting of one chignon is brown and fiery and is adorned with the image of Akṣobhya.[55] This is the *Sādhanā* of Mahācīnatārā.' According to the colophon,[56] the *Sādhanā* of Mahācīnatārā was restored from a tantra called the *Mahācīnatantra,* and is attributed to Śāsvatavajra.

The Hindus took over this goddess into their later pantheon; the *Tārārahasyā* of Brahmānanda who taught in the sixteenth century, and the *Tantrasāra* of Kṛṣṇānanda Āgamavāgīśa, of still more recent origin, contain iconographical descriptions of Tārā that are almost literally identical with that of Mahācīnatārā just quoted. By that time, the distinction between the Hindu goddess Tārā, wife of Śiva, and her Buddhist namesake had become completely blurred—if indeed it was ever rigidly adhered to. The two Hindu texts do not mention Mahācīna, etc., the originally alleged provenance of the goddess having either been forgotten or ignored.

Sādhanāmālā No. 141 describes the worship of the goddess Ekajaṭā (lit: 'having one chignon'), so do a few more *sādhanās* in this collection. The colophon of *sādhanā* 141, however, contains the cryptic words '*Āryanāgārjunapādaiḥ Bhoṭesūddhṛtam iti*', which B. Bhattacharya[57] renders 'restored from Tibet by Ārya Nāgārjuna', not the author of the *Mādhyamika-Kārikā*, but the famous Siddha from among the eighty-four Vajrayāṇa Buddhist sorcerer-saints, to whom many *sādhanās* are attributed.

The last text I want to adduce here seems to be the most

complete Hindu statement of tantric topics pertaining to Tibet, etc.; from among the extant Hindu tantric works (i.e. disregarding the aforesaid *Mahācīnatantra*, which is not known to be extant) the *Śaktisaṅgama-Tantra* contains a whole chapter captioned *Mahācīna-krama* 'the Method of Mahācīna'.

Śāktas all over India regard the *Śaktisaṅgama* as an extremely important text, and its popularity ranks second perhaps only to the *Mahānirvāṇa*. The text is fairly old—I would place it in the eighth to ninth century on some inner evidence: first, there is in it much preoccupation with Vajrayāṇa Buddhist terminology, quite a few mantras occur in the *Guhyasamāja* and other Vajrayāṇa works. We have '*vajrapuṣpeṇa juhuyāt*' ('he should sacrifice by means of the *vajra*-flower') in the 18th Paṭala, No. 17, which presupposes the entire notion of libations based on the adept's identification with *vajra*-hood; or '*vairocanāṣṭakaṃ pūjya tataḥ padmāntakān yajet*' in the 15th Paṭala, No. 38 ('having worshipped the eight forms of Vairocana he should offer sacrifice to the ones with '*-padmā*' at the end of their names i.e. the goddesses Manipadmā, Vajrapadmā, etc.); or again '*śūlarājā mahākrūra sarvabhūtapriyaṃkara, siddhiṃ saṃkalpitaṃ dehi vajraśūla namo'stu te*', 68th Paṭala, No. 18, i.e. 'O king with the trident (i.e. Śiva), great terrible one, bestowing favours on all the *bhūtas* (demons, etc.), give the desired success, *Vajra*-trident holder, be praised.' This one is particularly interesting, as it shows a combination of Hindu and Buddhist elements of equal power. Hence it seems the Vajrayāṇa literature was either contemporary with or still greatly in vogue at the time this tantra was composed, which would not be the case later than A.D. 1000; on the other hand, its doctrines are deeply influenced by the monistic interpretation of Śāktism initiated by Saṃkarācārya and his disciples (eighth century), hence I think it is quite justifiable to place it in between A.D. 900 and 1000. The Śaktisaṁgama is a large work and three-fourths of its total bulk has been published so far.[58]

I am giving a free rendering of the '*Mahācīna-krama* section in the *Śaktisamgama*, which is contained in the Second Book, Tārākhaṇḍa, Vol. XCI, G.O.S., p. 104 ff.[59]: The Goddess said to

Śiva: 'I desire to know the method of Mahācīna.' Śiva then replied: 'O Tārā, by the method of Mahācīna results are quickly obtained; Brahmā-Cīna, the celestial Cīna, the heroic Cīna, Mahācīna, and Cīna, these are the five sections or regions; the method of these has been described in two manners, as "*sakala*" (with divisions), and as "*niṣkala*" (undivided). That which is *sakala* is Buddhist, that which is *niṣkala* is Brahmin in its application.' Then Śiva seems reluctant to continue with the instruction, as this knowledge is not even obtainable by the *devas*, *yakṣas*, by saints and great scholars, etc. The goddess thereupon implores Śiva to be merciful and to reveal it nevertheless, and moved by her entreaties Śiva consents and continues. The initial portions of the *Mahācīnakrama* are pretty much the same as usual meditative procedure: a bath must be taken, the mind must be purified through '*japa*', etc., *tarpana* (offering of water) has to be made, clean raiments have to be donned; then, 'he should constantly worship the goddess, having bathed and having taken food (as contrasted to non-tantric procedures where fasting is enjoined previous to formal worship). At midnight he should bring his sacrifice through *mantra* (or, accompanied by the proper *mantra*, "*baliṃ mantreṇa dāpayet*", v. 28). Never should he dislike women, especially not those who participate in the ritual, and having entered the place for "*japa*", he should perform a great number of "*japa-s*". The adept should go to the woman, touch her, look at her, O Thou with the Gem in the Crest, he should eat betel-nuts and other edible ingredients (i.e. used for the ritual); and, having eaten meat, fish, curds, honey, and drunk wine as well as the other prescribed edible she should proceed with his *japa*. In this *Mahācīna*-method there is no rule about the directions (i.e. about which direction the aspirant has to face, etc.), nor about time, nor about the posture, etc., nor is there any rule for the choice of time for "*japa*", nor for invocation and sacrifice. The rules are made according to his own liking in this *sādhanā* of the great *mantra*, with regard to the garments worn, the posture, the general arrangements, the touching and non-touching of lustral water. And, O Queen of the Gods, he should anoint his body with oil, should always chew betel (*tāṃbulaṃ bhakṣayet sadā*), and should dress in all sorts of garments (as he pleases). He should undertake the *mantra*-bath (i.e. he should meditate on the *mantra* in lieu of any ritual, "*mantra-snānaṃ caret*"), should always take refuge in me. This, O Goddess, shall be the sage's bath according to the method of Mahācīna (*mahācīnakrame devi viprasnānamidam bhavet*). He should keep his mind free from apperceptions, i.e. in the state of "*nirvikalpa*" (*nirvikalpamanascaret*), he should worship using incense, white and ruby-coloured lotus leaves, vilva blossoms (or rather "the pericarp leaves of the vilva" as opposed to the green leaves of the vilva tree), and bherukā leaves, etc., but he should avoid (the use of) the (otherwise auspicious) tulsī leaf.[60] He should further avoid the vilva leaf—there is no contradiction here; he should use the vilva blossom, but should not use the leaf of the vilva tree, though I don't see why. It would be more natural if the text read "*arcayet*" instead of "*varjayet*", e.g. "*varjayed-vilvapātrañca*", vs. 37), and he should diligently avoid the abstention from drinking ("*maru*", a fast where no liquid is taken). He should not harbour any kind of (sectarian) malice, should not take the name of Hari (Viṣṇu), and should not touch the tulsī leaf. He should always drink wine, O goddess, and should always demean himself like the rutting elephant (or "like Caṇḍāla women", *mataṅgibhir vihāravān*; low-caste women are said to be particularly lascivious and given to amorous demeanour); he should, O goddess, do *japam* with singular attention.'[61]

'. . . the threefold horizontal lines of fine sandel paste mixed with *kesara* (*Rottleria Tinctoria*) seeds (*kucandanaṃ tripundraṃ ca tataḥ sakesaraṃ śive*, vs. 44) spread on his forehead, O Śiva, wearing a garland of skulls around his neck and the skull-bowl in his hand, he who is given to this *ācāra* (discipline) becomes a Mahācīnite (*Mahācīnakramī*, one following the *Mahācīna* method); always in a joyful mood, always serving the devotees, he wears . . . (here follows a lengthy enumeration of other articles, rosaries, etc.).' The goddess then expresses her doubts as to whether such rites are beneficent, and how Brahmins can practise them, these rites being obviously non-Vedic (*vedavihīnaśca ye dharmā* verse 49). In reply to this query of his spouse, Śiva winds up saying that Brahmins—or, as I understand it, people who insist on Brahmin ritual—are not entitled to these (*Mahācīna*) rites in this age (*kalau tatra niṣiddhaṃ syādbrāhmanānāṃ Maheśvari*, verse 50.) Those who follow the *Cīna* (identical with *Mahācīna*) rites are dear to him, if they perform their ablutions in the manner indicated earlier, and if they eat and enjoy the ingredients designed by him for the rite (*sarvameva hṛdaṃbhoje mayi sarvam pratiṣṭhitam*, verse 57). 'Cherishing these attitudes in his heart, his mind ever directed towards their fulfilment, abandoning any dualistic attitude, he becomes Lord of all *siddhis* (spiritual powers); Brahmā and Vasiṣṭha, as well as the other great seers, they all worship in the undivided method (i.e. the *Mahācīna-krama*) at all times. The worshippers of Tārā, O great goddess, they are the true Brahmins; in this age the great Brahma-knowledge is indeed hard to attain.'[62] This, incidentally, seems to suggest that the rites called 'undivided' (*niṣkala*) should be called Brahmanical—who could be more Brahmin-like than Brahmā the demiurge and Vasiṣṭha—and this in spite of the fact that their origin be located in Tibet.

Summarizing this chapter, we would have to say that mutual references in Indian and Tibetan texts are quite disparate. Whereas the Tibetans have looked to India as the *Phags Yul* (*Āryadeśa*) 'the Noble Land', not only as the birthplace of the Buddha, but as the locus of the original teaching, as the actual or stipulated centre of Tibetan culture, there is no reciprocity of any sort. Historiography being a virtually non-existent genre in the Indian tradition, tracts of an historical or quasi-historical character could hardly have gained the prestige of religious writings. The Tibetan 'Histories' of Buston and Tārānātha are religious histories; just as the Chinese pilgrims in India were solely concerned with places of pilgrimage and with Buddhist topography, Tibetan monks and laymen who visited India through the ages did so only as pilgrims to the shrines of their faith. With the exception of Mount Kailāsa in Tibet, there is no locality on the northern side of the Himālayas which would be of any interest to the Indian pilgrim. Thus, whereas it may be difficult to find any Tibetan text which does not mention India one way or the other, we have to thumb through tomes of Indian religious literature to find references to Tibet. Even these references, as was shown in this chapter, are of a non-geographical, quasi-mythical character. Any place or region located to the north of the Himālayas seems to stand for the highly esoteric, slightly uncanny, potentially unorthodox, heretical: whether it is Bhoṭa, Mahācīna, or Cīnadesa, the actual location of those regions is of no concern to the Indian hagiographer, not even to the tantric.

There is, however, a strong fusion of Tibetan and Indian elements in tantric literature, apparently both Buddhist and Hindu. Names and epithets of deities both male and female have Indian or Tibetan provenience, and in many cases it is hard to say where a god or a goddess originated. It is almost impossible to study this situation diachronically because in the final analysis even purely Tibetan gods and goddesses may have some sort of Indian background. The village deities of the pre-Aryans in India never died out. There is a strong tendency to banish gods, teachings, and other religious configurations, which oppose the general feeling of orthodoxy in India, and to place them beyond the mountains, possibly where they can cause no mischief. The erotocentric *sādhanā* called *Cīnācāra* probably got its name due to this tendency; types of religious exercise which could not be accommodated in the framework of Indian *sādhanā* were thus extrapolated into an inaccessible region.

We shall see in the next chapter how sanctuary topography assimilates extraneous elements, and how it cuts across the boundary lines in a tentative or potential fashion.

NOTES

[1] Monier Williams, p. 412, rounds it up: 'The central one of the seven continents surrounding Mount Meru (India in Buddhist texts named thus either from the Jambu trees abounding in it, or from an enormous Jambu tree on Mount Meru visible like a standard to the whole continent).' The Jambu tree is the *Eugenia Jambolana*, i.e. the Indian rose-apple tree.

[2] *Studies in Tantras*, Part 1, p. 46f.

[3] See *Studies in the Tantras*, Vol. L, p. 46, where he refers to lists of countries in tantric texts, in this manner: 'Bāhlika (Balkh), Kirāta (the hill tribes of the Himālayan zone), Bhoṭa (Tibet), Cīna (China), Mahācīna (Mongolia?) . . . ,' i.e. putting a question mark behind 'Mongolia' as a possible equivalent of 'Mahācīna'. We have to wait for the final word on the Mahācīna problem, which Professor Tucci and the Istituto de Estremo Oriente at Rome is likely to say in the near future.

[4] V, 20, Gītāpress edition.

[5] Nilakantha Sastri, *History of Southern India*, p. 222.

[6] The *Bhāgavatapurāṇa* in its present version is of the seventh or eighth century, according to V. A. Aggrawala; the *Skandapurāṇa* is much later, i.e. perhaps fourteenth century; the Tamilian *Periapuranam* which dates back to the ninth century provided much of the material for the huge *Skandapurāṇa* in its present form; South Indian dynasties were the founders of the Shailendra and other empires in South East Asia.

[7] For instance, a former sheriff of Madras City. It means 'Mother of Lourdes.'

[8] Vd. Schiefner, Tārānātha's *Geschichte*, passim.

[9] *Bharatīya Vidyā Bhavan*, Bombay, beginning 1955; the whole work is scheduled for ten volumes, six of which have so far been published. See also G. Petech's excellent *History of Medieval Nepal*, ISMEO, Rome 1960.

[10] Kalhāṇa's *Rājātaraṅgiṇī*, edited by Durga Prasad, Bombay, 1892, English translation by M. A. Stein, London, 1900, and another translation by R. S. Pandit, Allahabad, 1935. U. N. Ghoshal's *Studies in Indian History and Culture*, Calcutta University Press 1955, contains an elaborate account of the work.

[11] According to Bagchi, official correspondence was exchanged between China and Kashmir in A.D. 724, vd. *Sino-Indian Studies*, 1, 71; the Chinese official history, so Bagchi writes, says that 'the Emperor awarded the title "King of Kashmir" to Lalitāditya.' Vd. also R. C. Majumdar, 'Northern India Between 650 and 750', in *The Classical Age*, p. 133f.

[12] *Rājātaraṅginī*, ibid.

[13] They are a Himālayan tribe and have nothing to do with Cambodia.

[14] S. Levi, *Nepal*, II, 157f.

[15] See the account of Nepal given in the 'History of the T'ang Dynasty' in the *Journal Asiatique*, Paris, 1894, Part II, pp. 64–5; according to this, the author of Che-ki-fanche, compiled in A.D. 650, says that the kingdom of Nepal is really a Tibetan vassal state. Reference also R. C. Majumdar, 'Northern India During A.D. 650–750' in *The Classical Age*, p. 136.

[16] *Epigraphia Indica*, I, 122, the Khajuraho Inscriptions, listed in *The Age of Imperial Kanauj*, p. 42.

[17] Vd. Ferrand, *Relations des Voyages et Textes Geographiques Arabes relatifs a l'Extreme Orient du VIIIe au XVIIIe siècles*, Paris 1913–14.

[18] R. C. Majumdar, in 'Colonial and Cultural Expansion', Chapter XIV of *The Age of Imperial Kanauj*, Bombay, 1955, sums it up in the following manner: 'According to the chronicles of Tibet, her kings exercised political domination over parts of India during the period A.D. 750–850. The Tibetan King Khri-sron-lde-btsan (ruled from 755 to 797) is said to have subdued the frontier provinces including "China in the East and India in the South". His son Mu-khri-btsan-po (ruled 798 to 804) subjugated two or three (parts of) Jambudvīpa and forced the Pāla king Dharmapāla and another Indian king to pay tribute [my note: This might well be the 'Bhoṭṭa viṣṭi' or corvee referred to on the Khajuraho inscription]. The next important king Ral-pa-can (*circa* 817–836) conquered India as far as Gaṅgāsāgara which has been taken to mean the mouth of the Ganges. How far these Tibetan claims of conquest and supremacy in the Indian plains can be regarded as historical, it is difficult to say. We have no reference in Indian sources to any military campaign of the Tibetans in India or to their exercising political suzerainty in any part of the country . . .', p. 445.

[19] Majumdar, *An Advanced History of India*, London, 1958, p. 324; Majumdar thinks that the expedition was hardly directed against Tibet, but just against some refractory tribes in the Kumaon-Garhwal region—the Himālayan border region of Uttar Pradesh—with the object of bringing them under the control of the Delhi Sultanate.

[20] The somewhat obscure Bengali poet Prākṛta Piṅgala and his poetry was a sort of Brahmanical counterpart to the Buddhist *Caryāpādas* (vd. Chapter on 'Sandhābhāṣā'); it was cited by C. M. Ghosh, *Prākṛta-paiṅgalam*, *Bibliotheca Indica*, Calcutta 1900–2.

[21] 'Northern India During the Eleventh and Twelfth Centuries', in *The Struggle for Empire*, Bombay 1957.

[22] Informant Mr. Mohanlal Shah, Lohaghat, Dt. Almora. *The Linguistic Survey of India* lists four Bhūṭiya dialects for this area: Rangkas, Chaudangsi, Byangsi, and Janggal. The figures would not be valid now, due to the age of the *Survey*; each of these dialects is spoken by less than three thousand people, according to the *Survey*.

[23] As an example, I would adduce the amazingly similar diction in Angelus Silesius' *Cherubic Wanderer* and in the Hindu *Nārada Bhakti Sūtras*, cf. '*Fuenf-Stufen sind in Gott, Knecht, Freund, Sohn, Braut, Gemahl—wer weiter schreit' verwird, und weiss nichts mehr von Zahl*'. Silesius wrote in the seventeenth century; the Nārada Sūtras are about a hundred years earlier. Their doctrine of the '*bhaktikrama*,' i.e. the 'hierarchy of devotional experience', is fivefold and quite similar, i.e. *dāsabhāva*, the attitude of a servant to his master, *putrabhāva*, that of a son to his father, *bandhubhāva*, that between friends, *kāntabhāva*, that of a wife to her husband, and *madhurabhāva*, that of secret lovers towards a partner wedded to a different person.

[24] *Studies in the Tantras*, Calcutta 1939.

[25] H. P. Sastri quotes this passage in his *Catalogue of the Palm Leaf MSS. of the Darbar Library*, Nepal 1906. The tantra was written between the twelfth and fourteenth centuries.

[26] Cf. P. C. Bagchi, *Studies in the Tantra*, p. 45.

[27] The Sanskrit text has been published in Bengali script by the Varendra Anusandhāna Samiti, Calcutta 1898; the Bengali preface does not even mention the possible age—indeed it hardly could, for the work is '*apauruṣeya*', that is, not of human origin, spoken by Śiva to the goddess; the editors being orthodox Śāktas, the question does not arise for them anyway.

[28] *Rudrayāmala*, published in Bengali characters by the Varendra Anusandhāna Samiti, Calcutta 1895; vd. also A. Avalon, *Śakti and Śākta*, London 1929, p. 180.

[29] Avalon reads 'Buddhīsvarī,' i.e. the Preceptress of *buddhi*, the intellect. I do not see why this should be necessary, when the whole account centres round the Buddha as the prospective teacher of Vasiṣṭha.

[30] This is not quite so cryptic a statement as it may sound; the Atharvaveda had always had the flavour of relative heterodoxy; this is borne out by the fact that many Brahmins refer to the Veda as '*trayī*', i.e. the 'threefold', meaning the four *saṃhitā*-collections minus the Atharvaveda—the obvious reason being that this Veda is full of magic of the sort which is reprehensible to the Brahmin lore.

[31] Mahādeva is a synonym of Śiva. The identification of Śiva, the lord of Mount Kailāsa, and Buddha, is typical for the tendency of obliterate mythological distinctions between the Hindu and the Buddhist pantheon, from the side of the Hindus at least; this did not work the other way round. The Buddhist Vajrayāṇa deities are usually extremely hostile to their Hindu counterparts or precursors.

[32] *Raktapānodyatā*. I don't see why Avalon renders this as 'awe-inspiring' (p. 182, 'Cīnacāra'); the phrase indicates close relation to disciplines very much in vogue in Vajrayāṇa tantric practice.

[33] The only available MS. of the *Brahmāyāmala* is dated 1172 Nepal Samvat, i.e. A.D. 1052; it is written in old, hooked Newari characters, see H. H. Sastri, *Nepal Catalogue*, II, p. 60.

[34] *Himāvatpārśve*. Avalon translates this 'by the side of the Himālaya', which is inexact.

[35] Vd. Bagchi, *On the Sādhanāmālā*, p. 43, and B. Bhattacharya, *Buddhist Iconography*.

[36] *Sammoha Tantra*, or *Akṣobhyatārasaṃvāda*, preserved in MSS. in the Nepal Durbar Library; see H. P. Sastri, *Catalogue of the Durbar Library*, II, p. 183.

[37] (Folio 21a) '*Brāhmaṇo vacanaṃ śrutvā prajahāsata maheśvara, śṛṇuṣvāvahito vipra mahānīlāsarasvatī/ yasyāh prasādamālabhya caturvedān vadiṣyati, mero pascimakule tu colanāma mahāhradaḥ/ tatra jajñe svayaṃ devī mātā nīlogratārā, etasminneva kāle tu mero śṛngaparāyanah// japan jāpyaṃ samāsadya triyugam ca tataḥ sthitaḥ,*

mamorddhăvaktrannihsṛtya te jorasi vinirgataḥ// hrade cole nipatyâiva nīlāvarṇābhavat purā, hradasya cottarabhāge ṛṣireko mahottaraḥ// (Folio 21b) *akṣobhya nāma cāśritya muniveśadharaḥ śivah, yenādau japyate yātu satvasya ṛṣirīrita// viśvavyāpakatoye tu cīnadeśe svayaṃ śive, akāroparṭ(?) ākārastasyopari ca huṃkṛtih// kūrcabījasvarūpa sā pratyālīḍhapādābhavat, mahogratārā sañjāta cin (?) prabhāśrīmahākāla//'.*

[38] P. C. Bagchi, 'On the Sādhanāmālā', *Indian Historical Quarterly*, 1934.

[39] Bagchi, *Studies in the Tantras*, p. 44.

[40] Following 6b and 7a; The relevant verse is '*airakabhoṭāntacīnamahācīna-stathaiva ca*'.

[41] Mantras commencing with '*ka*' or with '*ha*'. See the chapter *On Mantra.*

[42] Appendix to *Studies in the Tantras*, p. 99.

[43] P. C. Bagchi, *Studies in the Tantras*, Appendix, p. 100.

[44] A. Avalon, Luzac, London.

[45] I do not know whether any such text exists; it is not listed in any list I have seen. Referring to an obscure or perhaps even non-existent work for doctrinary corrobation seems to have been a fairly frequent procedure among sectarian Hindus after the Hindu comeback in the seventh and later centuries.

[46] *The Karpurādistotram*-Hymn to Kālī, with three commentaries, published by Ganeshan, Madras.

[47] '*gṛhe sammarjanya parigalitavīryaṃ hī cikuram/ samūla madhyāhne vitarati citāyāṃ kujadine/ samuccarya premnā manumapi sakṛtkāli satatam/ gajāruḍho yāti kṣitiparivṛdhaḥ satkavivaraḥ/.*'

[48] '*Śaktiṣādhakayoḥ gṛhe manmathagṛhe maithunasamaye yonīliṅga-sangharṣa-vaśāt śaktiyonipatitaṃ viryaliptaṃ lomaṃ devyai samarpitaṃ kavi . . . bhavati.*'

[49] Contained in the same edition, vd. note above.

[50] Published Āgamānusandhāna Samiti, *Tantrik Texts*, Vol. XIV, Calcutta.

[51] '*dhanārthi prajapedvidyām parayoṣit samāgame, latābhāve samutsarya svaśu-kraṃ sādhakottamaḥ/ ā kṣabdhaṃ prajapenmantraṃ dharmakāmārthasiddhaye, iti Cīnakramenaiva Tārā śīghraphalapradā.*'

[52] '*Mahācīnakramenaiva Chinnamastā tu siddhidā.*'

[53] See B. Bhattacharya, *Buddhist Iconography*, III. This and two other manuscripts were found in Nepal, and the deities whose worship the test describes are all popular in Nepal, among Hindus and Buddhists alike.

[54] *Buddhist Iconography*, 76*f*/.

[55] *pratyālīḍhapādāṃ ghorāṃ muṇḍamālāpralambitām, kharvalambodarāṃ bhīmāṃ nīlanīra jarajitām/ tryambakaikamukhāṃ divyāṃ ghorāṭṭahāsabhāsurāṃ, suprahṛṣṭāṃ śvārūḍhāṃ nāgāṣṭakā . . .*

[56] Bhattacharya, *Buddhist Iconography*, p. 77.

[57] *Buddhist Iconography*, p. 80.

[58] *Gaikwad Oriental Series*, Nos. LXI, XCI, and CIV, general edition by B. Bhattacharya. The fourth volume is in preparation and ought to be out soon. The first three volumes do not contain any prefatory notes, and Professor

Bhattacharya promised a thorough introduction to the whole work with speculations about the age of the work.

[59] There are only two copies of the work in the U.S.A. so far as I could trace them, and I copied the chapter from the University of Chicago copy listed there under PK 2971 G 3, No. 91.

[60] The tulsī plant is sacred to Viṣṇu, hence not acceptable to the Śivites and Śāktas.

[61] The second *hemistich* of this verse, No. 42, is thus given: '. . . *devirjapaṃ kuryādananyadhīh,*' and the footnote says 'omitted'. The editor says in the preface that he would omit many passages which he thinks would be misunderstood, i.e. extremely left-handed statements. It will not be possible to supplement the missing word which is probably an adjective qualifying '*japam*' until one of the four available manuscripts, i.e. the ones the editor used, can be looked into.

[62] '*tadbhavahṛdayāsannaḥ sadā tadgatamanasaḥ, dvandvabhāvaṃ parityajya sarvasiddhīśvaro bhavet/ Brahmā caiva Vasiṣṭhaśca tathānye ca ṛṣīśvarāh, niṣkalakramamārgeṇa bhajanti satataṃ Śive. Tārābhakta maheśāni brahmaṇa parikīrtitah, brahmaviydā mahāvidā sarvatra durlabha kalau,*' verses 61–63.

4

PILGRIMAGE

ALTHOUGH pilgrimage figures importantly in the religions of India, it never had any canonical status in non-tantric traditions. In tantric literature and practice, however, both Hindu and Buddhist, pilgrimage and its corollaries—especially circumambulatory rites which are central to the pilgrims progress—have a much higher prestige, so much so that it might almost be called canonical, if that term could be properly applied to tantrism.

In making a survey of Indian centres of pilgrimage, one thing emerges most forcefully: at places which are not officially linked with the tantric tradition, tantric elements become evident at every step. And although we have to concentrate on shrines which are traditionally linked with tantric literature and precept, we have to bear in mind that local traditions in almost all shrines in India—their number is legion—have strong tantric elements, whether this is conscious to the priesthood and the laity visiting those shrines or not.

One tends to identify pilgrim centres as tantric which have the flavour of extreme, bizarre and esoteric austerity. But such painful prostrations, self-humiliations, and disciplines bordering on the masochistic as I described in another place[1] are not necessarily tantric. And yet, such somewhat elusive elements as the sprinkling of wine on the *prasāda* (food offerings distributed among the votaries) at Jagannāth, Puri, the shaving ritual for boys of certain castes at such widely disparate places as Jvalamukhi in the Panjab, and Palni in Madras State are definitely tantric in origin and connotation.

The local lore at the shrines of India is one of the most direct means of telling whether the place is fundamentally tantric or not. This takes us into the most important mythological complex connected with tantric shrines and tantric worship. The story of Dakṣa's sacrifice and of the subsequent events is pivotal to tantric sanctuary-topography, as is the mythology ascribed to each individual place of pilgrimage.

The most important myth of tantric relevance is, then, no doubt, the story of Dakṣa's sacrifice; it is told, in many minor and major variations, in all the Purāṇas, and in the Epic. It is imperative to pursue this particular myth in some detail; valuable information about its development has been furnished by D. C. Sircar.[2] In the tantric tradition, a centre of pilgrimage is called a '*pīṭha*', a 'seat' of the goddess; tantric literature rarely uses the more general word '*tīrtha*'; probably the distinction itself depends on the mythological relevance of the centre: shrines of the goddess are *pīṭhas*, sanctuaries of gods, or mixed shrines (i.e. where a god and a goddess are worshipped), are called *tīrthas* just as non-tantric worshippers would call them. '*Pīṭha*' seems to be a purely tantric term in the first place, although it has gained currency in other, not necessarily religious, contexts in the last two centuries; thus, several colleges teaching classical subjects in the Indian tradition are called *pīṭhas*, quite literally 'seats of learning', as for instance the Kashi Vidyāpīṭha, one of the best institutes of higher education at Banaras.

As Professor Sircar's treatment can hardly be improved upon, I shall reproduce it in portions, so far as it is relevant to our survey.

... The earliest form of the legend of *Dakṣa-yajña-nāśa* is probably to be traced in the Mahābhārata (XII, chapters 282–3; cf. *Brahmā Purāṇa*, ch. 39) and a slightly modified form of the same story is found in many of the Purāṇas (*Matsya*, ch. 12; *Padma*, *Sṛṣṭikhaṇḍa*, ch. 5; *Kūrma*, I, ch. 15; *Brahmāṇḍa*, ch. 31, etc.) as well as in the *Kūmarasaṃbhava* (I, 21) of

Kālīdāsa who flourished in the fourth and fifth centuries and adorned the court of the Gupta Vikramādityas. According to this modified version of the legend, the mother-goddess, who was the wife of Śiva, was in the form of Sati one of the daughters of Dakṣa Prajāpati. Dakṣa was celebrating a great sacrifice to which neither Sati nor Śiva was invited. Sati, however, went to her father's sacrifice uninvited, but was greatly insulted by Dakṣa. As a result of this ill-treatment, Sati is said to have died by *yoga* or of a broken heart, or, as Kālīdāsa says, she immolated herself and perished. . . . When the news of Sati's death reached her husband, Śiva is said to have become furious and hastened to the scene with his numerous attendants. The sacrifice of Prajāpati Dakṣa was completely destroyed. Śiva, according to some of the sources, decapitated Dakṣa, who was afterwards restored to life and thenceforward acknowledged the superiority of Śiva to all gods. . . .

In still later times,[3] probably about the earlier part of the medieval period, a new legend was engrafted to the old story simply for the sake of explaining the origin of the Pīṭhas. According to certain later Purāṇas and Tantras (*Devībhāgavata*, VII, ch. 30; *Kālikā Purāṇa*, ch. 18; etc.), Śiva became inconsolable at the death of his beloved Sati, and after the destruction of Dakṣa's sacrifice he wandered over the earth dancing madly with Sati's dead body on his shoulder (or, head). The gods now became anxious to free Śiva from his infatuation and conspired to deprive him of his wife's dead body. Thereupon Brahmā, Viṣṇu and Śani entered the dead body by *yoga* and disposed of it gradually. The places where pieces of Sati's dead body fell are said to have become Pīṭhas, i.e. holy seats or resorts of the mother-goddess, in all of which she is represented to be constantly living in some form together with Bhairava, i.e. a form of her husband Śiva. According to a modified version of this story, it was Viṣṇu who, while following Śiva, cut Sati's dead body on Śiva's shoulder or head piece by piece. The story of the association of particular limbs of the mother-goddess with the Śākta *tīrthas*, which may have some relation with the Tantric ritual called Pīṭhanyasa,[4] belongs, as already pointed out, to the latest stage in the development of an ancient tale. But the story may have some connection with Buddhist legends regarding the worship of Buddha's bodily relics and the construction of *Stūpas* in order to enshrine them (cf. *Select Inscriptions*, I, pp. 84, 102 ff., 120 etc.) as well as with those concerning the various manifestations of Buddha in the Jambudvīpa (cf. the list of 56 countries in the *Candragarbhasūtra*; I.C., VIII, pp. 34–5; BEFEO, V, p. 261 f.).

The tantric tradition of four *pīṭhas* was not known to occidental scholars until recently. Monier Williams seems to have had a vague idea about four shrines dedicated to the goddess. He wrote: 'There are also four celebrated shrines of goddesses: Mahālakṣmī at Kolapur, Bhavānī near Sholapur, Reṇukā at Matapura, Yogeśvarī about 80 miles from Ahmednagar.'[5]

Most of the early tantras, both Buddhist and Hindu, refer to four *pīṭhas*. Sircar thinks that the conception of the four *pīṭhas* may have been associated with the Buddhist tantric notion according to which the adept can rise to *mahāsukha* ('the great bliss') through the esoteric practices involving sex.[6] He quotes a Buddhist tantric text called *Catuṣpīṭhantantra* (the tantra of the four *pīṭhas*) and its commentaries, one of which was copied in A.D. 1145.[7] This text speaks of four *pīṭhas* as '*ātmapīṭha*' (the 'shrine of the self'—strange-sounding Buddhism indeed, but not infrequent in Sanskrit Buddhist terminology), *para-pīṭha* (the shrine of the supreme), *yoga-pīṭha* (which is self-explanatory), and *guhya-pīṭha* (the secret, esoteric shrine), and it deals with the various kinds of Vajrasattvas and their intercourse with the Yoginīs, with Prajñāpāramitā and others. 'This philosophical concept,' D. C. Sircar avers (p. 11), 'of the Catuṣpīṭha was either the cause or the effect of the early recognition of four holy places as *pīṭhas*.'[8] He adds in a footnote (ibid.), 'it is difficult to determine what relation the Catuṣpīṭha could have with the Catuṣpīṭha Mountain near Jajpur in Orissa, and with other Sahajayāna conceptions of "four", e.g. the *Caturānanda*, the four-fold bliss'.[9] The *Hevajra Tantra*, composed around A.D. 690,[10] enumerates the four *pīṭhas*, and to my knowledge this is the earliest enumeration: (1) Jalandharā (definitely near the present Jullundar, East Panjab); (2) Oḍḍiyāna (or Uḍḍiyāna), Urgyan in Tibetan, misspelt 'Udyāna', viz. 'garden' in the Bengali *Dohakośa* (ed. Shahidullah) in the Swat Valley; (3) Pūrṇagiri (the location is doubtful), and (4) Kāmarūpa (Kamrup in Assam—at present the only *pīṭha* 'in action').

The same tradition is followed by the *Kālikā Purāṇa* (ch. 64, 43–5), which calls them (1) Oḍṛā, 'seat of the goddess Kātyāyanī and the god Jagannātha, (2) Jalaśaila, seat of the goddess Caṇḍī and the god Mahādeva, (3) Pūrṇa or Pūrṇasaila, seat of the goddess Pūrṇesvarī and the god Mahānātha, and finally (4) Kāmarūpa, seat of the deities Kāmeśvarī and Kāmeśvara. These four '*pīṭhas*' are allocated to the four directions, but this is pure theory, and stands in accordance with the tradition to allocate every ritualistic locale to a direction of the compass, and hence to group them either in fours or in tens, sometimes in groups of eight (i.e. omitting the zenith and the nadir). In geographical reality, however, the distribution of the four main *pīṭhas* is very irregular indeed: Oḍḍiyāṇa, in the Swat Valley, is the only far-western site —Kāmarūpa and possibly Pūrṇagiri are in the extreme east, and Jalandharā again in the middle north-west (Panjab). None of the four *pīṭhas* is situated in the south, in spite of the fact that the Kerala region has a strong Śākta and tantric element in its culture; in some form or another Śakti is the tutelary deity of Kerala.[11]

I shall now present a token topography of tantric sanctuaries.[12]

The canonical tantric text listing the '*pīṭhas*' is the *Pīthanirṇaya* ('description of tantric seats'), also called the *Mahāpīṭhapurāṇa*; the latter name indicates that the work has a sort of mongrel position —it is a tantra by virtue of its dealing with properly tantric material, and a *purāṇa* by courtesy, as it were, probably because it can be said to describe its objects satisfying the '*pañcalakṣaṇa-s*,' i.e. the five criteria of a purāṇa.[13] The text lists 108 *pīṭhas*—following the tradition of the sacred number 108, on which there has been much speculation; the author does not seem to have been worried about the lack of choice—there are no repetitions of any place name, not even under the guise of a topographical synonym. Other tantric texts list *pīṭhas* not mentioned in this text, but it can hardly be established with complete certainty whether or not a *pīṭha* mentioned in one text is or is not identical with one of the same name in another. Thus, the *Kubjikā Tantra*[14] lists a *pīṭha* '*Māyāvatī*,' and so does the *Pīthanirṇaya*; they may be identical, but their respective juxtaposition with other *pīṭhas* of established location would indicate that they are not. Very often a general epithet is given to a proper name or a place name, and it is customary to use the epithet in lieu of the proper name, it being understood that the people who read the text are familiar with the nomenclature. But '*Māyāvatī*', i.e. 'full of *Māyā*' or 'like *Māyā*', (cosmic illusion or enticement) applies to at least three great shrines—Banaras, Ayodhya, and Brindavan—and once an epithet like this has been used for any location by a popular teacher or author, the epithet comes to stay.[15]

It does not become directly clear from the texts why the four *pīṭhas* (Oḍḍiyāṇa, Śrīhaṭṭa, Pūrṇagiri, Jalandharā) were almost unanimously accepted as the most outstanding in all tantric tradition, Buddhist and Hindu alike. I would hazard the guess that the high esteem for these four places might have something to do with the mythological eminence of the sites: a *pīṭha*, by mythological definition, is a site where a limb of the goddess fell to earth when her body was being chopped up by the gods (after the Dakṣa episode); at these four *pīṭhas*, however (though unfortunately not only at these four), the magically most potent limbs of Satī descended: her pudenda, her nipples, and her tongue.

The most important phenomenon of tantric pilgrimage, both as a concept and as a set of observances, is the hypostasization of pilgrim-sites and shrines: the geographical site is homologized with some entity in the esoteric discipline, usually with a region or an 'organ' in the mystical body of the tantric devotee. This sort of homologizing and hypostasy began early.[16] It became ubiquitous in the tantric tradition. Centres of pilgrimage fell well into this pattern and Hindu and Buddhist literature abound in examples of such hypostasization. Professor Eliade, who was the first to formulate it, put it thus:[17]

all 'contacts' with the Buddha are homologized; whether one assimilates the Awakened One's message—that is, his 'theoretical body' (the *dharma*)—or his 'physical body', present in the *stūpas*, or his 'architectonic body' symbolized in temples, or his 'oral body' actualized by certain formulas—each of those paths is valid, for each leads to transcending the plane of the profane. The 'philosophers' who 'relativized' and destroyed the immediate 'reality' of the world, no less than the mystics who sought to transcend it by a paradoxical leap beyond time and experience, contributed equally toward homologizing the most difficult paths (*gnosis*, asceticism, *yoga*) with the easiest (pilgrimages, prayers, mantras). For in the 'composite' and conditioned world, one thing is as good as another; the unconditioned, the Absolute, *nirvāṇa*, is as distant from perfect wisdom and the strictest asceticism as it is from . . . homage to relics, etc. . . .

The *Mantramahodadhi*[18] has a section entitled 'the *nyāsa* of the *pīṭhas* (*pīṭha-nyāsa-kathanam*). Literally, *nyāsa* is the process of charging a part of the body, or any organ of another living body, with a specified power through touch. For instance, by placing the fire-*mudrā* on the heart-region uttering the fire-*mantra* '*raṃ*', the adept's heart is made into the cosmic fire; and by meditating on a specific *pīṭha* with the *mantra* of its presiding 'Śakti', the very region (for instance the heart, or the navel, or the throat) wherein the Śakti is thus visualized is hypostasized or trans-substantiated, into that *pīṭha*. The tantric formulation would be: Meditating on the pilgrim-centre through visualizing its presiding deity in the prescribed manner, the locus of concentration in the yogi's body is charged with the spiritual efficacy of that very place. With the Buddhist tantrics, the pattern is transparent even on a purely doctrinal basis—for no 'place of pilgrimage' exist in an ontological sense.

Going back for a moment to the *Mantramahodadhi*, the section says: 'He should meditate on his body as the "*pīṭha*" by doing "*nyāsa*" of the tutelary *pīṭha*-deity. He should make "*nyāsa*" of the Naṃdūkā flower (*Clerodendrum Syphonantum*) in his base-centre (*ādhāra*); in the heart, there are all the *pīṭhas* of the earth, the ocean, the jewel island, and of the snowy palace (i.e. the Himālayas), if he can pull up the *Ādhāra-Śakti* there.'[19]

The Buddhist tantric *Caryāpādas*, all of which are contained in the *Tanjur* and many of which are extant in their old Bengali originals, are replete with hypostases. An example: 'The path along which the boat is to sail is the middle-most one in which both the right and left are combined, that is located between the Ganges and the Yamuna, and along this path which is beset with dangers the boat has to proceed against the current.'[20] All this is *Sandhābhāṣā* (intentional language) and is easily understood once the terminology is known. The 'Ganges' and 'Yamuna' are the left and the right ducts in the yogic body, the middle-most is the '*avadhūti*' or the central duct which has to be opened by the controls created through meditation.

The *Hevajra Tantra* gives a beautiful instance of hypostasis:[21] 'Vajragarbha said: What, O Lord, are these places of meeting? The Lord replied: They are the *pīṭha* and the *upapīṭha*, the *kṣetra* and *upakṣetra*, the *chandoha* and the *upachandoha* . . . etc.[22] These correspond with the twelve stages of a Bodhisattva. It is because of these that he receives the title of Lord of the ten stages and as Guardian Lord. Vajragarbha asked: What are these *pīṭhas*? The Lord said: They are Jalandharā, Oḍḍiyāna, Paurṇagiri, Kāmarūpa (Tibetan *gnas ni dza lan dha ra bśad, de bzhin du ni u di ñid, gnas ni ko la gi ri ñid, de bzhin du ni kam ru ñid*).' He then lists a further 32 places.

A Doha by Sarāha[23] illustrates the hypostasis in a poetical manner:

> 'When the mind goes to rest, the bonds of the body are destroyed,
> And when the one flavour of the Innate pours forth,
> There is neither outcaste nor Brahmin.
>
> Here is the sacred Yamuna and here the River Ganges,
> Here are Prayāga and Banaras, here are Sun and Moon.
> Here I have visited in my wanderings shrines and such places of pilgrimage.
> For I have not seen another shrine blissful like my own body.'

In a treatment of non-tantric pilgrimage, the circumambulation-pattern which now follows would perhaps not have to be included. However, in tantrism it is so much a part of the process of pilgrimage that it must form the concluding, if not the most important, section of this chapter.

We do not know if circumambulation was a custom in pre-Vedic India; aboriginal tribes all over India (especially the Santhals of Bihar) circumambulate their houses and shrines rather more frequently than the neighbouring caste-Hindu groups; but it is hard to say whether these autochthonous groups are preserving a pre-Aryan custom or whether they have simply taken it over from the Hindu ritual.

Tantric literature contains elaborate instruction about circumambulation, *pradakṣiṇā* ('walking clockwise'), and there is hardly a tantric text or manual lacking such instruction. Scanning the tables of contents of a dozen tantric texts at random, I found only one (the *Mantramahodadhi*, ed. Khemraj Śrīkriṣṇadāss, Bombay) whose table of contents did not list *pradakṣiṇā* as a section—though this popular manual does contain such instructions under different headings. I shall quote an example from the large '*Mantramahārṇava*'. The section is captioned '*pradakṣiṇā nirṇaya*', 'definition' or 'description of *pradakṣiṇā*', and it is listed among other '*nirṇaya-s*' preceding and following it, i.e. neither more nor less important than these: description of incense (*gandha-nirṇaya*), of fruit and flowers to be offered (*phala-puṣpanirṇaya*), of raiments to be worn (*vastranirṇaya*), then comes our *pradakṣiṇā-nirṇaya*, and others follow. These *nirṇayas* usually stand at the beginning of the text, (commencing on p. 8 in this particular manual—which is one of 731 folios in print). It says (vs. 289), 'now then the description of *pradakṣiṇā*: according to the *Liṅgārcanacandrikā* ("the moon-rays of Liṅga-worship"—an extant but hitherto unpublished text) one *pradakṣiṇā* for (the goddess) Caṇḍī, seven for the Sun, three (are to be done) for Gaṇeśa; four for Hari (Viṣṇu), for Śiva half a *pradakṣiṇā*'. This may seem strange in a tantric work, Śiva being the tutelary deity of all the tantras; however, the implication seems to be that because so many other bits of ritual are performed for Śiva and listed in other parts of the manual—there was no need felt for more than the minimum *pradakṣiṇā* which is half a circumambulation. This also seems negatively implied by the great number of *pradakṣiṇās* to the Sun, a Vedic deity not very close to the tantrics; apart from the water-oblation (*tarpana*) offered to the

Sun, there is only this sevenfold *paradakṣiṇā* mentioned in the manual. I surmise that the feeling of some tantrics has been that *pradakṣiṇā* was something essentially Vedic, and then the unspoken formula might be something like 'more (Vedic) *pradakṣiṇā*, less tantric ritual; more tantric ritual, fewer *pradakṣiṇās*'. If we test this hypothesis by the verse quoted here and by numerous similar passages it is certainly corroborated. Śiva has the greatest number of typically tantric rituals, Caṇḍī (identical with Cāmuṇḍī, Kālī, the Vajrayāṇa Buddhist goddesses, and the non-Aryan autochthonous goddesses in general) very many indeed as a typically tantric goddess and as the many-splendoured spouse of Śiva; Viṣṇu and Gaṇeśa have some very few purely tantric rituals, the Sun none, although the Vedic *tarpana* or water offering has been taken over into the tantric tradition without any change.

The next two verses are captioned 'the greatness of *pradakṣiṇā* for Śiva', and they run 'he who has performed formal worship and who does not do *pradakṣiṇā* for Śambhu (Śiva), his worship is fruitless, and the worshipper is a cheat (*daṃbhika*); (but) he who performs just only this one correct *pradakṣiṇā* with devotion (to Śiva), all worship has been done by such a man, and he is a true devotee of Śiva'.

In the Dravidian south, *pradakṣiṇā* seems to be particularly popular in the worship of indigenous deities. The Nāga deities—represented by snake-idols of various shapes and sizes on a plinth usually at some distance from the shrines of the main (Brahmin) deities, or under specific trees in the villages—are chiefly deities of fertility and the life-cycle. They are also installed on the *virikṣa-vivāka-manthapam* (Sanskrit *vṛkṣa-vivāha-maṇdapam*, i.e. 'tree-marriage-platform'—a platform erected around two intertwined trees which are fairly frequent all over India; such trees are said to be 'married'), which women circumambulate on Mondays in order to remove *Carppa Tosam* (Sanskrit *Sarpa-doṣa*), the curse of barrenness, a curse incurred by harming a snake—either directly or indirectly—as by some relative, ancestor, etc.[24]

However, *pradakṣiṇā* is the regular procedure on any temple visit, especially in the south, where the temples have spacious *prādakṣiṇās* i.e. ambulatories. The *pradakṣiṇā* is done immediately after the worship in the shrine, sometimes before and after. Also the idol—or rather, a small, portable replica of the idol in the shrine—is carried around those *prādakṣiṇās* every day by the temple priests, with *nāḍasvaram* (south Indian reed-horns, somewhat like a shawm) accompanying the procession. The musicians walk some distance ahead, the pious follow the image, several times on festive occasions.

Although '*piratakṣiṇam*' (Tamil for *pradakṣiṇā*) is known to most Dravidians who visit Brahmin temples, the indigenous Dravidian word is '*valttu*', from the Tamil root '*vāl*', to salute. The *Akkoraci-vacariyar*, a manual for Tamilian temple-officials, prescribes 'The Acariyar (head priest) comes to the temple 3 and 3/4 *nalikai* (i.e. about an hour and a half) before sunrise; after having completed his *anuṣthānam* (the initial observances), he washes his hands and feet, makes *piratakṣiṇam* by walking round the sanctum turning his right side towards it, salutes the (guardians of the gate) *tuvarapalakar*, Sanskrit *dvārapālaka*, the figures placed at each side of the entrance), and reaching the place in front of the sacred bull (Nandi—his image is found in every Śiva temple, facing the deity), pronounces the basic *mantra* and offers flowers.'

At the Somasundara Temple in Madurai (Tamilnad), some devotees circumambulate the shrine nine times, while a *pattar* (a sort of auxiliary priest) throws a flower on one each of the nine idols representing the *navagrahas* (the nine constellations) on their behalf. A monk or some other religious mendicant usually stands at hand who, for a small fee, will throw incense on a charcoal fire as an offering as the visitors perform their *pradakṣiṇā*. There are dozens of variations in the *pradakṣiṇā*-routine in different shrines, and there is much more heterogeneity in the south than in the north.

The more tortuous kinds of *pradakṣiṇā* are well known to tourists and photographers; on Mount Abu—the famous Jaina sanctuary in Gujarat—I witnessed a group of pilgrims in June 1955 who measured the entire ambiance of the sacred mount, roughly two miles, by constant prostrations in what they call the '*dehamāp*' method in Gujarati (i.e. the 'measure of the body')—facing the direction of the *pradakṣiṇā* they prostrate, then stand up, placing their feet exactly on the spot where they had touched the ground with their foreheads, then prostrate again and repeating the process until the *pradakṣiṇā* is complete or until they pass out. That particular *pradakṣiṇā*, I was told, takes an average of thirty hours; the pilgrims do rest in between, however, but they do not take any solid food until they have completed it.

I have not seen any texts, however, which would prescribe these painful kinds of religious observance. If there are, they would belong to the category of pilgrim's-pamphlets such as are distributed at the various shrines all over India; they are always in the vernacular, and have none but purely local status. No widely accepted instruction manual would recommend self-inflicted hardship of this sort.

A word must be said about the *pradakṣiṇā* of Mt. Kailāsa in Tibet. In 1951 over six hundred Indian pilgrims undertook the pilgrimage on the route Almora, Pituragarh, Garbiang, Lipulek, Taghlakot. The Hindus regard Mt. Kailāsa as the abode of Śiva and Pārvatī, '*Kailāsanātha*', '*Kailāsapati*', etc., being frequent names of Śiva, and common male proper names. The mythology Tibetan legend has woven round the mountain is unknown to the Hindu pilgrims,[25] and although the number of Tibetan pilgrims circumambulating Mt. Kailāsa and Manasarovar must be many times that of Hindu pilgrims, their mythological background and the sectarian motives are totally unrelated to each other—though the general purpose for both, as goes without saying, is the acquisition of *punya*, spiritual merit. The Hindu pilgrims perform this observance in three parts: first, they circumambulate Lake Manasarovar, and some of the more heroic among them even take a bath in its chilly waters; the ascent to the ambiance of the Kailāsa Mountain proper begins immediately at the completion of the *pradakṣiṇā* of the Manasarover, i.e. the latter's starting point to which the pilgrims return after this first circumambulation, is situated right at the foot of the mountain. The circumambulation of Mount Kailāsa takes about three days, that of Manasarovar a day and a half, so the total *pradakṣiṇā* lasts four and a half days. On the other side of Mount Kailāsa there is another lake only slightly smaller than Manasarovar; it is called *Rakkastal* by the Hindu pilgrims, and I think it is a local Kumaoni variety of *Rākṣastala*, 'lake of the *rākṣasas*' or demons; the pilgrims do not go near that lake, as its water is thought to be inauspicious (hence the name?); they only cast a glance *bandanī nazar*, 'the glance of veneration', and fold their hands; they are advised not to look at it more often than just that one instant.

There is no built-in theory, in tantric written tradition or in tantric oral lore, which would establish a hierarchy of thematic importance: these decisions seem to be left to the individual tantric. The scholar, I believe, cannot do much more than rely on some sort of intuition by analogy: in most Indian religious traditions there is such a hierarchy in the gamut of religious exercise (*sādhanā*). Meditation first, belief in the theological framework—with the devotional (*bhakti*) schools this might stand first—then ancillary exercises, then perhaps charity, then study and reading. The Upaniṣad enjoins 'listening, cogitating, meditating' *śrotavyaṃ mantavyaṃ nididhyāsitavyam* in this order, and the general understanding is that 'listening' is the least important, 'meditation' the most important step. It is by no means certain that this orthodox hierarchy holds for tantrism. Ritual of all sorts seems so much more important in tantrism than it does in non-tantric literature of the same level of sophistication, that it seems quite possible that tantric masters did regard activities like pilgrimage and circumambulation to be as nuclear to the process as, say, deep meditation. If the proportion of textual injunction can be a guide, these activities, which may be regarded at the most as accessories to the religious life, by non-tantrics, have not been given any shorter shrift than meditation proper. Just how central these activities are to the practising and succeeding tantric we are in no position to say; yet, we cannot omit them in a survey of the tantric tradition just because most modernistically oriented or 'philosophically' inclined students and votaries of a religion may regard them as marginal, or even inferior, pursuits.

NOTES

[1] 'Pilgrimage in the Indian Tradition', in *History of Religions*, Chicago 1963.

[2] D. C. Sircar, 'The Śākta Pīṭhas', *Journal of the Royal Asiatic Society of Bengal*, Calcutta 1948.

[3] The *Brahmāvaivarta Purāṇa*, an old work known to Albiruni, contains interpolations of a date later than the Muslim occupation of eastern India where the Purāṇa was modified: cf. I, 10, 121, referring to the caste called Jolā (from *Julāhā*, 'weaver') said to have originated from a Mlechha (Mohamedan) father and a girl of the Indian weaver caste. Op. cit. IV, 43, 25, referring to Siddha—*pīṭhas* associated with Sati's limbs should similarly be assigned to a date not earlier than the fourteenth or fifteenth century.

[4] Vide *Śabdakalpadruma*, s.v. *nyāsa*; cf. *aṅganyāsa* (touching limbs with the hand accompanied by appropriate *mantras*) and *śodhanyāsa* (six ways of touching the body with mystical *mantras*) from which the *pīṭhavinyasa* seems to have later evolved. Originally certain limbs were mentioned in connection with a tantric ritual in which the names of the *Pīṭhas* were afterwards introduced. In explaining *pīṭhanyāsa*, the *Vācaspatyam* says, '*pīṭhadevatānām ādhāraśaktiprakṛtyādinaṃ praṇavādinamo'ntena, hṛdaye nyāsabhede tantrasāraḥ*'. 'The specific *nyasa* on the heart (or "with the heart—*mantra*") depends on the deities of the *pīṭha*, on the Śakti presiding over the yogic-body centre, and on the *mantras* like *OM*, etc., says the *Tantrasāra*.' The association of the limbs of the *sādhaka* with certain localities may have given rise to the belief regarding the *Pīṭhas* arising from particular limbs of the mother-goddess. *Vācaspatyam* V/4344.

[5] Vd. 'Hinduism', p. 179. None of these shrines are identical with any of the classical tantric *pīṭhas*; and on this count there are at least 200 shrines of goddesses in India, of equal importance as the ones mentioned here. See D. C. Sircar's list in '*The Sākta Pīṭhas*' *JRASB XIV*.

[6] D. C. Sircar, 'The Śākta Pīthas,' p. 11, *JRAS*, XIV.

[7] Note cf. H. P. Sastri, Cat. Palmleaf and Selected Paper Manuscripts belonging to the Durbar Library, Nepal.

[8] This, of course, ties in with the important problem of the hypostasization of centres of pilgrimage, q.v. post.

[9] The mountain is a purely tantric shrine, and Orissa in general is a 'tantric' region *par excellence*.

[10] Vd. B. Bhattacharya, *Sādhanāmālā* II, p. xliii, and Snellgrove, *The Hevajra Tantra*, I, p. 14 f.

[11] Although D. C. Sircar's list in 'The Śākta Pīṭhas' is very elaborate and possibly exhaustive, he does not list three extremely interesting tantric pilgrim centres. They are shrines dedicatad to Śakti in her three forms as '. . . mother', Mukhāmbikā in North Cannanore on the Malabar Coast, the 'mouth-mother',

i.e. the idol shows the lower portion of the head only; then there is Hemāmbikā, the 'golden mother' in Palghat, South Malabar—the name has no bearing on the shape of the idol, which is probably quite unique in India. It consists of only two female hands protruding out of a little artificial well. The legend says that the officiating priest once cast lewd glances at the goddess when he was administering her ritualistic bath, and she sank into the water with shame, and has been concealing her full form in the water ever since, holding out her hands only for the benefit of the devotees. The third '*ambikā*' is the famous 'Bālāmbikā' 'girl-mother', a synonym of Kanyā Kumārī, the goddess of Cape Comorin—'Comorin' being a Portuguese corruption of Kumārī 'princess'; there is a convent of Belgian nuns at the place—India's southern tip; Christian missionaries have been there since the early eighteenth century; a Tamilian Catholic nun told me that the Christian belief was that 'Kanyā Kumārī', i.e. 'Virgin Goddess', was actually 'Kanyā Mary'. Many local Catholics entertained the notion that the goddess was none but the Virgin, usurped by the heathens for their purpose. To my knowledge, there is no literature whatever, so far, on these three Kerala shrines, in spite of the fact that south Indian tantrics—by no means only Kerala tantrics—hold the shrines in high esteem and that they have been well-frequented centres of tantric worship and pilgrimage for centuries.

[12] Dr. D. C. Sircar has compiled an excellent list in '*The Śākta Pīṭhas*'; the best account of places of pilgrimage—not only tantric—H. V. Glasenapp's '*Heilige Staetten Indiens*', published 1900 by Diederich in Jena; the beautifully illustrated book has long been out of print.

[13] Vd., W. Kirfel, *Das Purāṇapañcalakṣaṇa*, Bonn 1947.

[14] MSS. No. 3174 Royal Asiatic Society of Bengal. Also quoted in *Prāṇatosiṇī Tantra*, ed. Vasumati, Calcutta; both referred to in Sircar, *Pīṭhas*, p. 19.

[15] '*Māyāvatī*' seems to be pleasant to pilgrims. The Advaita Ashrama monastery in the Almora District, U.P., in the Himālayas, was founded only sixty years ago by Swami Vivekananda, on a site called 'Mayyāpeṭ' by the local Kumaoni population. The term is quite clear; it means 'stone of the Mother', *Mayyā-pat* (*-har*), as indeed there are some megalithic remains strewn all over the place, which have been worshipped by the villagers of the neighbouring Lohaghat and Champawat for at least three generations—(this information is due to a personal communication by Mr. Mohanlal Shah, of Lohaghat): The sanskritizing influence of the Ramakrishna Order soon made itself felt, and within less than three years after the foundation of the cloister, the place came to be referred to as '*Māyāvati*', and is known only under this name to the new pilgrims. It is also listed as such with the Indian Postmaster General. This sanskritized 'corruption' of a dialect proper name is very frequent in India, and a popular pastime of many pundits fond of punning.

[16] *Cf. Bṛhadāranyaka Upaniṣad*, I, i.

[17] M. Eliade, op. cit., p. 198.

[18] A text which I have been using throughout my research for permanent reference; this tantric anthology is, together with the *Mantramahārṇava*, the most reliable compendium of instructions for the tantric adept.

[19] This describes a specific, highly involved process of *nyāsa* practice which is of no importance to us.

[20] Śāntipāda, *Caryāgīti* No. 26, in H. P. Shastri's *Bauddha Gān O Dohā*.

[21] *Hevajra Tantra*, I vii/10 f.; D. Snellgrove, Vol. I p. 68 f., Vol. II p. 22 f.

[22] Snellgrove explains it thus: 'these are different kinds of places of pilgrimage, some of which are known as seats—*pīṭhas*—some as fields (*kṣetra*), some as meeting-places (*melapakā*), and some as cemeteries (*śmaśāna*). As for *chaṇḍoha* and *pilāva*, I have no explanation. The Tibetan transliterates the former and translates the latter as '*Thung chod*, drink and cut', as though *pilāva* were derived from *pi*, 'drink', and *lāv*, 'cut'. Vd. also Roerich, *Blue Annals*, pp. 980 and 983.

[23] *Buddhist Texts*, Cassirer, quoted in Snellgrove I, p. 37.

[24] Vd., Goblet D'Alviella, under 'Circumambulation' in *Encyclopedia of Religions and Ethics*, Vol. III, 657 ff.; an important summary of circumambulation as a religious rite in general. D'Alviella thinks the origin of circumambulation is to be found in a sun-cult.

[25] The battleground between Bon and Buddhist, and then between the conflicting Tibetan Buddhist churches; vd. Hoffmann, *Quellen Zur Geschichte der Tibetischen Bon-Religion*, Berlin 1943.

5

ON MANTRA

THIS IS, and has got to be, the longest section in our study. The uneven length of the various chapters in this book hardly needs an apology—the topics of a bizarre, esoteric tradition are 'uneven', the importance given to its branches is not of any logical sort; it is accidental, historical. In the body of tantric literature, *mantra* takes the largest portion; and as was pointed out earlier, Brahmins often refer to tantric texts as *mantra-śāstra.*

On the technical side, then, *mantra* is the chief instrument of tantrism; it has to be dealt with in greater detail and with more care than the more peripheral, though by no means less important, themes, as pilgrimage and circumambulation, etc.

In order to make this bulky chapter less cumbersome, it will be convenient to divide it into sections with different headings; these are self-explanatory.

i. Delimitation of mantra

Hindu, Buddhist, and Jaina believers in *mantra,* and many critical scholars virtually identify several loosely connected terms, or they bracket them together in a manner that would suggest synonymy. This has to be clarified right at the outset.

Mantric language is not 'intentional language' (*sandhābhāṣā*—see Chapter 6); the confusion is shared by Vidusekhara Bhattacharya, Benoytosh Bhattacharya, Gopinath Kaviraj, Roerich, and quite a few others. It arises, so I would think, from the fact of outward analogy: both *mantra* and *sandhābhāṣā* are cryptic, clandestine utterances, unintelligible to the non-initiate. On a more sophisticated level, the confusion could have arisen from the enormous amount of instructions and directions about the correct formation of *mantras*, which fill all tantric texts. Such secondary instruction is very frequently couched in *sandhā*-terms and works as a sort of mantric meta-language.

Mantra is also not synonymous with *kavaca* (protective formula, 'cuirass'), *yāmala* (a mantra-based on text), and *dhāraṇī* (a mnemonic formula containing *mantras*), or parallel developments.[1]

Finally, *mantra* is not a 'senseless mumble-jumble of words' a view expressed by European scholars in the last century, and held by Ārya Samājist and some other Indian scholars to this day. There is a twofold danger today by way of perpetuating this erroneous notion. The first stems from philology which would relegate *mantras* to the hocus-pocus dustbin; the second, to my feeling graver danger, comes from the side of contemporary analytical philosophers of the early Wittgensteinian type, and from the epigones of the early Ayer, for whom meaningfulness consisted in verifiability. I do not say that all votaries of logical empiricism would mete out such treatment to *mantra*; quite a few philosophers of the present-day British schools—Hampshire, Wisdom, Popper, and no doubt the late G. E. Moore—would probably include *mantra* in their study if they became interested in it.[2] There is, however, a wide gap between philosophers and such sympathetic psychologists as Jung or Kerenyi and their numerous followers. If analytical philosophy were given the proper formula, it might well accept *mantra* as an object of a special study. The formula would contain some such directive as this: *mantra* is meaningful not in any descriptive or even persuasive sense, but within the mystical universe of discourse; that is, it constitutes a particular phase of literary expression belonging to that discourse. *Mantra* is verifiable not by what it describes but by what it effects: if it creates that somewhat complex feeling-tone in the practising person, which has found its expression in the bulk of mystical literature such as tantra, then it is verified; or in other words, the principle of verification of *mantra* lies in its emotive numinous effect as well as in the corroboration of such effects in religious literature. With this principle in view I do not think either the philologist, the analyst, or even the logical empiricist philosopher could have any objection to the inclusion of *mantra* in the list of academical topics. Such scholars might join forces with the indologist and the cultural anthropologist to arbitrate whether a particular type of expression is 'mumble-jumble' or not.

ii. The history of mantra

There can be no doubt about the correct etymology of *mantra*. It combines the old Vedic (and Indo-European) root '*man*' 'to think' with the element *-tra*, i.e. the *kṛt*-suffix indicating instrumentality. Monier Williams lists the following meanings:[3] 'instrument of thought, speech, sacred text or speech, a prayer or song of praise; a Vedic hymn or sacrificial formula; that portion of the Veda which contains the texts called *ric*-, or *yajus*-, or *sāman*- as opposed to the Brahmaṇa or Upaniṣat portion; a sacred formula addressed to any individual deity; a mystical verse or magical formula (sometimes personified), incantation, charm, spell (especially in modern times) employed by the Śāktas to acquire superhuman powers; the primary *mantras* being held to be seventy million in number and the secondary innumerable (Ṛgveda I, 147, 4); consultation, resolution, counsel, advice, plan, design, secret; a name of Viṣṇu, a name of Śiva; the fifth mansion in astrology.'

All the meanings listed above excepting the last section commencing with 'consultation' are relevant to us; but of course there are additional and subtler meanings to the word than a dictionary can bring out. Monier Williams was not interested in Buddhism, hence none of the meanings he listed would cover the peculiar significance which *mantra* has in Buddhist and especially in Buddhist tantric usage; this will be shown here.

It is important to bear in mind that the use of *mantra* as a Vedic verse—any passage in the *saṃhitā* portion, that is—is the oldest and hence the most hallowed in India. When a Brahmin speaks of *mantra* without any qualification of the term, he always means 'a Vedic passage'. In modern vernaculars, I have found it to work this way: *mantra* used simply by a Brahmin scholar means 'Vedic passage', or by metonymy, the *saṃhitā* portion of the Veda as a whole. Whenever he means to refer to *mantra* as a tool or formula or vocalization different from that meaning—particularly when he wants to refer to the tantric complex—he will invariably use such partial duplication as '*mantra-yantra*', '*mantra-untra*' or even '*mantra-tantra*'.[4]

There are sections of pandits in India who try to limit *mantra* to signify 'Vedic passage' to the exclusion of any other usage. This is borne out by the twist the Ārya Samāj[5] has given to the time-honoured definition of an heretic '*nāstiko vedanindakaḥ*'[6] by changing the dictum into '*nāstiko mantranindaka*'.[7]

The word *mantra* did, however, obtain its extra-Vedic connotations and its extra-canonical charisma at a very early time. There is evidence of a well-founded body of mantric texts in the Pālī scriptures. The Mahāsanghikas had collections of quasi-mantric formulae called '*dhāraṇī*' or '*vidyādharapitaka*'.[8]

The importance of *mantras* as aids and tools for meditation was never expressly stated or stressed in Theravāda texts, but neither was their efficacy doubted. We find *paritta-s* or protective *mantras* in several Pālī texts[9] said to do service at banning dangers of all sorts, preventing or curing diseases, protecting from snakebite, evil spirits, preserving peace, insuring happy rebirth, wealth, etc. In another passage, the Buddha himself instructs Aṅgulimālā, the converted robber, to cure a woman suffering from the after-effects of a miscarriage, through pronouncing a healing *mantra* over her.[10]

If we extend the Vedic connotation of *mantra* to early Buddhism—and I do not see why we should not—then the entire category of solemn pronouncements (*udāna*) used in course of the various regular ceremonies of the Thera tradition (*patimokkha, upasampadā, pūjā*, as in Burma and Thailand today) could well be called *mantric*; i.e. the constantly repeated solemn reassurance formula 'may prosperity be through this truth pronounced',[11] and even the threefold formula of refuge, which has all the charismatic effect of a *mantra*, and canonical status in addition to it.

Of the numerous folklore etymologies attempted for *mantra* I shall quote only two; there are apparently different etymologies in different Indian vernaculars based on syllables accidentally similar to *mantra* or a part thereof; thus, the Bengali saint Ramakrishna Paramahamsa, who lived at Dakshineshwar near Calcutta in the last century, used to give his own etymology of *mantra* as Bengali *mŏn-tōr*, 'now (after the initiation) the mind (is) yours'.[12]

In a Buddhist Hybrid Sanskrit text we find this etymologizing: 'it is styled *mantra* because it gives joy to all creatures by all the sounds . . . and because it is the mind's (*manasaḥ*) protection (*trāṇa*)'.[13]

iii. *Attempts at a definition of* mantra

There are two ways of defining a word like *mantra*; formal and material. Traditional scholars have been trying to give material and functional definitions, the latter being a special type of material definition. However, as a definition must be exhaustive, no material or functional enumeration of constituents can really qualify as a definition, because all constituents of a complex term like *mantra* cannot be included in a short series of propositions; it would be a book, not a definition. Some contemporary thinkers would say that we cannot speak of definitions at all except for terms of pure science, mathematics, and theoretical physics[14] and that we can give descriptions only of terms belonging to a universe of discourse other than that of pure science. If this is accepted, then all the scholars whose attempts at defining *mantra* I shall now present have given descriptions only, because their interest was not formal, but material or functional. At the end of this section, I shall therefore try to give a rigorous, formal definition of *mantra*.

We find the explanation of *mantra* in its Vedic connotation in Pāṇini; the relevant passages have been collated and presented in a recent Indian publication[15] under the heading 'terms indicative of texts': 'Pāṇini has used in his *sūtras* the following terms associated with certain texts: (1) *chandas*, (2) *mantra*, (3) *ṛc*. . . . (*Chandas* denoted the sacred literature, as distinguished from *bhāṣā*, the spoken language). The term *mantra* had a more restricted scope, being applied to a sacred formula whether in verse (*ṛc*) or in prose (*yajus*), as opposed to *brāhmaṇa*. Thus the particular linguistic forms noted for *mantras* do not occur in the Brāhmaṇas . . . Brāhmaṇa stands for the *Brāhmaṇa* works, and "*a-mantra*" (*sūtra* III. 1.35) also points to non-*mantra* literature, or the *Brāhmaṇas*.'

H. Zimmer describes 'mantra' thus:[16] 'it is compulsion to form a pictorial image (*zwang zum Denkbild*) compelling beings to be as they are in their innermost essence. It is therefore knowledge (*Erkenntnis*), it is mutual inherence of knower and known . . . it is compelling force, magical instrument by which immediate reality—appearance of gods, the play of mystical powers—is wrought. . . . *Mantra* is power, not arguing and proposition, to which the mind could resist or from which it could withdraw. Whatever is pronounced in *mantra* is an event. If anywhere, then words are deeds in this realm.'

Zimmer was prone to use poetic language, but it is not too difficult to extract the implied facts from the flowery shell—what he meant to say was that *mantra* means to stand for a magical force which confers existential status to imagination contents—and this is certainly a true description of *mantra*, a believer's description if put in this manner.

Lama Anagarika Govinda,[17] also a believing exponent of *mantra*, gives a tidy description: 'the symbol word, the holy sound (Tibetan, *gzuṅs sṅags*) which, transmitted to the initiate by the preceptor, makes his personality vibrate in consonance and opens it up for higher experience'.

This description contains a very important point, often neglected by orthodox as well as critical scholars. I have heard pandits impugn the secrecy and therefore the importance of *mantra* on the ground that 'you find them all openly listed in so many books'; this is true, but the crux of the matter is that a syllable or a collection of syllables constituting a *mantra* is no *mantra* at all, because a *mantra* is something imparted personally by a guru to a disciple. Hence *OM* is no mantra at all, and the statement that it is, is one by courtesy, as it were. If the syllable *OM* is formally imparted by a guru to a disciple under the observance of a particular ritual, then alone it is a *mantra*. Hence, any description of a *mantra* would have to be prefaced by a clause like 'imparted in the ritual "R" by a guru of the tradition "T" to the disciple, the *mantra* "X" . . . etc.' I suggest this be called the '*mantric* rubric'; and it has to be understood even when it is not expressed separately in the treatment of a *mantra*.

Bose and Haldar describe *mantra* thus:[18] '. . . the *mantra*, which is the concentrated symbol of realization when received from one in whom the *mantra* is conscious energy, when repeated by a *sādhaka* (aspirant) elevates him to the same tune and becomes ultimately revealed to the adept *sādhaka*. These *mantras* are eternal and possess wonderful capacities. . . .'

In the glossary appended to that work, the short description of *mantra* is 'sacred letters to be recited at the time of spiritual exercise'.

In spite of the simple diction, this is not a bad description, as it covers two important aspects of *mantra*: its relation to the eschatological target stipulated in any particular meditative tradition, and the invariable concomitance of *bījas* (seeds) with liturgical action. Of course, 'letters', sacred or otherwise, are not recited; but the authors certainly mean the right thing.

B. Bhattacharya, without trying to define or describe the meaning of *mantra*, gives this summary: 'The *mantras* or mystic syllables constitute the backbone of tantric esoterism and of Vajrayāṇa. They are of innumerable variety, such as *bīja* (seed), *hṛdaya* (heart) . . .; these *mantras* are mostly a string of unmeaning [*sic*] words, but they sometimes disclose distinctly the influence of a language not unknown.'[19]

Referring to the Brahmin lore preceding Buddhism, one of India's most eminent historians, R. C. Majumdar, says about *mantra*:[20] '. . . the leaning of the Indian mind towards the worship of divinities and the awe and veneration for rituals and mystical utterances (*mantras*) reasserted itself. The belief in the efficacy of the Atharva-vedic *mantras*, the superhuman powers acquired by the mystics . . . could not be totally eradicated from the Indian mind, however arduous might have been the efforts of Buddha in that direction. The huge sacrificial literature that grew up in the post-vedic period permeated the Indian mind to such an extent that it was almost impossible to separate religion from ritualistic worship and mystical utterances (*mantra*). Buddha had to repeat his warnings to his disciples and devotees to disabuse their minds of the efficacy of the *mantra* rituals, but the sequel shows that he failed in his mission. . . .'

Majumdar was obviously not aware of the fact that the Buddha of the Pālī canon actually permitted the use of *mantra*, although probably with some reluctance.

N. N. Dasgupta, another historian of ancient Indian culture, says:[21] '. . . belief in the efficacy of *mantra* and other elements of esoteric practices as the easiest means for attaining salvation retarded the growth of spiritual ideas. . . .

'. . . in order to satisfy the ideas and sentiments of what is called the mass-mind, manifold ceremonies and rites of very popular and homely nature had to be incorporated, and *mantras* . . . introduced into the religion of the Buddha. . . . What is, to the ordinary or plebeian section of people, a religion, if it be not something that consists of belief in a pantheon of gods and goddesses and of the performance of rites and ceremonies and some esoteric practices along with the muttering of mystic formulas, etc., with which they had been hitherto only too familiar? . . .'

Eliade's chapter on *mantra* and *dhāraṇī* contains a concise description, certainly the most comprehensive one I have so far found:[22] 'the practical value and the philosophical importance of the *mantras* depends on two series of facts: first, on the yogic function of the phonemes, utilized as "supports" for concentration; and second, its tantric sphere properly: the working out of a gnostic system and of an internalized liturgy in the process of revaluing (*en revalorisant*) the archaic traditions pertaining to the "mystical sound".'

As a functional and material description, this statement can hardly be improved upon.

H. v. Glasenapp gives a short summary in the fashion of orthodox European indology, when he writes: 'all tantrism has been seen in the attribution of magical meaning to secret syllables (*bīja*) and utterances (*mantra*), and in the fact that the doctrine about these has actually been developed into a virtual "occult linguistic"—the *mantra-sāstra*. As early as in the Brāhmaṇa texts of the Vedic period unintelligible syllables like "*oṃ, hūṃ, khaṭ, phaṭ*" were known and metaphysical meaning was ascribed to them. Tantric literature has increased the number of these syllables to an immeasurable degree (*ins ungemessene vermehrt*) and has established quasi-scientific methods about how to combine these syllables either with one another or with meaningful words in order to unfold their dormant powers. The first emergence of these syllables and formulae in Buddhist literature can therefore be taken as a clue to the inceptive development of tantrism in the teaching of the Buddha.'[23]

Glasenapp, at least at the time when he wrote this book (1940), held that tantrism was originally Hindu and found its way into Buddhism surreptitiously. This view, of course, has long since been abandoned, and the contemporary trend is to the exact opposite, i.e. Buddhist tantrism preceding Hindu tantrism.

A. Avalon (Sir John Woodroffe) was a believer; the first, incidentally, among non-Asians to write on tantra. He describes *mantra* in the manner of the Hindu Śākta apologetics:[24] 'The *Viśvasāra Tantra*, Chapter II, says that the *Parabrahman*,[25] as *śabdabrahman*, whose substance is *mantra*, exists in the body of the *jīvātma*.[26] It is either unlettered (*dhvani*) or lettered (*varṇa*). The former, which produces the latter, is the subtle aspect of the *jīva's* vital *śakti*.[27] When the *mantra-śakti* is awakened through *sādhanā* (yogic practice) the presiding deity appears (e.g. to the adept), and when perfect *mantra-siddhi* (i.e. fruition of the *mantra*) is acquired, the deity which is *saccidānanda*[28] is revealed. . . . A *mantra* is composed of certain letters arranged in a definite sequence of sounds of which the letters are the representative signs. To produce the desired effect[29] *mantra* must be intoned in the proper way.[30] A *mantra* is not a prayer; prayer is conveyed in what words the worshipper chooses . . . *mantra* is not the name for the things the worshipper wants to tell the deity . . . if it were, the worshipper might just as well use his own language without recourse to the eternal and determined sounds, the *mantra* . . .

'. . . a *mantra* may, or may not, convey on its face its meaning. *Bīja*-(seed) *mantras*, such as *aiṅg*, *kliṅg*, *hriṅg*, have no meaning, according to the ordinary use of language. The initiate, however, knows that their meaning is "the own form" (*svarūpa*) of the particular deity whose *mantra* they are . . . every *mantra* is a form (*rūpa*) of Brahman . . . "*man*" of *mantra* comes from the first syllable of *manana*, and *-tr* from *trāṇa*, or liberation from the bondage of the *saṃsāra* or the phenomenal world.[31] . . . whilst, therefore, mere prayer often ends in nothing but physical sound, *mantra* is a potent compelling force, a word of power—the fruit of which is *mantra-siddhi*—and is thus effective to produce monistic perception and liberation . . . by *mantra* the sought for deity is attained and compelled. Though the purpose of worship (*pūjā*), religious reading (*pāṭha*), hymn-chanting (*stava*), sacrifice (*homa*), *dhyāna*, *dhāraṇa*, and *samādhi* (i.e. various stages of contemplation) and that of *mantra* are the same, the latter is far more powerful than all these. . . . The special *mantra* which is received in initiation is the *bīja* or seed *mantra*, sown in the field of the practicant's heart.'

H. V. Guenther writes about *mantra*:[32] 'The distinction between thing and name is perfectly clear in tantric literature. Whenever language signifies an object in its particularity, i.e. in its special reference, the Tibetan writer uses *-tshig* and that contains personal and nominal endings; if the object itself is referred to, he uses *-miṅ* or a name. The sounds themselves neither signify the particularity nor the object itself (*die sprachlichen Laute selbst bezeichnen weder die Besonderheit noch das Ding selbst*); vowels and consonants then have another function, which I am tempted to call a metalinguistic function—and this is the *mantra*.'

The most thoroughgoing descriptive enquiry into the import of *mantra*, from a modern anthropological angle, is contained in K. G. Diehl's book.[33] Without attempting a propositional definition of *mantra*, he comes very close to one in many places.

He stresses the instrumental quality of *mantra*, and although his immediate interest is southern India, what he says will hold for the entire realm of *mantra* use. Thus, he writes: '... the *mantras* are instruments. Partly they are without meaning and often they are not understood by him who reads them. They have fixed places in the ritual and varied effects and cannot be interchanged ... they are all indirect means of achieving something.'[34] 'Formulas (*mantras*), syllables (*bījas*), hold the gods and can be directed; in that way the performer of the rites draws into himself the divine, whereby alone he becomes fit for worshipping.'[35]

I shall now attempt my own definition of *mantra*: A *mantra* is a quasi-morpheme or a series of quasi-morphemes, or a series of mixed genuine and quasi-morphemes arranged in conventional patterns, based on codified esoteric traditions, and passed on from one preceptor to one disciple in the course of a prescribed initiation ritual.

This definition does not include any reference to the purpose or purposes of *mantra*, for the statement of purpose is a material statement, which must be excluded from a definition, which is a set of formal propositions of exceptionless validity. If there is a single exception to a statement, then that statement forfeits its claim to being a definition. As there is a conceivable exception with regard to the purpose of *mantra*, 'purpose' could not be included.[36]

iv. Genesis and construction of mantras

Although a definition of *mantra* may not include 'purpose' for the reasons shown, purpose must be the first point in the enquiry into the genesis of *mantra*. This is the easiest task, for there are only three possible purposes of *mantra*, divisible no doubt into many sub-categories. These are: propitiation, acquisition, and identification, or introjection.

Propitiation is the most primitive, and certainly the most ancient, purpose of *mantra*; some vocalization has to be found and fixed and used which would ward off unpleasant powers whatever they are, and would ingratiate the user with the pleasant ones. The emotional patterns of fear, awe, devotion, in fact all the *rāgas* or passions, provide the purpose of *mantra* as fulfilment of the need of propitiation, and as belief in the efficacy of propitiation.

Acquisition is the most widely ramified purpose of *mantra*: acquisition of things which are thought to be unobtainable or not so easily attainable through secular or other religious efforts; in short, acquisition of powers of control, which includes remedies, prophylaxes, all the occult *siddhi-s* and magical skills, and the tantric and yogic '*ṣaṭkarma*'.[37]

The most sophisticated purpose *mantra* can have is what I call identification or introjection. It fits every type of religious consummation envisaged in indocentric traditions, regardless of such vast doctrinary differences as between Hinduism, Jainism, and Buddhism. The most hallowed *mantra* of the Vedānta tradition is the *mahā-vākyam* or great dictum of the Upaniṣad, establishing identity of the individual with the cosmic soul *aham brahmāsmi*, 'I am Brahman'; and the meditational key-mantra of Vajrayāṇa Buddhism is *Oṃ śūnyatā-jñāna-vajra-svabhāvako 'ham*, 'I am of the nature of the *vajra* through the intuition of *śūnya*'; of the Hindu tantrics of the Śākta tradition *mantric* propositions establishing identity with the goddess, like *ahaṃ devī na cānyosmi*, 'I am the Goddess, none else'. The oldest and most tenacious form of *mantric* identification is the process of *bhūtaśuddhi*, 'purification of the elements', which is an obligatory observance for such disparate worshippers as the vedic priest and the Buddhist tantric. The *Mantramahodadhi* calls it a rite preliminary to the worship of a *deva*,[38] but this is misleading as it covers only the formal, and in this context the least important, aspect of *bhūtaśuddhi*. It is actually a step-by-step dissolution of grosser into subtler elements in the cosmographical hierarchy, and culminates in a visualized merger with whatever supreme being or state the particular tradition postulates. In this rite, which is a congeries of thoroughly standardized *mantras* and *mudrās*, a process of gradual involution is thought to take place whereby at first the body is identified with its various elementary sources; earth is associated with the sense of smell, water with taste, fire with sight, air with touch, and ether with sound: these individual functions of the subtle body (*liṅgaśarīra*) are 'merged', one by one, into their sources, the practicant then identifies the last element (ether) with the element-principle (*tanmātra*), sound, and with the ego (*ahaṃkāra*), the ego with *mahat* (the cognitive totum of the cosmos), and this into *prākṛti* (total nature); finally *prākṛti* is identified with the Brahman, the supreme absolute neutral deity. Then, to eradicate the negative, all sins are driven out through a special *mantra* aimed at the sins anthropomorphically visualized as a black man or another uncanny phantom; thus, partial, gradual, progressive merger leading to the final identification which is tantamount with the target of each tradition respectively is the ultimate purpose of *mantra*: and as it has doctrinal sanction as a means to realize the aim of the teaching, it is its most hallowed purpose. For even the humblest sorcerer who uses *mantra* for propitiation or for acquisition will readily admit his shortcoming—at least in India; he will emend, if pressed to do so, that the actual purpose of *mantra* ought to be something close to what I called identification, or introjection.

Next we have to look into the origin of the *mantra*; although the two overlap, this will have to be studied from a mythological and from a literary angle: outside these two, there is no locus where *mantras* originate. In the case of *dhāraṇīs* and *kavacas*, this is relatively easy: they are abbreviations of longer passages, contractions of longer canonical passages, of *sūtras* in the case of Buddhist *dhāraṇīs*. The tendency to contract passages of canonical literature into indefinitely smaller units seems to me to rest upon the ancient Indian scholastics' love of succinctness in spite of the risk of opacity; a famous adage ascribed to a number of teachers, mythical and historical, like Vyāsa, Śuka, Gauḍapāda, etc., says the commentators would rather sacrifice their own sons than add a single syllable in elucidation of what they feel is the shortest possible statement. Also, it appears to me as though this succinctness creates precisely the awe and the numinous feeling that goes with the use of *mantra*. *Mantras* of unambiguous origin are therefore the *dhāraṇī*-like *mantras* like the *Gāyatrī*, the *mahāvākyam-s* of the Upaniṣads, the Vajrayāṇa formula quoted earlier, and the like.

I say *dhārāṇī*-like, because they are not *dhāraṇīs*, but *mantras* properly, even though for all practical purposes they function as *dhāraṇīs* as well, i.e. as mnemonic aids. The term '*dhāraṇī*' is possibly a Buddhist term originally, it does not appear in Vedic literature at all in this sense; it must then have been taken over into Hindu tantric literature along with many other technical terms in vogue in Buddhist tantrism. These meaningful *mantras*, then, derive from specific doctrines: they have, like the *dhāraṇīs*, simultaneous but distinct functions, to impress the essence of the doctrine *in nuce* on the mind of the votary as a didactic device and a mnemonic aid, and to work as *mantras* proper, as alleged power-vehicles in the manner previously discussed.

The matter is considerably more difficult when *bīja-mantras*, i.e. the 'senseless syllables' of the old scholars, are concerned. Rejecting the entire time-honoured notion of senselessness, I am proceeding on the postulate that we have to find some mythical or literary origin that renders a plausible even though hypothetical explanation of any *bīja* under study, gibberish though it may appear to be. The notion which I thus impugn is not solely that of nineteenth-century occidental indologists, but goes back into ancient India, where opponents of sacerdotalism in general or of the use of *bīja-mantras* thought or taught that cunning priests had concocted them with the sole purpose of fooling gullible folks for their own aggrandizement. Bṛhaspati, the ancient mythical founder of the Cārvāka or Lokāyata school of materialists, said scoffingly in the Lokāyata (Cārvāka) aphorisms: 'the authors of the three Vedas are nothing but impostors, rogues and skrimshanks, when they pass their unintelligible gibberish, their "*jarbharī*" and "*turpharī*" for words of wisdom'.[39] Similar objections were not only made by the anti-religious Lokāyatas, but by many traditionalists; the Jainas were extremely critical of such usage, notwithstanding the fact that they introduced *bīja* in their own tantras. Most modern Hindus share this ancient disdain; the same holds for Theravāda Buddhists where they live in close contact with *mantra*-using Hindu groups like in Ceylon, and to a lesser extent in Burma. In colloquial Sinhalese, *mantra* means something like 'hocus-pocus'.

To exemplify my postulate: the ubiquitous *bīja* '*hrīṃ*', senseless though it looks at first sight, can be traced as to its mythological provenance; it is always used when a female deity is concerned, or extended to a male god when his image is to be conjured up together with his female counterpart, Śakti or Prajñā, or some other female attendant. Now the Indian root for 'modesty', 'bashfulness', etc., i.e. connoting the feminine virtue extolled as supreme since the Vedic period, is *hrī*. This *mantra's* provenance has its literary corroboration, and commentators of classical Hindu tantric texts have expressly stated it.[40] However, some *bīja-mantras* do not have any such literary corroboration; even then we must try to trace their mythological provenance. The latter is really more important, for after all the Indian commentators themselves had to think of some mythological theme that would tally with their explanation. I have not found such an explanation in canonical texts proper; if it is found, then it would of course be a primary source for the provenance of a *bīja*.[41]

We do not know how *bījas* were formed at first; we have to speculate. The orthodox explanation is the same with all believers in mantric tradition, Hindu, Buddhist, Jaina alike: the *mantra* shows itself through some process of supersensory perception, as a result of successful meditation, as intuition due either to such meditation or through the grace of the *guru* or the *iṣṭadevatā*;[42] it is either seen or heard in that manner; it is not the result of any discursive method of composition; it is revealed in a flash, never in part but always completely as one unit. Its fruition is either the result of *japa*,[43] or again an act of grace through supernatural initiation;[44] occasionally, it may be drug-induced.

So much for the believer's explanation of the origin of *mantra*—its construction as a verbal sound cannot interest him; on the contrary, he must deny the very possibility of its having been 'constructed' at any time—for being eternal and only revealed in time, 'construction' is precluded. It is now for us to suggest by what linguistic devices *mantras*, especially *bīja-mantras*, have been formed.

The first theory about the formation of *mantras*—first in the sense of most plausible—seems to be, without facetiously wanting to play *advocatus diaboli*, the one anticipated and suggested by the ancient and modern antagonists of the tantric tradition: that some early priests or other esoteric illuminati did concoct the *bījas*, and that they conceived the idea of using verbal sound clusters which are not intelligible to the non-initiate to mark off an inner circle of adepts. However, it does not seem likely to me that they made up the first *bījas* from a complete vacuum in the manner in which children concoct an arbitrary, secret language. They did take, it would seem to me, phonetic elements from divine names and from sacred texts and put them together under the compulsion of some emotional force, some state of trance, or some state of non-discursive contemplation. A good example for this hypothesis would be the *bīja* '*phaṭ*', called the *astra* 'weapon' *bīja* and used as an aggressive *mantra* from the earliest times. In the first place, the sound of *phaṭ*, to the Indian ear at least, conveys explosion onomatopoetically. According to Monier Williams[45] '*phaṭ*' is used for 'crack' as an indeclinable in the *Atharvaveda*, the *Vājasaneyī Saṃhitā*, and the *Taittirīya Aranyaka*. In Hindi *phaṭ* is a very common colloquial term for 'burst, explode', in both intransitive and transitive use. From this, a causative verb *phāṛnā* is formed. The motor-cycle rickshaw in Delhi is called '*phaṭphaṭā*' by its drivers; *phaṭkī* is a fire-cracker. Once a syllable like this has been accepted into esoteric usage, analogous syllables will readily follow. If the onomatopoetic datum can be linked with part of a meaningful morpheme, a more complex *mantra* would grow of their combination: thus, the Vedic *vaṣaṭ* and *vauṣaṭ* added to incantations meant to entice or to assuage the powers that be, might be quasi-morphemes formed out of the phonetic complex 'v/s', which conjures up in the Indian ear speed and superhuman acceleration (e.g. *vidyut*, Sanskrit for 'lightning', pronounced *bijjut* in most Prākṛts; and from this *bijlī* in Hindi, for both lightning and electricity), and the notion of power, force contained in the morphemes of *vaṣ*-; *vauṣat* might then be an intensification of *vaṣaṭ* through a sort of folk-*guṇation*.

The second hypothesis is psycholinguistic and based on an

extremely ancient Indian notion voiced in past Vedic times, as in Yāska's *Nirukta*,[46] that divinity is not fond of being accosted or even referred to by its actual name. The specific reference is to the word *indha* which stands for the god Indra in the *Chandogya Upaniṣad*; there Śaṃkara comments '*indha* for Indra, because the gods like to be called by indirect names'.[47] *Bīja-mantras* which share the initial of some deity's name might thus be explained as to their formation: *krīṃ* for Kṛṣṇa; *klīṃ*, the *kāma-bīja* of Madana, the Hindu Cupid; *śrīṃ* for the goddess Lakṣmī (Śrī). It is hard to say whether such formation was always conscious; it is conceivable that in the process of the original fixation of the *bīja*, the name that influenced the *bīja* phonetically was not then present to the mind of its promulgator—particularly when there were many synonyms of a particular divine name (like Śrī for Lakṣmī, Kāma for Madana).

A third hypothesis rests on the Indian conception of *spanda* 'vibration'; this is an aspect of *mantraśāstra* which seems to attract western admirers in a strong degree;[48] certain sounds in nature are felt to have a definite pitch for the aesthetically sensitive Indian ear. This is borne out by the fact that the names of three of the seven *svaras* or tones in the Indian dol-fa scale are animal names, designating the absolute pitch ascribed to these animals' voices (*riṣabha*, 'bull' for the d; *dhaivata*, 'kingfisher' (not certain), for a; and *niṣādha*, 'ox', 'bullock', for the b-natural. Now if we assume that the elements in action produce a pitch which creates *spandana* (vibration) 'audible' to the *mantra*-seer,[49] then he will probably evaluate the constituents of his *mantra* by means of a quasi-scientific allocation of their sound-vibration (*spandana*) to the element with which the particular deity is connected: thus, *raṃ* is the *bīja* of Agni (fire); *vaṃ* of Varuṇa (water); etc. *Mantra*-sounds and constituent phonemes of divine names are thus constantly rationalized throughout esoteric literature; cf. *ha* means Śiva; *ra* is said to be Nature (*prākṛti*); *i* means Mahāmāyā; *Nāda* is said to be the mother of the universe; the dot-grapheme (*bindu*) means 'dispeller of sorrow'. With this *bīja*, i.e. *hrīṃ*, the Lady of the Earth (Bhuvaneśvarī) should be worshipped.[50] *Ha* is the first syllable of Hara, a common synonym for Śiva; why *ra* is *prākṛti* is not quite so evident—it may be due to the phonetic dominance of the 'r' sound in the word *prākṛti* itself, or it may be a conscious or an unconscious synonym of *prākṛti* having *ra* as initial; thus *rā* means 'giving', 'gold', 'yielding in abundance, i.e. nature'; it also means 'amorous play', one of the main functions of Prākṛti or nature.

The obvious parallel in occidental, especially in neo-Platonic, thought is the 'music of the spheres', which some mystics or other specially gifted individuals can 'hear'.

Many more hypotheses might be worked out, but they would have to come from psychologists or theologians; psychologists might tell us 'how' *mantras* come about in a manner analogous to 'how' expletives come about or even 'how' poetry emerges; and the theologian might show us by way of axiomatic deductions that the orthodox mantric devotees' claim to *mantra* being revealed is justified in a theological context.

As to the construction of *mantra* within the textual framework the material is vast. Every tantric text, in all the three religions inculcating *mantra*, abounds in instructions about the correct form and pronunciation of the *mantra*; in fact, these instructions seem to be obligatory in every tantric text, although this is not directly enjoined in any canonical text I have seen.

There are two ways in which instructions about how to arrive at a *mantra* are given: the direct way, in which the *mantra* is simply listed in the text; and the indirect way, in which the instruction is couched in heuristic propositions using circumlocutory terms for *mantra*-constituents and *bījas* which are known only to the initiate or to scholars conversant with tantric terminology. These instructions are therefore in *sandhābhāṣā*, and they are the only *sandhā*-passages in *mantric* instructions of any kind; that is to say, instructions about *dhārāṇi*, *yāmala*, *kavaca*, *yantra*, and *maṇḍala*, are not couched in intentional language. The reason for this seems to be that secrecy attaches only to the *mantra* itself in a degree comparable to instructions on esoteric practices, especially of the left-handed variety. *Mantra* loses its power if revealed to the non-initiate.

The *sandhā*-terminology that has to be understood in these instructions is quite limited; it is the most frequent *bījas* that have invariable *sandhā*-names, and parts of the written letters constituting the *bīja*. I am listing the most important ones:

OM is called *praṇava, tāra, setu, bridge*, etc.
HRĪM is called '*māyā-bīja*'
RAṂ is called '*vahnī*' (fire, syn. of Agni), '*rakta*' ('red')
HŪṂ is called '*kūrca*' ('bundles', 'heap')
AIṂ is called '*vahnijāyā*' (i.e. wife of Agni—the Vedic termination *mantra* '*svāhā*' is said to be the exoteric name of Agni's consort); '*vāgbhāva*' ('she of speech-existence'), '*vahni-kāntā*' ('beloved of Agni')
KLĪṂ is called '*kāmabīja*' (i.e. *bīja* of Cupid), but more often simply '*kāma*' or any of its synonyms (*madana, manmatha, ratipati*)
KRĪṂ is called '*ādya*' (incipient)[51] and also *Kāli-bīja*'
ŚRĪṂ is called '*Laksmī-bīja*', or simply '*Lakṣmī*'[52]
HUṂ is called '*varma*' ('warrior')
PHAṬ is called '*astra*' (weapon, already discussed')
EM is called *yonī-bīja* ('womb-*bīja*')

Each deity has his or her *bīja*, which is used in the worship of the deity of whose total *mantra* it is a component part.

There is a vast number of other *bījas*, some of which are formed, as previously indicated, by the first letters of the name of the respective deity, i.e. *GAṂ* for Gaṇeśa, *DUṂ* for Durgā, etc.

I shall now quote two typical paradigms of *sandhā*-instruction for the formation of *mantras*, one from Hindu and one from Buddhist lore:

a) (Hindu): 'placing the lord of life (*prāṇeśa*) on the fiery one (*taijasa*) and adding to it *bheruṇḍa* (name of an attendant of the Goddess Kālī) and the *bindu* (dot on the *anunāsikā* symbol) the first *bīja* is formed; after this, proceed to the second *bīja*: by placing the dawn (*sandyhā*, intentional for *sa*) on the red one (*rakta*, intentional for *ra*) and adding to it the left eye (*vāmanetra*, intentional for *i*) and the *bindu*, the second *bīja* is formed; now listen (to the formation of) the third *bīja*: the Lord of the born things (*prajāpati*, intentional for *ka*) is put upon the light (*dīpa*, intentional for the fire-*bīja raṃ*); to them is added the cowherd (Govinda, synonym for Kṛṣṇa, here intentional for *i*). It gives happiness to the devotees. After making these three *bījas* add the word Parameś-varī in the vocative, and then the name of the beloved of Fire (*vahni-kāntā*, intentional for *svāhā*). Thus, o blessed one, is the mantra of ten letters formed. This Vidyā (i.e. female *mantra*) is the supreme goddess, the substance of all *mantras*.'[53]

The *mantra* thus arrived at is '*HRĪṂ ŚRĪṂ KRĪM PARAMEŚ-VARĪ SVĀHĀ*'.

b) (Buddhist): 'the *mantra* (of the Goddess Ekajaṭā) is now correctly established as instructed by Her; at the end of the one of "the nature of fire" (*hutāśana*, i.e. the *vahnibīja, raṃ*), parted by the fourth vowel (i.e. *i*), on its head the *bindu* is placed with the broken crescent (i.e. the *anunāsikā* symbol, crescent and dot above it), this *bīja* is the great *bīja*; now immediately listen to the second *bīja* (constituting the goddess '*Mantrā*'): *ā* to the end of *ta* (or *sa* according to the A mss used by the editor of the *Sādhanāmālā*) is joined the fire (i.e. *raṃ*, the *bīja* of Agni), parted by that very same vowel (i.e. *a*), together with *nāḍa* (lit. the cosmic sound, but meaning the crescent of the *anunāsikā* symbol), this is the second *bīja*; now I shall tell you with care the third *bīja*: *ha* is followed by the sixth vowel as its end (i.e. *u*), dressed with *nāḍa* and *bindu* (i.e. the *anunāsikā*). This best of the *bījas* gets the three worlds afire. Now I shall tell you the fourth *bīja* as told by the Buddha: at the end of *pha* (*ya* according to mss A) stands the pure, well pointed, saturatad half-letter that bestows all *siddhis*'[54] (that is *ṭa*; 'half' on account of its shape ट compared with ṭha ठ; its being well pointed and saturated is synaesthetic parlance very frequent in this kind of instruction. Archers and marksmen around Banaras exclaim '*ṭhaṭṭ*' when the arrow or the bullet hits its mark, a rather apt paraphrase of the 'weapon-mantra' '*phaṭ*' here indicated). 'The *bija* is "pure" in the sense of not having any vowel added to the inherent *a* in *pha*.'[55]

The complete *mantra* is therefore *HRĪṂ TRĀṂ HUṂ PHAṬ*.[56]

The votaries of *mantra* are, however, not too consistent about the secrecy of the *mantras* so laboriously camouflaged in these *sandhā*-instructions; there are numerous manuals which list them *in toto*; they are the '*bījakośas*' of the various *mantra* schools;[57]

there is certainly no *mantra* arrived at by means of *sandhā*-instruction, which is not listed in manuals like the *Mantramahārṇava* and the *Mantramahodadhi*. The Hindu tantrics' rationalization for this apparent lapse runs somewhat like this: the canonical tantric texts which give *mantra*-formation in the above manner insist that it must be kept inaccessible to the non-initiate, and the *bījakośas* or manuals are meant for the initiates and the gurus only; and as these do not contain reference to the *sandhā*-passages in the canonical texts, they do not infringe on the rule of secrecy.[58]

The Jainas did not use *sandhā*-terminology for their *mantra*-instructions, at least not in their main Tantra, the *Bhairavīpadmāvatīkalpa*. They list the *mantras* and their *bījas* directly and a eulogy on their merits follows; e.g. 'he should meditate on the *bīja trīṃ* in his mouth when engaged in dispute with his opponents; or on the shining letter *ra* that gives the particular *siddhi* desired.'[59]

v. Mantra *in use*

There are two alternatives for the use of *mantra*; as part of a ritual and as spontaneous meditation. Professor R. P. Tripathi's division into 'individual' and 'collective' performance can hardly stand,[60] for the number of participants in a mantric performance is in no way essential. We might make a division by purpose, inculcating any of the suggestions indicated in the previous sections, but there would then be too much overlapping: almost all *mantras* are multipurpose instruments, as will be seen in the table towards the end of this chapter.

The arrangement *OṂ HŪṂ PHAṬ* in Buddhist tantra is used for banning and exorcism, for meditation on any of the *dhyānī*-Buddhas, for the worship of the tantric goddess Kurukullā, and for preparing the mind to accept the truth of Voidness (*śūnyatā*); the Hindu mantra *AṂ HŪṂ PHAṬ* is used when chopping off the head of the sacrificial goat during Kālī and Durgāpūjā,[61] and for invoking the blessings of Bagalā, a local Bengali goddess; and in classical times in the event of manumission.[62] My own suggestion, i.e. that *mantra* is of but twofold use, 'ritualistic' or 'spontaneous', offers a rigid, formal division in which there is no overlapping.

The oldest use was no doubt ritualistic, contained in the Vedic chant as part of the *homa* sacrifice and after Brahmanical observances, and in all activities of the ritualistic order of the post-Vedic traditions, in the three autochthonous religions. Even in the more sophisticated 'individual' meditations aimed at the realization of the supreme state of wisdom declared by most of the schools, the *mantra-japa* (repetition, silent or otherwise) is rarely performed in a vacuum: it is part of the total meditation routine, along with *bhūtaśuddhi* (see above), purification, invocation of deities and *gurus*, blessings to the universe, *prāṇāyāma* (breath-control exercises), *laya* (yogic contemplation proper, a meditative process of merging the individual into the cosmic soul), *mantra-japa*, and *samarpana* (transferring the 'fruit', *phala*) of the meditative effort to the *iṣṭadevatā* (chosen deity) or the *guru*.

What I call the 'spontaneous' use of *mantra* is at least as frequent in the all-round incidence of *mantra* practice. The *mantra* is constantly 'japped'[63] without any other observance accompanying it. This is a truly ubiquitous performance: the monk and priest murmurs or thinks it without any particular occasion many times a day or whenever they commence any activity; the pious rikshaw-puller mumbles his *mantra*, which in northern India is '*Rām Rām*' when he lifts and transports loads. The same *mantra* may then be used by the initiates as part of the daily ritual. The ideal achievement is called '*prāṇajapa*', i.e. the incessant repetition of the *mantra*;[64] this is more frequent than one would think, not limited to the professionally religious, and practised by men and women on the land as in metropolitan Calcutta, Madras, and Delhi, even in 1964.

The instructions on correct pronunciation or intonation pertain only to the ritualistic use of *mantra*. This emphasis is extremely old; an entire section of the Vedic discipline deals with correct pronunciation, *śikṣā*, *sanyāsī* monks, and other religious specialists chant verses reminding them about the importance of *śikṣā*, in their daily observances.[65]

The tendency to add denominational or sectarian significance to the manner in which *mantras* are pronounced in ritualistic use seems to have originated in early Buddhism; no earlier instruction has been found. The *triśaraṇa*-formula of the Buddhist novices which, as I tried to show earlier, is in effect a *mantra*, is pronounced twice three times, i.e. once with the Sanskritized bilabial nasal pronunciation 'm' (*buddhaṃ śaraṇaṃ gacchāmi*, etc.) and following immediately with the pronunciation thought to be genuine Pālī, i.e. with a velar nasal 'ṅ' (*buddhaṅ śaraṇaṅ gacchāmi*).[66]

In lieu of any further elucidation, I shall now present an authentic statement, a translation of the Hindi preface to the large *mantra*-manual *Mantramahārṇava*, which is now being used by almost all practising *mantra* believers in Bombay and central India. In the north, the *Mantramahodadhi* (which, like the *Mantra-mahārṇava*, means 'Great Ocean of Mantras') seems to be more popular—it is smaller and older; excerpts of a little-known small manual are presented as a sample at the end of this chapter. The preface of the large and important *Mantramahārṇava*, then, reads:[67]

'Thanks to the grace of the Supreme Brahman we have now succeeded in completing this work. Especially, we have to offer our thanks to the almighty Śiva through whose benign glance the *mantra-śāstra* (*mantra*—text and doctrine) has been revealed—through which *śāstra* that people in former times were able to defeat the gods even, and having subdued them, made them do for them whatever they desired. Through *mantra-sāstra* demons like Rāvaṇa could give fight to Śrī Rāmacandra and other divine heroes. Through the *mantra-śāstra* people could vanish out of sight right in front of others. Through it, they could enter into and assume others' forms and bodies. Through it, they were able to move below water for thousands of *yojanās* (one *yojanā* is about five miles). Through it, they could move in the sky and visit the abode of gods . . . through it, they readily acquired the eight miraculous powers. . . . It is a very sad matter that today this wish-fulfilling jewel, the *mantra-śāstra*, has been lost to the world. The reasons for this loss are that first of all such valuable things are hard to obtain, for if any person possesses something of this (literature) he keeps it a secret and does not show it to anyone; and if one does lay hand on one text or the other, then it is garbled or a corrupted text (*aśuddh*), no one knows how to perform the accompanying worship properly, nor is anyone able to pronounce it correctly, or he does not know at what sort of place it is to be read—or else, only just the bare *mantra* may be available—then pray tell me, how can there be success in the performance? And due to this fact (of failure through incompleteness) the *mantra* yields no results nowadays; and then (modern) people say the whole thing is nonsense. But this idea (of *mantra* being nonsensical and futile) is a grave error on the part of intelligent people and scholars. It is a grave error, first because Śiva himself has proclaimed this *śāstra*, and its miraculous effects were witnessed by people. . . . But, the absence of exact directives (for the use of *mantra*), and you people's doubt and hardheadedness even in the (occasional) presence of such prescriptions, these are the reasons for the failure to achieve *siddhi* through the *mantras*. It must therefore be hoped that you will change your mind in this matter, and will no longer say that the *mantra-śāstra* is false. However, the practice of *mantra* was being kept secret, and also the courage to do the necessary *sādhanā* was lacking so it is in a way understandable why people conceived this negative notion . . .

'Now, with a view to removing all these errors this crest-jewel of *mantra-śāstra* has been born (*mantr śāstrmen śiromaṇi is mantra-mahārṇavkā janm huā*), the "Great Ocean of Mantras". But in order to enthuse the hearts of Vaiṣṇavas, Śaivas, and Śāktas alike, Paṇḍit Mantraśāstrī Mādhavray Vaidya of Allahabad has compiled this "Ocean of Mantras" with the aid of many ancient *mantra*-books. In order to please your personal *iṣṭa-devatā*[68] you will see that the complete worship and *mantra*-procedure of each god or divine aspect is always listed under one heading—not like in older books of this kind, where you have to turn the tome topsy-turvy (*ulaṭ palaṭ*) and then to run over anyway to the *mantra* experts to have unintelligible passages explained. This book here has it all: the *mantras* of your *iṣṭa-devatā*, the *nyāsa*, ritualistic 'touch', meditation, the worship of the *pīṭha*, the Śakti of the *pīṭha*, the construction of *yantra* (mystical diagram), of the altar, the installation of the deity, the sixteen ingredients and their respective location (on the altar), the laudatory hymns, in fact the complete fivefold arrangement will be found together in one place, so that you can perform the rites yourself just by having this book or by giving it to the Brahmin whom you want to perform it. You won't find a single *mantra* in the whole book which is not accompanied, at the very same place, by a complete description of all the preparatory and other ceremonies that go along with it. . . . Neither is there a single deity, demon, *yakṣa* (semi-demonic being), *gandharva* (divine minstrel), *kinnara* (a kind of genii), *yoginī*, *asparā* (nymph), daughter of a god, daughter of a Nāga (snake-spirit), *rākṣas*, (ghoul), or departed spirit whose complete method of worship and *mantra* you could not look up in this *Mantramahārṇava*, they are all in it. . . .

'Without having to turn the whole book inside out, you will also find the various *siddhis* listed along with their respective mantras. . . .

'To my understanding, this present book supersedes all other *mantra* manuals current today—it will be of equal use both for the deep scholar and for the layman, for it will give *siddhi* to both of them if properly used. . . .

'Then, why should you people mistrust the power of *mantra*: just as the Brahmins of yore acquired success and greatness due to *mantra-śāstra*, in the same manner you can acquire them today; through it, the various afflictions of this world will be removed and in the end you will reach the abode of gods and emancipation. Well, I do not have to say more than this—I just request you to let this swan-like book float on the tender lake of your hearts. . . .'

The editor's claims to the completeness of the text are hardly exaggerated. I am quoting a number of headings from the table of contents following the preface. There are roughly a thousand sections listed; about half of them deal with *mantra* proper, i.e. those ending in the word *-prayoga*, 'the use of . . .'; the rest are preparatory, descriptive, and controlling devices: The chanting of the auspicious invocation (*maṅgalācaraṇa*); the tantras used; the constellations and genealogies of the worshippers; the difference of the deity (to be worshipped) in the different world-ages (*yugas*); the necessity of knowing the ingredients essential for ritual; the examination of *gurus* and disciples; the greatness of the *guru*; a *guru* who should be abandoned; a disciple who should be abandoned; the determination of the auspicious moment for initiation; the determination of what should be eaten and what should not be eaten (i.e. dietetic injunctions); the determination of the right location for repeating the *mantra*; the importance of precise location for the repetition of *mantras*; the difference in time (for meditation) in relation to different locations; the signs of the location (*sthānalakṣaṇa*); the signs of a *liṅga* (i.e a piece of stone or a rock which would qualify to be installed as a *liṅga* for formal worship on account of its phallic shape); the signs of a cremation ground (viz. its qualification for tantric worship to be conducted on it or near it); the persons qualified for *mantra*; the criteria of a empty place (for worship); the criterion of a crossroad (as a possible location); the criterion of a cloister; the determination of the direction of the compass; the direction of the compass for the worship of Śiva; the direction for the worship of Tārā or Kālī (synonymous in this compound); the determination of the correct ritualistic bath; the determination of *tilaka* (paste-mark on the forehead); the determination of the *āsana* (sitting posture); and type of seat. The determination of the rosary; the greatness of the *rudrākṣa* (read-beads sacred to Śiva) rosary according to the *Padmapurāṇa*; the value of the *rudrākṣa*-rosary according to the number of *mukhas* (natural furrows in the beads); the manner of holding the rosary; the determination of the *gomukhī* (the rosary container); the determination of (the position of) fingers (while holding the rosary); the determination of *japa* (repetition of *mantras*); the determination of *homa* (libation); the location for conducting *homa*; the shape of the *homa* pit; the proof of successful *āhuti* (pouring of the ingredient into the fire during *homa*) based on the quality of the used ingredients; the description of auspicious embers; the examination of auspiciousness and inauspiciousness through the colour of the fire; the determination of the right foliage (palm-leaves) for the drawing of *yantras* (mystical diagrams); the determination of incense; the difference of incense materials for the different deities; thoughts about using the correct finger for incense offerings; determination of fruits and flowers (for worship); incense types which can be used for all deities alike; determination of *dīpa* (oil-lights and lamps); description of the dishes carrying the oil; determination of musical instruments (used for the worship); injunctions and prohibitions about polluted material (for worship); determination of raiments (to be worn for the *mantra* repetition and worship); instructions on circumambulation (of the place of worship or the *guru* see also previous chapter)); the value of circumambulating (the idol of) Śiva; consideration of *siddha-mantras*; the *siddha-cakra* (the circle of devotees assembled for tantric worship); the *cakra* formed for the purpose of *mantras* to subject enemies; consideration of 'enemy-*mantras*'; removal of obstructions to the efficacy of enemy-*mantras*; on *mantras* which can be efficiently used without previous ritualistic purification; on *mantras* for getting rid of (the effect of) curses; on *mantras* which yield *siddhi* in the *Kaliyuga* (the present, final age of the cycle); on *mantras* that may be used by all the four castes in the *kali*-age; considerations of *mantras* according to their gender (masculine, feminine, neuter); the defects arising from mispronouncing the *mantra*, and from splitting it in the wrong place; ten rituals for removing the defect incurred through these faults; the method of 'unfastening' (of undoing the undesired effect of *mantra* already pronounced); on the great merit of renouncing the enjoyment of women; the necessity of the Gāyatrī-*mantra* for all primary rites; the definition of the five limbs of the worship of deities; the signs of *mantra*-accomplished persons; the types of *mudrās* (hand gestures); eighteen *mudrās* in the worship of Viṣṇu; ten *mudrās* for the worship of Śiva; seven *mudrās* for the worship of Gaṇeśa; ten *mudrās* for the worship of Śakti; *mudrās* for the goddess Lakṣmī; five *mudrās* for Sarasvatī; one *mudrā* for Vahni (the god of fire, Agni); miscellaneous *mudrās*; etc., etc.

In the enumeration of *mantras*, each of the deities is assigned a multitude of different *mantras*; thus, the goddess Lakṣmī has *mantras* of one, two, four, and twenty-five *bījas*; the same holds for far less illustrious deities—a genie Vakratuṇḍa ('having a curved trunk', probably some form of Gaṇeśa) has one *mantra* of six and one of twenty-four *bījas*, etc.

vi. Classification of mantras*: formal and material*

Almost any number of classificatory schemes could be devised—and in fact have been devised—by orthodox traditions, viz. into *nyāsa-mantras* (*mantras* accompanied by ritualistic 'touch'), *hṛdaya-mantras*, *pītha-mantras* (assigned to the various centres of pilgrimage), etc.[69] However, such classifications are of little critical use because the classes overlap to a high degree. The only classification of the traditional type that might suggest a workable classification in an analytical sense is the one suggested by some Bengali Śākta-teachers, as Vimalānanda, the author of the commentary to the *Karpurādistotram*; Hariharānananda Bhāratī, the commentator of the *Mahānirvāṇa Tantra*: and Pandit Jaganamohana Tarkālaṅkāra, who commented on the *Mahānirvāṇa* and some minor tantric texts. It is the division into *hādi* and *kādi mantras*,[70] i.e. *mantras* commencing with the syllable *ha* or *ka*, respectively. As a formal division, the distinction would be true, but unreliable; the pandits use it as a sort of formal-cum-material division: *Hādi-mantras* are said to be used where the predominant purpose is liberation; *kādi-mantras* where the predominant purpose is mundane—or in our terminology, *hādi-mantras* are used for identification, *kādi-mantras* for both propitiation and acquisition. Unfortunately, the distinction is not always correct; there are many *kādi-mantras* used for identification and introjection, and many *hādi-mantras* for secular purposes in the tantras; it does not hold at all for the Buddhist *mantra* tradition. A few examples of Hindu *mantras* which would upset the *hādi-kādi* distinction as to purpose:

'*HRĪṂ GAṂ GAṆAPATAYE GAṂ HRĪṂ*', a *hādi-mantra* to Gaṇeśa, the elephant-headed son of Śiva, remover of obstacles, is used for the achievement of conjugal happiness;[71] no doubt a mundane purpose;

KRĪṂ KRĪṂ KRĪṂ HUṂ HŪṂ, a *kādi-mantra*, though used for magical purposes most frequently, is also used in preparing the mind for the state of oneness with Kālī in at least one passage.[72]

I shall now present a few classificatory schemes; these are based on sporadic textual and oral suggestions made by recent tantric authors, which I am trying to bring into some sort of a system:

[I] FORMAL CLASSIFICATIONS

a) *Symmetrical—asymmetrical* mantras

A *mantra* having the exact inverse arrangement of constituents on both sides of its centre would be a 'symmetrical' *mantra*; a *mantra* of the form a-b-c-d—centre—d-c-b-a; fixed *bījas* like *OṂ*, *Phaṭ*, *Svāhā*, constantly recurring *bījas* that have an unalterable position in the *mantras* (OṂ at the beginning mostly, *phaṭ* and *svāhā* only at the end) would not, where they occur, bar a *mantra* from being 'symmetrical' if its arrangement otherwise conforms to the schema; e.g. '*HRĪṂ KRĪṂ KLĪṂ CHINNAMASTĀ KLĪṂ KRĪṂ HRĪṂ*'[73] and '*OṂ HRĪṂ KRĪṂ KLĪṂ (OṂ) CHINNA-MASTĀ KLĪṂ KRĪṂ HRĪṂ PHAṬ*'[74] are both 'symmetrical'.

The proportion is very uneven; among one hundred *mantras* surveyed at random from Buddhist, Hindu, and Jaina tantras, only twelve were symmetrical, the rest asymmetrical.

There is no Indian term for these two categories. The only statement providing a rationale for extruding symmetrical *mantras* as a formal category I found in a manuscript titled *Kulapūjānirṇaya*, 'description of the Kula tantric initiates' worship', in the collection of the late Dr. Bhagaway Dass, Bh.R., at Banaras. The passage in question reads 'if the *bījas* are arranged parallelly from the centre of the auspicious *mantra*, through the *japa* (repetition) of such a *mantra* the disease of the world vanishes', '*sādhyamantramadhyasthānād ye bījassamānāntaras, tadvidham mantra-jāpe tu saṃsārarogo naśyati*'.[75] If this verse is a condensation of an authoritative tantric teaching, it would imply that 'symmetrical' *mantras* are classed as an emancipation-giving category; *saṃsāraroga*, 'the sickness of the universe', is a very frequent, stereotype short-hand, up to this day, for the delusions that bind men to worldly things.

Symmetrical mantras

HRĪṂ GAṂ GAṆAPATAYE GAṂ HRĪṂ[76]
HRĪṂ HRĪṂ HAṂ MAHĪŚĀYA HAṂ HRĪṂ HRĪṂ[77]
AIṂ HRĪṂ VĀJAYE HRĪṂ AIM (*Mahādevīmantra*)[78]
HRĪṂ HRĪṂ SIṂHĀYA MAHĀVALĀYA HRĪṂ HRĪṂ (*Siṁhamantra*)[79]

Asymmetrical mantras

OṂ KIṬI KIṬI VAJRA HŪṂ HŪṂ HŪṂ PHAṬ SVĀHĀ[80]
AMṚTAṂ ŚRAVAYA ŚRAVAYA SAṂ SAṂ KLĪṂ KLĪṂ HRŪṂ HRŪṂ HRAṂ HRAṂ HRĪṂ HRĪṂ DRAVAYA DRAVAYA HRĪṂ SVĀHĀ[81]

Tentatively, I would say that symmetrical *mantras* are more common in Hindu than in Buddhist tantras, and not represented in Jaina tantra.

by *Isomorphemic—heteromorphemic*

I suggest this classifying terminology with reference to the single and multiple occurrence of a *bīja* within a *mantra*; e.g. *KRĪṂ KRĪṂ KRĪṂ HRĪṂ HRĪṂ PHAṬ* is an isomorphemic *mantra*; *KRĪṂ HUṂ HRAṂ AUṂ SVĀHĀ* is a heteromorphemic *mantra*. The two categories are represented in about equal numbers in the total mantric literature of all the three religions. One might venture a hypothesis about the use of these categories; it seems to me that isomorphemism is used for emotional intensification. It is not meant to convey desire for quantitative increase of the object, i.e. if two *mantras* '*OM HRĪM KLĪM SVĀHĀ*' and '*HRĪM HRĪM AIM KLĪM SVĀHĀ*' are available for the identical purpose,[82] the later, isomorphemic *mantra* would be chosen if the practicant feels that the heteromorphic one would not create in him the emotional intensity necessary to see the exercise through, particularly if it requires a prolonged *japa* for fruition; but this is at best healthy guesswork.

Gopinath Kaviraj taught[83] that 'shorter, non-repetitious

mantras', i.e. *mantras* which I call hetermorphemic, require a larger amount of *japa* than 'long, *bīja*-repeating *mantras'*, i.e. my isomorphemic *mantras* aiming at the identical target. This, however, is disputable because there are just too many exceptions. In the examples adduced right above, the number of *japa* to be performed with '*OṂ HRĪṂ KLĪṂ SVĀHĀ*' and with the alternative '*HRĪṂ HRĪṂ AIṂ KLĪṂ SVĀHĀ*' is identical, viz. 150,000.[84] In other cases, the number of *japa* required for a heteromorphemic *mantra* is actually larger than that required for its isomorphemic alternative; thus, the Assamese *Kāmaratna Tantra* offers two *mantras* to ward off snakebite, *OM UJENĀTHĀYA OṂ ṚṂ NAMAḤ, HAKĀLĀYA MARDDĀDEBI AṂṚTA GARBHA DEBI OṂ OṂ PHAṬ SVĀHĀ, OṂ HRĪṂ HRĪṂ SAṂ KṢAMĀHAM* (isomorphemic), and alternatively *HRĪṂ OṂ KṢAḤ PHAṬ SVĀHĀ*[85] (heteromorphemic).[86] The latter is required to be 'japped' five thousand times, the former one thousand times. There is no difference whatever in the promised *siddhi*, i.e. warding off the entering of snakes into the house, and of snakebite itself, nor is there any indication as to the duration of power; its words, so the text says, are effective over the same length of time regardless of whether it has been achieved through the *japa* of the one or other *mantra*. It is from this and analogous cases that I have come to think that the choice may be with the idea of emotional intensification in the manner indicated above.

[II] MATERIAL CLASSIFICATIONS

A very large number of material classifications is possible; rather than listing them all, they can be easily construed from the charts at the end of this chapter.

I shall in this section sample but a few which convey the most typical features for classificatory schemes:

a) Meaningful—*bīja*—mixed:
For example, *NAMAḤ ŚIVĀYA*, 'Obeisance to Śiva', is meaningful. '*HRĪṂ KLĪṂ PHAṬ VAUṢAṬ* is of the *bīja*-type; and *KRIṂ VAŚAMĀNAYA PHAṬ* is a mixed *mantra*.

b) According to use:
nyāsa ('placing'), *pratiṣṭha* ('installation'), *hṛdaya* (mnemonic 'heart') and all the other types listed in the texts, and finally, in this classification according to use, 'mixed', i.e. *mantras* which are used for various purposes.

c) According to the traditions in which they occur:
Hindu, Buddhist, Jaina, mixed (*mantras* that are used in more than one of the three traditions). It is, however, highly doubtful whether there is any *mantra* at all which is not 'mixed' in this sense. The only *mantra* which does seem to be present in one tradition only is the *mantra* of Tārā in the *Sādhanāmālā* and other tantric Buddhist texts '*tuttāre ture*'; the *mantra* does not occur, to my knowledge, in the (Bengali) Śākta texts pertaining to the Hindu Tārā, a form of Durgā. The *Gāyatrī*, *Mṛtyuñjaya*, and other 'typically' Brahmanical *mantras* do occur in Jana tantras.

vii. Mantra *samples and their analysis*

As all *mantras* are listed in tantric literature, though not exclusively in it, the division into samples of Hindu, Buddhist, and Jaina provenance seems the most practical.

The procedure which I shall use to analyse *mantras* in this section, supported again by the charts (section viii), is as follows:

(i) the *mantra* is listed exactly in the form the text spells it, with possible variants in other texts, provided that the 'purpose' is identical in the alternative text;
(ii) its pronounciation in use is stated;
(iii) its purpose follows;
(iv) the method of *japa* is outlined;
(v) its frequency in literature and use is estimated.

A. *Predominantly Buddhist mantras*

OṂ ĀḤ HŪṂ. This is the asymmetrical '*mūlamantra*' (root-*mantra*) in all Buddhist tantric literature; there is no Buddhist tantric text which would not contain it. In the *Guhyasamāja* it is listed over five times, in the *Sādhanāmālā* over twenty times.

The pronunciation of the nasal in the first and in the last *bīja* is bilabial *m*, except among Bengali and some Maithili speakers, who invariably pronounce the *anunāsikā* as a velar *ṅ*.

The purpose of this *mūlamantra* is identification, and (rarely) propitiation. It is never used for acquisition.

The *mantra* has elicited much commentary in Buddhist tantrc as well as in secondary literature; it is extremely important in Tibetan worship and iconography. A modern believer's statement on it was given by Lama Anagarika Govinda:[87] 'we find painted on the Tibetan Than-kas the *bīja* syllables "of the body, of the speech, and of the mind", i.e. *OṂ ĀḤ HŪṂ*[88]—but only where Buddhas, Bodhisattvas, or great saints are depicted; these *bījas* are painted on the backs of the scrolls, onto the three correlated physic centres of the body (brain-throat-heart). The meaning of these three *bījas* conjoined into the *mantra* transcends the forms of individual symbolization (like that of Vairocana, Amoghasiddhi, Akṣobhya)—that is to say, these *bījas* are here applied jointly to the highest plain of experience, in which all the singular aspects of the *dhyānī*-Buddhas merge into one and vanish.'

I did not try to estimate the frequency of this *mantra*; it is no doubt among the two most frequent along with the well-known *OṂ MAṆIPADME HŪṂ*.[89] This is the famous arch-*mantra* of Tibetan Buddhism. In spite of much mystification, this mixed, asymmetrical, heteromorphemic *mantra* does not offer any difficulty: it belongs to the species of invocation *mantras* of Buddhas and Buddhist Prajñās (with Govinda, I am avoiding the term 'Śakti' for the female counterparts of the Buddhas) of the form '*OṂ* . . . (x vocative) . . . *HŪṂ*'—like *OṂ VAJRAḌAKE HŪṂ OṂ VAJRAPUṢPE HŪṂ, OṂ VAJRAGHAṆṬE HŪṂ*.[90] The form '*maṇipadme*' is simply the vocative of 'Maṇipadmā', a Buddhist Prajñā, Yoginī, or Ḍākinī. Although these is no mention of a goddess of exactly this name in the *Sādhanāmālā*, no difficulty arises in locating her. The male Buddhas have as their counterparts Prajñās usually of a different name (Akṣobhya-Locanā;

Amoghasiddhi-Tārā; etc.); but the name of the female counterpart is very often just their own name with the feminine ending: Vajradhātvīśvara-Vajradhātvīśvarī; Heruka-Herambā; Padmanārtteśvara-Padmanārtteśvarī; etc. The Buddha who would provide us the male counterpart for 'Maṇipadmā' is Maṇipadma Lokeśvara, drawn and described by B. Bhattacharya.[91] The image has decidedly feminine traits and might have been thought to represent a goddess by the Tibetans; this is hardly important, for there is no doctrinal objection to styling the female counterpart of any Buddha by using his name in the feminine form.

It is hardly necessary to dilate on the frequency of this *mantra*—books, houses, and rocks bear it throughout Tibetan and Tibeticized lands—and, if I may be pardoned for the romantic diction, it is the *mantra* most deeply inscribed in the Tibetans' hearts.

OṂ PICU PICU PRAJÑĀVARDHANĪ as in *Sādhanāmālā* I/167 (24), is one of the standard Buddhist Hybrid Sanskrit texts; it is directed to Vajrasarasvatī—one of the few deities taken into the Buddhist tantric pantheon from Hindu models without demotion of status. I would hazard a guess that *mantras* of deities taken over from the Hindu pantheon at any time (Gaṇapati, Sarasvatī, Mahākāla) tend to be isomorphemic like this one, and that heteromorphemic *mantras* are more frequent for purely Buddhist divinities. The purpose of this *mantra* is propitiation, and acquisition of intellectual acumen and rhetorical competence. The frequency of its *japa* is not specifically mentioned in the text, but the injunction is that it must be used 'with a glad heart'. Such instruction is very frequent—the necessary moods are prescribed more often than not: one must be fiercely disposed if a fierce *mantra* for a fierce god and with a fierce purpose is 'japped'; etc.

OṂ HŪṂ VAJRĀṄGE MAMA RAKṢA PHAṬ SVĀHĀ

Sādhanāmālā I/123, a *mantra* of Ekajaṭā, a goddess whose importance for Tibet has been stated by Indian Buddhist authors; she is referred to as *bhoteṣu rakṣitā*, 'preserved in Tibet', or also 'rescued from Tibet' (see Chapter 3).

The *mantra* must be pronounced or thought of 'slowly'. Its purpose is identification, which is also evidenced by the fact that it has to be preceded by this text described as 'the *mantra* of the body-speech-mind-basis'—*kāya-vāk-citta-adhiṣṭhāna mantra*. The *japa* of this mantra is 100,000 times.

OṂ ĀḤ PAṂ HŪṂ SVĀHĀ and *OM ĀḤ TAṂ SVĀHĀ*

In the *Advayavajrasamgraha*,[92] these are *mantras* to the Buddhist goddesses Paṇḍāravāsinī and Tārinī respectively. The *bījas PAṂ* and *TAṂ* contain the initial syllables of their names, and this is a frequent pattern among the Buddhist *mantra* compilers for invocation-*mantras* for all deities; the *mūlamantra OṂ ĀḤ HŪṂ* is the matrix, and the *bīja* of any deity—especially of a minor deity that does not have its own set of established *mantras*—is formed by using a syllable of its name, usually the first as in the case of these two *mantras*; this *bīja* is inserted between the *ĀḤ* and the *HŪṂ*.

Mantras of this pattern are very frequent throughout tantric literature, and their purpose is propitiation or acquisition. *Mantras* of identification never use this pattern.

B. *Predominantly Hindu mantras*

The only *mantras* which are exclusively Hindu are, as one would expect, such as refer to a deity not worshipped in any other tradition, as for instance Viṣṇu, Kṛṣṇa, or any other incarnation of Viṣṇu, and such regionally worshipped deities as Subbramanya (the Tamilian version of Skanda or Kārtikkeya, the war-god, son of Śiva and Pārvatī). But this is about all—Śiva in many of his epithets—Rudra, Mahākāla, Śaṃbhu, etc.—is worshipped in Buddhist tantric and partly even in Jaina tantric discipline. *Mantras* of pure identification with abstract referends—i.e. to the principle of Brahman or Śūnyatā—are common to Hindu and Buddhist tradition, though their borrowing from one into the other is not too frequent; the *Kāśīviṣālākṣī Tantra*[93] has a *mantra*

'*OṂ ŚŪNYAJÑĀNA KRĪṂ SVĀHĀ*', and it looks to me like a take-off on the ubiquitous Vajrayāṇa meditation *mantra OṂ ŚŪNYATĀJÑĀNA VAJRASVABHAVĀKO' HAṂ*, 'OṂ, I am identified with the *vajra* wisdom of the void', which we find in important Buddhist tantras—Guhyasamāja, *Sādhanāmālā*. The notion of *śūnya*, though by no means identical in philosophical import with *brahman*, is sufficiently close in its numinosity to it to warrant *mantra* similarity.

AIṂ KLĪṂ ŚRĪṂ KLAUṂ HASAUḤ KULAKUMĀRIKE ḤRDAYĀYA NAMAḤ
AIṂ HAIṂ HRĪṂ ŚRĪṂ KLĪṂ AIṂ SVĀHĀ ŚIRASE SVĀHĀ
AIṂ KLĪṂ SAIṂ ŚIKHĀYAI VAṢAṬ
AIṂ KULAVĀGĪŚVARAVĀGĪŚVARĪ KAVĀCAYA HŪṂ KLĪṂ ASTRĀYA PHAṬ

These are typical Śākta *mantras*—a series beginning with the root—*bīja* of the Śakti of the Hindu pantheon—in this case, the 'Vāgbhavā' or *bīja* of the goddess of speech, Sarasvatī. This arrangement occurs in the *Kaulāvalli Nirṇaya*[94] and is used for the 'worship of the virgin'.[95]

In Kerala, Tamilnad, and in the north, the initial *bīja* is pronounced a bilabial *m*; in Bengal, Mithila, and Bhojpur District, U.P., it is a velar *ṅ*.

The *japa* of installation *mantras* is done aloud, almost like a chant; I have witnessed a Kumārī-Pūjā (formal worship of a Brahmin virgin representing the goddess) at Bhatpara (near Calcutta), where the priests chanted the *mantra* in exactly the same manner, with the identical speed and volume, as the other, non-mantric, invocations. Gopinath Kaviraj of Banaras informed me that there is no objection to this, provided the *mantras* are used for *pratiṣṭhā* (installation) only.

The Vāgbhavā (*AIṂ*) is one of the most frequent *bījas*; the complete *mantra* assortment offered here does not appear in the text.

HRĪṂ KLĪṂ HRĪṂ or *KRĪṂ KRĪṂ KRĪṂ HŪṂ HŪṂ HRĪṂ HRĪṂ DAKṢIṆE*; in the *Karpurādistotra*;[96] the short symmetrical and the ten-syllable asymmetrical *mantras* to Dakṣiṇa-Kālī are interchangeable if they are to serve the same purpose, which is identification with the tutelary deity of the *Karpurādistotra*-Kālī. The first heteromorphemic *mantra* is very frequent in Śākta literature and I have come across it in all Śākta tantras which I surveyed; the alternative, isomorphemic *mantra* is listed in the *Mantramahārṇava*,[97] where it says it is described in the *Karpurādistotra* and in the *Tantric Texts Series* edited by A. Avalon; there may have been a different manuscript available to the compiler of the *Mahārṇava*, as quite a few manuscripts of it seem to be extant in western India.

HRĪṂ ŚRĪṂ KRĪṂ PARAMEŚVARĪ SVĀHĀ

This appears in the *Mahanirvāṇa Tantra*, where it is indirectly given through *sandhā*-instruction (see Chapter 'On Intentional Language'); and in the *Ānandalaharī*, vol. 1, a part of the *Saundaryalaharī* traditionally though incorrectly ascribed to Śaṃkarācārya. The *anunāsika* are definitely pronounced bilabial *-m-* in south India where this *mantra* is very much in vogue up to this day, as it is one of the obligatory *mantras* for the performance of the *Śrī-Vidyā*, the one tantric meditation fully sanctioned and used by orthodox Brahmins of the south; the reason for this connivance seems to be the fact that the most orthodox Brahmin teacher, Śaṃkarācārya, practised and recommended it—even if he is not the author of the *Saundarayalaharī*, a work which Brahmins in the south call a 'poetic disquisition on the *Śrīvidyā*'. Like many *mantras* referring to the goddess, this too is ten-syllabled; care is taken during the *japa* of such *mantras* that no *OṂ* is prefixed, as this would make it an eleven-syllabled *mantra*—the Śākta tradition regards this number as inauspicious; it would also exclude women, as no Dravidian women—not even Brahmins—use the *OṂ*. The *mantra* is listed both in the *Mantramahārṇava* and the *Mantramahodadhi*.

HRĪṂ NAMO BRAHMĀŚRĪ-RAJITE-SAPŪJITE-JAYA-VIJAYE - GAURĪ - GANDHĀRĪ - SARVALOKAVAŚAṂ-KARĪ - SARVASTRĪPURUṢA - VAŚAṂKARĪ - SUŚUDUD-UGHEGHEVĀVĀ - HRĪṂ - SVĀHĀ.

This *mantra* is listed in the *Mantramahodadhi* (70, 2); its referend is Śakti in her function as giving food and nutritive opulence; it is chanted at the temple of Chausaṭṭhī Devī at the Daśāśvamedha Ghāṭ, Banaras, once a year at the *Holi* festival (early in spring). The *Mahodadhi* is replete with long *mantras* (up to 108 and more syllables), which are mostly used for formal worship of different deities installed in shrines. The object of these long *mantras* is never identification; quite a few times it is acquisition, but mostly propitiation.

Many *mantras* show an interesting phenomenon of which this offers a paradigm: the duplication or multiplication of a syllable constituent of a meaningful word; as '*su su du du ghe ghe*'—of the vocative '*sudughe*' ('worthy giver of milk', fem.); the ensuing '*vā vā*' isomorpheme is probably a *bīja*, or else simply the duplication of the expletive '*vā*'. This phenomenon leads one to think that the entire mantric tradition of isomorphemic *bījas* could be an analogue of the process of multiplying constituent syllables of meaningful morphemes contained in the *mantra*. This would accord with my previous suggestion; that isomorphemes are used for emotional emphasis and reinforcement has been accepted in India on a line with the *pulaka* or *romaharṣana*, i.e. horripilation; the Indian word for 'stutter' is '*gadgad*' (both Sanskrit and modern vernacular), and in Hindi it has become an equivalent of 'extremely joyful' (cf. Hindi *we gadgad ho uṭhe*, 'they turned wild with joy'). It is hard to say if the root '*gad-*', 'to speak, sound', is at the basis of the word, or whether it is not some kind of onomatopoeia (cf. English, *cackle*; German, *gackern*).

C. *Predominantly Jaina mantras*

OṂ NAMO BHAGAVATĪ/ TRIBHUVANAVAŚAṂKARĪ SARVĀBHARAṆABHŪṢITE PADMANAYANE/ PADMINĪ

PADMAPRABHE/ PADMAKOŚINĪ/ PADMAVĀSINĪ/ PADMAHASTE/[98] *HRĪṂ HRĪṂ KURU KURU MAMA HṚDAYAKĀRYAṂ KURU KURU MAMA SARVAŚĀNTIṂ KURU KURU, MAMA SVARĀJYĀVAŚYAṂ KURU, SARVALOKAVAŚYAṂ KURU, MAMA SARVASTRĪVAŚYAṂ KURU KURU, MAMA SARVABHŪTAPIŚĀCAPRETAROṢAṂ HARA HARA, SARVAROGĀN CHINDA CHINDA, SARVAVIGHNĀN BHINDA BHINDA, SARVAVIṢAṂ CHINDA CHINDA, SARVAKURUMṚGAM CHINDA CHINDA, SARVAŚĀKINĪŚ CHINDA CHINDA, ŚRĪPĀRŚVAJANAPADĀMBHOJABHRNGĪ NAMO DATTĀYA DEVĪ NAMAḤ/ OṂ HRAṂ HRĪṂ HRŪṂ HRAUṂ HRĀḤ SVĀHĀ/ SARVAJANARĀJYASTRĪPURUṢAVAŚYAṂ SARVE SARVE ĀṂ DROṂ HRĪṂ AIṂ KLĪṂ HRĪṂ DEVI/ PARMĀVATĪ/ TRIPURAKĀMASĀDHINĪ DURJANAMATIVINĀŚINĪ TRAILOKYAṢKOBHINĪ ŚRĪPĀRŚVANĀTHOPASARGOHĀRIṆĪ KLĪṂ BLŪṂ MAMA DUṢṬĀN HANA HANA, MAMA SARVAKĀRYĀNI SĀDHAYA SĀDHAYA SĀDHAYA HŪṂ PHAṬ SVĀHĀ'.*[99]

This single *mantra* of 288 syllables occurs in the Jaina *Padmāvatīkalpa.*[100] I have never heard it pronounced, nor could I obtain any information about its pronunciation. It is, however, used by monks of the Śvetāmbara sect in the Gujarat. Its purpose is both propitiation and acquisition. With the exception of *BLŪṂ*, all *bījas* are common to Buddhist and Hindu tantra.

OM HRĀṂ HRĪṂ HRŪṂ HREM HRAIṂ HROṂ HRAUṂ HRAḤ DĀTARASYA MAMA ŚĀNTIṂ KURU KURU PADMĀVATYAY NAMAḤ SVĀHĀ.

This *mantra* occurs in the same chapter of the Jaina tantra, and has to be 'japped' either 108 or 12,000 times, though the respective merit of the different quantity is not mentioned in the text; in such cases it is perhaps understood that the greater quantity of *japa* confers greater merit in the same direction; this *mantra* is for acquisition of *śānti*, mental peace and the state of readiness for higher meditations towards identification; hence, 108 *japa-s* would give some amount of it, 12,000 *japa-s* a correspondingly greater amount, if there is any method in *mantras*. . . .

The arrangement of *bījas* according to the Sanskrit alphabet (a-i-u-e-) is frequent in all the three *mantra* traditions; this point, however, needs no more elaboration, as good work has been done on it by Woodroff;[101] more recently, Lama Govinda dealt with it, confining himself to Buddhist tantra.[102]

viii. Suggestions for diagrammatic listing of mantras

Bījakośas or *mantra*-lists in all the three traditions offer some sort of diagrammatic listing, displaying the purpose and the deity or some other facets of the *mantras* used. K. G. Diehl[103] prepared an excellent chart on the basis of a Tamil *mantra* manual which is in constant use by temple priests in southern Tamilnad.[104]

A complete diagram covering all mantras with all their functions, their occurrence in literature, their *japa*, etc., is theoretically possible, but its construction is hardly practical, not even for a limited number of *mantras*. Such a diagram would look like this:

mantra	text-occurrence	pronunciation	purpose	japa	deity, etc.
OṂ etc.	Ṛgveda . . . . . . to BHS etc.	*m* in western India, *au* in central India, ṇ in Bengal, etc.	propitiation, acquisition, identification, etc.	108, 1,000,008, etc.	impersonal

Such a diagram might serve as an encyclopaedia, but we would have to work out different types for critical purposes. The only feasible method seems to be the construction of several diagrams to be inspected successively, with only one indicator category at a time in the horizontal, and one other category in the vertical direction, with the *mantras* listed in a co-ordinative fashion:

(1)

Mudra: ('gesture')	*Deity:* Śakti	Śiva	Viṣṇu	Ganapati	Sarasvatī	Mahākāla	Vairocana
abhaya	HRĪṂ	HĀḤ	HŪṂ	GAṂ	AIṂ	HUṂ	HŪṂ
varadāna	O	O	O	GAṂ	KRĪṂ	O	O
jaladharā	O	O	O	O	TRĀṂ	O	O
yonī	KLĪṂ	OṂ	O	O	AIṂ	PHAṬ	OṂ ĀH HUṂ
kākinī							
aśvinī							
dhyāna							

Etc., etc., etc.

(2)

Text:	*Mudrā:* *abhaya*	*varadāna*	*jaladharā*	*yonī*	*kākinī*	*aśvinī*	*dhyāna* etc.
Mahānirvāṇa		RAṂ	VAṂ	YAṂ	KLĪṂ	O	OṂ
Tantrarāja		O	O	O	O	O	HRĪṂ
Kaulāvalli		OṂ	AIṂ	O	KLĪṂ	O	KRĪṂ
Karpurādi							
Guhyasamāja							
Sādhanāmālā							
Mañjuśrīmūlakalpa							

Etc., etc., etc.

(3)

Deity:	*Text:* *Mahānirvāṇa*	*Tantrarāja*	*Kaulāvalli-nirṇaya*	*Karpurādi*	*Guhyasamāja*	*Sādharāmālā*	*Mañjuśrī-mūlakalpa, etc.*
Śakti	HRĪṂ	HRĪṂ	HRĪṂ	HRĪṂ	HŪṂ	AIṂ	OṂ
Śiva				KRĪṂ			
Viṣṇu							
Gaṇapati, etc.							

Etc., etc., etc.

In this manner, a number of graphs with one item-type in each co-ordinate direction would be collated, and the aspects of each *mantra* relevant to any particular enquiry could be checked by collating the respective graphs. The categories would be co-ordinated on this model:

deity and *mudrā*, deity and text, deity and purpose, deity and *nyāsa* ('touch')
mudrā and text, *mudrā* and purpose, . . .
text and purpose, text and *nyāsa*, . . .
purpose and text, purpose and *nyāsa*, etc. . . .

ix. An exposé of a manual of mantras, *Mantramuktāvali 'Necklace of* Mantras'[105]

This is a small contemporary work, written in all probability by Vajraratna Bhattacharya of Muradabad in North India: In his short Hindi preface, the pandit says that need has been fẹlt by persons desirous of religious observance (*anuṣthāna*) for a *mantra*-manual, which would save them the trouble of finding the texts containing *mantras*, which are legion; hence, for the convenience of such people he has here compiled a commentary (to the) *Mantramuktāvali*, where the most important *mantras* are collated. However, he does not make it clear whether he wrote the actual text, or only the commentary which is in Hindi—the signature says 'Vajraratna Bhattacharya, editor and translator'—which may mean either translator from an *apauruṣeya* text[106] or translator from his own Sanskrit original. I believe the pandit himself is the author of the Sanskrit text.

The invocation *Śrī Rāmānujāya namaḥ* indicates that the author is a Vaiṣṇava[107] and a follower of the qualified monistic system of Rāmānuja; this explains the slant in favour of *mantras* of the Vishnuite tradition, but in due fairness it must be admitted that he has included Śivite, Śākta, and even some Buddhist *mantras*.

The first seventeen sections, all of them extremely short, deal with preliminaries and comprise all topics relevant to the use of *mantras* as has become customary throughout India by now. The various *mantra*-traditions (Buddhist, Hindu, Jain) have contributed their shares, in unequal degrees, to the present state of *mantra* usage, so that this little work seems to me representative by way of an all-over *mantra* synopsis.

The first section is captioned 'determination of weekdays' (*vāranirnayaḥ*). It says that *mantra* usage on Sundays creates a barbarian mind (probably a facetious allusion to an occidental custom), on Monday it yields success in all activities, on Tuesday it gives wealth, on Wednesday it causes distress, on Thursday it gives peace, on Friday it gives the power of subjugation (*vaśīkaraṇa*), on Saturday it diminishes intelligence (another swipe at the West?).

The second section 'Reflection on the day of the month' (*tithivicāra*) tells us that the use of *manṭra* on the first day of the lunation is futile and does not yield any result whatever, the second day gives wealth, the third day gives success in all efforts, the fourth day gives the power of subjugation, the fifth gives both wealth and knowledge, the sixth gives poverty, the seventh gives the power of 'blowing up' (*uccāṭana*), the tenth makes poor like the sixth, the eleventh again gives wisdom and success in all works undertaken, the twelfth gives the power of killing (i.e. through magic, *māraṇa*), the thirteenth causes son and wife to be destroyed, the fourteenth gives wealth once more, the new moon day causes quarrel, the full moon day yields universal success.

The third section deals with the 'success or failure entailed by the various months' (*māsaphalam*), commencing with the first month of the Indian year *caitra* (March–April) which causes the eyes to become weak. . . .[108]

The fourth section deals with the respective merit of the cosmic ages *yugavicāra*—but, true to all tantric tradition, each day represents the four *yuga-s* in its four parts; thus, *mantra* initiation given in the first age (*kṛta yuga*) gives the possession of Mahālakṣmī (vision of the goddess and wealth of which she is the presiding deity and, consequently, wealth).

The fifth section deals with the periods to be allocated to the various *mantra*-initiations; thus, in the *kṛta-yuga* one hour should be given to the practice of the *mantra*, etc. . . .

The sixth section *varṇa-vicāra* establishes the colour of the *mantra* to be given to the individual castes.[109] Thus, Brahmins ought to be given a red *mantra*, a black one to *kṣatriyas*, etc. It also states that if a wrong colour be assigned to a member of a caste, it will have dire consequences, e.g. if a Brahmin is given a *kṣatriya*'s *mantra*, he will contract leprosy, etc.

The seventh section is on the right choice of the month for initiation into *mantras* for the various castes, '*dīkṣāprayoga*'; thus, a Brahmin should be initiated in spring, a warrior in summer, etc.

The eighth section is titled *mantranirṇaya*, 'determination of *mantras*', but it deals specifically with the choice of the right lunation in the different seasons.

The ninth section, *āsanaprayoga*, is about the sitting postures (*āsanas*) required for the practice of *mantras*. If the seat is made of bamboo there is the risk of becoming poor, if it is made of stone there is a chance of falling ill (evidently due to a cold?).

Some inauspicious or harmful materials for the seat and their respective dangers are then enumerated. For beneficent seats, the skin of the black deer is praised as bestowing wisdom, and the tiger-skin for a seat is conducive to *mokṣa* (complete emancipation). If the seat be made of cloth, disease will be avoided, and the cloth should be rinsed with cow urine diluted with water and some chemicals prepared of specific herbs. A seat made of a blanket is pure and gives success in the mantric effort. For the worship of *devatās* (minor deities) through *mantra*, a white blanket should be used, for *abhicāra* (malevolent rites) a blue cloth is excellent—and multicoloured blankets can be used for all purposes.

The tenth section is called 'specifications of the directions' (*diśaviśeṣāḥ*). Thus, by sitting down facing the east enemies, etc., are subjugated. . . .

The eleventh section deals with the use of rosaries (*mālāprayoga*); thus, the use of *rudrākṣa*, red beads made of the dried berries of *Elaeocarpus Ganitrus*, conch, lotus, *kuśa* grass, etc., yields salvation, etc. . . .

The twelfth section instructs on the use of fingers *aṅguliprayoga*, not for *mudrās*, but of the individual fingers for counting *mantras* or telling beads; thus, if the thumb is used for commencing the *japam* or bead-telling, this will give *mokṣa* (salvation), etc. . . .

The thirteenth section is called *mālājapasaṃkhya*, i.e. on the number of *mantras* to be uttered or mentally repeated ('japped') by aid of the rosary. Thus, if the rosary be drawn over the thumb, the merit gained is the basic measure; if the rosary be drawn over the heart, it is five times greater; . . . if the rosary be made of *rudrākṣa* (*Elaeocarpus Ganitrus* beads) the merit is 100,000 times greater; if of gold, 10,000,000 times, etc. Finally, the use of a rosary made of Tulsī-leaves is 'limitless' (*tulsī-saṃkhya-amānāsti*), which statement once again displays a mild Vishnuite slant of the work—*tulsī* being the plant sacred to Viṣṇu, especially in his incarnation as Rāmacandra.

The fourteenth section is simply called *sādhanam*, 'the exercise', but it refers only to the way in which the rosary is to be used. It says that if liberation is to be achieved, the rosary should have twenty-five beads, and if all desires are to be fulfilled, it should have 108 beads.[110] It also warns the aspirant not to use the index finger, i.e. the index must not come into contact with the rosary at any point or else the entire process is futile and dangerous, and entails disease and poverty.

Sections 15–17 indicate auspicious dates, the allocation of initial letters of personal names to the various constellations and other astrological hints.

The listing of *mantras* begins in the eighteenth section, and here again the Vaiṣṇavite proclivity is palpable in that the author commences with the '*Tulasī-instruction-mantra*', referring to the Hindi *Rāmāyaṇa* of Tulsīdās—these are purely sectarian and regional *mantras* and have hardly any importance outside the Avadhī Vaiṣṇava fold. The *mantra* is actually a short prayer in Hindi *dohās* (quatrains) and the author comments that this *mantra* has to be given to each and every one who wants to use *mantras* of any kind. It is a meaningful, charismatic, metric invocation; e.g.: *OṂ āp nirañjan śaṅkar śeś, tahā diyo tulasī upadeś, nar nārāyaṇ lage kām, rām nām tulasī praṇām.* '*OṂ* thou art the whole Śaṃkara (Śiva), the stainless one, this is Tulsīdās's instruction. (The Deity as) Man and Nārāyaṇa (cosmic Man) are here (referred to). Tulsīdās prostrates to the name of Rāma.' It goes without saying that *mantra*-compilers with different sectarian and linguistic backgrounds would not pay heed to this author's claim about the importance of his incipient instruction.

The nineteenth section seems to be the most important one; it is captioned *sarva-deva-mantra*, '*mantra* of all gods'. Each *mantra* is followed by astrological data, i.e. the constellation during which the respective *mantra* will yield the desired result. The *mantras* listed in the section are:

OṂ hrīṃ hrīṃ Rāmāya namaḥ (Rāma-mantra)
OṂ Jānakī tṝm tāraka Rāmāya namaḥ (Rāma-Sītā-mantra)
OṂ kliṃ yaṃ Kṛṣṇaya namaḥ (Kṛṣṇa-mantra)
Gopījanavallabhāya vṝṃ svāhā (Kṛṣṇa-mantra)
OṂ Jānakī nṝṃ Rāmāya namaḥ (Sītā-Rāma-mantra)
OṂ klīṃ yaṃ dadhibhakṣaṇāya namaḥ svāhā (Bāladāmodaramantra)
OṂ klīṃ yaṃ rathāṅgavṛghacakrāya namaḥ (Cakrapāṇi mantra)
OṂ nṝṃ nṝṃ narasimhāya namaḥ (Narasiṃha-mantra); etc.

Altogether there are thirty-five *mantras*, all of which have an aspect of Viṣṇu as their target-reference. Quite a few of them are not unique to the Vaiṣṇava tradition, but are used in various other settings. In fact, their usurpation for such sectarian use and their description in this work, as Vaiṣṇava *mantras*, must be somewhat annoying to other tantrics. The diffusely used *mantra OṂ klīṃ vṝṃ brahmaṇe namah* is styled '*Mukunda-mantra*', *Mukunda* being an epithet of Kṛṣṇa; the *mantra* is equally applicable in the Śākta tradition and in any non-sectarian Hindu setting; among its constituents, only '*vṝṃ*' is a predominantly Vaiṣṇavite *bīja*; *klīṃ*, the *kāma-bīja*, has been listed above, in various settings, Hindu and Buddhist alike. No. 30 quotes '*OṂ klīṃ bhṝṃ brahmaṇe namah*' as another *Mukunda-mantra*, a crasser case still, '*bhṝṃ*' being a *bīja* of Brahmā and of Varuṇa, but not of Viṣṇu or his *avatāras*.

It is evident that the caption '*sarva-devā-mantra*', i.e. *mantras* pertaining to all gods, is intended to mean 'all gods of Vaiṣṇava interest'.

The twentieth section is styled *digbandhanam*, literally, 'binding the directions'. This is the term for a preliminary meditation obligatory for initiated monks of the *Paramahaṃsa* class, which becomes clear from the concluding line *iti paramahaṃsa-catvāri-maṭha-dīkṣā*, 'the initiation of *paramahaṃsa* monks of the four head monasteries' (Śrīngerī, Puri, Dvāraka, Badarīkāśrama), its object is to warrant spiritual safety during the time of *mantra*-practice, from supernatural beings inhabiting the four directions, including the *dikpālas* or guardian deities presiding over the directions. The *mantras* listed here are partly Vedic, '*Indrāya namaḥ*', '*agnaye namaḥ*', '*nairṛtyāya namaḥ*', '*Varuṇāya namaḥ*', etc. (i.e. 'obeisance to the guardians of the directions'—though here too Viṣṇu is brought in surreptitiously—'*Viṣṇave namaḥ*'—in spite of the fact that looking after any particular direction is none of his commitments).

The section proceeds to tell us that the use of *mantra* is futile if the accompanying *mudrā* (gesture) is not known.

Then follows the *Gāyatrī mantra*, which is the most sacred *mantra* in the Brahmin tradition, and the best known.

After this, the *mantras* particular to the monistic meditation of the *paramahaṃsa* monks are listed together with some *mantras* of kindred provenance, mostly Vedic in style; the author does not give any reference to the text from which he derives the *mantras*, but this can hardly be expected and has never been customary in synopses of this type. These are the *mantras*:

OṂ nīlagarbho haṃsaḥ—sohaṃ paramahaṃsaḥ—tattvamasi ahaṃ brahmāsmi. The latter two are the *mahāvākyam-s* or 'great dicta' of the Upaniṣads, declaring the identity of the individual with the world-soul, they are the basic meditation formulae of the monks ordained under the auspices of the northern monastic diocese, Badarīkāśram near Śrīnagar, Kashmir.

OṂ mahādevāya viṣṇomatano rudrastano mahītano[111] *rudra pracodayāt* (*The Śiva-Gāyatrī mantra*).

'*OṂ bhūh brahma klīṃ sohaṃ ātmatattvamasi ahaṃ brahmāsmi*

soham—paramatattvamasi aham brahmāsmi': these two are again the Upaniṣadi c*mahāvākyam-s*, as enjoined for the southern monastic diocese, the Śāradapīṭha at Śriṅgeri-Mysore.

Soham hamsa[112] *tattvamasi*, which is a modification of the *mahāvākyam*, used both in the western head monastery, the Dvārakapīṭha in the Gujarat, and the eastern head monastery, the Govardhanapīṭha at Puri-Orissa.

The twenty-first section, '*Śaṃkarapaddhati*', i.e. the 'method of Śaṃkara', shows *mantras* of the Śivite and Śākta traditions, but also, strangely enough, a Buddhist *mantra*. Usually, Buddhism is felt to be closer to Vaiṣṇavism in present-day India than it is to Śaivism, the Buddha being the ninth *avatāra* of Viṣṇu in the Puranic tradition which led up to modern Hinduism.

The *mantras* in this section are *OṂ soham hamsa* again, 'I am he—he is I'; next, '*nānyadbrahma tvampadamāyā asipadajīvoham brahma*', 'nothing else is Brahman, the word "thou" is *māyā*, so is the word "art", I am the *jīva* which is Brahman'. This *mantra* is then named the *mantra* for the *nirālambadīkṣā*, 'the initiation into the substratumless way', which the author calls the fifth state. This is rather cryptic; the author probably did not understand the origin of the '*nirālambana*', for he passes over it in his Hindi commentary. I would think that '*nirālambana*' refers either directly to the Mahāyāna concept of the propless state of mind which somehow slipped into a Hindu *mantra* manual—the fact that the ensuing *mantra* is avowedly Buddhist would seem to support this view—or else to the Gorakṣa tradition which is close both to Śaivism and to tantric Buddhism, and to which, moreover, this manual dedicates a short section. The 'fifth state' in this light would be less mysterious—'*turīya*' or the 'fourth state' being a synonym for *samādhi* or supreme mystical cognition leading to *nirvāṇa*; or, what amounts to the same thing, the 'fifth state' is one even superior to that of *sannyāsa*, which is the fourth *āśrama* (state of life) and the consummation of the Hindus' life, that of homeless mendicancy.

The next is our Buddhist mantra, *bhrakaṭā-bhrakaṭā-suta-mokṣapadam pratipie tabhubhyathatham prava citsavedinam mama mokṣam tatvabandhanāgniham*, and the verse adds, 'this is the

Buddhist initiation'. The *mantra* is interesting on all counts; it is partially meaningful like most of the non-*bīja* or mixed *mantras* listed in the Buddhist *Sādhanāmālā* and the *Guhyasamāja*. The meaningful words in the *mantra* are '*mokṣapadam*', 'the word *mokṣa*'; '*cit*' (mind-cognition); '*vedi*' 'altar', 'sacrificial layer', although garbled into a form '*vedinam*' as a spurious accusative, and an equally garbled form of '*agni*', 'fire'. '*Bhrakaṭa*' seems to be a Hinduized corruption of the name '*Bhṛkutī*', an important tantric Buddhist goddess (*yoginī*) or of one of her *mantras* spelt '*bhṛkatā*' in the *Mañjuśrīmūlakalpa*.

The remaining *mantras* of this section are perfectly clear in their allocations: *ādi-anta-sakalaṃ hrīṃ hraṃ sakalaṃ hāhaṃ sakalahi*—*Vidyā mantra*;[113] *Oṃ Oṃ hrīṃ glīṃ glauṃ gaṃ gāṃ*—*mantra* of the God Gaṇesa; *Oṃ hrīṃ klauṃ namaḥ sohaṃ*—*mantra* of Bhuvaneśvarī;[114] *Oṃ ram rāṃ rāṃ oṃ rum rūṃ ruṃ*—this is a *bīja-mantra*;[115] *Oṃ aiṃ auṃ oṃ gaṃ go gaṇapataye namaḥ*—another Gaṇeśa *mantra*; *Oṃ yaṃ yāṃ śaṃkah priya viduḥ saṃ haṃ hrīṃ vāgīsvarī dhīmahi tanno śaktih pracodayāt*—*mantra* of Sarasvatī;[116] *Oṃ bhūrbhuvaḥ sohaṃ*—*mantra* of Sadyojāta (Viṣṇu); and finally, *Oṃ bhṛṃ bhṛṃ bhṛṃ bhṛṃ bhasmāṅgī sarvāṅge vāgīśvarīmāstuti phaṭ svāhā*—*mantra* of Vibhūti (Sarasvatī).[117]

The twenty-second section is very short; it is the '*Vāgvādinī-mantra*', i.e. the *mantra* of the goddess of speech, Gāyatrī-Sarasvatī. It starts out with *oṃ*; then the verse explains that the *Ṛṣi* of this *mantra* is the demiurge Brahmā himself, to be meditated on in the head; the metre is Gāyatrī,[118] the *mantra* being (*oṃ*) *prīṃ hrīṃ vāgvādinī svāhā*.

The twenty-third section, quite short too, deals with the initiation and the *mantra* of the Gorakṣa-tradition. The initiation-*mantra* is *oṃ dvanthe hāth kaṇṭhari gare ruṇḍamālā hathe patr mukhe śrīgorakhabāla*; so far as the constituents are meaningful, they are not Sanskrit, nor even Hybrid, but simply some sort of mediaeval Nepali in which most of the sayings ascribed to Matsyendranāth and Gorakṣanāth have been handed down. The section concludes with a symmetrical six-syllabled *bīja* of Gorakṣa or Śiva, the tutelary deity of the Gorakṣa cult: *raṃ raṃ raṃ khaṃ khaṃ khaṃ*.

The twenty-fourth section is called 'the method of Sanatkumāra.'[119] The *mantras* listed here serve various purposes, meditative as well as ritualistic. This is a customary procedure: whenever there is a cumulative list of miscellaneous items, the text is captioned 'the method of X', X denoting some famous seer, or teacher.

The *mantras* listed are *oṃ hriṃ hrīṃ kṣoṃ phaṭ svāhā—Aghoramantra*; '*oṃ raṃ kṣaṃ raṃ kṣaṃ raṃ kṣaṃ raṃ chaṃ raṃ oṃ*'—the ten-lettered *Aghoramantra.*[120] This is a symmetrical *mantra* in spite of the apparent difference of the third and the ninth *bīja*, as *kṣ* and *c* are used interchangeably in vernacular *mantric* usage; no Hindi dialect distinguishes radically between '*kṣ*' and '*ch*', e.g. 'Lakṣman' and 'Lachman'.

Oṃ bhūrbhuvaḥ svaḥ klīṃ klīṃ śrīṃ śrīṃ śrīṃ phaṭ svāhā āsana upaviśya kṛṣṇāya namaḥ—Āsana-mantra.[121]

Tarhitachepamarhi—the *mantra* uttered when receiving alms (for medicants).

'*Oṃ yajñopavītaṃ vīryapavitram oṃ brahmāmantraprabhāvina*', '*oṃ bhūbrahmavīrya saṃbhumam—oṃ śivasandhyaśatani ca—ye mastake rakṣaṇe śikhābandhanaṃ karomyaham*'—the *mantra* for discarding the sacred cord.[122]

'*Oṃ brahmānāmasahasrāni viṣṇunāmaśatāni ca*'—the *mantra* for binding the hair tuft.[123] '*Oṃ brahmāśikhā brahmāputrī mataṅgī tapasvinī nejavantīyate mastake*'—the *mantra* for the *homa*-ceremony in connection with the sacred thread investiture;[124] '*oṃ rudravatī mātāśikhāchedaṃ karomyaham*'—the *mantra* used when parting the hair tuft.[125]

'*Oṃ graṃ grāṃ graṃ śānti oṃ klīṃ vraṃ vrāṃ vraṃ śrīmahāpuruṣasvāmine namaḥ*'—'*svāmidayāya namaḥ svāhā*'—the *mantra* uttered on assuming the '*kimvyādha—āsana*'.[126]

The twenty-fifth section is called 'Śivapatrikā' ('Document of Śiva').[127] This and the last (twenty-sixth) section belong to a class of instructions about the times of the day and the month to be chosen for auspicious actions and also such undertakings as the use of *mantra*, spells, invocations, and ceremonies of all kinds.

These last two sections explain which times are propitious for the practice of *mantra*, and they give a formidable list of dangers and risks involved if the '*ghaṭikā*' is not painstakingly adhered to.

It now remains to summarize this long and cumbersome chapter: in order to come to grips with the highly diversified yet unsystematic indigenous use of the term *mantra*, we had to borrow terminological devices from external disciplines. The reason for this is analogous to what was said earlier in the book about the necessity of employing terminology used by contemporary, analytical philosophy in Britain and America. Although, strictly speaking, no definition of a complex cultural and regional term as '*mantra*' is possible, we can attempt a description as close to a definition as cultural anthropology would permit.

The philological origin, historical provenance, the psychological importance, the liturgical function, and finally the sacerdotal specialization which constructed, transmitted, and preserved the use of *mantra* from an unknown age right into the present day, necessitate an elaborate and probably highly discursive treatment of this pervasive theme.

No doubt, *mantra* is a syndrome which the tantric tradition shares with non-tantric traditions in India and adjacent regions; there is hardly any theme studied in this book which would not also be found in orthodox, non-tantric traditions. However, it is very much a matter of relative emphasis; *mantra*, mystical diagrams (*maṇḍala*), pilgrimage and circumambulation, and initiation—all these are also parts of the non-tantric traditions. However, whereas they are marginal in those traditions, *mantra*, etc., are focal in tantrism, so much so that Indian terminology often identifies them with tantric lore. This explains why many learned Hindus refer to tantrism as '*mantra-śāstra*'.

In all the processes of tantric initiation, *mantra* is the nuclear element, the basic unit. It is in a way the atomic constituent of initiation as well as of the further practices and the consummation of tantric discipline. If we wanted to use, facetiously that is, the terminology of modern linguistics and of other sciences which believe in reduction to the smallest possible elements, the artifical language of the '-emes' (as phoneme, morpheme, lexeme, sememe, etc.) might provide a model: the *mantra* would be the 'tantreme'. To any scholar other than the diehard modern linguist and his followers such a neologism sounds pompous or funny, but it does bring home the great importance which *mantra* has in the tantric tradition.

In all Indian initiations, *mantra* or a pre-*mantric* substitute play an important part. In the initiation ceremonies of the tribal Bhils described by the late Father Koppers (*Die Bhils von Zentralindien*, Horn (Austria), 1948) the Santhals, and the Mundas in north-eastern India sacred formulae, partly intelligible, partly dyssemantic, are amply employed; even such fundamentally antagonistic traditions as Islam, once they enter and get established on Indian territory, seem to be susceptible to the *mantra*-pattern—the Muslim divine's *mantra* at the shrine of Baba Qalandar Shah in the State of Mysore is a garbled Arabic-cum-Indian set of quasi-morphemes. It is of course not possible to say with certainty that the idea of the *mantra* is a pre-Aryan one—and that the identification of the Vedic hymn with the *mantra* was a latter interpretation of *mantra* within the Aryan tradition.

Whatever the *mantra* terminology might have led up to, there is no doubt in our minds that a magical or sacred formula of some sort must have been one of the oldest and certainly most permanent elements of autochthonous Indian supernaturalism.

NOTES

[1] For an excellent treatment of these kindred topics, see L. A. Waddell, 'The Dhāraṇī Cult in Buddhism—its origin, deified literature and art', in *Acta Orientalia*, Leiden 1912, Vol. I; also F. W. Hauer, *Die Dharani im Noerdlichen Buddhismus*, Stuttgart 1927.

[2] For an intelligent, sympathetic survey of logical positivism and its relation to analytic philosophy, see M. J. Charlesworth, *Philosophy and Linguistic*

Analysis, Duquesne Studies, Philosophical Series, No. 9, Duquesne University Press, Pittsburgh 1961.

[3] The brackets in the quotation are Monier-Williams'.

[4] I am indebted to Professor Fang-kuei Li for the term 'partial duplication', a very frequent phenomenon in vernacular Indian languages; here only '*mantra-yantra*' are both meaningful, but the actual meaning of '*yantra*' in such duplicative usage is hardly conscious.

[5] A Hindu reform movement in vogue in the Punjab, founded last century by Swāmī Dayānanda Sarasvatī, whose doctrinary object it was to bar all scriptures outside the *saṃhitā* portion from canonical status, a sort of 'back to the Veda' movement.

[6] i.e. 'an heretic is one who denies the authority of the Veda'.

[7] i.e. 'an heretic is one who denies the authority of *mantra*', viz. Vedic or *saṃhitā* text.

[8] Perhaps best, 'the basket (-collection) of magical knowledge'.

[9] *Khuddakapāṭha: Aṅguttara Nikāya* IV, 67, *Atantīya Sutta, Dīgha-Nikaya* 32 passim.

[10] *Majjhima Nikāya*, 66.

[11] '*etena saccena suvatthi hotu*', *Ratana Sutta.*

[12] The Bengali pronunciation of '*mantra*' is almost '*montor*', '*tor*' being the second-person intimate possessive pronoun.

[13] '*sarvasattvarutaiḥ sarvasattvānāṃ modanan-manasas-trāṇa-bhutvācca mantro . . .*' *Sekoddesaṭika* by Naropa, G.O.S. XC, p. 6.

[14] B. Russell, Theory of Description, Theory of Types. P. F. Strawson, *Introduction to Logical Theory*; S. L. Stebbing, *Modern Logic.*

[15] V. S. Agrawala, *India as Known to Pāṇiṇī*, Lucknow 1953, p. 318.

[16] Heinrich Zimmer, *Ewiges Indien*, p. 81 f.

[17] Lama Govinda, *Foundations of Tibetan Mysticism*, Rider & Co., London 1961, p. 90.

[18] Bose and Haldar, *Tantras: Their Philosophy*, pp. 132, 223.

[19] B. Bhattacharya, *Buddhist Esoterism*, p. 55 f. This book was written in 1932, and Bhattacharya was not acquainted with F. Edgarton's research.

[20] R. C. Majumdar, *The Age of Imperial Kanauj*, p. 259 ff.

[21] N. N. Dasgupta, Buddhism: 'Doctrinal Changes in Vajrayāṇa and Kālachakrayāna', in *The Struggle for Empire*, p. 400 ff. Both the last two authors' articles from which the quotations are drawn are part of the Bharatiya Vidya Bhavan current publication *The History and Culture of the Indian People* scheduled for ten volumes, six volumes being in print by now. The first volume was published in 1951. It is interesting to note that all of the numerous contributors to this important publication series are overtly or covertly antagonistic to *tantra* and, *a fortiori*, antagonistic to *mantra*; they represent the contemporary Hindu renaissance on the academical side.

[22] M. Eliade. *Yoga: Immortalité et Liberté*, p. 217.

[23] H. V. Glasenapp, *Buddhistische Mysterien*, p. 18.

[24] A. Avalon, *Introduction to Tantra Shastra*, p. 81 ff.

[25] i.e. the Supreme Being of the Hindus, viewed as Logos pervades the human body in the form of *mantra*, potentially as it were.

[26] i.e. the individual manifestation for Śakti, not in the sense of a Bergsonian *élan vital*.

[27] i.e. the dormant Śakti or yogic power imagined to lie coiled up at the base of the spine, in the yogic body accepted by all esoteric traditions in India.

[28] Existence—consciousness—bliss: the classical 'definition' of the neutral Brahman in the Vedānta tradition.

[29] Avalon writes 'designed', but this is a misreading for 'desired'; the *Viśvasāra* says *icchita*, not *lakṣita*.

[30] This is incorrect; *mantras* are not always chanted, nor even murmured; in fact, most Hindu and all Buddhist tantric texts consign superior merit to *mantra* when it is meditated upon in silence, i.e. without lip movement.

[31] If Avalon is still taking the *Viśvasāra-tantra* as the basis for the last statement (it does not become clear whether he does nor not), then this is an interesting parallel to identical folk-etymology quoted above, from the Buddhist *Sekoddeśaṭika*: the *Viśvasāra* is about a hundred years more recent in origin than Nādapāda, hence there might be some influence palpable from the Buddhist folk etymology; unless indeed the *Viśvasāra*, or whatever other Hindu tantric text Avalon bases this etymology on, have hit upon the same etymology by accident, which is just as thinkable. The grammatical background of the authors of such texts would certainly prompt them towards this tempting pseudo-etymology.

[32] From a communication by Guenther (October 5, 1958) in reply to my request for his description of *mantra*. Additional correspondence with Dr. Guenther and some other specialists working in India has yielded interesting results on the purely Buddhist side which I would like to adumbrate here: the folk-etymology of Naropa in his *Sekoddeśaṭikā* seems to rest on a passage in the *Guhyasamājatantra*, which is one of the oldest Buddhist tantric texts and shows some amount of system; the *Mañjuśrīmūlakalpa* may be older yet, but it is no place to find descriptions of the meaning of *mantra*. The passage in the *Guhyasamāja* is *pratītyotpadyate yad yad indriyaviṣayair manaḥ, tan mano mananam kyhātam kārakatrāṇanārthataḥ, lokācāravinirmuktaṃ yad uktaṃ samayasaṃvaram, pālanām sarvava jraistu mantracaryeti kathyate* (ch. 18, p. 156, G.O.S. LIII). A sophisticated rendering which inculcates contemporary philosophical terminology would be something like 'that which comes about in relation to sense organs and sense objects is the mental make-up, this mental make-up is mentation and it is protective in function. The discipline of commitment (to the ultimate) called the liberation from worldliness, which is (protection) by its total indestructibility

is called *mantracaryā* (mantric discipline).' This verse is quoted in a Tibetan text *dPal Dus.kyi 'khor. lo'i 'grel.chen dri.ma med.pa'i 'od.kyi rgya.cher bśad.pa de.koh.na.-ñid snañ.bar byed.pa,* fol. 5b. in substantiation of the following statement: *mantra.la ma.na ni yid/ traya ni skyob,pa ste/ des.na yid skyob.pas sṅags zes bya'o,* '*Mantra* (*sṅags*) can be viewed from various angles: it is, at first, ordinary articulate speech which due to its participation in the subtle (*phra ba*) can provide an index to the latter. This aspect is summarized in the term *vajrajāpa* (*rdo rje'i bzlas.pa*) referring to four different aspects . . .' These, I believe, are exact equivalents of the Hindu division of 'sound' in the extensive *sphoṭa*-literature, i.e. the four types called *parā-paśyantī-madhyamā-vaikharī,* beginning with the unmanifested, subtle sound and ending in articulate speech. The description of *mantra* as '*vajrajāpa*' in Buddhist tantrism follows the reverse order, i.e. it begins with *brjod.pa*—'articulater speech'; the second is symbolism relating *mantra* to the five Tathāgata divisions and is called *dmigs.pa*: the third is pure form and is divided into the three indicator-*bijas OṂ ĀḤ HŪṂ,* its referend being the experience of pure sensation as the realization of man's latent potentialities, which is called *brdar.gyur*; and finally there is Buddhahood, here called *don dam.* All sounds and letters can be subsumed under the *ali-kali* scheme, i.e. the vowel series beginning with *a* and the consonant series beginning with *ka*; the '*ali-kali*' scheme is then said to be subservient to *OṂ ĀḤ HŪṂ.* It appears that the relevant Tibetan mantric texts take this hierarchical arrangement to be the foundation of all *mantras.* The *mantra* complex is summarized in a passage from *Jo bo Na ro. pa'i kyhạd. chos bsre. 'pho'i gžuñ. 'grel rdo rje. chan gi dgons pa gsal bar byed pa fol. loa,* which Prof. Guenther copied and of which he sent me his translation: 'The nature is motility (*rluñ,* Sanskrit *vāyu, prāṇa*). As is said in the *rdo rje 'phren ba*: "motility is enlightenment . . . from that non-manifest and subtle (motility) comes clear speech". The performance of actions and interactions of beings and objects is based on it. The division is speech, *mantra,* and motility. The nature of speech is the collection of words; by them everything is achieved. All *mantras* are subsumed under the *ali-kali* (scheme). The form of the *mantras* is: at the beginning (head) when there is no *OṂ,* but the *SVĀHĀ* at the end (tail)—this is called 'headless'. If there is *OṂ* at the beginning, but the *SVĀHĀ* is missing, such *mantra* is called 'tailless'. . . . The *mantra* which has got both head and tail is called 'serpent', the *mantra* which has neither is called 'abbreviation'. The nature of *mantra* are the three letters *OṂ ĀḤ HŪṂ.* The function of the *mantra* is the origination of the *lha'i sku* lit. 'god's body', Sanskrit (*devadeha*), but Guenther thinks 'it can only mean something like "awareness of the structure" and it sustains this body (e.g. the *lha'i sku*)day and night'.

The interpretation of *mantra* as protection of the mind is also mentioned in *Phyag.rgya, chen.po rnal.'byor bzi'i bśad.pa ñes.don lta. ba'i mig,* fol. 9, after the attainment of the state of *rtse gcig* (Sanskrit *ekagratā,* 'one-pointedness of the mind'); see Guenther, 'Levels of Understanding in Buddhism', J.A.O.S. 78/1, pp. 19 ff; and *Naropa*, Oxford University Press, London 1963, *passim*.

[33] Karl Gustav Diehl, *Instrument and Purpose—Studies on Rites and Rituals in South India*, Gleerups, Lund 1956.

[34] Ibid., p. 94.

[35] Ibid., p. 100.

[36] i.e. the case of expletive use of *mantra*, as when an initiate pronounces his *mantra* involuntarily or at least indeliberately under some kind of emotional stress or duress or in his sleep: in such a case, the particular emotion or its discharge is not the purpose of the *mantra*, but its cause; such a *mantra* has no purpose and thus provides an exception, preventing 'purpose' from being included in the definition; there may be other exceptions, too.

[37] Lit. 'the six works', viz. *Śānti*—the power to remove diseases and yield protection from the influence of evil constellations, curses, and bad actions in some previous existence; *Vaśīkaraṇa*—the power to bewitch men, women, gods, and animals and to get work done by them, or have desires fulfilled by them; *Stambhana*—the power of stopping others' actions, of stunning, and of preventing the effect of others' actions, even when they are already operating; *Vidveṣaṇa*—the power of separating friends, relatives, etc.; *Uccāṭana*—the power to make enemies flee in shame and disgrace, also to explode houses and dwellings; and the most gruesome one, *Mārana*—the power of killing and maiming by *mantra*.

[38] First *taranga* '*devārca-yogyatā-prāptyai bhūtaśuddhiṃ samācaret*'.

[39] '*Jarbharī*' and '*turpharī*' are obsolete Indian words which became unintelligible in later times and which appeared to the sceptics as meaningless word-jumble. Vide E. Frauwallner, *Geschichte der indischen Philosophie*, II, note 395, Vienna 1952.

[40] *Hrīṃ hrīrlajjārupatvāt*, '*hrīṃ*—because of Her being of the form of modesty'. Tarkalankara's commentary to the *Mahānirvāṇa* III.

[41] i.e. if a line like the one in the last note were found, not in a commentary, but in the commented text itself.

[42] The deity chosen for the object of meditation by the yogi.

[43] '*Japa*' means repetition of a *mantra*, a fixed number of times, accompanied by meditation on the object of the *mantra*—e.g. the *iṣṭadevatā* in any form—as inner image, as *yantra* or *maṇḍala*, as some state of identity, etc. ('*Japa*' may be made aloud, in a whisper, soundless but with the lips moving, and mentally without lip movements.) In all traditions unexceptionally, the value of silent *japa* is highest, of loud *japa* the lowest. Recitation and repetition of texts, mantric or otherwise, is, however, not *japa*, even if those texts contain *mantras*: *japa* is repetition of the *mantra* alone, in the indicated framework.

[44] The Hindu tantrics' term for initiation which not only reveals the *mantra* to the adept, but yields its consummation at the same time (i.e. not after prolonged practice of *japa* which is the usual process), is '*śāṃbhavī dīkṣā*', lit.

'initiation through Śiva himself'. Whenever a sudden realization of the supreme spiritual object is achieved, a '*śāṃbhavī dīkṣā*' is supposed to have taken place, even though it may not be mentioned in the hagiographical account. Śaṃkarācārya's statement that the supreme truth propounded in the Upaniṣad is realized and liberation reached the moment the *mahāvākyam* '*ahaṃ brahmāsmi*', '*tattvamasi*', etc., is understood, has puzzled orthodox Hindus ever since, because understanding these dicta is not really difficult, and they are common knowledge among Smārta-Brahmins (i.e. Brahmins belonging to the tradition inaugurated by Śāṃkarācārya in the eighth century A.D.); however, the enigma is completely solved if the *ācārya*'s statement is understood under the mantric rubric: the *mahāvākyam* being *mantra*, its 'understanding' and the simultaneous realization of the supreme goal is no discursive event; it presupposed '*śāṃbhavī dīksā*'; initiation into the 'meaning' of a *mantra*. Whether that be written down previously or not, it is essential and is part of my definition of *mantra*. The *guru* may be a human person or, as in the case of '*śāṃbhavī dīksā*' and in the case of Śaṃkarācārya's implication, divinity itself.

[45] *Sanskrit-English Dictionary*.

[46] The oldest extant commentary on the Veda-Saṃhitā.

[47] No word '*indha*' exists, though it is of course a corruption of '*indhana*', 'fuel for fire', from the root '*indh-*'; Indra is the god of lightning and the alluded connection is evident.

[48] Tucci, Lama Govinda, H. Zimmer frequently refer to *mantra* as vibration, cosmic or otherwise.

[49] *Mantradraṣṭā*, 'seer of *mantras*', is a synonym for *ṛṣi* or Vedic sage.

[50] *Varadātantra*, Ch. 6: '*hakāraḥ śivavācī syādrephaḥ prākṛtirucyate, mahāmāyārtha īśabdo nādo viśvaprasuḥ smṛtaḥ, duḥkhaharārthako bindurbhuvanaṃ tena pūjayet*'. '*Nada*' is the crescent forming the lower half of the *anunasika* symbol ◡; *bindu* is the dot forming the upper portion.

[51] Tantric scholars in India seem to be particularly fascinated by the phonetic similarity of the cluster *-kr-* with words known to them from other traditions; I have heard several tantrics in Bengal and Banaras muse about it, and Swami Hariharānanda Bhāratī, the Guru of the Bengali reformer Raja Rammohan Roy, in a letter to the latter, stated this view elaborately ('*Śānibārer chithi*' [Bengali], Calcutta, July, 1951); in his commentary *Vimalānandadāyini-Svārūpa-Vyākhyā*, to the *Karpurādistotram*, 2nd ed., Ganeshan, Madras, p. 11, Vimalānanda says *krīm, islāmadharmāvalambināḥ sādhakāḥ mokṣalābhakāmanayā arabīyabhāṣāyāṃ rūpāntaritaṃ* '*karīm*' *iti mantraṃ japanti, tathā khriṣṭhānadharmāvalambināh sādhakāh api* '*khraiṣṭ*' *iti mantram muktikāmanayā sadaiva japantīti*', i.e. 'the followers of the islam *dharma*, desirous of liberation, make *japam* of this *mantra* in the Arabic modification '*karim*', and the followers of the Christian *dharma*, desirous of emancipation, continuously perform *japa* of (this *mantra*) as modified into 'Christ'.

[52] Thus, when the instruction runs like this: 'then let him put Lakṣmī and Kāma in the third and fourth place', it means the *bījàs Śrīṃ* and *Klīm* form the second and the third quasi-morpheme in the total *mantra.*

[53] '*Prāṇeśastaijasārundho bheruṇḍavyomabindumān, samuddhṛtyā dvitīyamuddharet priye: sandhyā raktāsamārūḍhā vāmanetrendusaṃyutā, tritiyam śṛṇu kalyāni dīpasansthaḥ prajāpatih, govīndabindusanyuktaḥ sādhakānāṃ sukhāvahaḥ, bıjatrayante parameśvari sambodhanaṃ padaṃ, vahnikāntavadhī prokto daśarṇo' 'yam manuh sive, sarvavidyāmāyī devi vidyeyam parameśvari'. Mahānivanātantra,* 5th Ullasa, 10–13.

[54] '*Mantraśca kathyate saṃyak yathādevīprabodhakaḥ, hāntaṃ hutāśanasthaṃ ca caturthasvarabheditaṃ, bindumastakasanbhinnaṃ khaṇḍendusahitaṃ pưnaḥ: etad bījam (mss AC has "ekabījam", which does not change the sense substantially) mahadbījaṃ dvitīyaṃ śṛṇu sāmpratam: tāntam (śāntam in mss A) vahnisamāyuktaṃ punastenaiva bheditam; nādabindusamāyuktaṃ dvitīyaṃ bhavati sthiram. Tritīyaṃ tu punarbījaṃ kathayāmi prayatnataḥ, hāntaṃ ṣaṣṭhaḥ (mss. ANC sāntaṣaṣṭha) svarākrāntaṃ nādabindusamanvitam. Etad bījavaraṃ śreṣṭhaṃ trailokyadāhanād ahaṃ, kathatāmi caturthaṃ ca yathā buddhena bhāṣitaṃ—phāntaṃ) 'yāntam' in mss. A) śuddhaṃ sutejāḍhyaṃ sarvasiddhipradāyakam; Sādhanāmālā,* No. 124, *Ekajaṭā.*

[55] The correlative term in such usage is not 'impure' (*aśuddha*) but '*miśrita*' (mixed), such as is the standard usage in talking about musical scales, i.e. '*śuddha*' or pure for scales representing a single melody-type (*rāga*) and '*miśrita*' or 'mixed' for a melody-type utilizing more than one basic *rāga.*

[56] Or, with the alternative readings: *HRĪṂ ŚRĪṂ HŪṂ KHAṬ*—;

[57] For example in the *Tantrabhidhāna,* Vol. I, published by A. Avalon, *Tantric Texts.*

[58] The manuals, like our *Mantramahārṇava, Mantramahodadhi* and *Mantramuktāvali,* do of course give general references—they would say 'the *mantra* x as in the *Tantrarājatantra*'—but they certainly do not give an indication about the exact passages, pagination, etc. But then, Indian scholastic commentaries seldom give such exact reference.

[59] *Trīnkāraṃ cintayed vaktre vivāde prativādinām, trāṃ vā repham jvalāntaṃ vā sveṣṭasiddhipradāyakam'—Krodhādistambhanayantrādhikārah* 5, 3, of the *Bhairavīpadmavatīkalpā.*

[60] R. P. Tripathi, '*Mantraśāstron men niyat kriyāvidhiān*' (Hindi) in *Kalyāṇ,* March 1955, he uses the terms '*vyaktigat*' and '*samaṣṭigat*'.

[61] See *Kaulāvalinirṇaya,* 14th *Ullāsa,* 67.

[62] *Tantraloka,* Vol. III, Kashmere Series, see bibliography.

[63] Prof. Suniti Kumar Chatterji used this handy term somewhat facetiously in his lectures at Calcutta University many years ago; it is of course an Anglicization of '*japam*' or '*japati*', viz, repetition of the *mantra.*

[64] 'Pray ye without cessation' in the Gospels.

[65] i.e. the relevant passage of the *Taittirīya Upaniṣad* of the Black Yajurveda is chanted every morning: '*śikṣāṃ vyākhyasyāmah, varṇasvarah, mātrā balam*'—'may we learn correct pronunciation, of letter and sounds, the exact volume and force of the syllables'.

[66] This procedure is customary only in India and Ceylon; it is not known in Thailand, Laos, and Cambodia. It seems to me the idea that the nasal laryngal was the correct pronunciation of the Pālī *anusvara* originated among old-Bengali and old-Maithili speaking monks, perhaps in the Pāla era, when many abbots in Nālandā and Vikramaśīlā came from these areas; up to this day, Bengali and Maithili speakers pronounce every final nasal as *ṅ*.

[67] *Mantramahārṇava*, published in loose leaves, Bombay, Kshemaraj Srikrishnadass 1924.

[68] The 'chosen deity' of the individual aspirant, usually a particular form of Śiva, Viṣṇu, or Śakti.

[69] For an exhaustive treatment of the highly complex symbolism of touch (*nyāsa*), see my monograph, 'Die Berührngsusymbolik in Indischer Tradition' in *Studium Generale*, Heidelberg 1964.

[70] The distinction is canonical in tantric literature, but no operational significance attaches to it; the teachers using the distinction determined the respective purposes of *hādi* and *kādi mantras* quite arbitrarily; so far I have not found any text limiting *hādi* to identification and *kādi* to propitiation-acquisition *mantras*. Cf. . . . *pūrvārdhaṃ kādisaṃjñaṃ tu dvitīyaṃ hādisaṃjñakam, kādau tu vedakhaṇḍāni hādavapi catuṣṭayam* (*Śaktisaṅgamatantra, Kālikhaṇda*, 10–11) 'the first half intimates *kādi* (*mantras*), the second half *hādi* (*mantras*) *kādi* and *hādi* (*mantras*) both pertain to the Veda (are to be counted as parts of the Veda)'. All tantric texts claim Vedic authority. In the *Saktisangamatantra*, both the types are used for a number of purposes which overlap.

[71] *Kālīvilāsa Tantra*, 19.

[72] *Karpurādistotra*, sect. Vidyārājñīs, 1–5.

[73] *Kālīvilāsa*, 17.

[74] *Kālīvilāsa*, 19.

[75] *Kālīvilāsa*, 18.

[76] *Kālīvilāsa*, 20.

[77] *Niṣpannayogāvali, Herukacatustaya*, p. 21.

[78] *Bhairavīpadmavatīkalpa*, 2/8.

[79] *Kālivilāsatantra*, 200.

[80] *Niṣpannayogāvali, Herukacatuṣṭaya*, p. 21.

[81] *Bhairavīpadmavatīkalpa*, 2/9.

[82] It is probable that some mantric text does give an explanation; I have not found any so far.

[83] These two are used for acquiring rhetorical prominence and are directed to Vāk, the goddess of speech. Vide *Mantramahodadhi*, V/3 ff.

[84] This is from lecture notes obtained during his class at the Anandamayī Ashram, Banaras 1953.

[85] Mantramahodadhi. Ibid.

[86] *Kāmaratna Tantra*, 80–82, p. 110.

[87] *Foundations*, p. 231.

[88] The Vedas, Brāhmaṇas, Purāṇas and other literary categories list *mantras*, too, but there is hardly a *mantra* in earlier literature which is not also listed in tantric texts; cf. the *Gāyatrī mantra*, the most important of all Vedic *mantras* appears in its original form, and in sectarian modifications in the most important Hindu tantras, especially the *Mahānirvāṇa*, substituting the original '*dhiyo yo naḥ pracodayāt*' by such phrases as '*tan naḥ kālī pracodayat*', '*Devī tan naḥ pracodayāt*' 'may Kālī prod our intelligence'—'may the Goddess prod our intelligence', see also Lama Anagarika Govinda, *Foundations*, p. 232.

[89] The Tibetan pronunciation is quite unlike the Indian—the Tibetans pronounce it /*om ma ni peh me hön*/.

[90] *Sādhanāmālā* 157 *passim*, 129 *et al.*: *Advayavajrasaṃgraha*, section on *maṇḍala*, has '*OM VAJRAREKHE HŪM*'; *Guhyasamājatantra*, *Prajñopāyaviniścayasiddhi*—: Frequent occurrence.

[91] *Buddhist Iconography*, p. 180, No. 22.

[92] *Gaekwad Oriental Series*, Vol. XL.

[93] An unpublished text of late origin, which I saw in manuscript in the Government Sanskrit College (now Sanskrit University) Library at Banaras; the colophon shows the compiler as one Pandit Pañcānana Gaur of Midnapur in West Bengal; no date is given.

[94] *Tantric Texts*, No. 15, 40 ff.

[95] *Kumārī-Pūjā*: a lovely and impressive ceremony current all over Bengal and in other parts of India, though with lesser frequency; a girl of twelve, of a Brahmin family, is installed on the *pīṭha* like the image of Śakti, and is worshipped accordingly after the '*pratiṣṭha*' or installation ceremony; in this particular *puja*, the virgin represents the goddess Sarasvati. However, most Brahmins regard the presentation of their daughter for this ceremony as inauspicious (*akuśala*).

[96] *Tantric Texts*, ed. A. Avalon.

[97] No. 1002.

[98] It is thinkable that the *mantra* commences only after '*Padmahaste*', and that the vocatives preceding it are what some Śākta pandits call '*prārambhika*', i.e. 'inceptive' incantations, preceding the actual *mantra*; but I believe these are meant as an integral part of the larger *mantra*, because similar vocatives occur towards the end of it, and nothing not belonging to the *mantra* can be sandwiched between actual *mantra* portions, else the entire effect of the *mantra* would be destroyed, the *mantra* having to be *akhaṇḍita*, 'unbroken'.

[99] I am rendering the meaningful portions in English to show how very

contrary to the spirit of orthodox Jainism it sounds: it is perhaps analogous to the tantric Buddhist vis-à-vis the Theravāda sentiment. '*OṂ* salutation to you, goddess! O thou who keepest the three worlds spellbound, who art ornamented with all jewellery, (O) lotus-eyed, lotus-woman, lotus-splendour, who residest in the lotus stalk, lotus-dweller, lotus-handed One! *HRĪṂ HRĪṂ* make make my heart's deed, make, make, make, make my all-peace, make, make me subdue all realms, make, make me subdue all the worlds, make, make me conquer all damsels, dispel, dispel all troubles caused by departed spirits, goblins etc., destroy, destroy all disease, remove, remove all obstacles, annihilate, annihilate all poison, destroy, destroy all epilepsy, destroy, destroy all *Śākinīs* (in Hindu tantra, the *Śākinīs* are something like the Buddhist *ḍākinīs*; in Jainism '*Śākinī*' is a generic term for evil spirits in female guise); (O) Bee of the lotus feet of the victorious Pārśvanātha (one of the founders of Jainism), salutations dattāya (a spurious dative of masculine "*datta*", "given") goddess, salutation: *OṂ HRAṂ HRĪṂ HRŪṂ HRAŪṂ HRĀḤ SVĀHĀ*, subjugation of all people, kingdoms, women and men, all all *OṂ ĀṂ KROṂ HRĪṂ AIṂ KLĪṂ HRĪṂ* O goddess, Padmavatī, fulfiller of the desires of the three cities (a purely Hindu tantric notion, i.e., the three realms of cognition, conation, and volition), destructress of the doctrines of bad (i.e. heretical) people, resplendent of the three worlds, removeress of the misfortunes of Pārsvanātha *KLĪṂ BLŪṂ* my faults kill kill, all my works make successful, make successful *HŪṂ PHAṬ SVĀHĀ*.'

[100] *Padmavatīstotram*, 5th *pariśiṣṭha*, pp. 37–7.

[101] A. Avalon, *Garland of Letters*, p. 45 ff.

[102] Op. cit. p. 89.

[103] Op. cit. pp. 78–9.

[104] *Akoracivacariyar*, *Kriyakrama Jyoti* (Tamil), ed. Madras 1897.

[105] *Mantramuktāvali*, publ. Bombay 1937.

[106] Canonical or semicanonical texts are called 'of no human origin', i.e. divinely inspired in Hindu usage, if they are anonymous texts.

[107] Sectarian worshipper of Viṣṇu.

[108] From here on I shall be quoting only the first item of each section.

[109] There is a pun in the caption, *varṇa* meaning both 'caste' and 'colour'; also '*mantra*' here is to be understood as linked with its respective *yantra* (diagram), which usually confers its colour to the *mantra* superposed on it; otherwise, *mantras* are drawn in different, prescribed colours inside or outside the *maṇḍala*.

[110] I have never seen a rosary with twenty-five beads; also it seems to me this claim is not corroborated by other *mantra*-texts; 108 beads are very much the orthodox arrangement meant to aid *mantra*-meditation for the sake of liberation-*mokṣa*.

[111] '*Sandhi*' is adventitiously used or omitted in *mantra* listings.

[112] The title 'haṃsa' or 'paramahaṃsa', i.e. 'swan' and 'supreme swan', has two simultaneous explanations—first, there is the mythological analogy to the swan, which is supposed to be able to drink the pure milk alone out of a mixture of milk and water; and second, there is the esoteric explanation based on this *mantra* '*sah-aham*' meaning 'he is I', i.e. the *mahavakyam* 'great dictum', proclaiming the absolutistic identity; read back or repeated several times, *sa-haṃ* reads *haṃ-sa*, i.e. 'swan'.

[113] Here probably the goddess Sarasvatī, or the Śrīvidyā of the Śākta tradition.

[114] An epithet, 'Queen of the World', applied to Sarasvatī, Lakṣmī, and Śakti alike; here, however, the latter must be meant, this being the 'method of Śiva'. Also, '*hādi*' preceding '*kādi*' *mantras* indicate Śākta and Śivite provenience.

[115] The author does not say whose *bīja-mantra* it is; he obviously has the title of the section in mind, hence he means '*bīja* of Śiva (Śaṃkara).

[116] This is the Vedic *gāyatrī* form with the tantric addition as frequently shown in the *Mahānirvāṇa* and kindred tantras.

[117] Or more likely, Śakti, who is also called 'Vāgīśvarī', 'goddess of speech', in the *Lalitāsahasranāma*; also, Sarasvatī is not known to be meditated on as 'bhasmāṅgī' ('her limbs smeared with ashes'), which ointment seems to be reserved for Śakti, and of course for the Buddhist goddesses. Besides, '*phaṭ*' being the '*astra*' or 'weapon' *mantra*, it would hardly be used for Sarasvatī.

[118] *Gāyatrī* is the name of a metre, and of the chief Vedic *mantra*, and a name of Sarasvatī, the goddess of speech.

[119] Sanatkumāra is one of the four mythical '*kumara*' (youth)—seers who have the everlasting bodies of sixteen-year-old youths.

[120] *Aghora*, 'not terrible' in folk etymology, is an epithet of Śiva; the real etymology of the word is unknown and probably not Sanskrit at all.

[121] i.e. the *mantra* uttered when the posture (*āsana*) for mantric meditation is assumed; according to the sect to which the worshipper belongs, the last phrase is variable; *Kṛṣṇāya namaḥ* 'obeisance to Kṛṣṅa' is used by a Vaiṣṇava, '*Śivāya namah*' would be used by a Śivite, etc.

[122] Completely unintelligible in part.

Obviously at the occasion of entering the fourth state of life, *saṃnyāsa.* However, this is not the orthodox Brahmanical *saṃnyāsa-mantra*, which is quite different, i.e. the *Vira-jāhomamantra*. Also, the taking of *saṃnyāsa* being a Vedic ceremony, no late mantric Sanskrit could be used as in this *mantra.*

[123] On entering the third stage, *vānaprastha*, that of a forest-dweller and contemplative.

[124] On entering the first stage of the twice-born Hindu's life, that of celibate studenthood (*brahmacaryam*); this *mantra* is completely intelligible. It invokes the hairtuft hypostasized as the daughter of Brahmā, the goddess Mātaṅgī, the '*femme ascête*' and it assigns her place on the forehead.

[125] This refers to the life-cycle rite called *sīmāntonnayana*, the parting of the highcaste women's hair in the fourth, sixth, or eight month of their pregnancy.

[126] This is not clear to me; there is no '*āsana*' of that name to my knowledge; '*kimvyādha*' might be an epithet of Śiva in the Kirātārjunīya myth-complex, where Śiva appears as a hunter (*vyādha*).

[127] Or 'auspicious letter', if '*śiva*' is taken as an adjective; this possibility is not excluded by the fact that vs. 11 says 'thus it is written by Śiva,' as the idiom '*sivena likhita*' simply means 'authoritatively said'.

6

ON INTENTIONAL LANGUAGE (SANDHĀBHĀṢĀ)

IN THE past chapters frequent reference has been made to *sandhā-bhāṣā* (intentional language), pre-empting, as it were, the information contained in this section. It is certainly poor style to keep referring to a technical and highly involved subject before investigating it; but this is one of the cases where a full investigation presupposes familiarity with other topics—*mantra*, Tibetan-Sanskrit lexicography, and the philosophical background of the tradition, in our case.

Also, procedures of initiation seem to follow logically upon *mantra*, because it is the atomic constituent, so to speak, of initiation; and yet, this study of the badly structured, complex, and hence highly involved pattern of intentional language must follow our investigation of *mantra*, mainly because intentional language can be viewed as a specialized extension of mantric language, but also because scholars in India and the West have wrongly identified mantric and intentional language. It is for these reasons that we have to sandwich *sandhābhāṣā* (intentional language) between our study of *mantra* and of tantric initiation and it will be seen that it forms a natural link in spite of the stylistic procrastination which it entails.

This chapter, then, deals with *sandhābhāṣā* (intentional language) which is used in the tantras. This study is best divided into four sections: first, the meaning of the term will be established; next, I shall contend that *sandhābhāṣā* terminology follows two obverse semantic patterns; third, I shall present a list of frequent *sandhā*-terms; lastly, I shall single out one particularly important *sandhā*-word for textual exemplification. A short textual selection on *sandhābhāṣā* will be appended, which leans heavily on Professor M. Eliade's list,[1] adding only some material which has been published more recently.

It is important to note that *sandhābhāṣā* has nothing to do with *mantra*; *mantra*-language is often virtually identified with, or taken to be a particular branch of, *sandhābhāṣā* by Indian pandits. However, *mantra* (including *dhāraṇī*, *kavaca*, *yāmala*, etc.) is meant to be an excitant, prompting towards action or inducing a particular state of mind. *Sandhā*-words, on the other hand, claim to describe something; *mantra* tries to change something, it does not designate anything in nature; *mantra* is an injunction, *sandhā* terminology is descriptive or appraising, or both. Scholars might agree to subsume *mantra*- under *sandhā*-language by watering down the injunctive purport of *mantra*, but this is hardly conducive to clarity. I believe the distinction is both correct and important.

Up to this day, there are two views about the correct form of the word. Older scholars thought it was *sandhyābhāṣā* (twilight language); the more recent and to my mind the more probable reading is *sandhābhāṣā* (intentional language). After Eliade's treatment of *sandhābhāṣā*[2] it seemed sure that the form would no longer be disputed. However, Lama Govinda has since written about *sandhyābhāṣā* again[3]; he does not mention the controversy and it is thinkable that he might not be aware of it. Even more recently, Snellgrove seems to accept *sandhyābhāṣā*,[4] though I do not understand why he does so although his Tibetan text reads *dgons pa'i skad*. He translates the term as 'secret language' throughout, which would do for both *sandhyā* and *sandhāya* in a somewhat specious way. Snellgrove then avers[5] that the list given by Shahidullah and quoted by Eliade 'consists chiefly of terms not properly *sandhyābhāṣā*. Terms such as *lalanā*, *rasanā*, *padma*, *vajra*, etc., are by no means "hidden".' Snellgrove would not encounter this difficulty if he read *sandhā* instead of *sandhyā*, for though 'hidden' and 'secret' may be synonyms, 'intentional' is not a synonym of either; hence the terms quoted by Shahidullah and Eliade are genuine *sandhābhāṣā*. I also do not see what terms do qualify as 'hidden' on this count, for in another passage Snellgrove obviously does accept similar diction as eligible, when he states 'in this case even the literal is concealed beneath the jargon of their secret language'.[6]

A third view must be mentioned if only for completeness' sake. P. K. Banerjee thinks the term reads *sandhyā*, and that it is the proper name of a dialect spoken in a region of this name; he writes:

'. . . the tract to the southeast of Bhagalpur comprising the western portion of Birbhum and the Santhal Parganas is the borderland between the old Āryavarta (the Indian domicile of the Aryans) and Bengal proper, and was called the *Sandhyā*-country. Anyone who is familiar with the several dialects all closely resembling one another spoken in that region, cannot have any doubt as to their near relationship to the language used by the Siddhacharyas.[7]

V. Bhattacharya dismisses this view as 'mere imagination',[8] he is probably right, for the dialect called *sandhyā-boli* does not bear any more resemblance to the language of the Dohākośas (if that is what P. K. Banerjee had in mind when he spoke of the language of the Siddhacaryas) than any other of the numerous *boli-s* spoken in that area.

I shall outline the *sandhyā-sandha* controversy succinctly, and attempt to resolve it. The late Paṇḍit Haraprasad Shastri, the editor of *Bauddhagān o Dohā* (Bengali),[9] speaks about *sandhyābhāṣā* throughout his introduction. He wrote (p. 8): '. . . all the works of the *sahajayāna* are written in *sandhyābhāṣā*. *Sandhyābhāṣā* is a language of light and darkness, partly light, partly darkness; some passages can be understood, others cannot. That is to say, in this high order type of discourse on *dharma* words have another, a different meaning (viz. from their literal meaning); this is not to be openly discussed.'[10] H. P. Shastri then uses *sandhyābhāṣā* eighteen times; he was certainly not aware, at that time, of the possible alternative reading *sandhā*.

V. Bhattacharya contested this reading. He showed[11] that both Sanskrit and Pālī Buddhist texts use *sandhābhāṣā* throughout and that the few instances where he found *sandhyā* were wrong spellings.

P. C. Bagchi[12] accepted V. Bhattacharya's reading and added that *sandhā* was corroborated by the Chinese translation of the term which he transcribes *fang pien shuo*.

The Tibetan equivalent for *sandhābhāṣā* is *ldem por dgoṅs te bśad pa ni.*[13] The *Śatapitaka Tibetan-Sanskrit Dictionary*[14] gives both *sandhā* and *sandhyā* as the Sanskrit originals. It lists *dgoṅs skad—sandhyābhāṣā* with *Blue Annals* 2/85 as textual reference; *dgoṅs te bśad pa—sandhāya*-vacana for *Sandhinirmocana Sūtra* 7/18, 19, 23, 29; *dgoṅs te gsuṅs pa-sandhāya-vacana* for the same text, 7/25.

Eliade informs us[15] that Burnouf translates the phrase as 'enigmatic language', Kern as 'mystery', and Max Mueller[16] as 'hidden sayings'. Eliade himself prefers *sandhābhāṣā* and renders it '*langage intentionnel*'; *sandhyābhāṣā* which he gives as the Sanskrit original is obviously a misprint.[17]

In the *Chos byuṅ bstan pa'i padma rgyas pa'i ñin byed śes bya ba bzhugs so*, by Padma dkar po,[18] there is a most revealing passage which says:

'the secret tantric treatises were originally compiled secretly, and to teach and explain them to those who have not become worthy would be improper. In the meantime, they were allowed to be translated and practised; however, since it was not clarified that they were couched in enigmatic words, there arose such people who took the word accordingly (i.e. literally), and did perverse practice.'

It seems that Lama Anagarika Govinda is the only scholar today who does not accept *sandhābhāsā* and who persists in the other reading; I believe Professor Snellgrove would not really object to *sandhā* instead of *sandhyā*. Lama Govinda writes:[19]

'. . . their words (viz. of the eighty-four Siddhas) as well as their biographies are phrased in a particular type of symbolic language which is called *sandhyābhāṣā*. This Sanskrit expression literally means "twilight-language" and indicates that a double sense underlies its words, according to whether it is to be understood in its commonplace or in its mystical connotation.'

The lexicographical meaning of *sandhyā* is clear, it means 'twilight' or 'evening'. *Sandhā*, which I accept as the valid lexeme, is the shortened form of *sandhāya*, a gerund of *dha-* prefixed by *saṃ*. The shortened form is by far the most frequent, though the full form *sandhāya* does occur in important passages.[20] The dropping of the final *-ya* might best be explained on the model of Paliisms which are frequent in Buddhist Sanskrit.[21] Professor Edgerton suggests that *sandhāya* could be instrumental of *sandhā*,[22] which would certainly be borne out by Tibetan *dgoṅs pa*.

V. Bhattacharya thinks[23] that the word is a synonym of such non-specialized, non-tantric words as *abhiprāyika*, *abhipretya*, *uddiśya*, all of which imply 'meaning, connoting, denoting, aiming at, intending, referring to'. Buddhist Sanskrit texts of tantric and non-tantric provenience used these and other synonyms quite freely and interchangeably with *sandhā*. No charismatic value attaches to the word *sandhā*, in contrast to *mantra* and its synonyms.[24] The Tibetan texts translate all the synonyms of *sandhābhāṣā* by *dgoṅs pa*, just as they invariably translate synonyms for the charismatic *mantra* by *sṅags*.[25]

There are quite a few views about the purpose of *sandhā*- or *sandhyā*-language.[26] Nothing in the texts themselves, so far as I can see, gives a clue about the purpose of *sandhābhāṣā*. It is often eulogized and extolled,[27] but it is left to commentators and to the scholars to speculate on its purport. H. P. Shastri, Benoytosh Bhattacharya in his earlier writings, and most of the orthodox Hindu pandits known to me assume that *sandhābhāṣā* was used to camouflage such instructions as may be resented by the orthodox public, Buddhist and Hindu alike, and by all who are not initiated into the tantric lore; this would have seemed particularly important when Vajrayāṇa, Sahajayāna, and the other esoteric systems were in their nascent state.

The second view about the purpose of *sandhā*-language is the one held by most of the sympathetic Indian pandits: that it meant to be intelligible to the initiate adept only, and to prevent the non-initiate from dabbling with the implied practices, lest he should come to grief. This notion has its exact orthodox Brahmanical parallel and could have conceivably been derived or inspired from the Brahmin precept of *adhikāra-bheda*, i.e. the difference in instructional procedure and in the targets of meditative training according to the individual aspirant's capacities which are conditioned through metempsychosis or through a preceptor's act of grace. V. Bhattacharya probably shares this view when he writes:[28]

'... now, the beauty of the instruction (*deśanā-vilāsa*) of the Buddha, or their skill in showing the means for realization of truth (*upāya-kauśalya*), is that their instructions (*deśanā*) differ according to the degree of fitness of their disciples. Those instructions are mainly of two kinds; one, the object of which is to show the real state of things directly (*tattvārtha*), and the other, "intentional" (*abhiprāyika*), meaning thereby that it is intended to imply or to suggest something different from what is expressed by the words (*yathārtha*).'

Lama Govinda, one of our most recent authors, also shares this view though his emphasis is on a different point:[29]

'... this symbolic language is not only meant to protect the holiest from profanization by intellectual curiosity and from the misuse of yogic methods and psychic powers by the ignorant and the non-initiate; it was prompted chiefly by the fact that common parlance cannot express the highest experiences of the mind. ...'

The third view, jejune if not mildly malicious, is quite frequent in India; its proponents are people who are averse to religious experiment, and also some secular scholars. It is the view that *sandhā*-language was aiming to entice people away from orthodox observance and to lure them into the tantric web. Scholars who share this view are often eager to exonerate the tantric tradition by stressing the purely metaphorical meaning of the words regardless of whether the tantric authors and schoolmen intended a literal (*mukhya*) or a metaphorical (*gauṇa*) interpretation. I quote D. N. Bose[30] as a typical representative of this view:

'... the tantras indulge in [*sic*] *sandhyā*-language with double meaning on many occasions. These were catch-phrases to the common people in the old days when society was still in the making. The later tantrics have termed them as symbolic of yogic processes ... these terms are reflections of the amorous raptures of the mystic *sādhakas* whose joy resembles that of a lover meeting her [*sic*] beloved after long waiting. The simple meaning[31] of these terms is as follows: *madya* is the nectarine stream issuing from the cavity of the brain where the soul resides; *matsya* means the suppression of vital airs; *maṃsa* is the vow of silence; *mudrā* means the interweaving of fingers during religious worship, it is a physical process that is calculated to enhance the concentration of the worshipper; *maithuna* is meditation on acts of creation and destruction.'[32]

I would like to add what I regard as two additional possible purposes of *sandhābhāṣā*; so far I do not have any textual support for them, but I think they fit well enough into the mystical climate of medieval India. The one possibility I have in mind is that *sandhābhāṣā* might have been used as a mnemonic device; for undoubtedly, queer and eccentric phraseology tends to be more lastingly remembered and more readily recalled than plain matter-of-fact idiom or the dry, cumbrous philosophical terminology of the scholastic traditions, especially when the code language uses a captivating and emotionally potent idiom like the erotic. I would illustrate this point on a textual model like the following. The basic text reads:[33] 'Once upon a time the Lord of all Tathāgatas ... was dwelling in the vulvae of the *vajra*-woman'—an inceptive clause in several Buddhist tantras. The commentator explains the passage[34] '... the intuitive knowledge is the *vajra*-woman due to its nature as undivided wisdom (*prajñā, śes rab*) and "vulva" is (used on account of its) destroying all afflictions (*kleśa, ñon moṅs pa*).' It is certainly easy to remember the instruction conveyed by the text in this diction, a typical *sandhā*-diction.

The other possibility, the last of which I can think at present, is that *sandhābhāṣā* might have been meant facetiously, at least sometimes. The oft-quoted tantric passage,[35] repeated in various modifications in many tantric commentaries as well as by orthodox Hindus as a deterrent and an invective against tantric practice, is a case in point; it says: 'inserting his organ into the mother's womb, pressing his sister's breasts, placing his foot upon his *guru's* head, he will be reborn no more'. The passage exemplifies what I shall presently call 'afferent' *sandhā*. In the Hindu tantric parlance, the 'organ' is the contemplating mind, the 'mother's womb' is the *mūlādhāra* or base centre of the *yoga* body, the 'sister's breasts' are the heart and the throat centre (*anāhata* and *ājñā*) respectively, and the '*guru*'s head' is the brain centre (i.e. the thousand-petalled lotus *sahasrārā-cakra*, also called the *śūnya-cakra*), and the implied instruction is thus translatable: he practises mental penetration through the successive centres, and when he reaches the uppermost centre, he will not be reborn, as he has thereby attained *nirvikalpa samādhi*.

Now, I cannot dismiss the idea that the author was perhaps trying to annoy the orthodox; this *śloka* and others of its kind have the flavour of teasing the orthodox religious bourgeois. Even though *sandhā*-terminology must have been devised as a secret language when it was first put to use, it is very unlikely that orthodox pandits should not have known anything about the *sandhā*-pattern; and it is equally improbable that the tantrics in their turn should have ignored the likelihood of their opponents' awareness of this pattern of esoteric language. The passage quoted above hails from a period when *sandhā*-usage had long been well established; for even though the *Mahānirvāṇa Tantra* itself is one of the oldest Śaktā works, it was preceded by at least five centuries of Buddhist tantric literature and hence by a solid tradition of *sandhā*-usage. It is quite natural—even in India where humour does not find much scope in religious lore—that the heretic may begin to flaunt his peculiarities when constantly attacked and vilified by an orthodox majority. An intensified, and eventually a facetious, use of *sandhābhāṣā* would then provide the heretic—the tantric in this case with an apt instrument for such flaunting and perhaps a sort of linguistic catharsis.[36] If this was so, then the author of this particular *śloka* was no doubt successful, as the passage is being quoted up to this day.

It is also evident that lay people knew about the tantrics' *sandhā*-use of language, not only in India but even in Tibet. This is well borne out by the indignant words ascribed to Queen Tse spoṅ bža, who is said to have been a sworn enemy of Buddhism and an ardent votary of the Bon tradition:[37]

'. . . what they call "*kapāla*", that is a human skull placed on a rack; what they call "*basūṭa*", that is entrails spread out; what they call a "bone-trumpet", that is a human bone; what they call "sanctuary of the great field" (*mahā-kṣetra-tīrtham*?), that is a human skin spread out; what they call "*rakta*", that is blood sprinkled over sacrificial altars; what they call "*maṇḍala*", it is just gaudily sparkling colours; whom they call "dancers", they are men wearing garlands of bones . . . this is not religion (viz. *chos, dharma*), this is the evil India has taught Tibet.'

As an afterthought, it seems possible that the entire *sandhā*-tradition is due, eventually, to the love of paradox common to all religious jargon in India, in Vedic times and today. In each religious and philosophical tradition a specific idiom is developed and constantly used by its adherents. This happened to the tantric tradition, too, and the pressure from orthodox Hinduism and Buddhism might have enhanced and fossilized the use of *sandhābhāṣā*.

In assigning a purpose to *sandhābhāṣā*, the last word so far has been said by Eliade. I quote a few salient passages from his chapter on *sandhābhāṣā*, 'la langage intentionnel':[38]

'. . . the tantric texts are frequently couched in intentional language—a secret, obscure language with a double meaning, wherein a particular state of consciousness is expressed in erotical terminology, the mythological and cosmological vocabulary of which is charged both with *haṭha*-yogic and with sexual significance.'

Eliade thinks that *sandhābhāṣā* has a double purpose: to camouflage the doctrine against the non-initiate, and to 'project the yogi into the "paradoxical situation" indispensable for his spiritual training'.

I now proceed to establish that *sandhā*-terminology can be classified into two categories, which I shall call 'afferent' and 'efferent' respectively. The point of reference for these qualifiers is the central concept of tantric thought, i.e. the Absolute conceived as Paraśiva in Hindu and as Śūnya in Vajrayāṇa philosophy; or, on the eschatological side, the state of *kaivalya* (or *nirvikalpasamādhi* or any of its equivalents) in Hindu and that of *asaṃpratiṣṭhita nirvāṇa*[39] in Vajrayāṇa mysticism. A *sandhā*-term which employs object-language and 'intends' the conceptual or mystical absolute is an afferent term as when *lalanā* (woman) is to mean *nirvāṇa*. Conversely, a *sandhā*-term employing the philosophical or theological language and 'intending' an objective thing or event or an action is an efferent term, as when *bodhicitta* (*'la pensée d'Eveil'* in Eliade's rendition) is to mean '*semen virile*'.

In compilations of *sandhā*-words certain terms are often listed which should not actually be called *sandhā* at all; for although they are object-language lexicators, they had already acquired an established theological meaning well before *sandhābhāṣā* was systematized. Thus, *vajra* (*rdo rje*, 'thunderbolt') is not genuine *sandhā* when it stands as a synonym for *śūnya*, which it almost always does in Vajrayāṇa texts; it is, however, a true *sandhā*-term if it stands for *liṅga* (*membrum virile*).

To qualify as a *sandhā*-term, a word must therefore be either afferent or efferent in this definition; whenever a lexeme used in *sandhābhāṣā* is neither of the two, then it is not *sandhābhāṣā* in that particular context.[40]

I shall now exemplify *sandhābhāṣā*. I shall add (a) or (e) to each term, for afferent and efferent, respectively. It would not be practical to list afferent and efferent terms separately, for the former overwhelmingly outnumber the latter; in fact there seem to be only a few genuinely efferent *sandhā*-terms. This is but natural, for after all the tantras are not collections of manuals on sex; they are *mokṣa-śāstra* (*thar ba'i bstan chos*), doctrinal texts on spiritual emancipation; hence the major part of *sandhā*-terminology must needs refer to a spiritual universe of discourse. This does not in any way make the classification into afferent and efferent redundant, for the few efferent terms are immensely important and frequent, especially the *sandhā*-word *bodhicitta*, 'mind of enlightenment', which will be my paradign.

The *Hevajra Tantra* is so far the chief source for *sandhā*-terminology.[41] This text uses the following *sandhā*-words:

madana (Tib. *ma da na*) 'Cupid' (e) ⊃[42] *madya* (Tib. *chaṅ ba*) 'wine'

bala (Tib. *ba la*) 'power, mind-control' (e) ⊃ *māṃsa* (Tib. *śa*) 'meat'

kheṭa (Tib. *khe ṭa*) 'village' (a) *gati* (Tib. *'gro ba*) 'the way, abode, method'

prekṣaṇa[43] (Tib. *preṅ kha ṇa*) 'the act of viewing' (a) ⊃ *āgati* (Tib. *'on ba*) 'arrival, achievement'

astyābharaṇa (Tib. *rus pa'i rgyan*) 'ornaments of bone', or more probably a *tatpuruṣa* 'one who wears ornaments of bone' (a) ⊃ *niraṃśuka* (Tib. *ni raṃ śu*) 'without upper garment', i.e. 'unconditioned'

kaliñjara (Tib. *ka linñdza raṃ*) 'Kaliñjara', name of a sacred mountain in Bundelkhand (a) ⊃ *bhavya* (Tib. *skal ldan*) 'existence'[44]

kapāla (Tib. *thod pa*) 'a human skull' (a) ⊃ *padmabhājana* (Tib. *padma bha dza naṃ*) 'lotus-vase', i.e. the universe

tṛptikara (Tib. *tri pi ta*) 'one who satisfies' (e) ⊃ *bhakṣa* (Tib. *bza' ba*) 'food'

mālatindhana (Tib. *mā la tindha nam*) (obscure etymology) probably 'moonlight'; or 'jasmine wood' (Snellgrove's reading) (a or e) ⊃ *vyañjana* (Tib. *tshod ma*) 'consonant', i.e. as a *mantra*-constituent[45]

mūtra (Tib. *gci ba*) 'urine' (a) ⊃ *kasturikā* (Tib. *ka stu ri*) 'musk'; an ingredient for worship

sihlaka (Tib. *si hlar*) 'frankincense'; the olibanum tree (a) ⊃ *svayaṃbhu* (Tib. *raṅ byuṅ*) 'self-originated', the Absolute; a name of Śiva[46]

śukra (Tib. *bhu ba*) 'semen virile' (a) ⊃ *karpūraka* (Tib. *ka pu ra*) 'camphor', another ingredient for worship in tantric ritual

mahāmāṃsa (Tib. *śa chen*) 'human meat' (a) ⊃ *alija*[47] (Tib. text transcribes another word, vd. note 47) 'the vowel', viz. originating in the *varṇamālā* or mystical vowel series

bola(ka) (Tib. *bo la*) 'gum myrrh' (a) ⊃ *vajra* (Tib. *rdo rje*) 'the Absolute' *kakkola(ka)* (Tib. *kakko la*) n.p. of an aromatic plant, and of the perfume made from that plant (a) ⊃ *padma* (Tib. *padma*) 'lotus'[48]

Ḍombī (Tib. *g'yuṅ mo*) 'a lowcaste woman', i.e. of the washermen's caste (a) ⊃ *vajrakuli* (Tib. *rdor rje'i rigs*) the '*vajra*-class', or an adept of the *vajra*-class

Nati (Tib. *gar ma*) 'a female dancer' (a) ⊃ *padmakuli* (Tib. *padma'i rigs*) the '*padma*-class', or an adept of the *padma*-class

Caṇḍāli (Tib. *raṅ 'tshed ma*) 'a lowcaste woman', i.e. born from the union of a Brahmin mother and a lowcaste father (a) ⊃ *ratnakuli* (Tib. *rin chen rigs*) the 'jewel-class', or an adept of that class

Dvijā (Tib. *skyes gñis*) 'Brahmin lady' (a) ⊃ *Tathāgatī* (*de bžin gšegs pa*) 'female Tathāgata'

lalanā (Tib. *brkyaṅ ma*) 'a wanton woman' (a)[49] ⊃ *prajña* (Tib. *śes rab*) 'intuitive wisdom'; the female pole in the *prajñopāya* (*yab yum*) complex; the left artery in the yoga body, i.e. the *iḍā* of the Hindu tantras

rasanā (Tib. *ro ma*) 'tongue' (a) ⊃ *upāya* (Tib. *thabs*) 'the means', the method of realization; the male pole in the (*yab yum*) complex; the right artery in the yoga body, i.e. the *piṅgalā* of the Hindu tantras

avadhūtī (Tib. *kun 'dar ma*) 'a female ascetic' (a) ⊃ Nairātmyā (Tib. *bdag med*); her epithet being *grāhya-grāhaka-vivarjitā* (Tib. *gzuṅ ba daṅ 'dzin med ma*) 'she who is devoid of the condition of subject and object'; the transcendence of *prajñā* and *upāya*, the Void; the central artery of the yoga body, i.e. the Hindu *suṣumnā*

The *Dohākośa* and the Buddhist *Caryāpādas* of Kāṇha and Sarāha were written in Old Bengali and Apabhraṃśa, and most of them have been translated and absorbed into the *bstan 'gyur*.[50] They are replete with *sandhābhāṣā* and it can be said without exaggeration that the *dohās* contain hardly nything which is not *sandhā*-language. M. Shahidullah[51] compiled an interesting list of *sandhā*-words in his edition of the *dohākośa* and the *caryās*, from which I quote:

padma 'lotus' (e) ⊃ *bhaga* 'vulva'
uṣṇīśa 'diadem' (a) ⊃ *kamala* 'lotus', the universe
vajra 'thunderbolt', the absolute (e) ⊃ *liṅga* 'phallus'
ravi, sūrya 'sun' (a) ⊃ *rasanā, piṅgalā* 'the right artery' in the yoga body

ravi, sūrya (the sun) (e) ⊃ *rajas* 'the menstrual fluid'
śaśi, candra, 'moon' (a) ⊃ *lalanā, iḍā* 'the left artery' in the yoga body
bodhicitta (Tib. *byaṅ chub kyi sems*) 'the bodhi mind' (e) ⊃ *śukra* (Tib. *khu ba*) 'semen virile'
taruṇī 'a young damsel' (a) ⊃ *mahāmudrā* (Tib. *phyag rgya chen po*) 'the consecrated female partner'—(a complex, loaded term)
gṛhiṇī 'the house-wife', 'spouse' (a) ⊃ *mahāmudrā, divyamudrā, jñanamudrā*—synonymous terms (see Günther, *Naropa*, bibliography)
samarasa (Tib. *ro mñam pa*) 'coitus', 'identité de juîssance' (a) ⊃ suppression of thought, together with the stopping of breath and the retention of the sperm
karin 'elephant' (a) ⊃ *citta* 'thought', 'mind'

As illustrated in two of the above instances, a *sandhā*-term may have both afferent and efferent use according to the context.

M. Eliade gives a short but very systematic list of *sandhā*-terms from the *Dohākośa* tabling all the *sandhā*-implications.[52] He uses the = sign of equation between the terms; I shall, however, continue using the implication symbol ⊃, as = should be reserved for synonymity only, as between *prajñā* and *nairātmya*, for instance. This is Eliade's list:

vajra 'thunderbolt' ⊃ *liṅga, śūnya* 'voidness', 'the void', *vacuité*'
ravi, sūrya 'sun' ⊃ *rajas* 'the menstrual fluid' = *pingalā* 'the right artery' (⊃ *upāya* 'the means')
śaśin, candra, 'moon' ⊃ *śukra* 'semen virile' ⊃ *iḍā* 'left artery' ⊃ *prajñā*
lalanā 'woman' ⊃ *iḍā* ⊃ *abhāva* 'non-existence' ⊃ *candra* ⊃ *apāna* 'exhalation'; 'the digestive power' (according to F. Edgerton)[53] ⊃ *ñada* 'cosmic sound' ⊃ *prakṛti* 'nature' ⊃ *tamas* (one of the three gunas of the Sāṃkhya) ⊃ *Gaṅgā* n.p. ⊃ *svara* 'vowels' ⊃ *nirvāṇa*, etc.
rasanā 'tongue' ⊃ *piṅgalā* ⊃ *prāṇa* 'life force,' 'breath' ⊃ *rajas* (one of the three Saṃkhyan *guṇas*) ⊃ *puruṣa* (the Sāṃkhyan polarity principle of *prakṛti*, the principle of consciousness, the male principle) ⊃ *vyañjana* 'consonants' i.e. *kāli*—the series starting with *ka* ⊃ *Yamunā* n.p. ⊃ *bhāva* 'existence' (*être*), etc.
avadhūtī 'female ascetic' *suṣumna* 'central artery' of the *yoga* body ⊃ *prajñā* = *Nairātmyā*, etc.
bodhicitta 'la pensée d'Eveil' ⊃ *śukra* 'semen virile'

He also lists *taruṇī*, *gṛhiṇī*, and *samarasa*, but does not add any information to Shahidullah's list.

Japanese Buddhists of the Shingon sect frequently refer to *sáke* as '*hanyato*', i.e. *prajñā* 'supreme intuitive wisdom'; unless this is purely facetious usage, it may well be a genuine case of efferent *sandhā*-usage.

Glasenapp lists a few *sandhā*-terms without expressly mentioning the *sandhā* complex; he selects them from the *Hevajra-seka prakrīya*, but he obviously takes them to be of purely iconographical import. He writes:[54]

'. . . the text which lists these symbols makes the following equations: a cup or skull—the great void (*śūnya*); a club—the purity of body, speech, and thought; a begging-monk, (*bhikṣu*)—'*das Erleuchtungsdenken*' (*bodhicitta*); a pail turned upside down (*ghaṭorrdhva*)—concentrated thought which cannot be diverted by anything; a drum (*ḍamaru*)—proclaiming the holy texts; a plough (*hala*)—the eradication of the passions; a tortoise (*kūrma*)—the thirst for living, attachment in general (*tṛṣna*, Pālī *taṇhā*); a lion (*siṃha*)—pride, arrogance (*abhimāna, ahaṃkāra*).'

In conclusion, I shall now illustrate what I regard the most important *sandhā*-paradigm, the efferent *bodhicitta*. In non-*sandhā* usage, *bodhicitta* simply means the *bodhi*-mind, which causes no difficulty for translation. We find numerous examples of *non-sandhā* uses of *bodhicitta* not only in non-tantric texts, but in one of the most important and oldest Buddhist tantras. In the *Guhyasamāja Tantra*, the various Buddhas and Bodhisattvas, one by one, give their definitions of *bodhicitta*, none of which could possibly be construed as a *sandhā-term*:[55]

Lord Śakyamuni defines it thus:

'Neither the perception of the absence of existence in non-existence should be called perception, nor can the perception of non-existence in existence be obtained.'[56] (i.e. any longer, as *bodhicitta* is not discursive)

Vairocana explains *bodhicitta* saying:

'My *citta* is devoid of all (phenomenal) existence, and it is unrelated to the *skandhas*, *dhātus*, *āyatanas*, (unrelated) to the universe of subject and object, it is without being and has the nature of *śūnya* like all objects which are actually *śūnya*.'[57]

Akṣobhya says:

'*Bodhicitta* is without substance like ether, and it regards perpetually the objects as without origin, and in it there are neither objects nor objectness.'[58]

Ratnaketu's definition runs thus:

'that which understands all objects as non-existent and devoid of object-signs, but which originates from non-selfhood (*nairātmya*) of the objects, is called *bodhicitta*.'[59]

Amitābha puts it this way:

'As the *dharmas* have no origin, there is neither existence nor perception. It is called existence (as though by courtesy), just as ether is said to exist, although in reality it doesn't.'[60]

Finally, Amoghasiddhi explains:

'The *dharmas* are luminous by nature, and they are pure like the sky. The *citta* in which there is neither *bodhi* nor *abhisamaya* (i.e. neither intuitive realization nor discursive comprehension) is called *bodhicitta*.'[61]

In all these passages, *bodhinaya* is an exact synonym of *bodhicitta*; each of the passages is preceded by the words *bodhicittam udājahāra*, 'he took up *bodhicitta*', i.e. he proceeded to explain it.

In *sandhā*-usage, however, *bodhicitta* implies 'semen virile'. Here it is easy to trace the motive for this usage: *bodhicitta* as the *bodhi*-mind results from the union of *prajñā* and *upāya*, from commingling the supreme intuitive wisdom with the contemplative or redemptive effort; *prajñā* and *upāya* are meditated upon as the male and the female deity in copulation (Tibetan *yab yum*); then the notion of *bodhicitta* as 'semen' evidently follows. All *sandhā*-usage rests on analogues between metaphysical conceptions and physical events which have been taken as impressionistic models for those conceptions in course of the development of mystical language.

The central rule behind the left-handed rites, both Hindu and Buddhist, is the retention of semen during the sexual act. The tantric disciplines which involve carnal contact are not priapic although they look as though they were. The man who discharges semen is a *paśu*, an 'animal' in the *Mahanirvāṇa* and the *Yoginī Tantra*, whereas he who retains it during *maithuna* is *divya*, 'divine' according to the former, and a *vīra*, 'hero', according to the latter text. These Hindu texts are considerably later than the Buddhist Vajrayāṇa texts which teach seminal retention as the method of realizing the *śūnya*, and the teaching thus propounded in the Hindu tantras may well have been a modified take-over from Buddhist texts. However, whereas all Vajrayāṇa texts seem to insist on seminal retention as a *sine qua non*, Hindu tantras frequently do not include it in their notion of *maithuna*; this may be a reason why there is no *sandhā*-term that might imply 'semen' using a Brahmin equivalent of *bodhicitta* (as, for example, *kaula-citta, kaivalya, svajñāna*, etc.), and I think it can be claimed with fair certainty that there is no such term in Hindu tantric literature.

The most radical *sandhā*-use of '*bodhicitta*' is, I think, the passage 'inserting the *liṅga* (penis) in the *bhaga* (vulva), let him not discharge *bodhicitta*'.[62] The Sanskrit commentary to Kaṇhā's *Dohakośa* says:

'. . . in the innate state (the natural state, i.e. in that of *mahāsukha*) *bodhicitta* is originated (that is to say) semen is produced.'[63]

This basic instruction has to be taken into account even when a text could be interpreted to flout the injunction, as in 'having established union with the *Mudrā*, the most blessed preceptor places the *bodhicitta* in the lotus, the home of the Jinas'.[64] Here, if *bodhicitta* were to mean the *bodhi*-mind and *padmabhāṇda* the Absolute, then of course this passage would not exemplify *sandhā-bhāṣā*. However, this is very likely on account of the juxtaposition of *bodhicitta* and *padma* and the use of the verb *ni-viś*, which is a frequent *sandhā* combination; the *bodhicitta* should not be discharged into the *padma*, it must be kept under control as is the rule for all *yuganaddha* practices—and *niviś*—never means anything like 'to discharge'.

It seems clear from these examples that *sandhābhāṣā* entails a sort of systematic ambiguity; it is always possible to give a second, literal interpretation of the passages. This refers us back to the ancient scholastic distinction between *mukhya*, 'literal', and *gauṇa*, 'metaphorical', interpretation of texts, and the decision is left to the individual interpreter, true to the Indian maxim *yathecchasi tathā vṛṇu*, 'choose whatever thou desirest'.

It follows then that the orthodox Brahmin can impute the dichotomy between left-handed and right-handed practices even on the basis of *sandhābhāṣā* alone: the *mukhya* reading (e.g. *bodhicitta* always understood as 'bodhi-mind') would imply *daksiṇācāra*, 'right-handed discipline'; the *gauṇa* reading (e.g. if *bodhicitta* is always taken to imply 'semen virile') would imply *vāmācāra*, 'left-handed' rites. The main distinction between the orthodox Brahmin and the tantric Hindu or the Vajrayāṇa Buddhist could perhaps be sought in the difference of their attitudes: the orthodox Brahmin wants to categorize, he must know how to read a passage, i.e. *mukhya* or *gauṇa*; the tantric, on the other hand, refuses exegetical categorizing and chooses *sandhābhāṣā* as a means to counter the orthodox attitude.

NOTES

[1] Mircea Eliade, *Le Yoga: Imortalité et Liberté*, Paris, 1954, p. 251 ff., pp. 394–5, 'Le Langage Intentionnel'. The book has been translated into English by W. R. Trask; the English version has a few additional bibliographical references. Its title is *Yoga; Immortality and Freedom*, Pantheon Publ., New York 1958.

[2] Ibid., pp. 251 ff.

[3] Lama Anagarika Govinda, *Grundlagen Tibetischer Mystik*, Zürich, 1957,

pp. 45 ff; English version *Foundation of Tibetan Mysticism*, Rider & Co., London 1960.

[4] D. L. Snellgrove, *The Hevajra Tantra*, London 1959, Vol. II, pp. 60–4.

[5] Ibid., Vol. I, p. 25, footnote.

[6] Ibid., Vol. I, p. 101, footnote 2. It is not quite clear to me why Snellgrove regards the excellent list contained in this footnote as instances of 'secret language' when he refuses this epithet to Shadidulla's examples. It is conceivable that Snellgrove wants *sandha* to apply to phrases only, and not to individual terms; but he does not say so.

[7] Panchkawri Banerjee, *Viśvabhāratī Quarterly*, 1924, 265, quoted in V. Bhattachrya, 'Sandhābhāṣā' ve. n. 8.

[8] V. Bhattacharya, 'Sandhābhāṣā,' I.H.Q., IV, 1928, 288.

[9] Mahamahopādhyaya Haraprasad Śhastri, *Bauddhagān o Doha*, (Bengali) Vangiya Sahitya Parisad Calcutta, 2nd. ed.

[10] '*seṭi ei ye, sahajiya dharmer sakalbba'i sandhyā bhāṣāy lekhā. Sandhyābhāṣāy mane ālo andhārī bhāṣā, katak ālo, katak andhakār, khanik bujhā hay, khanik bujhā jāe na arthāt ei sakal uccu anger dharmakathār bhitare ekṭā anya bhāber kathāo āce.*'

[11] I.H.Q., IV, 1928, 295.

[12] P. C. Bagchi, 'Sandhābhāsā and Sandhāvacana,' *Studies in the Tantras*, Part I, Calcutta University Publications, 1939.

[13] I.H.Q., IV, 1928, 296.

[14] *Indo Asian Literatures*, ed. Lokesh Chandra, *Tibetan-Sanskrit Dictionary*, New Delhi 1959, Part 3, pp. 424–5.

[15] Eliade, *Yoga*, p. 250 (English version). He does not list any more exact reference.

[16] *Vajracchedikā*, *S.B.E.* XLIX p. 118. Mueller writes he is stating this on Chinese authority which he does not quote.

[17] Eliade, *Yoga*, pp. 251 ff. (French original). This was not corrected in the English translation which preserves *sandhyā* (p. 249).

[18] I am indebted for this passage to Dr. T. V. Wylie. It is copied from folio 103-b of a Bhutanese blockprint of the book, in Professor Tucci's collection. The passage reads '*gsaṅ sṅags kyi rgyud rnams gzhuṅ gis gsaṅ bar bya ba yin te/ snod du na gyur pa rnams la bshad ciṅ bstan du'aṅ mi ruṅ la/ bar du bsgyur zhiṅ spyod du gnaṅ gis kyaṅ/ ldem po'i ṅag tu bshad pa na khrol nas/ sgra ji bzhin du 'dzin ciṅ log par spyod pa dag kyaṅ 'byuṅ/*'

[19] *Grundlagen*, pp. 45–6.

[20] *Laṅkāvatāra*, Ed. B. Nanjio, Kyoto 1923, p. 134, *pratyātmadharmatāṃ ca sandhyāya* 'meaning the *dharma* called *pratyātma*'; p. 11, *anutpattiṃ sandhāya mahāmate sarvadharmāḥ niḥsvabhāvāḥ* 'with reference to their non-origination, Mahāmati, all *dharmas* are (said to be) without *svabhāvaḥ*' (independent nature).

[21] Cf. Pāli *aññā aññāya* (Skt. ājñāya), *Dhammapāda* 56; *abhiññā abhiññāya* (Skt.

abhijñāya), *Sumaṅgalavilāsinī* pp. 173, 313; *upādā apādāya*, *Dhammasaṅganī* pp. 877, 960; and Geiger, *Pali Literatur und Sprache*, 1916, para. 27.2 (*aya ā*); also in V. Bhattacharya, op. cit., p. 294.

[22] *Buddhist Hybrid Sanskrit Dictionary*, p. 557. Professor Edgerton lists a number of representative instances with his own and other scholars' interpretations.

[23] Op. cit., p. 294.

[24] By this I mean that the word *sandhā* or its synonyms are themselves never part of the texts using *sandhā*-terminology, whereas *mantra* and its numerous synonyms frequently do form parts of longer *mantras*.

[25] Lokesh Chandra, *Tibetan-Sanskrit Dictionary*, Vol. 4, pp. 643–4.

[26] To establish the possible purpose of *sandha*-language, it is irrelevant which of the two lexemes, *sandhā* or *sandhyā*, is accepted, for without much stretch of imagination both terms can be brought to designate the same notion-complex; whether we understand the denotatum to be 'twilight language' or 'intentional language', the tantric understands their meaning in use; for him, *sandhā* and *sandhyā* would probably be the sememe, if he were conversant with this particular controversy.

[27] D. C. Snellgrove, *Hevajra Tantra*, II. iii., Vol. II, pp. 60 ff. *Sandhābhāṣā* is styled *mahābhāṣā* and *mahāsamaya*, and *samaya-saṃketa-vistaram*, 'full of doctrinal intimation'; its obscurity is often stated, as in *durvijñeyaṃ Śariputra sandhābhāṣyam tathāgatānām*, *Saddharmapuṇḍarīka*, B. B., p. 29.

[28] *Sandhābhāṣā*, p. 294.

[29] *Foundations*, p. 46.

[30] D. N. Bose, *Tantras—Their Philosophical and Occult Secrets*, Calcutta 1956, p. 137.

[31] The 'simple' meanings are wrong. There is much disagreement among Indian devotees as to the actual and metaphorical meaning of the *pañcamakāras*, the 'five M's'. Bose's enumeration is the one I have encountered among some Bengali and Maithili tantric laymen. I could not trace it in any tantric text I have seen.

[32] The book has 'mediation'; an obvious misprint which I corrected.

[33] *Guhyasamājatantra or Tathāgataguhyaka*, ed. B. Bhattacharya, *G.O.S.* LIII, p. 1. '*ekasmin samaye bhagavān sarvatathāgatakāya-vāk-citta-hṛdaya-vajrayoṣit-bhageṣu vijāhāra*.' This is one of the standard openings of Buddhist tantras, though the *Guhyasamāja* passage probably set the example. It is not contained in the *Manjuśrīmūlakalpa*, the one text usually thought to antedate the *Guhyasamāja*. It is contained in the opening of the *Hevajra Tantra*, Snellgrove, Vol. II, p. 2. The Tibetan text reads *bcom ldan 'das de bzin gśegs pa thams cad kyi sku daṅ gsuṅ dan thugs gyi sñin po rdo rje btsun mo'i bha ga la bžugso*. The *Yogaratnamālā* of Kāṇha, which Snellgrove published *in toto* in the second volume of his *Hevajra Tantra*, explains this passage '*tad eva vajrayoṣitāṃ Locanādinam bhagāḥ*', that is to say, the

vulvae of *vajra*-ladies like Lacana etc. (p. 103). Snellgrove's translation '. . . the Lord dwelt in bliss with the Vajrayoginī . . .' is modest, but misleading (I, p. 47).

[34] *Jñānasiddhi by Indrabhuti*, G.O.S., XLIV, p. 53. '*hṛdayaṃ jñānam tadeva vajrayoṣit, abhedya-prajñāsvabhāvatvāt, tadeva bhagaṃ sarva-kleśa-bhañjanāt.*' This may be a pun on *bhaga and bhañja*—.

[35] '*matriyonau liṇgaṃ kṣiptvā, bhaginiṣtanamardanam, gururmūrdhni pādaṃ dattvā punar janma na vidyate.*' In this form, the verse is found in Tarkālamkāra's commentary on the *Mahanirvāṇa Tantra*, quoted in *Tantric Texts* IX, p. 10. preface to the *Kulārṇava Tantra*, ed. A. Avalon.

[36] A contemporary American parallel might not be inapposite: the 'beatnik' poet tries to annoy the square by somewhat analogous devices. This comparison does not entail any sort of value judgment.

[37] H. Hoffmann, *Die Religionen Tibets*, pp. 60–1; he translates from the *Padma bka'than yig*.

[38] *Yoga*, pp. 251–2 (French ed.)

[39] The doctrine of the complete identity of *saṃsāra* and *nirvāṇa*; this notion stems from the Mādhyamika schools and was absorbed and emphasized in tantric Buddhism and even in the not strictly Buddhist *sahajayāna*.

[40] e.g., *vajra* for *śūnya*—two philosophical synonyms; *avadhūtī* (a female ascetic) for *yoginī*—two object-language synonyms.

[41] Bagchi, *Studies in the Tantras*, p. 28; D. L. Snellgrove, *Hevajra Tantra*, II, iii., pp. 60 ff.

[42] I am using ($\supset$) for 'implies' as the symbol commonly used in modern logic.

[43] Loc. cit., has various readings, *prenkhaṇam*, *prekhyaṇam*, *prekṣaṇam*, *preṃkhaṇam*, in the four manuscripts Snellgrove used.

[44] Not 'unworthy' as Snellgrove translates it (I, p. 99), nor 'worthy' for *abhavya* and *bhavya*, respectively. Edgerton lists 'unable' and 'able' (B.H.S. p. 45, 407); in harmony with the quasi-pragmatic notion of the Buddhist *artha-krīya-kāritva* 'non-existence' and 'existence' can certainly be implied; but the classical Sanskrit *bhavya* and *abhavya* as 'worthy' and 'unworthy' does not fit here. *Sandhābhāṣā* does not seem to contain any directly evaluative adjectives; and this chapter certainly contains none.

[45] Not 'herbs'; Snellgrove ignores the *sandhā-implication* (loc. cit.).

[46] Snellgrove (I, n. 100) translates 'blood'; I cannot see why.

[47] Snellgrove translates 'rice product' (loc cit.) and the Tibetan transcription *sa le dzam* warrants this interpretation. However, I prefer to follow Bagchi (*Studies in the Tantras*, p. 28.) who reads *alija*, as Snellgrove's reading would not show *sa ,dhābhāṣā*, 'rice-product' and 'human flesh' (*sālija* and *mahāmāṃsa*) being on the same level of discourse (vd. note 40 *ante*).

[48] *bola* and *kakkola* are tantric terms for the male and female organs of generation; they are not *sandhā*-terms, but euphemisms; *vajra* and *padma* would be *sandhā*-equivalents for *bola* and *kakkola*. When standing alone, either *vajra* or

padma implies the Absolute. But whenever there is a juxtaposition, as in this passage, the dual aspect of the Absolute, *upāya* and *prajñā*, or *karuṇa* and *śūnya*, is implied.

[49] A slight emendation seems to be called for at this point: Buddhist tantric texts use *lalanā*, *rasanā*, *avadhūtī* as their triad, but *iḍā*, *piṅgalā*, and *suṣumnā* also occur in Buddhist texts though rarely. Hindu tantras, on the other hand, use *iḍā*, *pingalā*, and *suṣumnā* exclusively. Lama Govinda uses *iḍā*, *pingalā* and *suṣumnā* throughout his *Foundations*; this is astonishing, for he takes great care to distinguish Hindu from Buddhist terminology.

[50] Vd. Shahidullah, *Les Chants Mystiques de Kāṇha et de Sarāhā*, Paris, 1928; H. P. Shastri, *Bauddhagan o Dohā* (vd. note 9); and a recent, excellent Hindi publication by R. Sankṛtyayana, *Siddha Sarāhapada kṛta Dohā Kośa*, Bihār Rāṣṭrabhāsā Pariṣad, Patna 1957; the last work contains the Tibetan text in Nagari transcription and the Apabhraṃsa texts, as well as a Hindi translation on the opposite page.

[51] This list has been amended and extended by Eliade and Snellgrove, in their *Yoga* and *Hevajra Tantra*, vd. Bibliography.

[52] *Yoga*, pp. 252–3.

[53] F. Edgerton, 'Prāṇa and Apāna', *J.O.A.S.*, 78, 1958, 51 ff.

[54] H. V. Glasenapp, *Buddhistische Mysterien*, Stuttgart 1940, p. 103.

[55] *G.O.S.*, Vol. LIII, pp. 11 ff. In the introduction, B. Bhattacharya gives his own interpretation of the passages. My own translation is more literal than his.

[56] Ibid., p. 11. *abhāve bhāvanābhāvo bhāvanā naiva bhāvanā/ iti bhāvo na bhāvaḥ syād bhāvanā nopalabhyate.*

[57] Ibid., p. 12. *sarva-bhāva-vigataṃ skandha-dhātvāyatana-grāhya-grāhaka-varjitaṃ dharma-nairātmya-samatayā svacittam-ādi-anutpannaṃ śūnyatā-bhāvam.*

[58] Ibid., p. 12. *anutpannā ime bhāvā na dharmā na ca dharmatā/ ākāśam-iva nairātmyam-idaṃ bondinayaṃ dṛḍham.*

[59] Ibid., p. 12. *abhāvāḥ sarva-dharmās-te dharma-lakṣaṇa-varjitāḥ/ dharma-nairātmya saṃbhūta idaṃ bodhinayam dṛḍham.*

[60] Ibid., p. 12. *anutpanneṣu dharmeṣu na bhāvo na ca bhāvanā/ ākāśa-pada-yogena iti bhāvaḥ pragīyate.*

[61] Ibid., p. 13. *prakṛti-prabhāsvarā dharmāḥ suviśuddhā nabhaḥsamāḥ/ na bodhir-nābhisamayam-idaṃ bodhinayaṃ dṛḍham.*

[62] *Guhyasiddhi* of Padmavajra, fol. 59 of a manuscript in the collection of the late H. P. Shastri at the Oriental Institute, Baroda; *bhage liṅgaṃ pratiṣṭhāpya bodhicittaṃ na cotsṛjet.* A similar passage is found in the section *Guṇa-vrata-nirdeśa* of the *Subhāṣita-saṃgraha*, quoted in Bendall, Museon, IV–V, Louvain 1905, 77: *niṣpīḍya kamale vajraṃ bodhicittaṃ notsṛjet.*

[63] Shahidullah, *Dohākośa* No. 5 *sahaje bodhicittaṃ jāyate śukram utpadyate.*

[64] *Prajñopāyaviniścayasiddhi*, 3rd Paṭala, G.O.S. XLIV, *mudrā-yogaṃ tataḥ kṛtvā ācāryaḥ subhagottamaḥ/ niveśya padmabhāṇḍe tu bodhicittaṃ jinālaye.*

7

ON INITIATION

BY THE Hindu or Buddhist devotees, the pattern of intentional language is viscerally understood; though none but the scholars among them could or would hazard speculations about the origins of intentional language, it is, as it were, unconsciously operational with them. The same, of course, holds for *mantra*. In a critical study like ours, therefore, it was necessary to establish the status of *mantra* and of intentional language, before proceeding to the fundamental routine of the Tantric devotees' career, *dīkṣā* or initiation.

The word *dīkṣā* is defined as 'preparation or consecration for a religious ceremony, undertaking religious observances for a particular purpose and the observances themselves (Atharvaveda and other Vedic passages); dedication, initiation (personified as the wife of Soma in Ṛgveda 25, 26); any serious preparation as for battle; self-devotion to a person or god, complete resignation or restriction to, exclusive occupation with'.[1] The underlying root is *dīkṣ*—to 'consecrate, dedicate', and it may be a rare desiderative of *dakṣ*—'to grow, to increase, to be able, to be strong'.

The word *dīkṣā* is used in all Indian vernaculars and is one of common though slightly sophisticated religious parlance everywhere, but it retains its connotation as 'spiritual initiation' only, in the modern languages, the other meanings being no longer covered by the word in any of the languages.

The dictionary omits the most important aspect of *dīkṣā*, however, i.e. that its content must be a *mantra* of some sort, or that a *mantra* must be part of its content. A person may be initiated into the use, say, of a *maṇḍala*, a *yantra*, or into the performance of a *yajña* (ritualistic sacrifice), but along with it a *mantra* is invariably imparted. Herein lies an important difference between *dīkṣā* and *abhiśekha* 'anointment' for the latter never requires the conferring of a *mantra* on the neophyte.

The notion and the practice of *dīkṣā* is common to Hinduism, Buddhism, and Jainism alike; tribal groups who were listed as 'animists' and do not belong to any of the three high religions also employ a sort of *dīkṣā*, probably in emulation of their Hindu surroundings; the Todas of the Nilgiris in south India impart a regular *mantra* to their sons, in analogy to the *upanayana* (investiture with the sacred thread) ceremony of the twice-born Hindus; instead of the Gāyatrī, a *mantra* commencing with '*UṂ*' is given to the boy, in the Toda language.

In the state of Mysore (Chikmaghlur District), there is a shrine on top of a mountain, called 'Dattātreyapīṭha', i.e. 'mound of the sage Dattātreya', who was, of course, a Hindu seer, connected with the worship of the Trimūrti (Brahmā, Viṣṇu, Maheśvara). The local story goes that due to some quarrels among the officiating priests, a Muslim *sufi*, Baba Qalandar Shah, was asked to look after the mound; the tradition was then kept alive, and a Muslim *mahant* (abbot) has been in charge of the Pīṭha up to this day. He is chosen by his predecessor and trained by him; he gives him *dīkṣā* after the training is completed and although I did not succeed in recording the *mantra* used by the present Muslim *mahant*, it was quite clearly a mixture of garbled Sanskrit and Arabic. Also, the devotees visiting the shrine are blessed by the *mahant*, with an invocation containing elements of both the languages—there is '*OṂ*' and '*Bismillāhī*' in the lengthy *mantra*. Along with it, the *mahant* gives '*prasād*'[2] in exactly the same manner as Hindu priests do.

The notion of *dīkṣā* provides us, as a semantic by-product so to speak, with a definition of a *guru*—for a *guru* is one who has received *dīkṣā* from one or more *gurus*,[3] is capable of conferring, and has actually conferred *dīkṣā* on another person or persons. All other qualifications—spiritual maturity, age, renown, learning, etc.—are marginal to *guru*-hood. If the question 'who is a *guru*?' is put to any practising Hindu, he will usually say 'one who gives *dīkṣā*'. As we shall see a bit further down, the formal conferring of *dīkṣā* is not always regarded as prerequisite of *guru*-hood—yet it is implicit even when there is no formal act.

The types of *dīkṣā* correlate with the *adhikāra* or 'specific entitlement' of the conferee.[4] A person receives the *dikṣā* of the divine form or principle which he is fit to worship or approach. One and the same *mantra* may be used in various *dīkṣās*, according to the spiritual *adhikāra* of the adept and to the purpose of the initiation. Thus, the *Mṛtyuñjaya-mantra*[5] is used for initiation into the worship of Śiva-Paśupati; into the worship of Ardhanārīśvara, i.e. the hermaphrodite form of Śiva; into the worship of the goddess as in the *Mahānirvāṇa Tantra*; for removing illnesses (or, rather, for initiating a person who wants to achieve the capacity to cure illnesses); among the Vīraśaivites of Mysore, to initiate a Jaṅgama, a Vīraśaivite monk, into the Order of Liṅgāyats; and to initiate a person into miscellaneous Śaivite and Śākta rituals.

The study of *adhikāra-bheda*[6] is part of the daily schedule in almost all monastic training institutions in India. What the students learn are chiefly the *lakṣaṇas* or 'signs' by which to recognize what person is capable for a particular rite, as also what kind of meditation, etc., is likely to yield proper results for a particular aspirant.

I shall now list some important categories of *dīkṣā*.[7]

The distinction made by some Indian authors[8] between 'group' and 'individual' initiation is not really functional, because *dīkṣā* is strictly a one-to-one interpersonal process between one *guru* and one disciple. The fact that several persons are frequently initiated at a time does not mean that a 'group' *dīkṣā* is involved; it is usually done for convenience's sake, especially if the *guru* is a famous and well-sought-after teacher who consents to give *dīkṣā* to hundreds of people every year. What actually happens in such cases is that he assembles those whom he regards as having the same *adhikāra*; he then gives them the common instruction jointly; but, subsequently, each of the aspirants comes up to him separately and he whispers the latter's particular *mantra* into his ear; but this is no 'group' *dīkṣā*. The Hindu and the Buddhist alike distinguish very sharply, though perhaps not in a formulated manner, between group instructions, individual instructions, and *dīkṣā*, which is always a one-to-one affair. Group and individual instruction (*upadeśa*) may seem, to the outsider, very similar to a formal *dīkṣā*; but it is never the same. *Upadeśa* does not have the spiritual power of *dīkṣā* nor has it any charismatic function. In the whole history of *dīkṣā*, there has actually been only one known case where something like a genuine group-*dīkṣā* took place. That was when the medieval founderof the Viśiṣṭādvaita School, Śrī Rāmānuja, proclaimed the *mantra* '*OṂ NAMO NĀRĀYAṆĀYA*' to all the peope assembled at the Śrīraṅgam shrine, flouting the injunction of his own *guru* to keep the *mantra* secret and to impart it only to deserving and well-tested individuals. The Sthalapurāṇa[9] then says 'the *ācārya* thus gave *dīkṣā* to all the hundreds, all the hundreds were thus initiated at once'. Similar stories are told about Rāmānuja's Bengali counterpart Śrī Caitanya Deva, the famous Vaiṣṇava reformer. The *Caitanya Caritāmṛta*[10] narrates how the saint initiated thousands at the threshold of the Jagannātha Temple in Puri (Orissa); but the narrative is a complete analogy to the Rāmānuja episode and it seems almost beyond doubt that it is a copy, whatever the authenticity of the former story had been. Learned Hindu opinion rejects any such possibility, for individual conferring of *dīkṣā* is felt to be part of its definition. What has been said about *mantra*[11] holds, *mutatis mutandis*, for *dīkṣā* as well.

The most frequent use of *dīkṣā* is what is synonymous with *mantra-dīkṣā*; 'initiation with a *mantra*'; any practising Hindu may seek it, and I would guess that at least one in a dozen high-caste Hindus have obtained *mantra-dīkṣā* of some sort. The *gurus* are not always monks—some of them are householders who have acquired fame as spiritual teachers. This is how it works: a person feels the desire for 'spiritual practice',[12] goes for *darśan*[13] to several teachers and listens to them. He soon singles out the one whose teaching and personality appeal the most to him, and then he tries to get that teacher interested in him—he visits him frequently, brings gifts of food and clothing, and sounds his views about the possibility of *dīkṣā*. There is a lot of literature on this type of spiritual courtship.[14] When the prospective *guru* has acknowledged the *adhikāra* (spiritual qualification) of the prospective disciple, he selects an auspicious day for the ceremony by matching the horoscopes of the aspirant with his own and with the respective '*devatithi*'; this 'date of the deity' is the day and the hour in which any particular deity is easily accessible for worship. Establishing the *adhikāra* of an aspirant is virtually identical with finding the latter's *iṣṭadevatā*, i.e. the deity or divine aspect, meditating on which the aspirant will find congenial; and each deity as well as every divine aspect has its own *mantra*—this has to be imparted to the disciple at the right time.

At the appointed time, the disciple gets ready. He has to fast for twelve hours previous to his *dīkṣā*. He takes some fruits or some other presents as *dakṣiṇā* or sacrificial fee to the *guru*; princes usually give a gold *mohur* (seal), modern business men frequently hand a cheque on the prescribed *pātra* or tray—all in elaboration of the Vedic injunction that the *guru* has to be approached *samitpāṇi* (with firewood in the student's hand); poor aspirants may just bring a coconut or two plantains.

The initiation must take place at the *guru's* place. The *guru* sits facing the east or the south, with the disciple facing him. The *guru* first invokes his own *iṣṭadevatā* (chosen deity) and offers *puṣpāñjali*, a flower oblation. He then instructs the disciple in the mode of worship, the preliminary rituals, and warns him to keep the *mantra* secret; in certain cases, he also instructs the disciple on *prāṇāyāma* (breath control), *dhāraṇa* (fixing the mind on one point), and other techniques belonging to the general yogic tradition. He does not usually instruct him about *āsana*, 'sitting posture', for this is supposed to have been mastered before the *dīkṣā* takes place. Then the *guru* whispers the *mantra* into the disciple's right ear repeating it three times, and has it repeated three times by the disciple, first singly, then at one stretch.[15] The *mantra* must not be written down, else it loses its effect just as it would were it communicated by the disciple to another person previous to the attainment of its *siddhi* (fruition), that is to say, the *mantra* can be passed on in the process of *dīkṣā* only when the disciple has become a *guru* in his own turn after the *mantra* has yielded its results through continued practice; in the insiders' terminology, after he has become a *siddha* in his *mantra.*

The *mantra* having been imparted, the central part of the initiation is over. In some traditions, the *dakṣiṇā* (*guru's* fee) is handed to the *guru* only now. Finally, the initiate prostrates before the *guru* in the *daṇḍavat* manner, 'like a stick', i.e. lying flat on his face, his forehead touching the *guru's* feet. The disciple then rises to his feet, circumambulates the *guru* three times, and receives some *prasād* (sanctified food) from the *guru*—very often from the plate of food touched by the *guru* himself—thus converting it into *prasād.*

The initiate now leaves, worships at the shrine, takes another bath (he has, of course, taken a bath previous to approaching the *guru* for *dīkṣā*), and withdraws.

The process itemized here holds more or less for all kinds of *dīkṣā*, but some features are added in some other *dīkṣā* types: contemporary *mahants* (abbots) of the Sannyāsi and Udāsi Orders in northern India, as well as the Nāth Order in Nepal and Gorakhpur, hold that there are three fundamental categories of *dīkṣā*:

(a) the *yoga-dīkṣā*, initiating a person into the practices of *haṭha-* and *laya-yoga*; this is not a *dīkṣā* in the strict sense, for no *mantra* is given, although the Gāyatrī, the Mṛtyuñjaya, and other Vedic *mantras* are occasionally recited or meditated upon during these practices;

(b) the *upayoga-dīkṣā*, i.e. the *dīkṣā* for a particular (usually secular) purpose (*upayoga*); here, a *mantra* is given;

(c) the *jñāna-dīkṣā*, 'initiation leading to intuitive knowledge', this is reserved for monks and monastic novices. The *mantra* is that of the impersonal Brahman or Absolute; interestingly, the Brahman is referred to as *iṣṭadevatā* in this context just like the personal deities or the personal aspects of a particular deity.

These Orders as well as most of the practising Hindus stipulate the possibility of a *Śāṃbhavī-dīkṣā*, i.e. a '*dīkṣā* given (directly) by Śiva' (the term is used even by worshippers of Viṣṇu, for Śiva is the god of meditative praxis). This notion seems to arise from the presence of persons who satisfy all the phenomenological criteria of a *siddha*, or who have spontaneously achieved a spiritual status which can otherwise be reached only through the prescribed process: *dīkṣā*—practice of *mantra*—fruition of the *mantra*. In such a case, Śiva himself is said to have given the *mantra* to the person in question. The most fascinating, and, in Bengali and other active modern Hindu circles, best-known case of a *Śāṃbhavī-dīkṣā* was the conversion of the young Naren Datta into the later Swami Vivekananda. The *Rāmakṛṣṇa Caritāṃṛta*, compiled by the schoolmaster who recorded the events round the Bengali saint Śrī Ramakrishna Paramahamsa, tells us how one morning the great saint placed his foot on the chest of the unwary and unaware young man from the worldly city of Calcutta; Naren fainted and lost consciousness for a long time. When he woke from this state of deep trance, the young man was a transformed soul. This event was later on retold by the *Swami* himself, and it is referred to as a standard instance of a *Śāṃbhavī-dīkṣā*, the moral of this frequent reference being that these things happen even in our own urban age. Disciples of the late Ramana Maharshi, at that sage's *ashram* in South India, write and tell similar tales of their own immediate experiences in the vicinity of the saint: much of it is too similar to the above-mentioned report about the conversion of the young Naren to preclude the likelihood of acquaintance with the prototypical event. The Ramakrishna Mission is an all-Indian and an international institution, and devotees of that organization have sought out other saints of the modern Hindu Renaissance. The words of Ramakrishna have been translated into English, the works of Swami Vivekananda were partly written in English by the Swami, and at this time hagiological information and communication throughout modern India is perfectly amazing—all the professional 'saints' in the India of our day, consciously or unconsciously, imitate Swami Vivekananda.

Initiation into the worship of specific deities does not always mean that the initiate desires to obtain any particular boon from that deity. Quite frequently, worship for worship's sake needs a *dīkṣā*, especially where a person is not entitled to a specific worship which he would like to perform, by birth and caste. In Tamilnad, we have the Śiva-Tikṣai, i.e. Tamil for the Sanskrit *Śivadīkṣā*; it is the ceremony whereby a person is made fit to worship Śiva in accordance with the rules laid down by the *Śaiva-Āgama* texts. These texts divide Śaivites into four groups: those who have received *Camaya* (Sanskrit *Samaya*) or occasional *dīkṣā*; those who have received *viśeṣā*—or special *dīkṣā*; those who have received *Nirvāṇa*—or 'emancipation'—*dīkṣā* (identical probably with the *jñānadīkṣā* of the northern schools); and '*acarigay*', i.e. 'preceptor's' *dīkṣā* which includes the anointment as an *acariyar* or preceptor, capable of bestowing any of the three other *dīkṣās*. Such a person must be an '*Aticaivar*' (Sanskrit *Ādiśaiva*), in order to have the *adhikāra* for such exalted functions; i.e. he must be descended from the *gotras* (patriclans) of the five *ṛṣis* (seers) who were born from the five faces of Śiva, i.e. Kauśika, Bharadvāja, Kaśyapa, Gautama, and Agastya.[16]

The Vīraśaivites of Mysore[17] are given *dīkṣā* at least twice in their lives, at birth and at the age of eight. Śiva who resides in the disciple is 'extracted' by the *guru* and returned to him, together with the appropriate *mantra*, in the shape of a *liṅga* which he carries round his neck forthwith and which he worships in his daily observance.[18]

In the same sect, there is also a kind of temporary *dīkṣā* during which the initiate is 'bound', because *dīkṣā* contains the tying of *kappu* or *kaṅkanam*[19]—when the *kappu* is removed, the *dīkṣā* and its obligations are thereby also rescinded.[20]

The Tamilian manual for temple worship by Akoracivacariyar says: 'worship of Śiva is twofold, viz. *ātmārtham* and *parārtham*. *Ātmārtham* is worship to receive benefit for one's own self and *parārtham* is worship on behalf of and for the benefit of others'.[21] *Ātmārtham* may be performed by anyone who has received *dīkṣā* and has as its object of contemplation the *liṅga* received from the *guru* during the *dīkṣā* ceremony, or a temporary earthen *liṅga*.

Parārtha is worship of other *liṅgas* in temples and other sacred places. The two terms, however, do not stand for different sets of rites like home rites and temple rites, for *ātmārtha* as well as *parārtha* is performed bilaterally at home and in the temple; but both types of worship are confined to persons who are qualified to officiate through *dīkṣā*.

Abhināvagupta's *Tantrasāra* gives an epitome of *dīkṣā* in its first chapter after enumerating the qualifications of a *guru*. The text says that *dīkṣā* is 'the giving of *mantra* by the *guru*'. At the time of initiation the *guru* must first establish the 'life of the *guru* in his own body';[22] this 'life' is the 'vital force' (*prāṇaśakti*) of the Supreme *Guru* (i.e. Śiva) whose abode is in the thousand-petalled lotus. As an instrument wherein divinity is symbolized, a *yantra* (mystical diagram) is used, and the body of the *guru* is meditated upon as an additional symbol, by the disciple. The day prior to the actual *dīkṣā* the *guru* should seat the prospective initiate on a mat of *kuśa*-grass. He then does *japa* of a 'sleep'-*mantra* (*suptamantra*) into the candidate's ear, and ties his hair-tuft into a knot. The disciple, who should have fasted and abstained from sexual activities of any sort, repeats the *mantra* three times, prostrates himself before the *guru*, and then retires to rest. Initiation, which follows (the next day) 'gives spiritual knowledge and destroys sin'. 'As one lamp is lit at the flame of another [lamp], so the divine Śakti, consisting of the *mantra*, is communicated from the *guru's* body to that of the disciple. Without *dīkṣā*, *japa* or the *mantra*, *pūjā*, and other rituals are entirely useless.' (ibid.)

The preliminary ceremony described here by Abhināvagupta is not known by me to be in vogue; possibly this refers to a Kashmirian *dīkṣā* variant, as do many of the injunctions given by the Kashmiri teacher. The procedure in vogue at the present time is outlined at the end of this chapter, based on a recent text.

The idea of initiation is as old as the Veda, although the term *dīkṣā* is not used until much later; however, the more general term *saṃskāra* very frequently has the same connotation as *dīkṣā*. The most important and ubiquitous *saṃskāra* is the investiture with the sacred thread, the *upanayana*, which I would class as a *dīkṣā* without any hesitation. The ceremony clusters round the *gāyatrī-mantra* which is imparted to the student.[23] The *brahmacārin* (initiand) used to reside and board at the *guru's* house and render many personal services such as 'tending the fire and the cows' of the teacher. The *Chandogya Upaniṣad* (iv. 4.) gives an elaborate account of the rules for admitting a disciple. In the *Maitrayānī Upaniṣad*, certain types of persons are dissuaded from seeking initiation, and the relevant instruction for the prospective *guru-s* is 'this knowledge should not be imparted to a skeptic, one who is not clean, etc., etc.[24] Professor R. B. Pandey, one of the best known authorities of Hindu ritual in India, uses 'initiation' throughout for *saṃskāra*—he never uses the word '*dīkṣā*' as it has a distinct tantric flavour.[25]

The most authoritative Hindu tantric text dealing with *dīkṣā* is no doubt the oft-mentioned *Mahānirvāṇa Tantra*;[26] the tenth chapter which comprises two hundred and twelve verses deals exclusively with *dīkṣā*. This work has been accepted as the most important scripture among the Śāktas of Eastern India. It was probably written in the seventh century, and Śaṃkarācārya appears to have been acquainted with it. It contains a few references to Mahācīna and there can be no doubt that the authors were conversant with earlier Buddhist tantric literature. Certain pre-initiatory vows listed in that chapter are strongly reminiscent of the *bodhisattva*-covenant.[27]

On the Buddhist side itself there is a vast amount of *dīkṣā*-literature, preserved mostly in Tibetan with sporadically extant passages in Buddhist Hybrid Sanskrit; no Vajrayāṇa text omits copious instruction about *dīkṣā*. Anaṅgavajra's *Prajñopāyaviniścayasiddhi*[28] advocates *dīkṣā* which involves lefthanded rites. It says here that the preceptor should be approached by the disciple accompanied by the *Mahāmudrā*, the great female co-adept,[29] who appears 'charming to the sight and who is profusely decked with ornaments.' The disciple then worships the preceptor with a lengthy eulogy, after which he requests the latter to bestow *dīkṣā* upon him so that he may forthwith be regarded as belonging to the *kula* ('family') of the Buddhas, as their true offspring. The *guru*, after having ascertained the spiritual qualification (*adhikāra*) of the postulant, grants the requisite *dīkṣā* after associating the disciple carnally with the Mahāmudrā in the presence of the *kula*-assembly. Finally, the *guru* imparts the five *mantras* of the *dhyāni*-Buddhas to the neo-initiate, and instructs him on *saṃvara*, the restraint imposed on all *bodhisattva-s* not to enter *nirvāṇa* themselves, but to continue taking birth and guiding mankind.

Partly as a feed-back from the literature of the Westernized Hindu Renaissance into the vernacular, and partly no doubt as a continuation of the tradition of commentary, we find that learned and pious Hindus during the past two decades have been making increasing use of manuals, short statements, and of succinct instructional material published by specialists in the vernacular. A very fine specimen of this trend is Pandit Ramadatt Shukla's booklet, *Hindi Tantrasāra*, 'the essence of *tantra* in Hindi'.[30]

In a conversational, yet by no means unsystematic, style the author provides us with a check list, so to speak, of material pertinent to *dīkṣā*. Rather than giving a literal translation of this lengthy section, covering over fourteen pages of close type, I shall conclude this chapter with an excerpt from Shukla's *dīkṣā* chapter, following the original as closely as possible. The repetition of *mantra* without *dīkṣā*, is bad, he says; through *dīkṣā* divine knowledge is acquired and sins are destroyed, therefore initiation is called *dīkṣā* (one of the age-old *ad hominem* folklore etymologies which are so popular in India: '*dī-*', a morpheme similar to *divya* ('divine'), and '*kṣa*', the morpheme identical with the root '*kṣi*' ('to destroy')—*mantras* which are used from sight, after having seen them in a book, are fruitless and will not yield results in thousands of years unless a *guru* has imparted them.

Mantras given to *śūdras*, members of the low caste in the orthodox structure, must not contain the *mantra OṂ*; the *gāyatrī*, and the *mantra* of the goddess Lakṣmī are forbidden for the *śūdra*. Quoting the *Varāhī-tantra* the author then says that *śūdras* are entitled to the *mantras* of Gopāla (a name of Kṛṣṇa), the goddess Durgā, the sun-god, and the god Gaṇesa.

He then gives a very large section to the consideration of the astrological data pertinent to the initiation of any individual. In addition to this, omens of various kinds are either conducive or detrimental to successful initiation; for instance the dreamed sight of an elephant, a bull, a rosary, the ocean, a snake, a tree, a mountain, a horse, a mango, meat, alcoholic beverage, are auspicious, and forbode *siddhi* (spiritual success).

A day before *dīkṣā* is to be given, the *guru* should call his disciple and, having seated him on a clean *kuśāsan* (a seat made of a specific kind of grass), he should bind the disciple's hairtuft, pronouncing the following *mantra: oṃ hili hili śūlapāṇaye svāhā.* Then the disciple should repeat this *mantra* three times when he goes to bed, and carefully avoiding any nocturnal emission he should meditate upon the *guru* and should sleep on a bed made of *kuśa*-grass again, he should remember what dreams he has had and should report them to the *guru* in the morning.

Some months of the year are auspicious for *dīkṣā* others are not; most tantric texts hold that February/March are highly auspicious, and the hot months are inauspicious or at least dangerous. Similarly, certain days of the week are auspicious others are not: *dīkṣā* on Sunday brings wealth, on Monday peace, on Tuesday early ageing, on Wednesday it gives physical beauty, on Thursday it gives wisdom, on Friday good luck, and on Saturday it brings about the destruction of fame and glory. Analogous recommendations and cautions for the various dates of the month, the various moon phases, etc., follow.

The place for *dīkṣā* should be a cowpen, the house of the *guru*, a temple, a forest, a garden, the banks of a river, a mango or *vilva* tree, the foot of a mountain, and, of course, the shores of the Ganges—these places make *dīkṣā* 'ten million times successful'. The following locations are forbidden for *dīkṣā*: Gaya, the famous Buddhist shrine and the Hindu shrine connected with obsequial rites, (qv. the chapter on Pilgrimage), certain regions of Assam, East Pakistan (Chittagong), and some other geographical locations.

However, in the concluding lines of this study Shukla declares (page 8 quoting the *Samaya-tantra*): 'whenever the Lord *Guru*, out of his own sweet will, calls his disciples and gives them the *mantra*, then there is no need for considering auspicious signs, astrological perquisites, etc. At such a time, the day, the constellation, the stars, the place, and the location—all of these are auspicious.' And this is an ancient, typical, and unchanged procedure: the proper authority, the most highly qualified persons, have superceded the restrictions incumbent on all those who have not achieved his status.

NOTES

[1] Monier Williams, p. 480.

[2] The food offered to the deity of the shrine (Dattātreya and Anusūyā in this case) which is then distributed among the audience—a *sine qua non* of all religious ceremonies in India.

[3] Any number of *dīkṣā-s* is permissible, and necessary for different purposes. The Skaṅdapurāṇa tells the story of the Avadhūta monk who was given *dīkṣā* by no less than thirty-three *gurus* (i.e. thirty-three *dīkṣās*), one of whom was a crow.

[4] The problem of *adhikāra* in tantric literature and practice has been dealt with in the Chapters on *Mantra* and on Intentional Language.

[5] '*Tryaṃbakaṃ yajāmahe sugandhiṃ puṣṭivardhanam, uruvārukamiva bandhānanmṛtyor mukṣīya māmṛtāt*'. 'We worship the three-eyed one, the fragrant, the increaser of growth, liberate us from death like the Uruvāka flower is (liberated) from its bondage, but not (i.e. don't separate us) from immortality'. This *mantra* is quoted both in Vedic and tantric literature.

[6] 'Distinction as to the individual adept's capacity'—i.e., for a particular kind of ritual or meditation.

[7] The *Mantramahārṇava* lists over two hundred classes of *dīkṣā*.

[8] B. Bhattacharya, V. Bhattacharya, R. B. Pandey.

[9] Each south Indian and many north Indian temples have a text kept by the headpriest, which gives the mythological and historical background of the sanctuary and which is recited once a year together with the canonical texts—this is the *Sthalapurāṇa*, i.e. 'Purāṇa of the Place'.

[10] Bangiya Sahitya Parishad, Calcutta.

[11] See previous chapter 'On Mantra'.

[12] This term is used throughout by English-speaking Hindus—it is the rendering of the Indian '*abhyāsa*', which has acquired exactly the same connotation as Greek *askēsis*.

[13] Literally 'sight', i.e. visiting a great man, particularly a religious teacher or a deity in a shrine.

[14] In English translation, the 'Gospel of Ramakrishna', published Ramakrishna, Math, Mylapore, Madras, translated by Swami Nikhilananda, provides an excellent example of this ancient tradition.

[15] 'A' standing for the *guru*'s utterance, 'B' for the disciple's repetition—the procedure is thus: AB, AB, AB, AAA BBB.

[16] Kāmikāgama, preface of Sanmuka Suntarar; Gopinatha Rao, 'Elements of Hindu Iconography', II, 1–10 ff.

[17] A sect founded by Bāsavācārya in the fourteenth century; they are strictly dualistic monotheists and deny the element of Śakti altogether, which opposes them to the other southern Śaivites who proclaim the total identity of the Śiva and Śakti principles.

[18] Vd. Nandinath, *A Handbook of Vīraśaivism*, 66 ff.

[19] These are strings of *darbha*-grass tied around the wrist or the neck; the string tied around the wrists of bride and groom during the Vīraśivite wedding ceremony is also called '*kaṅkanam*'.

[20] This removal is called '*tiksai nivarti*' in Tamil, i.e. '*dīkṣā nivṛtti*'.

[21] Akoracivacariyar, *Śrī Parartta Nittiya Pujaviti*, 1.

[22] Abhināvagupta, *Tantrasāra* 1, '*svadehe gurujīvanaṃ sthāpayedguruḥ*', which means that he has to verify intuitively whether he is fit to give *dīkṣā* at this particular time and occasion.

[23] '*Om bhūr bhuvaḥ svah tatsavitur vareṇyam bhargo devasya dhīmahi dhiyo yo naḥ pracodayāt*'. Frequent in all four Vedas.

[24] Maitrayāni Up., Chi. 1, '*asūyakāyānṛjave 'yatāya. . .* ;' vd. also R. B. Pandey, *Hindu Saṃskāras*, p. 9.

[25] Professor Pandey is a sympathizer of the Ārya Samāj, a modern sect which tries to reinstate the Veda as sole authority and is extremely antagonistic towards the tantric tradition.

[26] The *Mahānirvāṇa Tantra* has been translated into English tolerably well by A. Avalon and the edition is easily available, published by Ganesh & Co., Madras 1953; I therefore do not quote from the said tenth chapter which contains a solid number of rules pertaining to '*dīkṣā*'.

[27] E.g. to resist entering *nirvāṇa*, for the benefit of mankind.

[28] G.O.S. edition, p.3.

[29] Note the conscious hypostasy and identification of the cosmic principle with the female co-initiate.

[30] Ramadatt Shukla, *Hindī Tantrasār*; Kalyan Mandir, Katra, Allahabad 1958, Chapter '*Dīkṣā—Prakaraṇ*'. This work, of course, has not much but the title in common with the famous Sanskrit treatise *Tantrasāra* by Abhināvagupta.

8

POLARITY SYMBOLISM IN TANTRIC DOCTRINE AND PRACTICE

IT MIGHT seem strange to some students of comparative religion that the section on religious symbolism should follow that on initiation; academical methodology might suggest that the theoretical or ideological parts of a particular study should come first, or last, or should, at any rate, be kept together rather than spread over the whole study. However, academical methodology, when conceived as a rigid mould, tends to be not only sterile but very often misleading. This would be the case particularly in our investigation: tantrism is so heterogeneous in its constituent themes and so erratic, or at least adventitious, in its literary and in its operational institutions—if indeed we can speak of such institutions—that a preconceived methodology, informed by the study of simpler and more organized forms of religion in India and elsewhere, would be insufficient and erroneous. Thus, it may seem to the unwary student of comparative religion that symbolism should be bracketed with philosophy, or with the linguistic contents of a religion. This cannot be done here, because the polarity symbolism which we are going to investigate in this chapter is much less a conceptual construct than it is a configuration or, to use a down-to-earth expression, a shooting target for the tantric initiate. It is not presupposed by him in the way in which he presupposes an absolutistic world-view; rather, it is worked out by him as a consequence of his initiation; and it is for this reason that this section must follow that on *dīkṣā*.

The problem of the present section is this: both Hindu and Buddhist tantrism visualize their respective noumena[1] as a supreme non-duality (e.g. *advaita* in Vedāntic Hinduism and *advaya* in tantric Buddhism), which can be expressed only in terms of a diametrical polarity due to the common axiomatic notion that the supreme is inexpressible and non-communicable in itself, i.e. that it is totally transcendent (or totally immanent, which amounts to the same in Indo-Asian religious thought). The tantrics have chosen the one paradigm that is no doubt singularly fitting, both from a psychological and a mythological angle, to illustrate this polarity, i.e. man and woman, or rather man and woman in their cosmicized version, god and goddess. Thus the creative—or, to be more precise, the emanative—function of the noumenon is polarized into the static and the dynamic aspect, a speculation common to all ancient cosmosophies in one way or the other. The Indian and the Tibetan mystagogue had to assign these aspects to either the male or the female, respectively, and the initial choice was, to my feeling, arbitrary: whoever came first among the system builders in the tantric tradition, Buddhist or Hindu, probably assigned the static principle to the male, the kinetic principle to the female, or vice versa: the later systematizers, whose loyalties were with the other religion, might have inverted these respective ascriptions, either intentionally or more or less unconsciously.

On the surface, then, the situation is this: the Hindus assigned the *static* aspect to the male principle, the *dynamic* aspect to the female principle. The tantric Buddhists in India (Luipā, Sarāhapā, Indrabhūti, Lakṣmīṅkarā) were not quite at one between themselves about this assignment, but they tended to fall in line with the non-Buddhist trends round them, for it seems probable that the matrifocal atmosphere in which they flourished (Bengal in the East, Oḍḍiyāṇa in the west—the latter being linked with an Amazon-like tribe in the legend) was indirectly conducive to assigning the *dynamis* to woman.[2] The Indian and Tibetan

Buddhist tantrics did the opposite of the Brahmin paṇḍitas: they assigned the dynamic aspect to the male, the static to the female principle.

Finally, both the Indian and the Tibetan theologians alike assigned 'wisdom', 'realization', 'beatitude'—in short, all cognitive terms of spiritual consummation—to the static, and 'compassion', 'method', 'energy', etc., i.e. all conative terms in this universe of discourse, to the dynamic. This is the situation from which we have to proceed in our investigation, for it is axiomatic for all concerned: the Hindu pandit—regardless of his sectarian affiliations or sympathies—identifies 'power', 'energy', etc., with the feminine—*śakti* is a feminine noun—and *śakti* is the proper epithet of all Hindu, Buddhist, and Jain goddesses for him: he is not aware that the term *śakti* does not apply to Buddhist tantric female deities. When a Brahmin guide explains the various female deities on the Vajrayoginī temple at Khajuraho, he calls them 'some *śakti*'; so do all other Hindu scholars, however learned. The reason for this seems quite simple: Mahāyāna and tantric Buddhism have been historically so much removed from modern Hinduism that their languages and their nomenclature have become totally alien to the Hindu scholar. By extension of Hindu semantical usage, any female deity would be called a *śakti* regardless of her denominational provenance. The imperturbable, static, supreme principle of pure wisdom is male, it is *śiva*. The contrary notion obtains with the Tibetan scholar[3] for this follows from his ubiquitous identification of wisdom (Tibetan *śes rab*, Sanskrit *prajñā*) with the cosmic mother (Tibetan *yum*) and of the 'means' (Tibetan *thabs*, Sanskrit *upāya*) with the cosmic father (Tibetan *yab*); the latter is invariably a form of the Buddha, and the former is being called a 'Buddha-Śakti' by Indians or indologists—a wrong term, but deeply ensconced in Indian religious parlance.

Among scholars, two views have been held—that Buddhism was influenced by non-Buddhist Indian tantric or similar ideas in the process of creating the Vajrayāṇa school which was then transplanted into Tibet; the other, more recent and nowadays more usually accepted view is that tantric notions, especially the ones using sexual polarity symbolism, are originally Buddhist and that the left-handed Hindu tantric schools derived their inspiration from them. Both views have much to commend them and the final word has yet to be said.

I have come to hold a slightly modified view, with regard to this problem. I think that the Vajrayāṇa Buddhists created or absorbed two types of deities, chiefly female, i.e. genuine '*Śaktis*' in the Indian sense, female 'energies' which retain their purely dynamic function in Tibetan Vajrayāṇa (e.g. *rdo rje phag mo*—Vajravarāhī, 'the Vajra-Sow'); and also, goddesses who embody the theologically genuine Vajrayāṇa concept of the static *yum* (cosmic mother) who is also *śes rab* (*prajñā*, total wisdom), viz. the quiescent apotheosized Prajñāpāramitā. I also think that many of these deities belong to the popular, pre-systematized pantheon of Indian origin: 'Indian' as opposed to the hazardous standard dichotomy of 'Aryan' versus 'Dravidian'. To use the anthropological terminology of modern Indian and western scholars, many of these deities belong to what M. N. Srinivas and many of his American colleagues call the 'little tradition', the 'big-and-little tradition' terminology going back to Redfield and Radcliffe-Brown.

My argument rests on certain iconographical observations: there are numerous icons which show the goddess trampling or dancing on a male deity. The *dhyānas* (meditations or visualizations prescribed for the initiate) of these goddesses always describe the situation as a potentially hostile or toxic one,[4] as trampling down and dancing upon some demon or, in tune with the anti-Hindu-pantheon attitude of the Vajrayāṇa iconographer, on some Hindu god, thus annihilating him. But the Vajrayāṇist was never conscious of a totally different alternative significance which might have been underlying the models for these icons. In the Hindu *Śākta* tradition, the goddess dances on Śiva, her spouse—not to destroy him, but to symbolize, for the devotee, the basis of its cosmosophy: *śivaḥ śaktivihīnaḥ śavaḥ* 'Śiva without Śakti is a corpse——' (*Mahānirvāṇa*, *Kulārṇava*, etc.) the great dictum of Hindu tantrics.

Dancing upon the male might not seem to be an act of excessive tenderness on supercilious scrutiny, but it ties in with the secular Indian notions of *sṛṅgāra*, the erotic sentiment. Copulation in which the female partner takes the active part, *maithuna viparīta* (lit. obverse intercourse), is mentioned in all classical tracts of erotic didactical literature (*Kāmaśāstra*), and the phrase 'dancing upon the lover' is said to occur in pre-Sanskritized Tamil literature.[5] The pattern seems to be well ingrained in the naive poetic sentiment of contemporary devotees of the tantric tradition.[6]

One particular Buddhist icon seems to lend strong support to my view. It represents a goddess Gaṇapatihṛdayā, 'she who is the heart of Gaṇeśa' or 'she whose heart is Gaṇeśa', i.e. who constantly meditates on Gaṇeśa.[7] Here, a Hindu deity—the popular god Gaṇeśa, son of Śiva and Ūmā, has been matched with a true *śakti*. Her *dhyāna* reads: 'Gaṇapatihṛdayā is one-faced, two-armed, exhibits the boon-granting gesture and that of fearlessness, and she is in a dancing attitude.' On the other hand, the much more famous Buddhist goddess Aparājitā tramples upon Gaṇeśa in the true Vajrayāṇa fashion when it comes to dealing with Hindu deities. This dual phenomenon seems to prove my point: the Buddhist tantrics utilized two different types of goddesses—pure Indian *śaktis* (like Aparājitā), which preserve their dynamic function in their new Vajrayāṇa locale, as well as other Indian, Buddhist and non-Buddhist models (like Tārā or Locanā) which came to function in a manner more representative of the polarizing doctrine of Vajrayāṇa (as Prajñāpārāmitā, Nairṭyā, etc.): these goddesses came to be purely Buddhist in conception, they fulfil the notion of absolute quiescence, and are far removed from the offices of a *śakti*. Iconographically, these are shown in a sitting posture. Now our rather exciting Gaṇapatihṛdayā seems to me to hold a middling position, and I would suggest that goddesses of her type represent a transitional stage: they stand between the non-Buddhist Indian *śakti* and the purely Buddhist (especially the Tibetanized) *prajñā* (*śes rab*) concept.

Summing up this problem, Tibetan Buddhism must have had the choice, originally, to attribute the dynamic function to either the male or the female cosmic principle, because both patterns were then available in Indian models. We shall then have to guess why Tibetan Buddhism finally ascribed the dynamic function to the male principle, the static function to the female principle. Three possible causes could be averred as influential on a first glance, i.e. Indian, perhaps Chinese, and autochthonous shamanist (Bon). My own feeling is that the Indian models, although they were negligible in the purely Indian context, would have sufficed to cause the respective canonical ascriptions of the Tibetan Buddhists. As I said earlier, the original ascription was probably arbitrary; this, however, is an anthropological statement, as it were. It cannot suffice for an analysis on a more abstract level, and this is one of the cases where indology has to fall back on the time-honoured devices of Indian classical philology.

Let us commence with the pre-Buddhist situation in India. The polarity has its philosophical background in the Sāṃkhya system, the oldest systematized metaphysical school in India. Its founder Kapila—if he were an historical personality at all—might have flourished in the eighth century B.C., for any but the two oldest Upaniṣads (i.e. the Bṛhadāranyaka and the Chandogya) either refer to him by name or they show strong traces of Sāmkhya ideology. The most important codification of the Sāṃkhya system is due to Īśvarakṛṣṇa, who lived in the second century A.D. Sāṃkhya is a radically dualistic philosophy; it explains the universe as consisting of two and only two principles, i.e. inert nature (*prakṛti*) and the pure, conscious principle (*puruṣa*). Whatever happens in the universe, happens in and through *prakṛti*; *puruṣa* does not act—it is the pure witness. *Prakṛti*, however, could not act—or more precisely, nothing can happen in *prakṛti*, which is the repository of all actions—if *puruṣa* were not there. The analogy would be, in chemical terminology, that of a catalyzing agent. No Sāṃkhya philosopher ever tried to explain the paradox; it seems to be a postulate of intuition rather than of discursive reasoning.

Now the proto-Indian, or at least the pre-Aryan, cultures of India were replete with mother-worship; it was the female deity that ranked supreme, and that encroached on the Vedic doctrine of the Aryan invaders and settlers, whose own religion was patriarchal in the extreme, hostile to the *magna mater* atmosphere which they encountered at every step of their advance, and which made them assign a somewhat trifling position to goddesses. But in the course of time the powerful feminism in worship and ritual, autochthonous in India, reasserted itself and modified the Vedic notions of male supremacy to an ever greater extent.[8] On the philosophical side, the dualistic *Weltanschauung* of the Sāṃkhya which was in vogue with a large section of the sophisticated of pre-Buddhist India, tied in handsomely with the older, indigenous predilection. We do not know how and when popular imagery and speculative proclivity blended into the tantric pattern, but one fact emerges with clarity: *Prakṛti*, the active principle, *natura naturans*, and the goddess of pre-Aryan India were merged into that Indian religious style which we encounter forthwith; and so were the inactive conscious, witnessing *puruṣa* and the (Vedic?) male deity. The indigenous element having reasserted itself, it found its most refined diction in the words of the tantric scholar and the poet, based on what by his time had become fundamental doctrine[9]: 'If Śiva is united with Śakti, he is able to exert his powers as lord; if not, the god is not able to stir. Hence to you (the Goddess), who must be propitiated by Hari, Hara, Virañci (Brahmā), and the other gods, how can one who has not acquired merit be fit to offer reverence and praise?'

Another ancient paradigm of the cosmic woman as agent is the myth of Viṣṇu as Mohinī, the seductress,[10] which is as old as anything in the Indian tradition could be. When the milk-ocean was churned by the gods and the demons, and the immortality drink (*amṛta*) had been finally obtained, the gods and the demons were to get an equal share by previous contract.[11] In order to prevent the demons from getting their rightful portion of the potent potion, Viṣṇu assumed the guise of the great enchantress (Mohinī), and danced between the gods and the demons, dispensing the nectar to the gods as she whirled round; by the time the demons realized what the dancer was up to, it was too late.

The idea that woman has to initiate courtship is probably pre-Aryan Indian. It was the most tenacious of all related ideas—up to this very day Sanskrit and Sanskritized poetics (*kāvyaśāstram*) prescribe that the girl has to come to the tryst and prepare the rendezvous—this is the concept of the *abhisārikā* (lit. 'she who approaches'). Courtship initiated by the male is *sthūla* (crude, rustic). This complete reversal of the Vedic and Epic tradition must have come from some indigenous source, by sheer default of other possibilities.

Modern Indian scholars so far were satisfied with the *fait accompli*: the Vajrayāṇa Buddhists (Indian and Tibetan) homologized their cognitive concepts—*śūnya* (the void), *prajñā* (supreme quiescent wisdom), *nairātmya* (non-self-hood), and also their conative notions—*karuṇa* (active compassion), *upāya* (the method). As to the fusion of ancient, popular beliefs with mystical speculation, the prevailing view is the one commonly held in comparative religion: that the doctors contrived a mythology for the lay public, and that they in turn derived unconscious inspiration from ancient mythical residues. Thus, B. Bhattacharya gives a somewhat simplistic summary of the problem as he sees it: 'Buddhism, we should not forget, was a mass-religion and the mass is not expected to be so intelligent as to grasp the real philosophical significance of *Prajñā* and *Upāya* or of *Nirvāṇa*. The priests found a great deal of difficulty in making the mass understand the meaning of *Nirvāṇa*, to the attainment of which every Bodhisattva strives. They invented a word for *Śūnya*: it was *Nirātmā*, that is something in which the soul is lost. The *Bodhicitta*[12] merges in *Nirātmā* and there remains in eternal bliss and happiness (*Mahāsukha*). The word *Nirātmā*, it may be noted, is in the feminine; the *Nirātmā* is therefore a *Devī*, in whose embrace the *Bodhicitta* remains. The masses well understood the significance of *Nirātmā*, and this feminine aspect—an outcome of the *Mahāsukha* doctrine—in the doctrine of *Nirvāṇa*, gave rise to Vajrayāṇa.'

Bhattacharya glosses over the fact, that the then popular *Nirātmā* was an extension of some pre-Aryan Indian mother-goddess christened with a sophisticated name, and that it was the goddess that was well understood by the masses, *not* the significance of the doctrine; neither is the feminine aspect an outcome of the *Mahāsukha* (Great Delight) doctrine—but the *Mahāsukha* doctrine is, conversely, the outcome of the merger of popular and speculative elements which had taken place many centuries previous to the formulation of this doctrine. The fact that *Nirātmā* was imported, or re-evaluated by the Tibetans in the Lamaistic pantheon does of course not in any way conflict with this statement. The Tibetan *bdag med ma* is definitely a purely Buddhist goddess, not a superimposition on some pre-Buddhist Tibetan deity in the sense of the earth deities *sa bdag*, Bon or other forms of pre-Buddhist Tibetan religion. I believe that those deities of the Tibetan Buddhist pantheon, which translate a learned term from Indian Buddhist cosmology, are wholesale imports from across the mountains; other Tibetan deities, not connoting a sophisticated scholastic concept of Vajrayāṇa Buddhism may or may not be transmuted pre-Buddhist deities.

Further down, he says, 'but the most thorough-going worshipped the gods in embrace, in union with their *Śaktis*, or as the Tibetans describe it—in *Yab-Yum*'.[13] This is a considerable over-simplification. It has been pointed out that the *śakti* concept is not known in Tibetan Buddhism. This may be disputed, but if the *Yum* is identified with *śes rab* (*prajñā*, supreme wisdom) in Tibetan Buddhism, then the assumed homology with *Śakti* is wrong. If *Śakti* figures at all in Buddhism, she does so only in specific stylistic imports discussed earlier in this chapter.

In the Hindu tantric ontology, the Sāṃkhya background has been forgotten, but its influence is evident. Many Indian scholars (S. K. Chatterji, V. Bhattacharya, V. S. Agrawala) think that it is a direct continuation of Sāṃkhya; but this can hardly be correct unless it is stated in some such sense as, say, that Bertrand Russell 'continues' the philosophy of Heraclitus. Too much has accrued in between Sāṃkhya and Tantra—most of all, the entire bulk of gynocentric mystosophy, and on an entirely different level, Buddhism. If we juxtapose the Hindu and the Buddhist tantric philosophies, we shall have an instrument for distinguishing their basic outlook, more than any iconographical comparison could provide, for there is too much mutual borrowing and overlapping of icons; the same holds for *mantras, yantras,* and the entire apparatus of tantric worship. This, then, is the simplest representative schema:

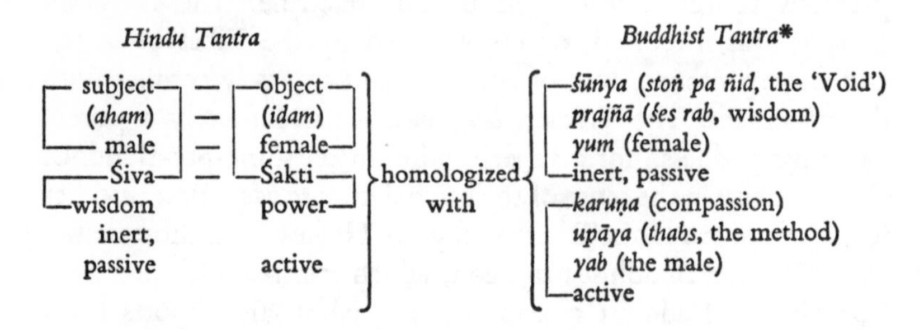

I shall now proceed to exemplify the diverse Indian traditions, so far as they are relevant to our problem.

S. B. Dasgupta gives a summary of the situation[14] from which I quote the relevant passages:

'*Śūnyatā* (the void, voidness) and *Karuṇa* (compassion) are widely termed as *Prajñā* (*śes rab*, supreme wisdom) and *Upāya* (*thabs*, the method) respectively in tantric Buddhism. *Śūnyatā* is called *Prajñā* simply because it represents perfect knowledge . . . *Prajñā* is passive by nature, the religious inspiration is derived from the active emotion of compassion, which serves like the means of the expedience (*upāya*) for the realization of the highest goal. *Prajñā* is the one universal principle, the oneness as the suchness (*tathatā*) underlying the diversity of the phenomenal world, while the *Upāya* is the principle that brings down our mind again and again to the world of particulars[15]. . . . The use of the term "*Prajñā*"

* In Buddhist tantra, the homologized terms have to be arranged in a single direction, because there is no real ontology in Buddhism; everything is either subject (as in later Mādhyamika) or object (Sarvāstivāda, Vijñānavāda); there is no consistent dichotomy of subject-object in any Buddhist school. This dichotomy remains, in even the most radical Hindu monistic systems (and Śākta-Tantra at times claims to be such a system), the basic dualism of Sāṃkhya lingers on. Buddhism is the one and complete break-away from the Sāṃkhyan background, except in the trivial matter of the Buddhist love for categorizing, to which there are few exceptions anywhere in Indian scholasticism.

for "*Śūnyatā*"[16] is well known in Buddhist philosophy and literature, they are often treated as synonyms; but the use of the term "*Upāya*" for *Karuṇa* seems to be somewhat technical. . . . We find that these conceptions of *Prajñā* and *Upāya* are already there from the time of Aśvaghoṣa. It is said in his *Mahāyāna-śraddhotpāda-sūtra* that Enlightenment *a priori* has two attributes, viz. (a) Pure Wisdom (*prajñā*), and (b) Incomprehensible activity (*upāya*? *karuṇa*?). Later on the word *Upāya* is found widely used in Mahāyāna texts for *Karuṇa*[16]. . . . In the *Hevajra Tantra*[17] *Upāya* and *Prajñā* have been described under the imagery of the Yogin and the Mudrā (the female companion-adept) who stand for *Karuṇa* and *Śūnyatā* respectively. In all classes of Buddhist Tantras (i.e. Indian and Tibetan) the most important matter is the stress on this union of *Prajñā* and *Upāya*, either in the philosophical sense or the esoteric yogic sense. The authority of renowned Buddhist teachers like Vimalakīrti and others has often been quoted . . . i.e. that *Upāya* is bondage when unassociated with *Prajñā*, and even *Prajñā* is bondage when unassociated with *Upāya*; both of them again become liberation when associated with each other. Their commingling through the instruction of the competent teacher, like the inseparable co-existence of the lamp and the light, will conduce to success . . .'

Later on, Dasgupta illustrates the point thus, '. . . the goddess Varāhī (*rdo rje phag mo*) who represents *Prajñā* (*śes rab*) is spoken of as of the nature of knowledge, whereas the god Heruka representing *upāya* (*thabs*) is spoken of as the knowable; the circle of perfect purification (*avadhūtimaṇḍala*) is formed by the combination of both knowledge and the knowable. From all these it is evident that *Prajñā* is conceived as the absolute knowledge, which is negative and passive, whereas *upāya* is the positive and active principle. *Prajñā* is conceived as the female element while *upāya* is conceived as the male element.'

In the rich *sandhā*-imagery of Buddhist tantric texts, the dynamic part of the male principle finds its individualized counterpart in the male lover who takes the active part in the yogic love-act in contrast to the Hindu tantrics' tradition, where it is the female partner who takes the active part. Anaṅgavajra puts it rather graphically, 'soon after he has embraced his female partner (*mudrā*), inserted his organ into her "*vajra*-house" (efferent *sandhā*-term for the vulva; *vajraveśapravartana*), drinks from her lips sprinkled with milk, makes her speak cooingly, enjoys rich delight, and makes her thighs quiver, Cupid (that is) man's adamantine nature (*vajrasattva*), will become manifest'.[18]

The division of labour is pretty well marked in the two tantric traditions: the redeeming function is assigned to the dynamic principle and its mythological manifestations. That is to say, the Buddhist *upāya* (male) and the Hindu *śakti* (female) in all their guises (*bodhisattvas*, Buddhas; the Hindu redeemer-goddesses) guide the adept. This is so deeply ingrained in the Hindu mind, that the redeeming function remains with the *śakti* even when the Hindu has borrowed Buddhist goddesses who, in their own circle, are of course passive. I chanced upon an interesting example of this trait in a preface to the *Tārā-svarūpa-tattva*, a hymn to the Hinduized goddess Tārā. It is a contemporary work and the Buddhist origin of the goddesses mentioned is no longer conscious to the author, Paṇḍit Śyāmānanda Kaulakalpataru. The Paṇḍit uses the *Tārā-Upaniṣad* as the basis of his own composition; the *Tārā-Upaniṣad* is a late apocryphal work (about fifteenth century A.D.) and is in vogue with Bengali and Maithili tantrics. He says: 'she who makes transcend (*tarānewālī*) the threefold misfortunes caused by natural, supernatural, and spiritual forces, is called "Tārā" . . . through this Vidyā[19] the soul is protected from the five afflictions, i.e. ignorance, selfishness, passion, hatred, fear of death. The difference between Kālī and Tārā is but one of name (i.e. there is no difference between Kālī and Tārā: this is probably said by way of reassuring suspicious Hindus for whom Kālī is the more familiar name [my comment]) . . . inside Tārā there are three Śaktis: Nīlasarasvatī, Ekajaṭā and Ugratārā.[20] Tārā readily gives wisdom (*jñān*) and is therefore called Nīlasarasvatī (i.e. the goddess of wisdom; he does not explain the "*nīla*" i.e. "blue"); she is called Ugratārā (i.e. the terrible Tārā), because she liberates the devotees who desire only liberation from the most terrible misfortune, namely the fetters of existence, and she also destroys the mundane and natural misfortunes of those devotees who have worldly ends in mind; and because she gives the state of supreme at-one-ment (this is Eliade's term for "*kaivalya*"), she is called "Ekajaṭā" (i.e. "having one chignon"). The quintessence of all this is that the knowledge of the goddess as "Tārā"—as of her who makes transcend (*tārayati*) is that of her as of the form of Brahman, helping transcend the ocean of existence.'[21]

Such pseudo-etymologies are the usual device in explaining names of deities whose provenance is no longer understood. We know that Ekajaṭā, Nīlasarasvatī, and Ugratārā are Buddhist tantric goddesses *par excellence*; each of them epitomizes the Tibetan *śes rab* (Sanskrit *prajñā*) in the *rgyud* (tantric) tradition of the Tibetan canon.

The Hindu notion of the male being identified with the inert, the passive, is brought out in the theme of Śiva being the goddess's mattress, or her footstool; it found its most fascinating diction in the famous *Saundaryalaharī*, traditionally but incorrectly ascribed to Śaṃkarācārya (eighth century A.D.). In Professor Norman Brown's rendition: 'in the midst of the Ocean of Nectar (where) covered with groves of heavenly wishing trees (is) the Isle of Gems, in the mansion of wishing jewels with its grove of *nīpa* trees, on a couch composed of (the four gods) Śiva (and the others), your seat a mattress which is Paramaśiva—some few lucky ones worship you, a flood of consciousness (*cit*) and bliss (*ānanda*).'

In tune with the absolutist style, which is the one common factor of Buddhist and Hindu tantric philosophy, the goddess has not only her own characteristics but those of Śiva also. All over India, especially in the south, we find the hermaphrodite representation of Śakti as Śiva or vice versa, the *Ārdhanārīśvara* (i.e. 'the Lord who is half woman'.). The *Saundaryalaharī* says that the goddess is the whole of Śiva (i.e. as the cosmos and the process of its evolution, as well as herself—Professor Brown's diction). The verse says: 'you are the body of Śiva with the sun and moon as your pair of breasts, your self I take to be the flawless self of Bhāva (i.e. Śiva), O Blessed Lady; hence as you reciprocally realize each other as complement and essence, this union exists of you two experiencing supreme bliss with equal savour' (Brown's translation).[22] '*Samarasa*', which Eliade renders *identité de jouissance* following Shahidullah,[23] is literally used, with exactly the same meaning, in Buddhist tantra, and it is conceivable that the Buddhist is the older model.

On the Hindu side, the position of Śakti was summarized by Brown:[24] 'The feminine principle, or *śakti* (power), personified as the goddess Devī, is the first and supreme principle of the universe. It includes both the spiritual and the material principles and hence may be understood to comprise both soul (*puruṣa*) and nature (*prakṛti*) of the Sāṃkhya system. As such it is equivalent to the neuter brahman of *advaita* (monastic) thought. The feminine principle in conjunction with the masculine principle, but with the masculine principle always secondary and subordinate to the feminine, creates the cosmos by exercising its power to produce change.' 'Creates' is not too well chosen; the final clause reveals the conception more adequately, for 'creating' does not exist in Indian thought in any sense of '*creatio*', i.e. '*ex nihilo*'; 'manifestation', 'emanation' or a similar term should be agreed upon instead of 'creation', whenever Indian thought is under discussion. In the Tibetan Buddhist tradition, the symbolized polarity is far more homogeneous and more pervasive than in India. Whereas institutionalized tantrics formed but a small section within Hinduism and Buddhism in India, every Tibetan Buddhist can be called a potential tantric. This finds its formal corroboration in the fact that the *rgyud* literature is canonical for all Tibetan Buddhists; tantric literature in India is canonical only to the tantrics themselves.

As shown earlier in this chapter, the Tibetans invariably assigned the dynamic function to the male, the static to the female metaphysical principle, and the essential homologies are: (1) *Buddha or Bodhisattva*: male (*yab*) = *upaya* (*thabs*); the method, the manner, the way (here a purely theological term; in common parlance, *thabs* also means 'occasion') = *karuṇa* (compassion). (2) *The Goddess* (I avoid 'Śakti' for reasons stated earlier and to be elaborated presently) = the female (*yum*, mother) = *prajñā* (*śes rab* supreme wisdom) = *śūnya* (*stoṅ pa ñid*, the Void).

The homology is rigid—there is no differing assignment throughout the entire *rgyud* literature, as Professor H. V. Guenther confirms. This means that it is more rigid than in Hindu tantric literature, where there are a few instances in which the dynamic function is assigned to Śiva (the male principle), as for instance in the *Periyapurāṇam*, a canonical text of Tamil Śaivism; also, the static function is assigned to the female principle in at least two passages in the *Mārkaṇḍeya Purāṇa, Caṇḍīpātha.*

The Tibetan Buddhists' fascination with the symbolized polarity is most strikingly evident in their *yab yum* iconography. Precursors of this iconic pattern are to be found in India, no doubt —erotic sculpture had been produced by Hindu artists at least as early as A.D. 300, probably even earlier. The stereotyped *yab yum* icon, however, seems to be purely Tibetan, or Nepalese, Buddhist. The goddess sitting astride on the god's lap, facing the god, is nowhere seen in Hindu sculpture, and not even in purely Indian Buddhist sculpture. There are scores of variants of posture in the erotic symbol sculpture of India, but the one typical of the *yab yum* is not found anywhere, to my knowledge, in Indian sculpture proper.

The Indian yogis who provided the earliest hagiology for the Tibetans were the eighty-four *siddhas* (yogis, magicians). Among them, Tillopa (the first elder of the spiritual lineage of Marpa, Naropa, and Milaraspa) was entirely Indian in his style; it is very likely that he had not even heard about the Tibetan developments of Buddhism (he lived in India in the seventh or eighth century). In his meditations—all of which were translated into Tibetan from the rustic Old Bengali original—he identifies himself with the Void (*śūnya, stoṅ pa ñid*), very much in the manner of a Brahmin monist identifying himself with the Brahman, the neutral supreme being. He says, 'I am void, the world is void, all the three worlds are void, in this pure natural state (*sahaja*) there is neither sin nor virtue.'[25] With him, the notion of polarity cannot yet have been too strong, although his *dohās* are full of erotic imagery—yet the ascription of the dynamic function to the female pole was still at best a dormant idea. His view, for the Buddhist interpreter, is presaged by the Mādhyamika preceptor Nāgārjuna's *śūnyavāda*; the latter did not yet conceive of any polarity in a tantric sense. The fact of the Tibetans attributing Vajrayāṇa notions of polarity to Nāgārjuna is due to their confusion between the *Siddha* Nāgārjuna who lived in the eighth century and the great Mādhyamika dialectician of the first or second century, in whose days there was hardly any trace yet of what could be called tantric Buddhism, unless we assume, with the Buddhist tantrics, that Asaṅga was the real author of the *Guhyasamāja*.

Now the immediate problem is the terminological and functional assignment of the *yum*, the female deity. Hindu scholars, as we have seen earlier, constantly speak of *Buddhaśaktis*. I have tried to show that only a special type of Indian pantheonic imports can be called '*śaktis*', i.e. goddesses like Nīlāsarasvatī, Aparājitā, and the *ḍākinīs* (*-mkhah 'groma-*). The Tibetan *Prajñā* (*śes rab*) is simply no *śakti*. Lama Govinda puts it somewhat radically, but, so I feel, with full justification: '. . . the conception of Śakti, of divine power, of the female-creative potentiality of the supreme god (Śiva) or of one of the many subordinate (Hindu) gods plays no role of any sort in Buddhism. Whereas the notion of power (*śakti*) is the pivot of interest in Hindu tantrism, the central idea of tantric 'Buddhism is realization: *prajñā* (*śes rab*) joined to *upāya* (*thabs*).

. . . to incorporate oneself into the driving forces of the cosmos and to utilize them for one's purposes, may be an objective of the Hindu tantras, but it is none of the Buddhist ones. The Buddhist has no desire whatever to incorporate himself into any driving forces, but to rid himself of them, as they keep driving him about in the *saṃsāra* (the phenomenal realm) . . .

' "From the union of Śiva and Śakti unfolds the world (*śivaśaktisamāyogād jāyate sṛṣtikalpanā*)", says the *Kulacuḍāmani Tantra* (an important Hindu work). But the Buddhist does not seek the unfoldment of the world—rather he seeks its regression into the "unborn, unformed" which is at the basis of all unfoldment—the "*śūnyatā*" (*stoṅ pa ñid*), the Void) . . .'[26]

The Lama does some injustice to Hindu tantra in this matter, for the Hindu tantric wants very much the same, subject only to a different diction. He wants to merge into the *Paraśiva* (the supreme Śiva), which is a state of complete quiescence—his use of *śakti* is intermediary—and, on the metaphysical level, Śakti herself merges into the *Paraśiva* at the point of the cosmic dissolution.

The Lama's account of the problem on the Tibetan Buddhist side is perfectly candid. He says that the *yab yum* imagery does not conjure up sexual notions with the Tibetan Buddhist, for this symbolic significance is utterly germane to the religious atmosphere of Lamaism. I do not know if he and Professor Glasenapp, whom he quotes, are right in claiming that 'associations of a sexual nature are strictly excluded' in this symbolism. Again, this seems largely a semantical matter: sexual contact does take place in certain meditations of the *rgyud* tradition, as it does in its Indian counterpart, the left-handed tantric exercises. But if 'physical' is to mean 'conscious of physical ramifications' then the Lama is right, for it seems to be a fact that advanced adepts do not have such consciousness in the pursuit of such exercises; but then 'physical sexuality' might just mean 'physically expressed sexuality', or 'sexuality acted out physically', i.e. without any reference to the attitude and the motive behind the process—in which case the Lama is wrong because these exercises have been performed, both in India and in Tibet, up to this day.

He then continues: 'We must not forget that these iconological representations (i.e. the *yab yum* images) are not representations of ordinary human beings, but that they emerged from meditative imagery. In this state there is no longer anything "sexual" in the conventional sense of the term, but there only exists the supra-individual polarity of all that occurs, to which both the mental and the physical (which is but an aspect of the mental anyway) are subordinate; this polarity, once it has reached the highest level of absorption or integration—the thing we call illumination (viz. *bodhi*)—is cancelled and becomes *śunyatā* (*stoṅ pa ñid*). This is the state called "*mahāmudrā*" (*phyag rgya chen po*; the "great *Mudrā*").'

I now believe that any speculation on why the Tibetan Buddhists made so much of their particular choice has to be made in full awareness of a paradox which has not yet drawn the attention of Buddhist scholars, so far as I can see. This is all the more amazing, as the paradox is very obvious indeed: the Tibetan doctrine teaches that *śes rab* (*prajñā*, the deified supreme realization) is static and *thabs* (*upāya*, the deified method) dynamic. But Tibetan iconography takes little cognizance of the doctrine: for the *yab yum* icon behaves in direct contradiction to the doctrine—the *yum* sits astride of the *yab*, the latter sits in *padmāsana* (lotus posture) or *vajrāsana* (*vajra*-posture); in these postures, no movement is possible—whereas the posture of the *yum* suggests intensive motion to even the most casual observer.[27] Hence, in spite of the inversion of the Indian notion on the doctrinary level, the Tibetan iconographers modelled their *yab yum* in functional analogy with Indian *maithuna* sculpture.[28] This does not have to be a conscious analogy and probably is not, unless it could be shown that Tibetan artists learnt their trade in India or from Indian sculptors; and that they retained the iconographical convention with regard to its functional aspect (i.e. the male as passive and the female as active partner in the act of yogic copulation). All this is at best a learned guess. The main argument against the conjecture of Indian tutelage dominating Tibetan iconography would be that Tibetan artists obtained their precise instruction on every detail of their work from indigenous Tibetan sources,[29] just like Indian sculptors have taken great pains to fashion their idols in exact conformity with the *śilpaśāstra*, the instruction manuals which have almost canonical force for the Indian iconographer.

A point of equal importance illustrating the basic paradox between doctrine and iconography is the representation of the *bhāva* (attitude of mind) of the *yum*: though she appears to be the partner in the *yab yum* icon, she is never shown in a *ghora* (fierce) attitude. Now fierceness or ferociousness usually symbolizes the dynamic principle; the Tibetan iconographer proceeds in consonance with the doctrine, when he shows the male deity as fierce; the *lha chen po* (Mahākāla) looks very fierce indeed, even when shown in *yab yum*; but his female partner looks benign and mild. The same holds for all the deities depicted in *yab yum* in the Tibetan iconographical lore.[30] The only fierce goddesses in Tibetan iconography are the ones which I referred to as genuine 'Śaktis' earlier in this chapter: but they stand alone, and have no erotic contact with a male deity.

From these observations two alternative answers might emerge: first, although Tibetan doctrine assigns the dynamic function to the male, the static to the female, Tibetan Buddhist iconography pays no heed to this doctrine, for reasons I do not know; second, the Tibetan iconographer may feel that the static function of the goddess is sufficiently represented by her peaceful mien when juxtaposed with the fierce male deity. If this is true, then it would mean that the Tibetan Buddhist iconographer does not feel that the active part in the act of copulation is exhaustively symbolical of the dynamic function, and that the general *bhāva* (attitude) is a more efficacious symbol of the static. This would mean a radical divergence from his Indian colleague. Heinrich Zimmer states the situation in a manner which would make the iconographical paradox less flagrant:[31]

'. . . this *yab yum* icon is to be read in two ways. On the one hand, the candidate is to meditate on the female portion as the *śakti* or dynamic aspect of eternity and the male as the quiescent but activated. Then, on the other hand, the male is to be regarded as the principle of the path, the way, the method (*upāya*), and the female, with which it merges, as the transcendent goal; she is then the fountainhead into which the dynamism of enlightenment returns in its state of full and permanent incandescence. And finally, the very fact that the dual symbol of the united couple is to be read in the two ways (with either the male or the female representing transcendent truth) [Zimmer's parenthesis] signifies that the two aspects or functions of reality are perfectly equal in rank: there is no difference between *saṃsāra* and *nirvāṇa* (i.e. the bound state of the phenomenal world and the state of detached perfection) [my parenthesis], either as to dignity or as to substance. *Tathatā*, the sheer "suchness" is made manifest both ways, and for true enlightenment the apparent difference is non-existent.'

This would actually mean a complete cancelling of the paradox, but the trouble is that Zimmer's statement, in this form, is not borne out by doctrine. First, nowhere in Vajrayāṇa texts is the *yum* to be meditated upon as *śakti*. Second, while it is no doubt true that in the final merger the *yab* and the *yum* are one—this is an ontological statement, not one on the level of tantric practice. I think Zimmer glossed over the basic differences between the Hindu and the Buddhist tantric tradition; if there were such a person as a tantric who is both Hindu and Buddhist, a meditation such as Zimmer hints at would be conceivable. Unfortunately, however, there is not a single text that would support Zimmer's super-eclectic notion; nor did he list any textual reference. The truth of the matter is this: the Hindu tantric meditates on *śakti* as energy, and on Śiva as quiescent wisdom—and he knows they are ontologically one, for tantrism is as monistic as a doctrine can be. The Tibetan Buddhist tantric meditates on *Prajñā* (*śes rab*, *yum*) as static and on *upāya* (*thabs*, *yab*) as dynamic, and he asserts that there is no *ontological* distinction whatever between them. The *yab yum* or the Indian Śiva-Śakti *maithuna* (i.e. sexual embrace) icon does not represent the ontological oneness, though it points towards that oneness; but it represents our mystagogical polarity, and it presents it differently in the two traditions. This, Zimmer did not see, probably due to his extreme fondness for Asian mystical syncretism, which ignores systematic distinctions. In his statement, quoted above, the upper portion is Hindu tantrism, the lower is Buddhist Tibetan or Vajrayāṇa tantrism. The two are not the same. Zimmer, like many old-time indologists, wrote how he thought things ought to have been, not how they were.

The purely doctrinary side is no doubt monistic; it has been recently summed up by a Japanese scholar,[32] 'In this sense, both *paramārthasatya* (i.e. the unconditioned, absolute truth or existence) and *saṃvṛtisatya* (relative, phenomenal truth or existence) are inseparably united with one another (*yuganaddha*, *abheda*), and there results *apratiṣṭhita-nirvāṇa* (i.e., the *nirvāṇa* which is not "fixed", i.e. which is not different from phenomenal existence). Accordingly . . . it is said to be similar to (the concept of) *upāya-prajñā* or *mahākaruṇā-śūnyatā* (i.e. the terms basic to this discussion).'

Evans-Wentz, in a note on the 'All-Good-Mother' (*kuntu bzang mo*) as mentioned in the *Bardo Thodol*,[33] also uses *śakti* in the slipshod manner which has been in vogue among Buddhist as well as Hindu scholars and which I believe to be a real obstacle in the way of clarification of the involved issues. He writes: 'The tantric school holds that every deity, even the Supreme, has its *śakti*. A few deities are, however, commonly depicted as *śakti*-less—for example, Mañjuśrī, or Mañjughoṣa; though there may be, as in the instance of the *Prajñā-Pāramitā* (often called the Mother) which this deity holds, some symbolic representation of a *śakti*. This is, apparently, a doctrine of universal dualism. In the final analysis, however, all pairs of opposites being reviewed as having a single source in the Voidness of the *dharma-kāya* (*chos sku*)—the apparent dualism becomes monism.'

The obscurity of the above is due to Evans-Wentz's inexact terminology which is similar to Zimmer's. The correct notion, inadequately expressed here, is simply that there is dualism on the level of mystical practice, on the level of a heuristic polarity, and there is monism on the ontological level. To use a somewhat facetious gastronomic analogy, the mystical adept is interested in *filet mignon* and sparkling burgundy, the ontologist is interested in food and drink. The tantric is no metaphysician, neither is the yogi. Metaphysics (ontology) is of secondary concern for them, admitted at best by courtesy.

Eliade, discussing the *Hevajra Tantra*, describes the situation with precision:[34] 'this is a state of unity obtained by doing away with two polar contradictory notions, *saṃsāra*, the cosmic process, and *nivṛtti*, absolute arrest of all process; one transcends these two notions by becoming conscious that the ultimate nature of the phenomenal world (*saṃkleśa*) is identical with that of the absolute (*vyavadāna*); hence one realizes synthesis between the notions of formal existence and of the non-formed, etc. . . . the tantrist is concerned with *sādhanā* (spiritual practice); he wants to "realize" the paradox expressed in all the images and formulas concerning the union of opposites, he wants concrete, experimental knowledge of the state of non-duality. The Buddhist texts had made two pairs of opposites especially popular—*prajñā* (wisdom), and *upāya* (the means to attain it); *śūnya*, the "void", and *karuṇa*, compassion . . . Tantrism multiplies the pairs of opposites (sun and moon, Śiva and Śakti, etc.), and attempts to "unify" them through techniques combining subtle physiology with meditation.'

With all this, it is clear that Indian texts provide a complete source for the Tibetan ascriptions male-dynamic—female-static. This, however, does not explain *why* the Tibetans made the choice they did make, and why they did not canonize the view which was so much more prevalent in Indian sources (i.e. the obverse ascription). It can hardly be assumed that the Tibetans made a random choice, and I shall now present what I have come to see as possible grounds for their choice.

The late Nebesky-Wojkowitz suggested[35] that the autochthonous deities (*sa bdag*) of Tibet might have been deeply ensconced in the Tibetan minds previous to the advent of Buddhism; and if it could be shown that the predominant setting in the pre-Buddhist Tibetan pantheon was patrifocal, the pattern might have proved too strong to be subverted. Similar processes have taken place in India at all times. Pre-Aryan Indian deities were absorbed into the Brahmin pantheon; or, more precisely, any popular god became identified with a genuinely Brahmin deity whose features or functions were not too dissimilar: Durgā was a native Bengali goddess, so was Caṇḍi or Cāmuṇḍī in Mysore, or again Kālī in Bengal, and they all were gradually identified with the consort of the Vedic Rudra, Rudrānī—which was fortunate for her, for in the Veda the great god's spouse had been rather colourless. In south India the Tamilian Vallī became the wife of Subbramaniya, who, himself a Dravidian god, was soon identified with the war-god Kārttikeya, the son of Śiva and Pārvatī. Scores of parallel instances can be adduced; in the anthropological diction of this decade, 'little tradition' deities merged into the 'big tradition' pantheon.

Professor H. Wilhelm suggested[36] that the Tibetans might well have preserved their notion of the male being the dynamic element subsequently transferring this notion into a Buddhist context, because, unlike in India, there was no basis for a reaction of autochthonous elements against a superimposed dogmatic strucsure which opposed these elements. In India the Vedic patrifocal tacerdotalism clashed with the powerful native matrifocal environment, and though the former subdued the latter on the doctrinary level it had to come to terms with it in later days when this sentiment reasserted itself in what might well be called the tantric revolution. Now, if the Tibetan sentiment at the time of the advent of Buddhism was patriarchal, there was indeed no need for any such reaction: the Tibetan converts to Buddhism would then quite naturally choose those texts and those preceptors from India which fell in line with a partiarchal trend.

If the Tibetan choice was prompted by non-Indian sources, then the first idea that comes to one's mind is the pre-Buddhist Bon. However, I do not think that we can find much relevant information here. The purely shamanistic Bon of the earliest times was hardly sophisticated enough to envisage a problem of such complexity; and the later, systematized Bon of the *Tsher mig*[37] was so thoroughly suffused with Buddhist ideas that whatever might appear in this work and in other works of systematized Bon in connection with our problem can hardly reflect a genuine Bon notion.

The other non-Indian influence might have been Chinese. Though we cannot be sure whether it was the *yin-yang* complex that seeped through into the Tibetan Buddhist *yab yum* concept, certain parallels can obviously be shown. One must always bear in mind, however, that the polarity male-female is ubiquitous in the world's religious, mystical and magical traditions; that its parallel occurrence at any place may be independent invention; and even striking similarities in diction or formulation in different regions cannot preclude the possibility of indigenous origination—for the simple fact that the possible homology-combinations are not too numerous. Thus, if we have, say, the terms 'static', 'dynamic', conscious', 'inert' to be ascribed to 'male' and 'female', the possible, combinations total about a dozen. Hence, when we list analogies of this kind, we have to do so without forcing them into a Procrustean bed. For example, if the male element is shown to be dynamic and the female static in Taoism, and the same relation obtains in Tibetan Buddhism, the most we can say is 'here is a parallel'. This would be a trivial cautioning, were it not for the fact that scholars of merit have fallen into the temptation of drawing inferences on the basis of similarity in diction. I feel that any Taoist ascription of the dynamic to the male principle, if indeed there be such a formulation in Taoist texts, might not have been strong enough as a single influence to counterbalance the one wielded by the Indian doctrine even if it could be shown some day that there was a direct influence of Taoist ideas on Tibetan tantric Buddhism. Some of the most outstanding authorities on Taoism, among them H. Wilhelm at the University of Washington, hold that there is definitely an historical and thematic connection.

Finally, it is conceivable that the *Kālacakra* system was a possible prompter of the Tibetan paradox. We know that the *Kālacakra* (Tibetan *'Dus kyi khor lo*) was not Indian in origin, in spite of its considerable influence on Indian tantric developments, both Hindu and Buddhist. Its place of origin is not really known; the legendary origin is either Zahor, or Śambhala, or Oḍḍīyāṇa, but the actual location of these areas is not known with the exception of the last, which is the Swat Valley according to most scholars including G. Tucci.[38] However, it seems certain that the *Kālacakra* did originate somewhere to the west of Tibet and to the north-west of India. I am quoting from the only text available to me, following S. B. Dasgupta:[39] 'The Lord Śrī Kālacakra is saluted as of the nature of *Śūnyatā* and *Karuṇa*; in him there is the absence of the origination and destruction of the three worlds, he is the unity of knowledge and the known. The goddess Prajñā, who is both with and without form, is embraced by him; bereft of origin and change, he is immutable bliss . . . he is the father of the Buddhas, possessing the three *kāyas* (bodies)—the ultimate original Buddha, the non-dual lord.'

This passage sets the scene: the non-dual Buddha principle is quiescent, because once the monistic standpoint is taken the polarity has disappeared; '*Prajñā*' is the epitome of the static in Buddhist tantra, and if she is 'embraced by Kālacakra', the couple must be seen as *yab yum* for purposes of mystical practice and, *a fortiori*, for the iconographer. The description of *Kālacakra*-Buddha in this quiescent manner must then have had a different effect on Indians and on Tibetans: the quiescent, static male found a congenial atmosphere among the tantric Hindus, and in fact among all Indian adepts to whom this ascription was germane: *Kālacakra* was simply identified with Śiva.[40] The Tibetans no doubt realized that the god's description in the *Kālacakra* text was static; but they would reject it in an ontological statement, albeit of a monistic nature—the mystical or 'practical' aspect being more important: hence—'*Prajñā*' (*śes rab*) is embraced by *Kālacakra*.

I shall now summarize my own conclusions:

(a) No definite and certainly no single reason can as yet be given for the Tibetan Buddhists' choice in attributing the static to the female, and the dynamic to the male cosmic principle.

(b) In the Indian sources which were instrumental in creating the Tibetan canon there were considerable traces of the same ascription: many of the Indian Vajrayāṇa teachers ascribed the dynamic to the male (*upāya, karuṇa*) and the static to the female principle (*prajñā, śūnyatā*), yet the majority of Indian texts shows the opposite ascription in line with the general Indian tradition.

(c) Taoism shows a tempting parallel to the Tibetan notion.

(d) Pre-Buddhist Bon did not have any such problem of sophisticated complexity; systematized (or Buddhicized) Bon is not helpful as it absorbed virtually everything on the doctrinary side from Buddhism.

(e) The *Kālacakra* (*'Dus kyi khor lo*) teaching is ambiguous, as it does not make an unequivocal ascription.

I feel this much can be safely said: the Tibetan teachers did not have to incorporate any non-Indian sources to reach their ascription in the *yab yum* polarity. They laid stress on such Indian scriptures and teachings as would corroborate their notions, which may well have been much older than Buddhism in Tibet. These notions might have had their origin in a number of causes, which jointly prompted the Tibetans to select those Indian teachings which homologized the dynamic with the male and the static with the female: and some of these causes may lie in the preceding suggestions.

NOTES

[1] I use the term 'noumenon' instead of a less esoteric but theologically loaded term: the 'divine' will not do for Buddhism; the 'absolute' is too scholastic and non-charismatic; the 'noumenon', being the correlative of the 'phenomenon', seems to be the most expedient choice.

[2] The legend of Matsyendranāth, the semi-mythical founder of the 'Nāth' order of yogins, is told in varying form in all parts of India and especially in Nepal, where he is regarded as a tutelary deity. Matsyendranāth is kept as a more or less voluntary captive of a tribe of Amazon women, sporting with their queen in pleasant oblivion of his sacred mission, until his great disciple Gorakhnāth rescues him; Matsyendranāth is one of the eighty-four Siddhas or magician-saints in the Tibetan Vajrayāṇa tradition, and is one of the spiritual ancestor-*gurus* of Naropa and Milaraspa (vd. Gruenwedel, Tārānātha's *Edelsteinmiene*). I suspect that the identification of power and energy with the female principle and the use of the word *śakti* to denote female deities is based on the fact that in pre-Aryan India as well as among the Kerala Dravidians, up to this day, woman has been the active partner in all love-play and in the act of procreation; the same holds for the Nāgas and other tribes in Assam; tantric literature and practice originated in those regions and has been in vogue there to a far greater degree than in any other area in India. Similar views were held by Professor Suniti K. Chatterji, and by the late B. S. Guha of Calcutta.

[3] I put this question to Thubten Norbu, elder brother of the Dalai Lama, and found that the ascription of *prajñā* to the female, and of *upāyā* to the male noumenal aspect is quite axiomatic with him, although the Gelugpa denomination does not attend too much on the polarity pattern; Norbu was not aware that the Hindu notion was the reverse. Similarly, hardly any Hindu paṇḍits know that Vajrayāṇa Buddhism holds the opposite view as an axiom.

[4] Vd. *Sādhanāmālā* A 230, *et passim*; the goddesses Vajravarāhī, Aparājitā, Prasannatārā, and many others trample on male figures; or they dance upon them, though the dancing is often so crude that no classical pose could be discerned, hence 'trampling' may be a justified description; this may also account for the term *samākrāntā* '(she is in a pose of) attack', common in the *dhyānas*.

[5] I have this information from Paṇḍit Ananta Shastry of the Tamil Sangham Library, Madras. He said he saw the phrase in a manuscript of the Tirukurral, one of the oldest extant Tamil works; I did not, however, find it in the translation available to me. However, the idea is fully in vogue in Dravidian folkloristic genres, and the idiom is frequently used in the medieval devotional hymns of Manikavaccakar, Jñānasambandha, and other Śivite saints of the Tamilian tradition.

[6] Dr. P. C. Roy, a Bengali medical practitioner in Banaras, a man of no particular literary background, recited to me a poem which he had composed in praise of Durgā, the Divine Mother—the tutelary deity of Bengal. A passage in it ran somewhat like this: 'seeing that the most beautiful ornament for her spouse's breast would be her own lotus-feet, she placed them both on his chest and danced her dance'.

[7] *Buddhist Iconography*, Plate XLII d; the *dhyāna* is contained in the *Dharmakośasaṇgraha*, Fol. 48, quoted ibid. p. 158 '*gaṇapatihṛdayā ekamukhā dvibujhā varadā abhayā nṛtyāsanā*.'

[8] The latest among the many speculations on this highly exciting subject is the one of M. Eliade, which is exceedingly well reasoned and sober; tentatively, I am accepting his arguments, and shall therefore not dilate on the matter at present; vd. *Yoga—Immortality and Freedom*, Pantheon, New York 1958, p. 348 ff.

[9] Translation of Norman D. Brown, first verse of *Saundaryalaharī*, *Harvard Oriental Series*, Vol. 43, 1958. '*Śiva śaktyā yukto bhavati śāktaḥ prabhavitum/ na cedevaṃ devo na khalu kuśalaḥ spanditumapi/ atastvāmārādhyaṃ hariharavirañcyādibhirapi/ prānantuṃ stotuṃ vā kathamakṛtapunyaḥ prabhavati*' (p. 49 ibid.).

[10] The story, in its most detailed version, is contained in the *Viśṇu Purāṇa*, first part; but there is hardly any Purāṇa which does not adduce it in one form or the other, and there is scarcely a paurāṇic or tantric text which does not allude to it.

[11] There may be some link to a saga-complex of Indo-European origin; cf. the cheating of the giants out of their fees after they had built Valhalla; or, even more closely, the descent of Thor into the giants' palace in the guise of the latter's bride—both stocks-in-trade in Germanic mythology.

[12] For the homology of *bodhicitta*, the Bodhi-mind, with *semen virile*, see the chapter on Intentional Language (*supra; sandhābhāṣā*).

[13] B. Bhattacharya, *Buddhist Iconography*, pp. xv, xvii, xix.

[14] *Tantric Buddhism*, p. 100 ff., *et passim*.

[15] Dasgupta minimizes the role of *upāya*; he overlooks the fact that *upāya* is a cosmic principle rather than an individual accessory ever so hallowed. He obviously thinks of the Hindu concept of Śakti, as identified with *Māyā*, the phenomenal universe, homologized with the goddess, who is thence Śakti, *Māyā* and temptress; for *Māyā*, in spite of its metaphysical use, remains a mildly pejorative term. Its Vedic use was simply 'magic'—Indra's *Māyā* is often spoken of in the *Ṛgveda*; Śaṃkarācārya derives it from the root *mi*—for 'fade', 'dwindle'.

Up to this day, it is *Māyā* that has to be overcome, in popular religious parlance, it being a sort of Hindu analogue to temptation. Yet the analogy between the Hindu and Buddhist (Vajrayāṇa) concept is less justified here than anywhere else. The Hindu conception of the dynamic (female) and the Buddhist one of the dynamic (male) do not coincide in their soteriological function; the Hindu stresses the distinction between *saṃsāra* (the worldly existence) and *kaivalya* (emancipation), whereas Vajrayāṇa Buddhism stresses the identity of *saṃsāra* and *nirvāṇa* systematically and rigorously. Somewhat facetiously, one might say that the Hindu *dynamis* (Śakti, *Māyā*), tempts the adept away from emancipation, the Buddhist *dynamis* (*upāya*, *karuṇa*) tempts him towards emancipation—there being not the slightest difference between *saṃsāra* and *nirvāṇa*, the question of tempting away from the supreme goal simply does not arise.

[16] The Tibetan *stoṅ pa ñid* and *śes rab* are, of course, used synonymously, in exact analogy with the Sanskrit terms, throughout the Tibetan canon: synonymity of terms plus synonymity of relations between terms in Sanskrit have their exact counterpart in the Tibetan renderings; this would be a trivial statement were it not for the one exception which constitutes our particular problem, i.e. the obverse assignment of the static and the dynamic functions to the male and the female cosmic principles, respectively, in the two traditions. Unfortunately, the *Mahāyānaśraddhotpādasūtra* is almost certainly a Chinese invention.

[17] '*kṛpopāyo bhaved yogī mudrā hetu-viyogataḥ, śūnyatā karuṇābhinnaṃ bodhicittam iti smṛtam*' *Hevajra Tantra*, Paṭala X, Ms. p. 30 (A). The commentary says that the state of mind that feels the self-sameness in all beings is compassion, and it is the means (*upāya*) as it is the method for attaining perfect enlightenment; this is also 'the yogin himself', i.e., his cardinal principle. The adept companion-woman (*mudrā*) is *Prajñā* (*śes rab*), for she is *śūnyatā* (*stoṅ pa ñid*), the Void in the sense of the non-production of beings because nothing can originate either from the self or from others or from the combination of both or from something other than their combination. ('*kṛpe'ty ādi/ sarvasattveṣu ātma-samatā-cittaṃ kṛpā saiva paramopāyaḥ/ samyak-saṃbodhiprasādhanopāyatvāt/ sa ca yogī/ yogināṃ pradhānadharmatvāt/ mudrā prajñā cāsāvityāha/ śunyatā sarva-dharmānām anutpādāḥ/ katham anutpādaḥ śūnyatā/ āha/ hetu viyogataḥ svataḥ parata ubhayato'nubhayataḥ sarva-bhāvānām anutpatteḥ/ anutpāda-lakṣaṇa śunyatā/ saiva paramā prajñā*' *Hevajraprājnikā*, MS p. 41 (B). Quoted in *Tantric Buddhism*, p. 103.)

[18] Tr. H. V. Guenther, in *Yuganaddha*, p. 45; Anaṅgavajra's *Prajñopāyaviniścayasiddhi*, 38–40, G.O.S.

[19] *Vidyā* in the tantric vocabulary means a goddess or any female being whose contact or worship is conducive to the visualized target; see also the chapter on *Mantra*.

[20] '*Antargat*' which may also mean 'constituent of'. These three goddesses figure importantly in the *Sādhanāmālā* and in other important Buddhist Vajrayāṇa texts.

[21] *Śrī-Tārā-Svarūpa-Tattva*, Kalyāṇ Mandir, Prayāg, pp. 3, 4.

[22] '*śarīraṃ tvaṃ śambhoḥ śaśimihiravakṣoruhayugam/ tavātmānam manye bhagavatī bhavātmanamanagham/ ataḥ seṣaḥ śeṣityayamubhaya sādhāranatayā sthitaḥ sambandho vāṃ samarasaparānandaparayoḥ*', *Saundaryalaharī*, vs. 34.

[23] M. Eliade, *Yoga-Immortalité et Liberté*; and M. Shahidullah, *Les Dohakoshas*.

[24] N. Brown, *Saundaryalaharī*, p. 6.

[25] '*hau suṇṇa jagu suṇṇa tihua (na) suṇṇa/ nimmala sahaje na pāpa na puṇṇa*' *Doha* No. 84, M. Shahidullah, ed.

[26] Lama Anagarika Govinda, *Foundations of Tibetan Mysticism*, Rider & Co., London 1959, pp. 99–104. For the best treatment so far of the *Mahāmudrā*, see H. V. Guenther's *The Life and Teachings of Naropa*, Oxford University Press, 1963.

[27] This configuration is not revoked by the fact that a substantial percentage of *yab yum* icons shows the male standing rather than sitting; for although the male can play the dynamic part in such congress, the fact that the impossibility of his being the active partner in the sitting postures was not seen by the Tibetan iconographers suggests that they did not attach any cognitive importance to the obvious difference.

[28] See B. Bhattacharya, *Buddhist Iconography*; H. Zimmer, *The Art of Hindu Asia* (Bollingen Series), where some excellent *maithuna*-reliefs are reproduced; also in Stella Kramrisch, *The Art of India*; and J. Auboyer, *Khajuraho*, Mouton & Co., The Hague 1960.

[29] Evans-Wentz, *The Tibetan Book of the Great Liberation*, Preface.

[30] B. Bhattacharya, *Buddhist Iconography*, *passim*.

[31] H. Zimmer, *The Philosophies of India*, Meridian, New York 1958, p. 557.

[32] Hakuyu Hadano, 'Human Existence in Tantric Buddhism' (Japanese with English summary), in *Annual Reports of the Faculty of Arts and Letters*, Tohoku University, Sendai 1958.

[33] Evans-Wentz, *The Tibetan Book of the Dead* (*Bardo Thodol*), p. 121, note 4.

[34] M. Eliade, *Yoga-Immortality and Freedom*, p. 269.

[35] Personal communication, October 5, 1957.

[36] Personal communication, May, 1959.

[37] H. Hoffmann, *Quellen zur Geschichte der tibetischen Bon Religion*, *passim*.

[38] The *Blue Annals* make ample reference to the *Kālacakra*; Roerich, *Blue Annals*, II, 753–838.

[39] *Kālacakra-tantra*, with a commentary '*Laghu-kālacakra-tantrarājā-ṭika Vimalaprabhā*', preserved in Mss Cambridge University Library No. 1364, quoted in S. B. Dasgupta, *Tantric Buddhism*, p. 73.

[49] *Rudrayāmala*, III, 83 ff., ed. Vacaspati Press, Calcutta 1937; section captioned '*Śivacakram*'—Śiva is here addressed as Mahākāla, which epithet is probably older than the *Rudrayāmala* and which is current in all parts of India. Professor Poppe mentioned identification of 'Mahagala' with an ancient god of the forge, in Mongolia.

9

SĀDHAKA AND *SĀDHANĀ*: THE ASPIRANT AND THE OBSERVANCE

THE central *sādhanā* of tantrism, Buddhist and Hindu alike, is the exercise of sexual contact under tantric 'laboratory' conditions. It is irrelevant, in the final analysis, whether these *sādhanās* were or are literally performed, or whether they are hypostasized entirely into mental configurations. The Hindu tantric tradition makes some distinction between the *sādhanā* that is performed on a purely mental plane and that which involves actual handling of the ritualistic 'ingredients' including woman, meat, and wine. The Hindu schools usually refer to the latter as the left-handed (*vāmācāra*), to the former as the right-handed (*dakṣiṇācāra*) tradition, which is also called the worship through 'substitutes' (*pratinidhi*)—i.e. where the actual ingredients are replaced by other ingredients of a type normally held to be less risky: wine is replaced by some non-alcoholic liquid, meat and other aphrodisiacs by vegetables and cereals, and sexual contact (*maithuna*) by the meditation on the conjunction of the *kuṇḍalinī-śakti* with the Supreme Śiva in the thousand-petalled lotus on the upper end of the central yogic duct (*suṣumnā*).

Although no tantric text makes this distinction, it seems to me that there is a discrepancy between 'substitute' and 'right-handed' worship. The 'substitute' type of *sādhanā* replaces one or more physical ingredients by another, or other, physical ingredients; 'right-handed' practice tends to eschew physical ingredients altogether, replacing them by processes of internalization. To be more precise, I think that 'right-handed' practice is a wider term which often subsumes 'substitute' *sādhanās*, but the 'substitute' *sādhanās* are by no means co-extensive with right-handed practices. There is a lot of difference, after all, between using milk rather than wine for a ceremony, and meditating on wine or milk, without drinking either. The tantric *ācāryas* refer to both these types of *sādhanā* as *pratinidhi* and *dakṣiṇācāra*, but this is clearly due to a lack of terminological precision. From the texts it becomes quite obvious what the words mean: *dakṣiṇācāra* and *vāmācāra* refer to the position of the female partner in the ritual in relation to the yogi; in practices where she sits on his left, the ingredients (*sāmagrī*) tend to be physically used, and where she sits on his right, the use either of substitutes or of meditation on the ingredients prevails. Yet, as in all topics relating to the tantric tradition, there is no hard and fast rule which would apply without any possible modification.

I have not seen any Buddhist tantra which uses the term *makāra* as denoting the ingredients of esoteric practice; we find *pañcatattva* (the five essences) frequently, but it is never quite sure whether the term does not refer to any other of the Buddhist pentads. All Hindu tantras, on the other hand, seem to refer to the five M's, commendingly or disparagingly as the case may be. Let us hold on to this, for it seems to provide a definite criterion for distinguishing Buddhist from Hindu texts in marginal cases. However, a more pervasive criterion is available: Hindu tantras make much of the dispositions (*bhāvatraya*), of which I have not found anything whatsoever in purely Buddhist tantras. The Indian doctrinary tendency being to incorporate in subsequent texts—again commendingly or disparagingly—any known previous terminology referring to a particular topic, we may perhaps see an additional point here for the more recent origin of Hindu tantrism.

The three dispositions are hierarchically arranged: the lowest is usually the animal-disposition (*paśubhāva*); next is the heroic disposition (*vīrabhāva*), and the divine disposition (*divyabhāva*) most frequently ranks supreme. I would tentatively suggest that the term *paśu* (animal), no doubt derogatorily used in this scheme, derives its connotation from the south Indian Śaivites, where the triad is 'the Lord, the bound-one, the fetter' (*pati-paśu-pāśa*), the folk-etymology[1] connecting *paśu* (animal) with *pāśa* (fetter, bond rope) is pervasive in later religious literature, not only in the south. The epithet Lord of *Paśu-s* (*Paśupati*) for Śiva is very old, and I have little doubt that the original term had nothing disparaging about it.

The *Rudrayāmala*, one of the most reliable treatises on Hindu tantrism, distinguished three types of tantric *sādhanā*, adding '*kulācāra*' (the practice of the tantric in-group) to right- and left-handed worship. It enjoins 'in the morning the bath and the *sandhyā* are performed, and at daytime *japam* is done, a woollen seat is to be used, and milk and sugar are to be eaten, the *rudrākṣa* rosary is used, a plate of earthenware (lit. stone) (is made and used). One's own wife (only) is enjoyed—this is right-handed practice.[2] The understanding is, however, that one's own wife (and no one else) should be enjoyed if celibacy cannot be kept—for continence ranks higher than legitimate indulgence.

Left-handed practice is considerably less philistine; it enjoins what is a real inversion of the injunctions for right-handed practice: 'I shall proclaim left-handed practice, the supreme *sādhanā* of Durgā; following which the adept obtains *siddhi* speedily in this *Kali*-age. The rosary should be made of human teeth, the bowl (or plate) of a man's skull; the seat of *siddha*-skin, the bracelet of woman's hair. The sacrificial ingredients saturated with wine, meat, etc., are to be eaten, o beloved. His solid food is young fish, etc., the *mudrā* (here gesture) is the "Vīṇā-sound"—(*vīṇā-rava*) gesture (possibly the *vīṇā-mudrā* usually given to the goddess Sarasvatī Vīṇāpāṇī ("Holder of the Vīṇā"). Ritualistic intercourse is held with a woman who is not one's wife (the literal translation "another's wife", though lexicographically correct, may be a distortion of anti-tantric writers and interpreters), and women of all castes are equally eligible. Thus is left-handed practice described which bestows all *siddhis*, o Benign Goddess.'[3]

Left-handed rites defy the usual time-schedules; worship can be done at any time, preferably at midnight (when other worship is more or less avoided); there is no rule about the time for bathing and evacuating. There are no caste-restrictions all castes are viewed alike. Yet there is certainly an anti-Brahmin undertone in these instructions—very few Brahmins would undertake *vāmācāra* worship unless they were prepared to court complete ostracism. In Mahārāṣṭra, even the term Śākta has an unpleasant connotation; *vāmācāra* is identical with gross fornication—not only in Marāṭhī usage but virtually in all languages with the exception of those spoken in regions of tantric predominance (Bengal, Assam, Kerala—although even there the Hindu Renaissance is gradually effecting a pejorization of the terms).

The *kulācāra*, the third division according to the *Rudrayāmala*, is a more opaque matter. It seems to unite and transcend both the right- and the left-handed traditions in a sort of dialectical synthesis. Some authors identify *kulācāra* with *Rājayoga*,[4] though a Rājayoga with a left-handed slant. The text is terse 'I shall now propound *kulācāra* performed by the best yogins: if one worships always and everywhere the *kula*-woman, the *kulaguru*, and the *kula*-goddess, o Great Goddess, this is called *kulācāra*.'[5]

Now the 'three dispositions' are usually—though not always—allocated to the three types of worship. The *Kālīvilāsa Tantra* says 'Listen to the three dispositions, o Devī, they are classified as the divine (*divyabhāva*), the heroic (*vīrabhāva*), and the animal-like (*paśubhāva*). The first is god-like, the second is intensely exciting, the third is always pure and shining white.'[6] Notice that the animal-like disposition is not being disparaged; the categories seem almost value-free, and if this was really meant to be so, then it was an intellectual achievement of no mean order. However, all texts do not display this degree of sophistication—there is a derogatory tone in the more frequent evaluations of a hierarchical order, as in 'the disposition, o Lord, is threefold—*divya*, *vīra*, and *paśu*; the first (i.e. the *divyabhāva*) is the best, giving total perfection, the second (i.e. *vīrabhāva*) is mediocre, the third (*paśubhāva*) is totally objectionable'.[7] The Hindu tantric tradition assumes that every kind of worship—i.e. Vedic, tantric, or heretical—falls under either of these three dispositions. It is probable that the famous triadic elaboration of types of behaviour and action in the eighteenth canto of the *Bhagavadgītā* provided a powerful precedent for the tantric triads under investigation. It is not necessary to stipulate a more recent origin of the *Gītā* than Professor S. N. Dasgupta did; the fact that the *Gītā* triads have not affected Buddhist tantras is not really a puzzle, for the Hindu tantrics were naturally more open to schemes propounded in earlier Hindu lore. The Hindu tantrics' desire to be taken seriously within orthodoxy might well be accountable for this rather striking analogue.

There is hardly any practising Hindu who does not know the nomenclature 'the five Ms' (*pañcamakāra*) or 'the five essentials' (*pañcatattva*) which are used as synonyms, though more stigma attaches to the first term. It seems to me that tantrics themselves avoid using *pañcamakāra* in their conversation with non-tantric Hindus; the term *pañcatattva* is more respectable, but also less well known in this connotation.[8]

The five Ms are enumerated many times in all tantras of Hindu provenance. Although some Hindu tantric texts speak derogatorily about the use of wine, fish, sex, as singular terms, I have not found any tantric text which would deny the *pañcatattva* or *pañcamakāra-sādhanā* an important place in the ritualistic hierarchy. Many passages pronounce eulogy (*praśaṃsā*) upon the five Ms, but many just state them without any value judgment, as for example 'wine, meat, fish, and parched grain as well as sexual union, this pentad of Ms applies in the union of Śiva and Śakti.'[9] The ambivalence of the 'animal'-status lends itself to all sorts of speculation. Ghilḍayāl, for instance, argues like this: the animal-status is the original status. Man is the foremost among the animals, but as long as he does not obtain intuitive insight or wisdom he will remain an animal. Transcribing the phrase into Nāgarī characters, he says: 'that is why occidental scholars call him a "rational animal".'[10] As long as a man entertains the idea of duality, he must needs think that things and persons are either good or evil. This idea, however, entails animality, and so long as it lasts he will have to do his *sādhanā* with the animal-disposition, and so long he will not be able to perform *sādhanā* as a hero or in the divine disposition.

Now the idea that the notion of duality entails being animal-like is canonical; the Upaniṣad teaches that the gods use him as their beast of burden who views himself as different from them, and for that different from anything else. Ghilḍayāl then muses: 'If a person cannot even get on the back of an ass, then even if he climbs on to the back of an Arab steed and is not killed in the attempt he is sure to get his bones broken.'

The 'dispositions' are by no means conceived as static. The individual can and must progress from the lower to the higher dispositions, if possible during one lifetime, and the idea seems to be that a person starting off with *sādhanā* in the lower dispositions advances automatically into the higher reaches providing he does well with what he starts with, and does not try to begin higher up.

As in all Indian criteriology, the tantras provide lists of standards (*lakṣaṇa*) whereby the aspirant can negatively test his disposition. The criteria are eight, and they are called fetters (*pāśa*): 'hatred, doubt, fear, shame, backbiting,[11] arrogance from the notion of belonging to a good family (*kula*—lit. just 'family', but the sense is best given in my paraphrase), conformity (*śīla*), arrogance about one's caste (*jāti*), bound by these fetters one is a *jīva* (an individual, a human being), free from them one is Sadāśiva (the God Śiva in his highest phenomenal aspect)'.[12]

Whereas the first three or even the first five are common stock with non-tantric moralists, Hindu and Buddhist, the last three are tantric paradigms. That there should be no pride in one's descent and in one's ancestors has of course often been sung by non-tantric saints of India. But the flavour here is definitely anti-caste, or at least anti-Brahmanical. That *śīla* should be denigrated, would seem strange at first: for it means, among other things, discipline and *sādhanā* are based on discipline. However, it is understood in a different sense: not discipline in itself is animal-like, but the fear of social opprobrium in the event of a lapse of outward discipline, or etiquette; it is for this reason that I paraphrase the term as conformity, or conformism.

The notion—unorthodox no doubt when judged by the Brahmanical code—that there is no real caste, or that caste is a fiction, is well documented in much non-tantric literature,[13] but the tantrics are much more emphatic about it. They do what Nietzsche wanted to accomplish . . . '*eine Umwertung aller Werte*', a revaluation of all values. Mircea Eliade uses his own neologism 'revalorization' when speaking about yoga and tantra, and though I do not know if Nietzsche was at the back of his mind when he coined the word, Eliade's term is certainly most fitting.

Ghilḍayāl likens the three *bhāvas* to the three physical ages of human life—childhood, adolescence, adult life. Just as there is a progression of knowledge from the three Rs to whatever wisdom and skill a man may acquire, *sādhanā* progresses in an analogous fashion: the child has to stick to conventional worship, to the Vedic sacrifice and the orthodox observance; the adolescent learns a sort of compromise *en route* to contemplative perfection: he uses the *pratinidhi* or substitute tantric worship, right-handed *sādhanā*, that is, directed towards tantric meditation objects, but without the use of the five ingredients commencing with the letter M. Adult age then ushers the supreme *sādhanā*, left-handed tantric observance utilizing the five ingredients 'literally'.

There is a possible distinction between the *paśu* and the other *bhāva-s* according to the way in which they interpret the meaning of the five Ms. The texts are sufficiently equivocal about the matter: whether a *paśu* means a *sādhaka* who has been taught to view the five ingredients in a *paśu*—fashion—(viz. *mada* as coconut water instead of wine, etc.) or whether it means one who by his own initial choice has come to view the substitute-ingredients (*anukalpatattva*, *pratinidhi*) as more beneficial is left open to the interpreter. A tantric might well hold the view that most persons —Hindus and Buddhists, that is—shy away from the actual ingredients (*pratyakṣa tattva*), because they are *paśus* as yet, regardless of whether their preceptor has instructed them in this direction or not.

It appears that it is not really important what the specific materials are, provided their function as 'substitutes' is realized.

The *Kulacūḍāmaṇi Tantra*, the *Bhairavayāmala*, and most of the important tantras list divergent ingredients. Avalon[14] lists a few, saying 'these have been variously described and sometimes as follows: in lieu of wine the *paśu* should, if a Brahmin, take milk, if a Kṣattrīya, *ghee*, if a Vaiśya, honey, and if a Śūdra a liquor made from rice. Coconut water in a bell metal utensil is also taken as a substitute. Salt, ginger, sesamum, wheat beans (*maśakalāi*) and garlic are some of the substitutes for meat; the white *brinjal* (egg-plant), red radish, *masur* (a kind of pulse, i.e. *masur dāl*), red sesamum and *pāniphala* (a water plant) take the place of fish. Paddy, rice, wheat, and grain generally are *mudrā* both in the *paśu* and the *vīra-sādhanā*. In lieu of *maithuna* there may be an offering of flowers with the hands formed into the *kacchapa mudrā* (the tortoise-like *mudrā*), the union of the *karavīra* flowers representing the *liṅga* and the *aparājitā* flower representing the female organ, or there may be union with the *sādhaka's* wedded wife.' As usual, Avalon gives no reference, but it is almost certain that he got this information from some Bengali tantric (hence, *maśakalāi*, a Bengali culinary term).

A late manual, also of Bengali origin, enumerates the initial or elementary ingredients (*ādya-tattva*). It lists hemp (*vijayā*) as *ādyamada* (original wine), ginger (*adraka*) as *ādyaśuddhi* (original purity) as meat, lemon (*jaṃbirā*) as *ādyamīna* (original fish) processed paddy (*dhānyaja*) probably the popular Bengali *mūlī* or puffed rice as *ādyamudrā* (original *mudrā*), and finally the devotee's wife as *ādyaśakti* (the original *śakti*).

It would seem that the disposition of the individual devotee has been viewed as functional by many tantric authors; the sacred office itself renders the 'ingredient' pure and extends ritualistic purity to the aspirant. Outside worship, every human being may be called a *paśu*, but in the act of meditation only those are *paśus* who choose the *paśu*-rites, and we have by now realized that *paśu* in tantric tradition means the conformist to non-tantric, orthodox ritual—which is the Vedic ritual and observance for the Hindu, and the *śrāvakayāna* for the Buddhist. Such an attitude is implied in a rather beautiful *śloka* in the *Uttara Tantra*, quoted by Avalon.[15]

'When there is no ritual, she should not even mentally touch another male; but during the ritual, o Goddess, she should satisfy him like a *hetaira.*' This verse, incidentally, is one of the rare instances in tantric literature, where the instruction is given to the female partner, the *śakti* or *mudrā*; for in spite of the assumedly matrifocal atmosphere of the tantras, it is the male that is assumed to be lewd and who has to be curbed through the appropriate instructions.

Whatever the variant readings and evaluations of *paśu-* and *divya-bhāva*, there is no doubt in my mind that the central attraction and aspiration of the tantric lies in what the Hindu *ācārya* called *vīrabhāva*, i.e. the heroic attitude. It is the central theme in all enumerations (i.e. standing between *paśu* and *divya*, regardless of whether *paśu* or *divya* are mentioned first). I would like to put it this way: what the tantrics really *mean* when they talk of their ultimate *sādhanā* is *vīra-sādhanā*, the meditation routine of the 'hero'; both *paśu* and *divya* are approximations to *vīra-sādhanā*; *paśu*, a derogatory, and *divya* a laudatory, one. The fact is that eventually the *paśu* and the *divya* trainees undergo, or ought to undergo, the *vīra* ritual which uses the active, actual ingredients, the five Ms. My statement is at present based on a purely formal consideration: both the *paśu* and the *divya*, and apart from them *all* Hindus and Buddhists who know about tantrism, regard it as *the* tantric exercise, and whatever falls short of it, is not central. This may be noted in a resentful or in a commending mood, but the fact remains that tantric *sādhanā* in common parlance means exactly what *vīra-sādhanā*, the 'heroic' mode of worship, means in technical language.

It is, of course, understood that an aspirant can successfully practice only the *sādhanā* that accords with his 'mood'—i.e. *paśu-sādhanā* with the animal '*bhāva*' or 'mood', etc.

There is an interesting passage on the transition from *paśu-* to *vīra-* worship. It is found in one of the most widely accepted texts, from which we have already had occasion to quote.[16] It says: 'the person who is to take *dīkṣā*, him the *guru* should tear about and should beat up. If he (the prospective disciple) does not show any signs of dismay, but on the contrary thinks that the *guru* is now about to bestow his grace upon him; and, if thus thinking, he displays such phenomena as horripilation, trembling of his eyes and his voice, then this is an indication that the disciple is ready for the initiation (viz. for the initiation that effects his transition from *paśu-* to *vīra-sādhanā*, or from the worship through 'substitutes' to that through the actual five Ms).

Ghilḍayāl premits a laudatory poem to his chapter on the *vīra*-attitude; I am not sure if the poem is his own or a quotation—he does not indicate anything to that effect. But the verse certainly sums up the elated, or even euphoric, attitude the tantric entertains about the prospects of *vīra*-worship, and about the concomitant heroic attitude . . . 'at his left sits the beauteous damsel, given to dalliance, at his right stands the bowl of liquor; in front of him the vessel containing *mudrā* (parched kidney bean or another preparation thought to be aphrodisiacal), and the hot meat of the wild boar; the propounder of the true *guru*'s words is the *vīṇā* (the ancient Indian string instrument, with a lute-like tone) with sweet and appealing sounds (lit. sweet with *rasa* or aesthetic sentiment); the road of the *kaulas* (i.e. the tantric adepts who all belong to the "*kula*" or family of initiates) is particularly profound, and is inaccessible even to yogis. Surrounded by abundant spirituous beverage, I am intent upon worship through enjoyment, I am about to commence upon the path of many methods, I have relinquished the company of *paśus*, I am relying on Bhairavī (the goddess). Content at the *guru's* feet, I am Śiva, I am Śiva.'[17]

When the *kaula*—a term which is now almost synonomous with *vīra* when used in the tantric in-group—says that his specific training puts him above the yogi—or, as in this text, that his own path is inaccessible to yogis, he means the yogis of all other schools and tendencies, but, more likely, the classical, orthodox yogis of the Patāñjala school. The reason for this is clear—but there is a strange paradox: he does not thus denigrate—at least not overtly—the *haṭha*-yogi, although *haṭha*-yoga (admitted even by its own votaries) is a training inferior to *dhyāna*-yoga or meditations towards enstasy, *haṭha*-yoga being considered (even by most *haṭha*-yogis) as preparatory to the less somatocentric forms of contemplation. The tantric derives most of his physical routine from the semi-historical father of *haṭha*-yoga, Matsyendranātha (Macchindranāth, Gorakhnāth's *guru*; the Buddhist tantric tradition enumerates him with the eighty-four *siddhas*; some scholars want him to be identical with Luipa, the Buddhist Sahajayāna preceptor),[18] and Eliade rightly observes that all tantrism presupposes mastery of the intricate *haṭha*-yoga training.

The hallmark of '*vīra*'-attitude is that the *vīra* does not regard himself as numerically separate from the object of his worship or the entity meditated-upon. As long as the devotee regards himself as numerically different from that supreme object, he is still a *paśu*. In fact, this implicit monistic attitude is the covert criterion of the *vīra-sādhaka*. This criterion is shared by the *divya* or divine worshipper, and it seems to me that the very fact of its being a common criterion obliterates an important difference between the *vīra* and the *divya*. It would also seem that the distinction between the *vīra* and the *divya* is tenuous. Epithets used for the one are equally used for the other, but they are not used for the *paśu*.

The risk of social approbrium and ostracism is particularly strong in the *vīra*-method, and the *sādhaka's* resolution has to be pretty firm. Ghilḍayāl quotes: 'Let all kinsmen revile me, let wife and sons forsake me, let people ridicule me on sight, and let the kings punish me. Let Lakṣmī stay on or leave me, I shall not relinquish this path. He who has this sort of devotion, he will acquire the *siddhi* of the left-handed path.'[19]

Returning once more to the Vasiṣṭha story (fully given in Chapter 3), which apparently provides the one extant and powerful link between Hindu tantric *sādhanā* and Vajrayāṇa, its hero being a *sādhaka* between, or perhaps within, the two traditions, let me revert to a passage omitted in the earlier account of the episode:

(Vasiṣṭha then continues in considerable bewilderment—see Chapter 3): 'How is it that these heaven-clad (i.e. naked) perfect sages are intoxicated by the drinking of blood? They take wine and meat and they sport with beautiful damsels. Constantly filling themselves with meat and wine, their eyes look red. These Great

Siddhas, who can bestow boons when pleased, and who can destroy when angered, with their anti-Vedic methods, who can rely on them? How can the mind be purified by this sort of process? Without the Vedic observance, how can there be *siddhi*? (*manaḥpravṛttireteṣu katham bhavati pāvanī katham vā jayate siddhirveda-kāryam vinā prabho*?)'.

The Buddha answered thus: 'O Vasiṣṭha, listen to the esoteric in-group method (*kaulamārga*), by the mere acquaintance with which a person becomes like Rudra (Śiva) himself in a short time. I shall give you the essence of this method. First of all, the *vīra* should be completely free from the *paśu*-attitude, pure, discriminating. He should completely avoid the company of *paśus* (which means of people following the Vedic ritual), should stay in solitude, and should get rid of the seven inner enemies such as lust and anger, etc. He should practise *haṭha*-yoga. He should study the Vedas and should understand their essence fully. He should direct his mind to virtuous deeds, should practise *prāṇāyāma* and should gradually destroy the outgoing tendencies of his mind. His body will begin to perspire—this is the lowest stage.'

The lowest stage is the *paśu*-stage: and it clearly means *both* the Vedic and the Patāñjali-yogic practice, as well as *haṭha*-yoga. This is important, because in spite of Patāñjali's and his followers' assertion that their teachings and disciplines are Vedic, presaged in the Veda, there has always been considerable suspicion amongst Vedic ritualists about Patāñjali's method. I recall a conversation with Professor V. Raghavan, no doubt one of India's most outstanding Sanskritists, and an orthodox Brahmin. He takes strong objection[20] to the notion that spiritual emancipation can or should be reached through yogic processes. He says that any person who fulfils the moral and the ritualistic observances laid down in the Veda reaches *mokṣa* at the end of his life and will not have to continue the circle of birth and death. This seems to be the attitude of the majority of learned orthodox paṇḍits in Hindu India. In other words, there is a marked aversion to super-erogatory efforts *en route* to emancipation, from the axiomatic shackles of metempsychosis. This aversion is directed even against Patāñjali and other orthodox forms of yoga—but tantrism is anathema and felt to be downright scandalous by the orthodox paṇḍits, especially where left-handed rites are involved. The paṇḍit's argument against these rites runs somewhat like this: the fact that a set of instructions is given in Sanskrit does not in itself guarantee that these are valid and emulable instructions. If a book or a chapter starts: 'Śiva says' or 'the Devī says', this does not guarantee that it has any canonical status whatever. It is only the consensus of learned, orthodox (i.e. Vedic, Brahmanical opinion), and the tradition of every specific opinion which makes a text acceptable as either *śruti* or *smṛti*.

All this, from the *vīra*, i.e. the left-handed 'hero's' viewpoint, is the talk of the *paśu*. From the orthodox Brahmin viewpoint the tantric is a self-appointed *vīra*, though it is he who really is a *paśu* who gives his passions free play. The controversy is semantic yet fundamental and is bound to stay.

Before we proceed, let us repeat that the *vīra* considers *both* the Vedic *and* the Patāñjala yoga procedure as *paśu*—hence the injunction to practise *prāṇāyāma* (breath control,)[21] one of the salient features of Patāñjali's course, is included in the practices incumbent on one who is still a *paśu*. The *vīra* is explicit about the Vedic observance being *paśubhāva*, but he does not mention Patāñjali or orthodox yoga. It seems to me that tantric authors wanted to have an ally in Patāñjali's followers as well as in *Haṭha-yoga*—and although tantric apologetics constantly assert the conformity of tantric with Vedic injunctions, they know they have already antagonized the Vedic traditionalists so strongly that it hardly matters if they describe their observances as *paśu*-ritual.

The Buddha then continues his instruction to the Brahmin sage: 'In the next higher stage, the body begins to tremble; this is the middling stage. In the last, the highest stage, the body of the contemplative begins to levitate. In this manner, through the fruition of *prāṇāyāma*, the worshipper becomes a (true) yogi. Thereupon he should undergo a vow of silence, and should meditate in solitude on Śiva, Kṛṣṇa, Brahmā, etc., and should imagine that they are as fickle as the wind. Then the *sādhaka* should establish his mind in the primordial Śakti, who is of the essence of cognition (*citta*). Then the *sādhaka* should assume the attitude of the great *vīra* and should worship the Śakti-circle, the Vaiṣṇava-circle, the nine planets, and the supreme goddess of the *kula* (Kulakātyāyanī). She is the foundation of intuitive wisdom (*jñāna*) and of bliss (*ānanda*). She is that eighteen-armed goddess Raudrī, who is fond of mountain-like heaps of wine and meat. All the great gods obtained their power of manifestation, preservation, and destruction through the grace of that *Magna Mater*, and she can be obtained only through the *vīra-sādhanā* which crystallizes in *cīnācāra*. One who thus proceeds obtains the occult power of attraction in one month, in two months he becomes as knowledgeable and learned as Bṛhaspati (the Vedic god of speech, knowledge, and the sacerdotal skills), after four months the practicant becomes as powerful as the Lords of the Directions, after six months he becomes like Cupid (note the high rank sexual attractiveness and success is given in this discipline), after six months he is as powerful as Rudra (Śiva) himself. In six months, a Brahmin, if united with a Śakti, can become a full-fledged yogi.'

The last statement is quite revealing: *śakti-sahita* may of course mean 'together with Śakti' in the sense of 'through the offices of Śakti', i.e. the goddess, whom he worships, *Sahita*—also having instrumental import. I don't think that this is implied, but simply that he does *cīnācāra* or *vīra-sādhanā* which involves worship in union with *śakti*—i.e. in *yuganaddha*, as the exact parallel to the Buddhist Vajrayāṇa's union with the *mudrā* (*phyag rgya*). Why a 'Brahmin'? Brahmins are the main target of the *paśu*-parlance. They are often excluded from tantric *sādhanā* altogether—which works both ways, as the orthodox Brahmin would not stoop to such things as *vīrācāra*—'left-handed' (*vāmācara*) is a term of overt abuse for all orthodox Hindus. Now unless Brahmin here means just a learned or well-disposed person in general—a virtuous man much in the sense the Buddha uses the term in the Pāli canon—it must be an expression of the tantric proselytizing zeal which I found to be quite subtle. 'Even Brahmins are accepted'—a concession of no mean importance—for in a way the Brahmin *qua* Brahmin is the arch-foe of the tantrics: he has usurped the monopoly of Vedic ritual and of the Vedic lore, he legislates on what is orthodox and what heretical, and he prevents seekers from finding the spiritual ends of life if they do not happen to be twice-born.

'If', so the 'Śiva in the form of Buddha' continues his instruction, 'not even Śiva himself can accomplish anything, how much less so can human beings with their frail minds?'

In this manner the Buddha-formed Śiva made Vasiṣṭha do the *vīra-sādhanā* and as the latter performed the worship of the Mother, of the Universe through the five ingredients beginning with M., i.e. *madya* (liquor), *māṃsa* (meat), *matsya* (fish), *mudrā* (parched grain or kidney bean), and *maithuna* he became a complete yogi.

Now Ghilḍayāl in his paraphrase uses *śakti* instead of *maithuna* as the fifth M. The original reads correctly *maithuna*; this is perhaps a Freudian slip of the pen—*maithuna* is, of course, *with* the Śakti—but *śakti* commences with the palatal sibilant, not with m. This corroborates my reading of 'united with *a* Śakti' rather than 'through (worshipping) Śakti' in the above section.

Mudrā in Hindu tantra means parched grain or kidney beans—any cereal aphrodisiac—or believed aphrodisiac; in Buddhist tantra[22] it means the female partner or adept; in Hindu and Buddhist non-tantric literature it most frequently means a ritualistic gesture. But it is strange that these four very different meanings have not been sufficiently stressed. It will not be inapposite to list the four meanings systematically:

mudrā	non-tantric Hindu	non-tantric Buddhist[23]	tantric Hindu	tantric Buddhist
	ritualistic gesture, esp. constituent of *pūjā* or formal worship		parched grain, kidney bean, any cereal aphrodisiac used as the third m-ingredient	the female partner in the enstatic process

Now the chief apologetic argument of modern tantrics is somewhat like this: the five Ms are inveighed against both by scholars and laymen—as dirty (*gandā*), taboo, or not amenable to religious treatment except under sacerdotal sanction which removes their poignance and their importance. But, so the tantric apology continues, when viewed candidly these things are the most important in human life and all religious texts have dealt with them directly or indirectly. Why, then, should not specific religious texts state them systematically and evaluate the possibilities for spiritual advancement? Ghilḍayāl, a very typical tantric apologetic, puts it this way (p. 28) 'sexual enjoyment is established as an excellent matter. If it is necessary for every living being, if it is a natural act, then its performance is a natural worship, that is to say, it is the worship of the World Mother.'[24]

Tantric apologetics like to adduce non-tantric canonical texts which corroborate their view; Ghilḍayāl (p. 31) quotes the *Śatapatha Brāhmaṇa* as saying: 'the joyous embrace of man and woman is the *agnihotra* sacrifice' (i.e. the pouring of the oblation into the *agnihotra* fire, one of the ritualistic acts obligatory for the Vedic Brahmins). Then there are scores of tales about gods and goddesses who did not prevail against the arrows of Cupid, and the Purāṇas are full of these narratives; the story of Viṣṇu as Mohinī, of the birth of the War God through Pārvatī's seduction of Śiva the eternal ascetic—a mythological episode made into one of the most famous poems by Kālīdāsa in his *Kumārasaṃbhava*. Of course, the apologists would suppress the orthodox matrimonial presuppositions. There is a passage in the *Bṛhadāranyaka Upaniṣad* which tells how a man should court and consummate a woman—and here there is no reference to whether they are married or not; orthodox paṇḍits aver that it refers to the married man courting his own spouse; but even if this does not follow from the text itself, the vast majority of *śruti* or canonical texts presuppose marriage to consummation. To this the tantric would answer that the tantric consecration of a Śakti is of higher order than a marriage ceremony in the Vedic tradition—the fact that it is not accepted by a society ruled by self-styled legislators in matters of moral right and wrong does not concern them.

Ghilḍayāl then says that all religions offer important eulogies on sex, covertly or overtly as the case may be, and he says about

Buddhism (p. 32): 'the Buddhist took to this *vīra*-path so extensively, that there is probably not a single Buddhist tantra which does not mention *vīrācāra*.' Indeed there is no such Buddhist tantra. Buddhist texts do not use the term '*vīrācāra*'—but all the instructions contained in the '*anuttara*' (the 'unexcelled') category of Buddhist tantras would be called '*vīrācāra*' by the Hindu tantric.

To summarize the meaning of *pañcamakāra*: they are the five things commencing with the letter m: *madya* (liquor), *matsya* or *mīna* (fish), *māṃsa* (meat), *mudrā* (parched kidney bean, parched grain or any other cereal prepared in a manner which is thought to be aphrodisiacal), and *maithuna* (sexual union). The reference is general—tantrics use it descriptively, orthodox Hindus disparagingly. If these five Ms are materially used, and the relevant instructions are being taken literally, then Hindus call this *vāmācāra* or 'left-handed practice'; if they are taken in some metaphorical, indirect sense then they refer to it as *dakṣiṇācāra* or 'right-handed practice'. The right-handed tradition is also called somewhat ambiguously worship through substitutes (*pratinidhi*).

I now proceed to describe the preparation for and the performance of the *sādhanā* of the five Ms. Left-handed tantrics today use several texts as their manuals, i.e. the two great *yāmala-s*, the *Rudrayāmala*[25] and *Brahmāyāmala*; the *Mahānirvāṇa Tantra*, the *Kulārṇava Tantra*, the *Yoginī Tantra*, and any of the collection of *mantras* available to the *sādhaka*,[26] as for example the *Mantramahārṇava* or the *Mantramahodadhi* with which texts we are already familiar.[27] Only quite recently some comprehensive instruction manuals were published, which contain both procedural instructions and the *mantras* as well as the texts which are to be recited. I am here following such a recent manual published in Sanskrit and Hindi. It is called *Vāmamārga*, i.e. simply 'the left-handed path'.[28]

As in most non-tantric *sādhanās* and observances of the ritualistic or meditative order, the instructions proceed in two parts, the first half (*pūrvārddha*) being preparatory, the second half (*uttarārdha*) being the central instructions.

The *pūrvārddha* (first half) starts with morning-observances (*prātaḥkṛtya*). The *sādhaka* has to get rid of sleep and inertia, then sit up straight on his bed, starting immediately to worship his *guru* in the thousand-petalled lotus (*sahasradala-kamalacakram*).[29] The accompanying invocation is quite orthodox, and the progression from the milder, more general, texts to the more radically tantric ones is very gradual. This initial invocation reads 'obeisance to the true *guru*, the destroyer of the fetters of phenomenal existence, giver of the sight of wisdom, to the giver of (sensuous) enjoyment and liberation. To the blessed *guru*, who is the supreme Brahman in human form, the remover of ignorance, the light of the *kula-dharma* (i.e. the *dharma* of the tantric in-group), obeisance.'[30]

He then offers a flower to the preceptor-couple (it being understood that the tantric preceptor is worshipped together with his own wife or his anointed Śakti), and mutters the *mantra* 'to [name of his specific *guru*] the Lord of Bliss and to [name of the *guru*'s consort] the mother Śakti I offer worship, and I offer this ether-like flower, obeisance.'[31] This is followed by various *mudrās* together with the enunciation of the corresponding element—*bījas*,[32] as *yaṃ* for air, *raṃ* for fire, and *laṃ* for earth, as he inserts these *bījas* repeating the same invocation.

Next, the *sādhaka* should murmur the *bīja aiṃ*—which is the *bīja* of the goddess—from ten to a hundred times.

This is followed by the worship of his chosen deity (*iṣṭa-devatā*, the Tibetan *yid dam*), and the procedure is quite analogous to that of the just completed worship of the *guru*. The offerings consist of consecutive oblations of flowers, incense in paste form (*gandha*), incense sticks (*dhūpa*), lights, and *naivedyam*, which is a libation of various constituents like milk, sugar, rose-water, etc. These oblations (*arpanam*) are by no means purely tantric—every Hindu employs them for formal worship. However, the incantations which follow them are culled from tantric texts, and the name of the chosen deity—a goddess in this case—is filled into the *śloka* which says 'worship unto the sustaineress of the universe, to the One of all forms, to the original . . . (here the name of the goddess is pronounced in the dative) . . . to thee, the doer and the remover (or destroyer), worship.'[33]

Only after this should the *sādhaka* leave his bed, placing his left foot on the floor first as he gets out (the left being the auspicious side in the tantric tradition—outside of which Hindus share the suspicion about 'getting out of bed with one's left foot' with many occidentals)—he should then clean his bowels, cleanse his teeth with twigs of the *nīm*-tree, and should then proceed to the ritualistic bath (*snānam*) which is obligatory for the tantric devotee as for all practising Hindus.

The tantric's bath is hardly different from that of the ancient Vedic Brahmins, and this may be a peace-making device through adoption of orthodox forms by the tantrics; these are frequent in all sections of the tantric cult—including the sporadic choice of purely Vedic *mantras*. Our manual says (p. 45) 'after rinsing his mouth the *sādhaka* should enter a water expanse (i.e. a pond, tank, or river, or the sea if it is near at hand); he should stand, the water reaching to his navel, and should take a dip fully immersing himself. Then he must do three more *ācamanam* (rinsings) meditating on these *mantras*: *ātmatattvāya svāhā* (to the self-essence, *svāhā*) and *śivatattvāya svāhā* (to the Śiva-essence, *svāhā*).[34] He then inscribes the *kulayantra* (i.e. the simple triangular *maṇḍala* which is the basic diagram of all tantrics) into the water expanse before him (i.e. he draws his fingers over the surface of the water as if he drew the diagram); he inscribes (viz. in the same hypothetical manner) the *mūlamantra* (i.e. the "*bīja*" (seed-*mantra*) of his chosen goddess) into it and mutters this seed-*mantra* twelve times. He then contemplates the water inside the (imagined) triangle as being of the form of lustre, and he sprinkles drops of it as *arpanam* (oblation) to the sun.'

The last act duplicates the ancient Brahmin tradition of offering certain things imagined to partake of a hierarchically higher substance into that substance (i.e. the sense of hearing into the cosmic ether, the act of speaking into the fire, etc.)—this is the important observance of *bhūtaśuddhi* (purification of the elements).

Next, the *sādhaka* settles down for his *sandhyā*,[35] which differs considerably from its orthodox model. He invokes the holy places (*pīṭhas*), making the *aṅkuṣa-mudrā* with his hands,[36] chanting the verse 'O Gaṅgā, Yamunā, Godāvarī, Sarasvatī, Narmadā, Indus, and Kāverī (i.e. the seven holy rivers), deign to be present in this water', referring to the *sandhyā*—water which he keeps in a vessel in front of him.[37] Next, he pronounces the *mūla-mantra* (the basic *mantra* of his chosen deity) again, twelve times over this libational water. The chief difference between the tantric *sandhyā* and the orthodox Hindu *sandhyā* consists in the contents of the concomitant meditation. The main point of departure is that tantric *sandhyā* uses the thought construct of the mystical body as conceived in the Hindu and Vajrayāṇa Buddhist esoteric systems, i.e., the notion of the central duct surrounded by the two peripheral ducts which penetrate the *cakras* on their way to the experience of union in the higher *cakra* thought to be located beneath the cranium (i.e. *suṣumnā*, *īḍā*, and *piṅgalā* in Hinduism, *avadhūtī*—Tibetan *kun 'dar ma, rasanā*—Tibetan *ro ma*—and *lalanā* —Tibetan *brkyaṅ ma* in Vajrayāṇa). In tantric *sandhyā*, the *sādhaka* draws up the libational water through the *īḍā* (which is to the left of the *suṣumnā*), and lets it out through the *piṅgalā* (to the right of the *suṣumnā*).[38] The *īḍā-piṅgalā-suṣumnā* do not even enter orthodox Vedic *sandhyā*. He then imagines that his hand is as hard as a diamond (*vajra*) and pronouncing the seed-*mantra phaṭ* he pours water over this hand—thereby driving out the sin-man (*pāpa-puruṣa*) from his body.

Next, he offers *ārghya* (libation to the sun) uttering the *mantra* '*Oṃ hrīṃ haṃsa ghriṇi sūrya idam ārghyam tubhyaṃ svāhā*' which would mean '*Oṃ hrīṃ* o Sun take this *ārghya* libation for thee *svāhā*'—if '*ghriṇi*' were a verbal form of *grah* which it is not.[39]

The next preparatory meditation is that on Gāyatrī. 'Gāyatrī', in the first place, is a Vedic synonym of Vāk or Sarasvatī, the goddess of speech and learning, the spouse of the demiurge Brahmā. It is also the name of a Vedic metre, and the *Gāyatrī par excellence* is the *mantra* universally accepted as the most sacred by all orthodox Hindus. This *mantra*—on the orthodox count—must not be used by male persons who do not belong to the three upper castes and who have not been invested with the sacred thread; nor must it be used by any woman, of whatever caste. I have so far not been able to decide whether the *Gāyatrī-mantra* is used by tantrics in its original form, or whether only a modified *Gāyatrī* is used by them. Some tantrics personally known to me use it no doubt, others use a modified version of it, or they simply use a tantric verse in the *Gāyatrī* or a similar metre. For instance, our manual prescribes this verse as the tantric's *Gāyatrī* '(I worship) in the morning the red-coloured, two-armed princess, who holds a *kamaṇḍalu* [the water-container used by all ascetics, usually made of a hollow coconut] full of lustral water, who wears a pure garland, dressed in the skin of the black antelope, seated on a swan, with a pure smile'.[40]

The *sandhyā* is followed by *tarpana*—in the same order as in orthodox Hindu ritual; *tarpana* is the pouring of (lustral) water into water—into a pond, tank, river, or the sea—another instance of *bhūtaśuddhi* (purification of the elements). In order to consecrate the water which is to be poured into the natural expanse, he pronounces the water-*bīja* (seed-syllable) *vaṃ* and does the *dhenumudrā*[41] above it, thus transubstantiating it into nectar (*jal ko . . . amṛtmay kare*, p. 50). He utters a formula in propitiation of his *guru's guru* (*parameṣṭhiguru*), and to the *gurus'* wives or Śaktis. The latter clause is the only important difference between tantric and orthodox *tarpana*. The *tarpana*, here as in orthodox Hinduism, invokes the blessings of the tutelary deity, and establishes a permanent spiritual bond between the tutelary deity and the *sādhaka's guru*, as well as the *sādhaka's* family and clan (*gotra*). The only other difference seems to be that the tutelary deity of the tantric is always Śiva and Bhairavī (Śiva's Śakti), whereas in orthodox Hinduism the tutelary deity varies according to the *gotra* of the householder who performs *tarpana*; Śiva and Bhairavī are perfectly acceptable and quite frequent *kuladevatās* or tutelary deities with non-tantric groups as well, especially in the Himālayan tier.

The ritual preceding the actual five-letter rite is very much along orthodox lines, and I shall point out the deviations only; all this is still part of the 'first half' (*purvārddha*), i.e., the preparatory portion of the injunctions.

When performing the purification of the seat (*āsana-śodhanam*)

—i.e. the mat or deer skin or whatever is used as a seat for meditation—the formula of obeisance is 'worship unto Kāmarūpa' (*kāmarupāya namaḥ*); Kāmarūpa is one of the main *pīṭhas* (i.e. seats, centres of tantric worship, common to Buddhist and Hindu tantrics) and is located in Assam (the region is an administrative district even now, viz. Kamrup). The *sādhaka*'s seat is now hypostasized into the great seat (*mahāpīṭha*) of the goddess.

Along with it, he worships the *ādhāra-śakti* (i.e. the primordial matrix which is represented both in the lowest centre of the yogic body, as well as manifested in the yogi's seat, which at this point symbolizes the base (*ādhāra*) of his universe. The *mantra* (non-existent in the orthodox tradition) for this item is '*klīṃ* worship to the base-*śakti*-lotus seat' (*klīṃ ādhāraśaktikamalāsanāya namaḥ*).

As to the material proper for the seat, the *Gandharva Tantra* (seventh chapter) makes some definite suggestions: 'when a seat of black antelope skin is used, it gives *mukti* (liberation); a tiger skin gives both *mukti* and wealth to the *sādhaka*; for the fulfilment of the mind's desires a woollen *āsana* is the best; and particularly an *āsana* of red wool yields one's heart's wishes. For the fruition of the *mantra* and for the worship of the goddess Tripurasundarī (a magically highly potent form of Śiva's spouse), the *āsana* should (also) be of red wool; the *āsana* should not be longer than two cubits, not wider than one cubit and a half, and three fingers high. A married man should not use a black antelope skin . . . etc.' (the rest being specifications as to the possible dangers of using various kinds of material for the seat).

The *sādhaka* should then sit on the seat either in the lotus-posture (*padmāsana*) or in the heroic-posture (*vīrāsana*). The former is quite familiar from Buddhist iconography, and well known to occidental yoga-fans.

As to the postures to be taken, tantric teachers and texts seem to be quite pedantic about them; the orthodox Hindu uses whatever *āsana* he finds comfortable.[42]

Rāghavabhaṭṭa, an important tantric scholar of the eighteenth century, says: 'for *japa* (repetition of the mantra), *pūjā* (formal worship) and similar pursuits the *āsanas* to be taken are the *padmāsana* (lotus posture), the *svastikāsana*, or the *vīrāsana* (the heroic posture)—otherwise these observances will not bear fruit'.[43]

Although the classical text containing instructions for *āsana* is the *Gheraṇḍa Saṃhitā* ascribed to Matsyendranātha, the semi-mythical founder of *Haṭha-yoga*, most tantras contain such instructions too, not usually at variance with the *Gheraṇḍa Saṃhitā*. Thus, the *Gautamī Tantra*[44] simply says: 'both feet are placed on both thighs—this is *padmāsana*'. The conciseness of the instruction implies that readers are already familiar with this *āsana*, which is considerably more tortuous than this note would tell. The *Sammohana Tantra*[45] says: 'the yogi places one of his feet upon the ground, the other on the opposite thigh—this is the *vīrāsana* (heroic posture)'. This, too, is an oversimplification which would appear a strange thing in a tantric text otherwise so meticulous about details. The simple fact is, however, that all tantrics are supposed to be familiar with the *haṭha*-yoga tradition and its *āsana* training, which is fundamental to all yogic practice.

Paṇḍit Vaidyarāj adds an interesting footnote, but does not tell us where this instruction comes from; I believe it is tantric oral lore: The worship of the gods, when performed at daytime, should be done facing the east (this much is Vedic), if at night, facing the north; but the worship of the goddess and of Śiva must always be done facing the north.[46]

The next item is most certainly a deviation from the orthodox process of worship: it is called *vijayā-grahaṇa* (the taking of *vijayā*). *Vijayā* is hemp (*Cannabis Indica*, containing the same chemical agent as marijuana). Orthodox Brahmins especially around Banaras and Allahabad take hemp (which is called *bhāṅg* in Hindi, and—interestingly—*siddhi* (also meaning occult power) in Bengali) regularly on Friday, but it is not a part of their formalized ritual. *Vijayā* (lit. that (feminine) which gives victory, or simply victory) as a feminine principle is a Sanskrit euphemism—quite apt as a term for the euphoric feeling caused by the drug—of considerable age; Paṇḍit Gopinath Kaviraj of Banaras informed me that it is mentioned once in the *Śatapatha Brāhmaṇa* which would take it back to about 800 B.C.

An important matter has so far escaped scholarly attention: the time that elapses between this part of the tantric's meditation in the first half (*pūrvārdha*) and the climax of the ritual in the second half (*uttarārdha*), i.e. the administration of the five Ms, is just long enough to get really 'high' on the drug—i.e. one hour and a half. This is very important in the Indian scene, where the spiritual postulant has to overcome enormous cultural inhibitions; *Cannabis Indica* certainly does the trick, and I think Professor M. Opler is over-cautious when he assumes that the fifth *makāra* (sexual union) is never really performed because of social strictures being deeply ingrained.[47] What G. M. C. Carstairs' informants told him about the *kānchulī* practice of left-handed yogis—i.e. that they did undress and have intercourse as part of their worship—would indeed be unlikely in such an exceedingly puritanical region as Rajasthan, but for the effect of *vijayā*.

The taking of *vijayā* is preceded by these observances: the *sādhaka* places the bowl of hemp on the foundation, i.e. the equilateral triangle drawn on the ground-*maṇḍala* in front of him, and purifies it with this *mantra*: *Oṃ hrīṃ*, o immortal goddess (or o nectar-formed goddess), thou who art risen from nectar, who showerest nectar, attract nectar, bestow *siddhi* (occult power), and bring my (particular) chosen deity into my power, *svāhā*.[48] Next, the *sādhaka* mutters his root-*mantra* (i.e. the *bīja* of his chosen deity) seven times, and then makes the following *mudrās* over the *vijayā*-bowl: the cow-*mudrā* (*dhenumudrā*), the womb-*mudrā* (*yonimudrā*), the calling-in-*mudrā*(*āvāhanī mudrā*), the fixing-*mudrā* (*sthāpinī mudrā*), the hypostasizing-*mudrā* (*saṃnidhāpinī mudrā*), the obstructing-*mudrā* (i.e. the *mudrā* that repels evil forces, *saṃnirodhinī mudrā*), and the bringing-face-to-face *mudrā* (i.e. with the chosen deity, *sammukhīkariṇī mudrā*).[49] Then, the *sādhaka* meditates on the *guru* whom he imagines seated in the uppermost centre (*sahasradala cakra*, the thousand-petalled lotus imagined at the cranium), and contemplates the *mantra* '*aṃ*, o (name of the *guru*) Lord of Bliss, I offer this libation to the foot-stool of the *guru*, obeisance to him'.[50] Along with this *mantra*, he touches the *vijayā*-bowl to his forehead through the essence-*mudrā* (*tattva-mudrā*); this he repeats three times. Then he mutters this *mantra*: '*aṃ* speak speak, o Speaker (feminine) of Speech (i.e. Sarasvatī), establish thyself firmly on the tip of my tongue, o thou who bringest all truth under control, *svāhā*',[51] meditating on the primordial power thought to be coiled up at the base-centre (the *kuṇḍalinī-śakti*) as pouring the *vijayā* as an oblation into her opened mouth; just before this, he touches his heart three times with the *tattva-mudrā*, holding the *vijayā*-bowl and offering its contents to his chosen deity with the root-*mantra* of this specific deity. He then drinks the potion. In some regions, especially around Banaras, *bhāṅg* is prepared with sugar and molasses and kneaded into rather tasty little balls—in which case the tantric devotee swallows them one by one.

Now the question must arise as to why *vijayā*, a far less innocuous ingredient of the tantric circle than, say, fish and meat and parched kidney-bean, is not included in the five Ms. The answer given to me by some tantrics, that there is no term for *Cannabis Indica* commencing with the letter m, is childish; any number of words starting with m could be given this connotation—just as *mudrā* became one of the five Ms, although no cereal had ever been called *mudrā* before. I believe the reason is simply that were *vijayā* administered as one of the five Ms, it would forfeit its purpose: the five Ms are taken in quick succession, i.e. within about half an hour; but *vijayā* would take its effect only an hour and a half later, when no effect would be desired or useful. Also—and about this I feel quite as strongly as Professor Opler—the general inhibition of the Hindu pious is so great that the *makāras* would just not come about were there not a de-inhibiting factor preceding their use.

The irony about it all is that *vijayā* is the only actual aphrodisiac; the four edible and potable *makāras* are ascriptive aphrodisiacs—i.e. tradition has declared them to be that—and the reason why this proven effect of *Cannabis Indica* is subdued by the tantric paṇḍits may well be that the Ms *must* be *uttejaka* (aphrodisiacs) in order to qualify for the preparation for the final M, *maithuna* or union. Now although *Cannabis Indica* (*bhāṅg*) is known by its Hindu votaries to be an aphrodisiac this does not conflict with its exclusion from the ascriptive *uttejaka* ingredients belonging to the ritual of the five Ms in the pious Hindu mind.

There are several parallels to this type of official declaration of the effects of some food on the spiritual development of aspirants. I was specifically puzzled by the south Indian (*smārta*-caste) Brahmins who have a powerful ritualistic aversion to onions, because they are official aphrodisiacs; but instead of onions they make abundant use of *hīṅ* (*asafoetida*) in their kitchens, which is a victual with an ominous odour, and obviously a more powerful aphrodisiac than onions: Ayurvedic medicine administers *asafoetida* against impotence, and not onions (it has to be added that there are ritualistic prohibitions which are considerably relaxed where medical treatment is involved).

The next few items are quite analogous to the orthodox ritual, except that the bulk of the *mantras* used are tantric; even so, quite a few *mantras* are orthodox Brahmanical *mantras* of Vedic provenience. The *Mṛtyuñjaya-mantra* is pronounced in a focal position, i.e. during the 'purification' of the five Ms, and, strangely enough, the *mantra* used for the 'purification' of the assembled *śaktis* (viz. the female partners present during the rite), is nothing but the Vedic invocation of Viṣṇu to make the womb fertile—a *mantra* used in the Vedic marriage ceremony.[52] Strange, because the purpose of the *pañcamakāra* practice is certainly not conception, but the very opposite—immersion into the *Brahman*-essence, which is the consummation of a process of involution, not of procreation. I have asked some knowledgeable tantrics why these *mantras* are used. The only satisfactory answer I got was again from Mahāmahopādhyaya Paṇḍit Gopinath Kaviraj at Banaras: the womb of the *śaktis* must be 'in-tact', as he put it (using the English phrase in his Bengali exposition), for a woman with a barren womb is not entitled to function as a *śakti*, just as an impotent man is not entitled to any form of yoga or *sannyāsa* (monastic ordination).

Then follows the instalment of the various 'bowls' (*pātram*) which contain the ingredients for the ultimate ritual—i.e. the four victual-*makāras*, and other ingredients like clarified butter (*ghṛtam*) milk, honey, etc., all of which are also used in orthodox worship. The most important *pātram* is called *śrīpātram* and contains five kinds of flowers (*durva*, *akṣata*, the rose, *barvara*, *aparājita*), over which lustral water is sprinkled as the *mantras* are muttered.

The *mantras* used during the instalment of the *śrīpātra* are very interesting indeed and deviate completely from Vedic usage; the deities invoked are largely common with those of the Buddhist Vajrayāṇa pantheon; so is the joining of the letters of the Devanāgarī alphabet in various orders to the *mantras*, called '*akṣaramālā*' (garland of letters), transplanted into the Vajrayāṇa tradition.[53] I shall select only a few of those *mātṛikā-nyāsas* which accompany the setting of the *śrīpātra*; *mātrikās* are used in various garland-arrangements throughout the entire tantric ritual.[54]

As the *sādhaka* traces his *maṇḍala* with rice-powder, or other materials like cinnabar or sesamum seeds, he invokes the four great 'seats' (*pīṭha*) of the tantrics, which are common to the Buddhists and the Hindus,[55] '*puṃ*, adoration to the *Pūrṇaśaila*-seat—*dīṃ*, adoration to the Uḍḍiyāṇa seat (Uḍḍiyāṇa- Oḍḍiyāṇa- Tibetan-Urgyan)—*jaṃ*, adoration to the Jalandharā seat—*kaṃ*, adoration to the Kāmarūpa seat'.[56]

The *sādhaka* then worships the 'six-limbed goddess' (*ṣaḍāṅgī*) at each corner of the *maṇḍala*, which has the basic *maṇḍala*-shape—of all tantric *maṇḍalas*—the triangle with the apex downwards representing the female, the one with the upward apex the male aspect of the deity, the integration of the two triangles symbolizing the union of the two (*yuganaddha*: Tibetan *zung 'jug*). The formula for the worship of the six-limbed goddess' (i.e. the goddess symbolized by this *maṇḍala*) is '*hraṃ*, adoration to (Her) heart—*hrīṃ*, *svāhā* to (Her) head—*hrūṃ*, *vaṣaṭ* to (Her) hairtuft—*hraiṃ*, to her amulets, *hūṃ*—*hrauṃ*, *vauṣaṭ* to Her three eyes—*hrāḥ*, to her palms and backs of her hands, *phaṭ*.'[57]

Then, the *sādhaka* worships the ten '*kalās*' with their respective *mantras*:[58] a *kalā* is a segment, literally, but here each of them symbolizes an auxiliary goddess, see neither as an attendant of the *great* Śakti, whom the complete *maṇḍala* represents, or as a partial aspect of the same '*dhūṃ* worship to Dhūmrā (the Smoke-coloured One), *aṃ* worship to Accisā, *jvaṃ* worship to Jvālinī (the flame-like One), *viṃ* worship to Visphuliṅgiṇī (the ember-like One), *suṃ* worship to Suśrī (the blessed Śrī), *sūṃ* worship to Sūrapā (the liquor-drinking One), *kaṃ* worship to Kapilā (the reddish-coloured One), *haṃ* worship to Havyakavyavahā (the name is etymologically unclear—unless it is a Sanskritized corruption of some non-Indo European name, it means something like 'she who is carried (or carries) oblations and poetical things' (?)).[59]

He then proceeds to worship the *kalās* in the other parts of the *maṇḍala*, with analogous *mantras*. Among them there is a goddess Marīcī—well known to Vajrayāṇa Buddhism; her *sādhanā* is described in *Sādhanāmālā* A, pp. 156–7. She is also worshipped in Tibet: 'Marīcī is invoked by the Lamas at the advent of the morning, showing her connection with the sun . . . Marīcī is . . . regarded as a consort of Vairócana himself . . . Marīcī is always said to be residing in the womb of a *caitya* (*mchod rten*), whereas Vajravarāhī (*rdo rje phag mo*) being an abbess may reside anywhere.' The *mantra* for Marīcī is '*oṃ marīcyai māṃ huṃ svāhā*', Śāntideva (*zhi ba lha*) gives her *dhāraṇī*. . . .[60]

The installation of the *śrīpātra* is concluded by a very poetical incantation,[61] and by this meditation: 'aiming at realizing the universal manifested Brahman (*sakala brahma*—as opposed to the unmanifested, neutral *niṣkala brahma*), contemplating the copulation of Śiva and Śakti and imagining that the *rasa* (liquid, juice—i.e. the divine sperm) is caught in the *śrīpātra* and commingles with the flowers and other ingredients which form the contents of this bowl, he then worships the Śrī-bowl with incense and more flowers'.

The installation of the *pātras* (bowls), commencing with the most elaborate, the *Śrīpātra*, is followed by the worship of the *sādhaka*'s own chosen deity (*iṣṭadevatā*, *yid dam*). For this, he first makes the *kacchapa-mudrā* (the 'tortoise'-gesture), and then he takes a sandal incense stick and a flower into his hands. He then places it near his heart and meditates on his chosen deity. He then 'takes it up along the *suṣumnā*-channel from the base-*cakra* to the thousand-petalled lotus, and then worships it in that highest position' (p. 83). This means that he utilizes the general tantric method of imagining the coiled-up dormant power to rise and enter the hypothetical uppermost centre at the cranium. He then repeats the secret *mantra* of his chosen deity—i.e. the *bīja* (seed-syllable) imparted to him by his *guru* during *dīkṣā* (initiation). The mode in which this repetition (*japa*) is done is quite intricate and elaborate, but it is common to all tantric procedure—i.e. the *akṣaramālā* (garland of the letters of the Nāgarī alphabet) is prefixed to the *mantra*, and then the supreme *bīja Oṃ* is prefixed and affixed to the *mantra*, so that the actual form of the *mantra* during meditation on the chosen deity is '*aṃ* xyz *aṃ*' '*āṃ* xyz *āṃ*' '*iṃ* xyz *iṃ*' '*uṃ* xyz *uṃ*', and so on through to '*kṣaṃ* xyz *kṣaṃ*' and then backwards to '*aṃ* xyz *aṃ*'. Such is the tradition with which I am personally familiar. Vaidyaraj (p. 88) uses the whole garland first, then inserts the *bīja*, and then uses the garland in reverse order, and tells the *sādhaka* to repeat this process seven times.[62] He then worships his rosary with the *śloka*: 'O rosary, rosary, great rosary: Thou of the form of all *śaktis*, the four groups, [i.e. the four objects of life—*dharma*, *artha* (gaining and preserving mundane goods), *kāma* (satisfaction of the desire for creature comforts), *mokṣa* (liberation)] are all deposited in thee, be thou the giver of *siddhi* to me.'[63] He then does *japa* (repetition) of his chosen deity's *mantra* with the beads of the rosary, 108 times. He ends his *japa* with the verse 'thou keepest hidden the most secret of the secrets, accept thou the *japa* made by me; let *siddhi* be mine, o Goddess, by thy grace, of Maheśvarī'.[64]

At the conclusion of the first half (*pūrvārdha*), the preparatory rites, the *sādhaka* makes the dedication of the self—a mental observance common to all Hindu and many Buddhist meditational routines—he offers himself and all his observances to the chosen deity with a formula which includes the name of the chosen deity and ends with . . . *sarvaṃ brahmārpanaṃ bhavatu*, 'all this be given over to the *Brahman*'. The formula winding up the first half is unexpectedly aggressive and sounds like a good transition from the exoteric to the esoteric half of the tantric ritual: 'whomsoever I touch with my foot, whomsoever I glance at with my eye, he may become (my) slave, even though he be like unto Indra'.[65]

We now proceed to the second half (*uttarārdha*). Let me add that the nomenclature '*pūrva . . .*' '*uttara . . .*' is systematically ambiguous, for in this juxtaposition the terms also mean inferior and superior. Thus we have, for example, *pūrva-mimāṃsa*, the system of sacerdotal and ritualistic speculation ascribed to Jaimini, followed by *uttara-mimāṃsa* which is a synonym of Vedānta, which has the ultimate and hence the highest place in the enumeration of the six orthodox systems of Brahmanical learning.

The ritual proper coincides with the formation of the *cakra*, the circle of male and female *sādhakas*, or in tantric phraseology of the Śivas with their Śaktis. It is a genuine circle, for the participants sit in a circle, each *sādhaka* has his Śakti on his right side in the case of right-handed tantric ritual, and on his left in the case of the ritual we are presently describing—which, I hasten to repeat, is the core of tantric ritual in general. Thus, the *uttarārdha* begins with the worship of the *cakra* by its participants—(*cakrārcana*).

The relevant text gives this instruction: 'the *sādhakas* and the Śaktis are given sandel paste (i.e. sandel-paste is put on their foreheads in the form of a *tilaka*, a vertical streak), and then they should sit in the formation of a circle. The *sādhaka* and the Śakti should sit together or each (pair) on one seat in the prescribed order. Then they should place a flower into the *guru*-bowl and offer the bowl to the *guru*.'[66]

However, in practice this initial part of the *uttarārdha* proceeds more often than not on fairly conventional lines—conventional in the orthodox sense. It is only in one place, in Orissa, that I personally witnessed a *cakra* where the *sādhakas* and their Śaktis sat in a circle in conformity with this text and other equivalent instructions. The tantric paṇḍit would say that the instructions are one thing and their execution is another thing, as time changes. Vaidyaraj puts it this way:[67] 'but the customary procedure (*pracalit praṇāli*) is this, that as the worship commences only the male *sādhakas* take part in the *cakrācarcana* (the worship of the circle). The Śaktis sit separately in some other place. When the male *sādhakas* begin *tarpana* (vd. above) which is different from the *tarpana* in the first half, in the sense that the texts recited and the *mantras* used now are more expressly left-handed—or afferent in my own terminology—than for *tarpana* in the first half—so Vaidyarāj, some lad "goes to the place where the Śaktis sit" (e.g. in their separate circle) and he worships them and does *tarpana* for them (because women are not entitled to perform *tarpana*). For married *sādhakas* this ends their connection with the Śaktis, during the worship of the *cakra*. The *mantras* now used for the *tarpana* are '*aiṃ*, I make *tarpana* for the supreme *guru* and his wife, adoration'[68] repeating the *mantra* for the second and third generations of his preceptors and for their wives. Then the *sādhaka* meditates on Śiva as Ānandabhairava (the Blissful Terrible One) in his heart, which means that he imagines that deity seated in the 'heart' which is of course not the physical heart but the hypothetically stylized twelve-petalled lotus (*anāhata-cakra*) located in the cardial region. The *mantra* that goes along with it is nothing but the slightly extended *Śrīvidyā*—the central *mantra* of the earliest systematized Hindu tantrics.[69] The *Śrīvidyā* is a non-semantic *mantra*—a *bīja*-concatenation. Risking the wrath of the goddess, the Paṇḍit Vaidyarāj also printed it in his manual, so I do not hesitate to repeat it: '*haṃsakṣamalavarayūm ānandabhairavāya vaṣaṭ tarpayāmi svāhā*.'[70] Vaidyarāj spells it '*hasakṣamala* . . .' but the instruction given in the *Saundaryalaharī* insists on the *anunāsikā* (the nasalization), and the *Saundaryalaharī* is considered the canonical text for the *Śrīvidyā*. W. Norman Brown also has '*haṃsa* . . .'.

The *tarpana-mantra* for Bhairavī, the Śakti of Śiva, is most interesting: '*sahaṃkṣamalavarayīṃ ānandabhairavyai vauṣaṭ tarpayāmi svāhā*'. The *tarpana*, like all acts of libation and oblation, is done on '*svāhā*', ever since Vedic times.[71] We see that the '*haṃ*' and the '*sa*' are inverted, and that the ending is an artificial accusative feminine ending, contrasting it with the equally artificial masculine *-ūṃ* ending in the formulae for the (male) Ānandabhairava. Vaidyarāj prints it '*sahakṣamala* . . .': here, too, omitting the *anunāsikā* over the '*ha*'. The *sādhaka* then meditates on his own chosen deity 'in his heart', pronouncing its specific *mantra*, adding 'I offer *tarpana* to Her with Her weapons, with carrier-animal, with family, *svāhā*'.[72] According to Vaidyarāj (p. 103), the *sādhaka* does *tarpana* to his chosen deity in his heart—five or seven times. Tantrics round Banaras, however, do the actual *tarpana* to their chosen deity just as they do it to *their gurus* and to Ānandabhairava, etc.

The *arpana* is followed by the purification of the essences (*tattva-śutddhi*) which at this stage means a ritualistic purification of the body organs: Śiva and Śakti are invoked with lengthy *mantras* to purify the visible and the subtle body (*sthūladeha* and *paradeha*). Then, the goddess is meditated on as *surā*, i.e. as presiding over the liquor used in the five Ms. The text for this meditation is given by Vaidyarāj (p. 104), from the *Kaulāvali Nirṇaya*: 'O thou (goddess) who wast churned from milk-ocean, (thou) the best of (products of) that ocean: There the goddess "liquor" was born, assuming the form of a virgin; her countenance as (white as) cow-milk, (she) emerged from the *kula*-nectar. Having eighteen arms, lotus-eyed, born on the summit of bliss, (and thence also originated) bliss as Maheśvara. From their union comes forth Brahmā, Viṣṇu, and Śiva. Therefore I drink thee with my total personality, o goddess of liquor.'[73] The *kula*-nectar (*kulāmṛta*) is a controversial term, and I have met at least two interpretations of the word, by tantrics. One was given to me by Śrī Bhairavanātha, a tantric *sādhaka* from Darbanga, who attended the Kumbhamela at Allahabad in 1954: 'the *kulāmṛta* is the spiritual essence of the five *makāras*; it is none of the physical *makāras* nor is it all of them together. It is the cosmic residuum caused by Śiva's and Śakti's eternal copulation, which is again reflected in the meditation of the *śāktas*.' Another tantric, whose name and provenience I do not recall, but who must have had some status as he participated in the monastic procession, explained the term somewhat like this: 'the *kulāmṛta* is nothing but the *amṛta* (nectar) produced by the churning of the milk ocean, but it would not have any special significance for the tantric *sādhakas* were it not for the fact that Śakti herself, in the form of the maiden, was the main product of the churning process. She, being the chosen deity of the tantrics, must be worshipped along with the foundation (*ādhāra*) from which she originated, which is the *kula*-nectar, i.e. it is *amṛta* (nectar) for the *kula*, those initiated in the tantric tradition (*kulāmṛta* as *kulāya-amṛta*).' Other tantrics whom I met seem to indicate that the *kula*-nectar is the liquid which emerges from the contact of Śiva and Śakti. Among Assamese tantrics worshipping at Kāmarupa (one of the great 'seats') the *kulāmṛta* is identified with the *rajas* (menstrual fluid) of the goddess—the great *kula*-convention in that area takes place at the time of the goddess's *ṛtu* (menses) which is set for August-September.

The senior *sādhaka* who presides over the *uttarārdha* of the ritual is called the 'Lord of the Circle' (*cakreśvara*). He is not necessarily the *guru* of any of the participants, but just a person (and his Śakti—who may either be his wife or his initiated partner) of respect and seniority in the *kula*. The bowls (*pātra*) are offered to him and his partner as representatives of the individual participants' personal *guru* who cannot be present at all occasions. The *cakreśvara* thus functions as a vicarious *guru*. I do not think that there is any objection, in principle, to the actual *guru* of a person or persons presiding as *cakreśvara* at a *cakra* where his disciple, or disciples, participate.

As the *sādhaka* is about to drink the *surā* (which is the *madya*, liquor, or the third M) he says: 'I sacrifice' (*juhomi*); as he does so, he mentally draws the coiled-up energy of the *kula* (*kulakuṇḍalinī*) from her seat in the basic *cakra*; this time, however, he does not draw her up into the thousand-petalled lotus in the yogic cranium, but instead he brings her into the tip of his tongue and seats her there, and at this moment he drinks the beverage from its bowl, and as he drinks he impresses the thought on his mind that it is not he himself who is drinking but the *kulakuṇḍalinī* now seated on the tip of his tongue, to whom he is offering the liquid as a libation.

In the same manner he now empties all the other *pātras* (bowls) as he visualizes that he feeds their contents as oblations to the goddess—for the *kulakuṇḍalinī* is the microscosmic aspect of the universal Śakti.

This, then, is the process of using the first four Ms—and before we proceed to the delicate fifth and last one let us summarize the procedures of ritualistic consummation of the four Ms (fish, meat, liquor, and *mudrā*):

(a) the preparations consist of various processes of symbolic purification (*tarpana*, *śuddhi*, *arcana*, etc.).

(b) the actual taking of the ingredients is accompanied by meditation on the vicarious nature of the observances—i.e. that it is not the *sādhaka* as an ephemeral individual who takes them, but that they are being fed to the goddess residing in his body as the *kulakuṇḍalinī* (the coiled-up lady of the *kula* or tantric in-group);

(c) along with the acts of taking the four Ms, the *sādhaka* also does silent *japa* (repetition) of his own *bīja*, i.e. the secret *bīja* given to him by his *guru* which is the *mantra* of his chosen deity.

Thus, mentally, the *sādhaka* does two things simultaneously: he keeps up the thought of feeding the *kulakuṇḍalinī* at the basic level of mentation, and he repeats his specific *mantra* as he eats and drinks the four *makāras*.

Let us always bear in mind, that whatever the manner in which ritual is conducted in India—and *a fortiori*, in Buddhist Tibet—the postulated target is never to be sought in the enjoyment of the used materials; it is not at any time a hedonistic motive that directs the ritualistic acts. We are not here concerned with the possibility and the occurrence of frauds: for even if over ninety per cent of all tantric *sādhakas* had been and were seekers of pleasures which they could not otherwise find, this study does not purport to deal with possible or actual misuse. Sacrifice is the perennial hallmark of Indian worship and ritual, and, by extension, of all India-originated meditation. By sacrifice is not meant what the occidental use of the word suggests—sacrifice by way of charity, altruistic effort at the expense of one's own betterment, etc.—it is always the actual or symbolic pouring of some sort of liquid or solid food into a chemically simpler, but cosmically more pervasive, receptacle, whether it is the Vedic *nitya* ritual of pouring clarified butter into the *homa*-fire under prescribed incantations, or whether it is the feeding of the *kulakuṇḍalinī* through the four Ms in the tantric discipline. 'Chemically simpler' has to be understood in this specific context not as a facetious idiom, but as a term which tries to rephrase the *sādhakas'* axiomatic notion: water and fire are simpler and more universal than the food offered into them; the liquor and the meat offered to the *kulakuṇḍalinī* in the ingestive process of the worship through the five Ms are more specific, less simple, less general, than the*kulakuṇḍalinī* which is the microcosmic aspect of the universal matrix. 'Simple' for the tantric—and by feasible extension, for non-tantric Hindus and Buddhists as well, is at least psychologically, if not semantically, synonymous with 'universal', 'absolute', *via* 'non-composite' (Sanskrit '*sama*'—as a prefix denotes simplicity, oneness, equality, universality).

The purpose of immersing the more complex and specific into the more simple and universal, epitomized through the ritual of *bhūtaśuddhi*, is the postulated actualization, through ritual, meditation, yogic discipline, etc., of the cosmic fact of oneness propounded in the canonical texts, in the *mahavākyams* or great dicta of the Upaniṣads: all this is Brahman, thou art that, the conscious self is Brahman, etc. In other words, for the *sādhaka* (i.e. the practising Hindu or the practising Buddhist) oneness is not a mere thought-construct requiring intellectual or emotional assent, it is something to be actualized, something about which one can and must do something. That doing is the elaborate series of acts and thoughts, guided by traditional disciplines and training, which reenacts the cosmic fact of oneness, postulated by the Hindu and the tantric Buddhist.[74]

There are certain indications about ritualistic etiquette. The *sādhaka* should not produce any sound with his mouth when eating and drinking the ritual food; he should not spill a drop of the beverage; he should have eaten something before he takes the drink—else it makes for poisoning; this seems to mean that he should take the fish and the meat before the liquor, for fasting is enjoined for the day preceding the formation of the *cakra*. He should not touch what has been polluted through touch (i.e. *ucciṣṭam*, any food that has come into contact with the mouth, directly or indirectly); he should not raise the bowl with any sort of noise, he should not make any noise when he fills the bowl; he should not empty the glass at once (not in a 'skoal' fashion, that is), nor should he turn the bowl round as he fills it; the married *sādhakas* should not drink more than five bowls of *mada*, for the adepts who drink more are likely to lose out on their *siddhi*. So long as his sight does not become unsteady, so long as his mind does not become unsteady (lit. so long as he does not make his gaze and his mind 'go round'), so long he may go on drinking—if he drinks more than that it is the drinking of *paśus*.[75] Then there is an interesting prohibition, from which one might infer that malpractices have been frequent even at the time when Hindu tantrism was being codified. The *Mahanirvāṇa Tantra* has this warning: 'He who introduces (lit. makes enter) *paśus* into the *cakra* out of love, fear, or passion, falls from the *kula-dharma*, and goes to hell, even though he be a *vīra*.'[76] This is followed by a verse warning against caste-distinctions in tantric ritual: 'He who makes a caste distinction out of caste-pride when in the *cakra*, he goes to a fearful hell, be he the most excellent among the knowers of Vedānta.'[77] This is a fling at the monastic Vedāntins, the followers of Śaṃkarācārya who, like their master—in spite of their making much of being beyond caste—keep discriminating on the basis of caste.

The fifth of the *makāras* is performed in accordance with the following instructions: the *sādhaka* should draw a triangle-*maṇḍala* on the couch, pronouncing this *mantra* '*oṃ āḥ* o well done "line" o *vajra* "line" *hūṃ phaṭ svāhā*'.[78] This is also a Buddhist tantric *mantra* and is well known to Tibetan tantric adepts; Dezhung Rinpoche and Phrin las Rinpoche of the Sakya monks in Seattle recognized it immediately. It is significant that the *mantra* initiating the central exercise should be a Buddhist *mantra*.

The *sādhaka* should then perform mental worship of the basic Śakti (*ādhāra-śakti*), whose microcosmic aspect is the *kuṇḍalinī* coiled up in the base-centre (*mūlādhāra*) of the yogic body, injecting her image into the centre of the triangular *maṇḍala* on the couch, with these (unpronounced, mentally repeated) words:

'*oṃ hrīṃ* worship to the basic Śakti (and to the) lotus-seat (i.e. the couch)'.[79] Then the *sādhaka* worships the couch with this *mantra*: '*Oṃ* o couch, thou art like the corpse, thou art to be utilized for the ritual (*sādhanīya*) by the *sādhakas*; hence the *mantra* is here recited, be thou (o couch) our *siddhi*-giver.'[80]

Thereafter the *sādhaka* sits down on the couch alone and does *japa* of the *mantra* of his chosen deity (*mūlamantra*) for a while, the duration of which is left to him.

Then his Śakti is called in; if she has not been consecrated previously, the *sādhaka* whispers the *bīja* '*hrīṃ*' into her ear three times. He then bathes her, puts fragrant oil into her hair, combs her, dresses her in a red robe and makes her sit down on the couch. He then sprinkles water from the *samānārghya*-bowl[81] over her head and recites this *mantra*: '*Aiṃ klīṃ sauḥ* worship to the goddess of the three cities (Tripurā), purify this Śakti, make this Śakti mine, make (her mine), *svāhā*.'[82]

When the Śakti has been thus purified, the *sādhaka* does the *nyāsa* of the six limbs (*ṣaḍanga-nyāsa*), i.e. he touches her forehead, eyes, nostrils, mouth, her arms, and her thighs with his right hand, pronouncing the *mātṛkās* (the letters of the Sanskrit alphabet, q.v. above), as also the seed-*mantra* of his chosen deity.

If the Śakti has not been participating in the four preceding *makāras*—which is the case in most *cakras* in northern India today where the Śaktis sit separately—he feeds her betel-nut in a betel-leaf (*tāṃbula*), touches her pudenda for an instant, and mutters the syllable *aiṃ* one hundred times. We must remember that *aiṃ* is the most intimate *bīja* of the goddess (vd. On *Mantra*). I am now quoting our manual in literal translation: 'viewing the Śakti as Gaurī (i.e. the spouse of Śiva) and himself as Śiva, he should pronounce the root-*mantra* of his chosen deity and should offer the father-face into the mother-face'.[83] This does not refer to the act of kissing—osculation being no part of the Hindu tantric practice proper—but to ritualistic copulation. 'During the act, he should (mentally) recite the verse "*Oṃ* thou goddess resplendent by the oblation of *dharma* and non-*dharma*, into the fire of the self, using the mind as a sacrificial ladle, along the path of the *suṣumnā*-duct (q.v. above) I who am engaging in harnessing the sense-organs, constantly offer (this oblation)." '[84]

The *sādhaka* keeps reciting this *mantra* mentally: 'he creates the attitude of the oneness of Śiva and Śakti, his mind becomes unruffled[85] and he repeats (mentally) the syllable-*mantra* (i.e. the letters of the alphabet) along with the aforesaid *mantra*. In the end, he 'abandons his sperm' (*śukratyāg kare*) with the following *mantra*: '*Oṃ* with light and ether as my two hands, I, the exulting one, relying on the ladle, I, who take *dharma* and non-*dharma* as his sacrificial ingredients, offer (this oblation) lovingly into the fire, *svāhā*.'[86]

The main difference between the Hindu and the Buddhist tantric *sādhanā* seems to have been that the Hindu tantric ejects his sperm, the Buddhist Vajrayāṇa adept does not: '. . . *bodhicittaṃ notsṛjet*' '(placing the *vajra* in the lotus) he should not let the *bodhicitta* (*byang chub kyi sems*) go'. There are obviously exceptions on both sides; the *Hevajra Tantra* which deals extensively with the dance of the yoginīs (*kha 'gro ma'i gar*)[87] does not indicate the necessity of retaining the sperm. The general rule, however, does seem to hold; that the Hindu tantric releases the *bīja* with the final *svāhā*—the formula that concludes all oblations and libations in the Indian tradition—the Buddhist Vajrayāṇa adept retains it, aiming at stabilizing the esoteric three jewels (*triratna*, *nor bu gsum*)—breath, thought, and semen—in a simultaneous act which, when successful, yields the state of oneness in duality, the *yuganaddha* (*sku grub zung 'jug*) of which the *yab yum* is the icon.

No one, I think, has tried so far to explain this difference in the execution of the central *sādhanā* in tantrism. To my knowledge, there have been no Hindu apologetics; it would seem proper that a Hindu tantric, acquainted with the fact that the Vajrayāṇa adept 'stabilizes' where he emits, should give some sort of explanation, particularly as Hindu tantrics are extremely sensitive to criticisms on points of ritualistic procedure. I think the reason for the absence of such Hindu comment is that tantrics in India are not aware of the difference because they do not bother to read Buddhist tantras, of which very few are available in Sanskrit.

I shall, however, try an hypothetical explanation: the Buddhist tantric's concern is purely esoteric, his method experimental. He has no stake in ritual *per se*, and the notion of sacrificial oblation and libation means little if anything to him. His preceptors taught the spiritual and magical potentiality of the control of breath, thought, and sperm, and the importance of their retention. For the Hindu, on the other hand, the notion of ritualistic sacrifice is all-important. In fact, the idea of sacrifice (*yajña*) being at the base of every religious act has remained focal in Hinduism, though the interpretations have changed. Yet, just as the Upaniṣads were a quasi-philosophical rendition of the *saṃhitā* portion of the Veda, the tantras provide a psychological or therapeutical interpretation, if you wish, of the Vedic and Upaniṣadic lore. The ritualistic ideal of the Hindu is abandoning, renouncing, giving up of all the ingredients used, at times including one's own life. Nothing is held back, ever so dear and important. The same holds for the Buddhist, no doubt—that the Buddha and the Bodhisattvas renounce is the keynote of the Jātakas and other Buddhist legends—but this giving up is, in his case, bereft of the fundamental notion of ritual; this, from any Buddhist angle, is as it should be, for the Buddha broke away from the Brahmin ritual.

If this be acceptable, then it must follow that no ritualistic ingredient including the ingredient which constitutes the fifth M can be held back—it, too, has to be abandoned into the fire of sacrifice, in whatever manner the fire is conceived. The Hindu tantric's argument would be: if the liquor and the meat and the fish and the parched cereal are given as libations and oblations to the goddess as *kulakuṇḍalinī*, then the fifth ingredient has to be given to the goddess, too, his Śakti being the embodied goddess.

Whether the Buddhist retention or the Hindu emission is more conducive to the achievement of the spiritual postulate—*mokṣa*, *nirvāṇa*—is a mute point and cannot be discussed by anyone at all; there are no instruments for comparison. This much seems certain to me, that both practices are, under the laboratory conditions of the yogic training and environment, highly numinogenic, if another neologism be excused; they both engender the intensive, euphoric, oftentimes hallucinatory and perhaps psycho-pathological feeling which goes with religious experience—or which *is* religious experience.

I shall conclude with a few quotations which support the practice of the five Ms within the tantric tradition. It must be said that some Hindu tantras do not mention the *pañcamakāra* at all, others hint at them in an opaque manner, whereas at least one important tantra (the *Kālīvilāsa*) is directly antagonistic towards left-handed rites culminating in the five Ms; and it has been said in other places that non-tantric Hindu sources deny any merit to the *sādhanā* involving any of the five ingredients, but especially wine and woman. Paramahamsa Ramakrishna, the famous Bengali saint of the late nineteenth century, used to warn his disciples asking them to stay away from the two great evils, *kāminī kāñcana*, woman and gold, in spite of the fact that he himself had been initiated into tantric *sādhanā* by the Bhairavī Brāhmaṇī, a woman-tantric of his day.

'He who worships Caṇḍī (i.e. the goddess) without the five Ms, the four (goods), i.e. long life, knowledge, splendour, and wealth, they perish for him.'[88]

'Liquor, meat, fish, *mudrā*, and copulation, these, o Goddess, are the five Ms, which give the favour of the gods (or which are dear to the gods—this is how Paṇḍit Vaidyarāj interprets it).'[89]

'With liquors, meats, fish, *mudrā* and copulation with women, the great *sadhu* should worship the Mother of the Universe.'[90]

'That liquor which is called "release—giver" in the world, in all actions, that liquor's name, of goddess, is *tīrtham* (i.e. lustral water, or place of pilgrimage; probably connected with the root *tr*, *tar*, for "transcend"), —it is indeed difficult to obtain.'[91]

We have now reached the end of the central and the most delicate topic of the tantric tradition. It now remains to be seen how tantrism can be operational as a practised religion. The last chapter is a teleological summary. It should also serve as a mild sedative after the five Ms.

NOTES

[1] An actual derivation of *pāśa* from *paśu* seems possible; occasionally, folk-etymologies do coincide with actual derivations.

[2] *prabhāte snāna-sandhyādi madhyāhne japa īśvari, ūrṇam-āsanam-ātmārthaṃ bhakṣyaṃ pāyasa-śarkaram, mālā rudrākṣa-saṃbhūtā pātraṃ pāśana-saṃbhavam, bhogaḥ svakīyā-kāntābhir-dakṣiṇācāra ityayam. Rudrayāmala*, quoted in *Pañcamakār tathā Bhāvatraya*, by Paṇḍit Deviprasad Ghilḍayāl, Allahabad, 1954. We shall refer to it frequently in this chapter.

[3] *vāmācāraṃ pravakṣyāmi śrīdurgā-sādhanam param,*
yaṃ vidhāya kalau śīghram mantrikāḥ siddhibhāg-bhavet;
mālā nṛdantasaṃbhūtā pātraṃ tu naramuṇḍakam,
āsanam siddha-carṃādi kaṅkanaṃ strī-kacodbhavam;
dravyam-āsavāttv-āḍhyaṃ bhakṣyam māṃsādikam priye,
carvaṇaṃ balamatsyādi mudrā vīṇāravaḥ kathā.
maithunam parakāntibhiḥ sarva-varṇa-samānatā,
vāmācāra iti proktaḥ sarva-siddhi-pradaḥ śive.
(*Rudrayāmala*)

siddha-carma may literally mean the skin of a *siddha*, but it probably means just the skin or hide which the *siddha* uses for his *āsana*; i.e. a tiger skin or the hide of another animal.

[4] Thus Ghilḍayāl, op cit., p. 2, '*kulācāra*' is Rājayoga and it is connected with the esoteric portion (*antaryāg*) of the five Ms.

[5] '*Kulastrī*', I think, is simply the ordained female partner participating in the left-handed rite. Ghilḍayāl thinks the term refers to the goddesses presiding over the six centres visualized in the yogic body; the *kulaguru* is the preceptor in the ritual, i.e. the *cakreśvara*, the presiding priest in the rite; Ghilḍayāl thinks the term refers to the supreme Preceptor—i.e. Śiva—who resides in the fifth centre (lotus), called *ājñācakra*; the *kuladevī* must be the presiding goddess; Ghilḍayāl thinks it means the *kuṇḍalinī*, i.e. the coiled power thought to be dormant at the base of the spine in the postulated yogic body.

[6] *śṛṇu bhāvatrayaṃ devi divya-vīra-paśu-kramāt,*
divyaśca devavatprāyo vīras-coddhata-mānasaḥ,
paśubhāva sadā devi śuddhaśca śucivat sadā.
(*Kālīvilāsa* T., 6–4/10)

[7] *bhāvastu trividho deva divya-vīra-paśu kramāt,*
ādyabhāvo mahādeva śreyān-sarva-samṛddhidaḥ,
dvitīyo madhyamaścaiva tritīyas-sarva-ninditaḥ.
(*Bhāvacūḍāmaṇi*)

[8] *pañcatattva*, moreover, applies to several doctrinary pentads, both in Hindu and Buddhist lore, tantric and otherwise.

[9] *madyaṃ māṃsaṃ tathā mīnaṃ mudrā maithunameva ca,*
makāra-pañcakaṃ sevyaṃ śiva-śakti-samāgame
(*Merutantra* 1/59)

[10] op. cit., p. 5, '*islīye usko paścātya ācāryon ne* rational animal *arthāt tarkvitark karke apnā mat sthir karnewālā paśu kahā hai.*'

[11] Monier Williams lists only 'disgust, abhorrence, etc.'. But it seems to mean something like slander in this enumeration; the tantrics were constantly on the alert, being obnoxious to outsiders—hence perhaps the identification of abhorrence with slander.

[12] *ghṛna śaṅkā bhayaṃ lajjā jugupsā ceti pañcamī*
kulaṃ śīlaṃ tathā jātir-aṣṭau pāśāḥ-prakīrtitāḥ,
pāśa-baddhaḥ smṛto jīvaḥ pāśa-muktaḥ sadāśiva.
(*Kulārṇava Tantra*)

[13] Thus, *Bhaviṣyapurāṇa* 42/41–45 explains that as all the four castes descend from one and the same universal ancestor distinctions between them are spurious; this, of course, is a very late text, probably of the eighteenth century.

[14] *Shakti and Shākta*, p. 609.

[15] *Shakti and Shākta*, p. 621, *pūjākālaṃ vinā nānyam puruṣaṃ manasā spṛśet, pūjākale ca deveśi veśyeva paritoṣayet.* Strangely enough, Avalon does not give a translation of the *śloka*, but paraphrases it as though he felt shy about it—an unusual feature. He gives a very free and watered-down rendering, viz. 'outside worship the mind is not even to think of the subject, as is said concerning the Shakti in the Uttara Tantra'.

[16] *ākṛṣṭastāḍito vā'pi yo viśadaṃ na yāti ca,*
guruḥ kṛpaṃ karotīti muda sañcintayesadā.
ānanda kampanonmañca svaranetrādivikriya,
yeṣāṃ syustatrayogyañca dīkṣā saṃskāra karmaṇi.
(Gh. 18, *Kulārṇava*, 22, 24)

[17] *vāme ramā ramana-kuśalā dakṣiṇe cālipātram,*
agre mudrāścaṇakabaṭakā sūkarasyoṣṇamāṃsam.
tantrī viṇā sarasamadhurā sadguroḥ satkathāyām,
kaulo mārgaḥ paramagahano yogināmapyagamyaḥ.

alipiśitapurandhrī bhogapūjāparoham,
bahuvidhakulamārgo'rambhasaṃbhavito'ham.

paśujanavimukho'haṃ bhairavīmāśrito'ham
gurucaraṇarato'haṃ bhairavo'haṃ śivo'haṃ.
(Ghilḍayāl, p. 19)

[18] vd. S. B. Dasgupta, *Buddhist Esotericism, passim.*

[19] *nindantu bandhavaḥ sarve tyajantu strīsutādayaḥ,*
janā hasantu mām dṛṣtvā, rājano daṇḍayantu vā,
Lakṣmīstiṣṭhatu vā yātu na muñcāmi pathantvidam.
Evaṃ yasya dṛḍhā bhaktiḥ sa vāme siddhimapnuyāt.

[20] Personal conversation at Madras, April 1957.

[21] Vivekananda, throughout his eight volumes, waxed eloquent on *prāṇāyāma* as not being breathing exercises, but as 'control of the *prāṇa*, the vital force, of which breathing is but the most visible limb'. That is true. But it is also just pure breathing exercises, and this is certainly the more frequent meaning in tantric literature.

[22] Dale Saunders, in his *Mudrā* (Bollingen Series 1960), does not include the meaning 'parched kidney-bean', although his otherwise excellent book deals with tantric patterns throughout.

[23] *Mudrā* has no special significance in non-tantric Buddhism to my knowledge; certainly not in Theravāda Buddhism. I do not claim that the specific technical meaning in each section is the exclusive meaning there used; i.e. it is conceivable that *mudrā* means ritualistic gesture occasionally in Buddhist *tantra.* However, it *never* means the aphrodisiac food in Buddhist *tantra* the Tibetan translation is always *phyag rgyas* which never means any sort of food, though it does mean both the female partner and ritualistic gesture.

[24] The Hindi text reads, . . . *iskā karnā prakṛti (jagadambā) pūjan hi to hai.* It utilizes the technical meaning of *prakṛti* as nature and 'natural' in its identification with the *śakti*, the *jagadambā*, i.e. the World Mother.

[25] The text has been published; *Rudrayāmalam (uttara-tantram)*, Calcutta 1937.

[26] A *sādhaka* once again is any person who does *sādhanā*, i.e. religious, but, from the layman's viewpoint, supererogatory efforts towards the achievement of the supreme intuitive realization postulated by the Indian religious traditions. I have used the word throughout the book, there being no adequate English equivalent for it.

[27] See the chapter 'On Mantra'. Both the texts are available.

[28] *Vāmamārga*, by Paṇḍit Vanśīdhar Sukul Vaidyarāj, Tantraśāstrī, Kalyān Mandir, Katrā, Allahabad, U.P., 1951. I have seen a similar, slightly larger manual in Bengali. I do not know if there are any manuals in Dravidian areas where there is left-handed worship. Śrī T. K. Menon, a tantric of Palghat, Kerala, told me that there is such a manual in Malayalam, but it is not printed and it is circulated only among initiates (personal communication, Palghat, 1954).

[29] On the six *cakras* A. Avalon's *The Serpent Power* is still the standard work; it was reprinted by Ganeshan and Co., Madras 1954. The text on whose basis the book is written is a tantra named 'the description of the six *cakras*' (*ṣaccakra-nirūpaṇa*) which is appended in the Sanskrit original in Avalon's book. The Buddhists refer to the *cakra* in the cranial region as the *śūnyacakra*, the *cakra* of Voidness. It is in this region that the esoteric process of *yuganaddha* (*zung 'jug*) is meditated upon, just as the Hindu tantric visualizes the union of Śiva and Śakti in this centre.

[30] *bhavapāśavināśāya jñānadṛṣtipradarśine/*
namaḥ sadgurave tubhyaṃ bhuktimuktipradāyiṇe//
narākṛti parabrahma-rūpāyājñānahāriṇe/
kuladharmaprakāśaya tasmai śrigurave namaḥ
(*Rudrayāmala* III)

[31] *Vāmamārga*, p. 43 f, *amuka ānandanātha amukī śaktyambā śirapādukāṃ pūjayāmi ākāśātmakaṃ puṣpam samarpayāmi svāhā*. The same invocation is repeated with different flowers each of them linked with one of the cosmogenic aspects of the ritual at a time; and each time the *bīja* of the 'element' in question is added; i.e. '. . . *laṃ pṛthivyātmakaṃ puṣpam*' (*laṃ* being the earth *bīja*' '. . . *laṃ* this earth-like flower'; '*yaṃ vāyvātamakaṃ puṣpam*' '*vaṃ* this wind-like flower'; '*raṃ vahnyātmakaṃ puṣpam*' '*raṃ* this fire-like flower', etc. The *bījas* of the elements are exactly the same in the Tibetan *mantra* (*sṅags*) tradition (personal information Dezhung and Phrin las Rinpoche at Seattle): *kaṃ*, ether, *vaṃ*, water, *raṃ*, fire, *laṃ*, earth, *yaṃ*, wind.

[32] *bīja* lit. 'seed' (see chapter On *Mantra*) a non-semantic syllable and the key element (or elements) of a *mantra*. The Tibetans use the same term *sa bon* when they refer to these syllables. Almost the entire Tibetan corpus of *mantras* is composed of Tibetan transcriptions of these Indian *bījas*; I doubt if there are any indigenous *bījas* in Tibetan *sṅags kyi theg pa* (*mantrayāna*).

[33] *namaḥ sarvasvarūpinyai jagaddhātryai namo namaḥ/*
ādyāya (*amukyai*) *te kartryai hartryai namo namaḥ//*
(*Brahmayāmala*, quoted in *Vāmamarga*, p. 45)

[34] *svāhā* is the terminal constant in all Hindu and much Buddhist ritual and in *mantras* which accompany oblations and libations, actual or metaphorical. The Tibetans pronounce it *soha*. Brahmin folk etymology explains *svāhā* to be the name of the spouse of the demiurge Brahmā, who presides over all Vedic sacrifices. The actual etymology of this ubiquitous *mantra* is unknown, but I think the combination *su* + *āha* 'well-said' would be a reasonable clue.

[35] *sandhyā* means twilight, both dusk and dawn, at least in ritualistic terminology. The two *sandhyā*, i.e. at dusk and at dawn, are the minimum observance requirements for the Hindu. *Sandhyā* consists of a number of meditations and of

the recitation of Vedic *mantras*, the Gāyatrī *mantra* of the Ṛgveda being the central text of the *sandhyā*.

[36] The elephant-hook *mudrā*, a *mudrā* which is used only in the Hindu tradition. It is described in the *Tantrasāra*, the most authoritative text on *mudrā* formation in Hindu tantrism: 'making the middle finger straight and placing the index upon the central mount (i.e. below the middle finger, having placed it (the index) in a slightly bent manner, when he has thus joined it to the mount beneath the middle finger) this is called the *ankuṣa-mudrā*'; *ṛjvīñça madhyamaṃ kṛtvā tarjanī madhyaparvaṇī, samyojyakuñcayet kiñcit (mudreṣāṃkuṣasaṃjnikā)*.

[37] *gaṅge ca yamune caiva godāvarī sarasvatī/ narmmade sindhu kāverī jale'sminsannidhiṃ kuru// Vāmamārga*, 47

[38] Some tantrics also meditate on holding the lustral water for a while in the *suṣumnā*, before emitting it through the *piṅgalā* (personal communication from Śrī Devicharan Dube, Ll. B., a lay tantric devotee of Sīgrā, Banaras).

[39] On *svāhā, hrīm, krīm*, etc., see On Mantra.

[40] *prātabrāhmhīṃ raktavarṇāṃ dvibhujāñca kumārikāṃ/ kamaṇḍaluṃ tīrthapūrṇamacchamālāṃ ca bibhratīm// kṛṣṇajināmbaradharāṃ haṃsārūḍhāṃ śucismitām/ Vāmamārga*, 49.

[41] the cow-*mudrā*, 'which gives nectar' described in the *Tantrasārā*: entwining the fingers of both hands into each other, palms one towards the other, the two little fingers and the two ring fingers are then placed upon their opposites' forepart—then the index and the middle finger follow the same procedure with their opposite fingers, *anyonyābhimukhāśliṣṭhā kaniṣṭhānāmikā punaḥ/ tathā ca tarjanīmadhyā dhenumudrāmṛtāpradā*.

[42] It should be noted that *āsana* may have any of these three meanings: the surface upon which the seat is spread; the seat proper, viz. the material of which it is made; and finally the posture which the *sādhaka* takes for his practice.

[43] *Vāmamārga*, p. 53. Vaidyarāj does not quote the Sanskrit original, but gives a Hindi rendering, from which this statement has been translated.

[44] Same procedure as in note 42. The soles of the feet have to be turned up, as the right shin is placed over the left calf.

[45] Same procedure as in notes 42 and 44.

[46] Ibid., p. 53, *devatāoṉ kī pūjā din meṉ pūrvābhimukh aur rāt meṉ uttarabhimukh karnī cāhiye. Parantu devi aur śiv kī pūjā sadā uttarābhimukh karnī cāhiye.*

[47] M. Opler's review article of M. Carstairs' *The Twice Born* (Hogarth, London, and Indiana Univ. Press, Bloomington) in *American Anthropologist*, 1959.

[48] *oṃ hrīṃ amṛte amṛtodbhave amṛtavarṣiṇi amṛtam ākarṣaya siddhiṃ dehi amuka iṣṭadevatā me vaśāmānaya svāhā*. This *mantra* is listed both in the *Mantramahārṇava* and the *Mantramahodadhi* and I presume Vaidyarāj quotes it from there (p. 53).

[49] These are typically Hindu tantric *mudrās*. They are not contained in Dale Saunders' *Mudrā*, and so far I have not seen them listed in Buddhist tantric works.

The *mudrās* used in Vajrayāṇa Buddhism tend to be much simpler; another indication of the more recent origin of Hindu systematized tantra—ritualistic items tend to become more and more complex in the course of their development.

[50] *aiṃ amuka ānandanātha śrīgurupādukāṃ tarpayāmi namaḥ, Vāmamarga*, 54.

[51] *aiṃ vada vada vāgvādini mama jihvāgre sthirībhava sarvasattvavaśaṃkarī svāhā—Vāmamārga*, 54. The use of *sattva* in this phrase as 'living being' has a strong Buddhist flavour, for in canonical Hinduism *sattva* has an overwhelmingly strong philosophical connotation as truth (*sat, satya, sattva*); the Hindu term for 'living being' is usually *prāṇī*. Though I have not found this particular *mantra* in the Buddhist *Sādhanāmālā* I suspect it is a Vajrayāṇa *mantra* taken over into Hindu tantric lore along with many other Buddhist *mantras*.

[52] *Oṃ viṣṇuryonīṃ kalpayatu tvaṣṭā rūpāni piṃśatu ā siñcatu prajāpatirdhātā garbhaṃ dadātu te oṃ garbhaṃ dhehi sinivāli garbhaṃ dhehi sarasvatī garbham aśvinau devāvadhattāṃ puṣkarasṛjau*. 'Oṃ Viṣṇu shall form the womb, Tvaṣṭā shall grind the forms, Prajāpati shall besprinkle, Dhātā may place the foetus for you. Oṃ Sinīvalī place! (preserve, protect—all these being various Brahmin interpretations) Sarasvatī place! (preserve, protect)—Aśvins, the twin-gods, lake-born ones, should deposit the foetus (in the womb).' This verse is found in the Rgveda, the Yajurveda, and all the Śrauta-sūtras (the texts dealing with domestic ritual). The *Bṛhadāranyaka Upaniṣad* repeats it in the last *vallī*; it is to be pronounced by the husband before he cohabits with his wife for offspring. There are *mantras* in the same Upaniṣad which prevent conception, so the tantrics would not have to have their own *mantra* for such purpose. It remains mysterious why this *mantra* would be used in the *cakra*; I suspect that it is just a grave misunderstanding on the part of the tantric preceptors, partially caused by their eagerness to use and perpetuate Vedic material.

[53] We all observe the great fervour with which the Tibetan Lamas repeat the letters of the alphabet, both Tibetan and Nāgarī, in the style of *japam*, i.e. as repetition of a *mantra* or of any other sacred formula. The Lamas seem to attach more sanctity to the Nāgarī alphabet, however.

[54] *nyāsa* (lit. placing down, depositing) is the process of placing one meditational entity into another, and this applies both to actual, physical, and to imagined entities; *mātrikā* is what I call a systematically ambiguous word in tantric literature, i.e. its equivocality is intentional. It means a little mother, a little (or minimal) measure of any kind including metrical units; from the first meaning derives the purely tantric use as a goddess, usually auxiliary to some central deity male or female (as the *ḍākinīs—kha 'gro ma*); the second meaning yields the notion of the cosmic matrix symbolized by the 'garland of letters' which is thought to verbalize the cosmic process in tantric *sādhanā*.

To exemplify the *mātrikā-nyāsa*, we must adduce some instances from the tantric tradition; they form an invariable part of the complete tantric *sādhanā*

and I have seen no tantric text—Hindu or Buddhist alike—which would not dilate on this use of the alphabet:
—the *prāṇāyāma* (breath control) of the tantric uses the *mātrikā* as time-measures for the processes of inhaling (*pūraka*), exhaling (*recaka*), and retaining (*kumbhaka*) of breath: he mentally repeats *aṃ āṃ iṃ īṃ uṃ ūṃ ṛṃ ṝṃ lṛṃ lṝm eṃ aiṃ oṃ auṃ aṃ aḥ* to control the duration of *pūraka*; *kaṃ khaṃ gaṃ ghaṃ ṅaṃ caṃ chaṃ jaṃ jhaṃ naṃ taṃ thaṃ daṃ dhaṃ naṃ taṃ thaṃ daṃ dhaṃ naṃ paṃ phaṃ baṃ bhaṃ maṃ* for the *kumbhaka*, and from *yaṃ raṃ* . . . to the final *kṣaṃ* for the *recaka*; there is another intermediary exercise probably meant as an aid to calming the mind. It is called *kara-nyāsa* and it falls in line with other *aṅganyāsa* (the touching of parts of the body with one's hands or fingers pronouncing a *mantra* for the purpose of steadying the body and the mind for meditation): here, the *sādhaka*, touching the named fingers with their opposites on the other hand, says '*aṃ kaṃ khaṃ gaṃ ghaṃ ṅaṃ aṃ:* worship to the two thumbs (*anguṣṭābhyāṃ namaḥ*), *iṃ caṃ chaṃ jaṃ jhaṃ naṃ iṃ svāhā:* to the two indices (*tarjanibhyāṃ svāhā*), *uṃ taṃ thaṃ daṃ dhaṃ naṃ uṃ vaṣaṭ* to the two middle-fingers (*madhyamābhyāṃ vaṣaṭ*), *eṃ taṃ thaṃ daṃ dhaṃ naṃ aiṃ huṃ:* to the two ring fingers (*anāmikābhyāṃ huṃ*), *oṃ paṃ phaṃ baṃ bhaṃ auṃ vauṣaṭ:* to the two little fingers (*kaniṣtābhyāṃ vauṣaṭ*), *aṃ yaṃ raṃ laṃ vaṃ saṃ śaṃ ṣaṃ haṃ laṃ kṣaṃ aḥ phaṭ:* to the palms and the backs of the hands (*karatalakarapṛṣtābhyāṃ phaṭ*).

Another *nyāsa* is the *nyāsa* of the six parts of the icon of the deity worshipped: '*aṃ kaṃ khaṃ gaṃ ghaṃ ṅaṃ aṃ*': worship to the heart (*hṛdayāya namaḥ*): *iṃ caṃ chaṃ jaṃ jhaṃ ñaṃ iṃ svāhā:* in the head (*śirasi svāhā*), *uṃ taṃ thaṃ daṃ dhaṃ naṃ uṃ vaṣaṭ:* to the protuberance on the head (*śikhāyay vaṣaṭ*), *eṃ taṃ thaṃ daṃ dhaṃ naṃ aiṃ huṃ:* to the armour (*kavacāya huṃ*; this cannot refer to the amulet worn by the deity, because the instruction for the *nyāsa* is 'on the shoulders', i.e. the *sādhaka* touches his shoulders when he pronounces this formula, the place of contact being vicarious for touching the respective part of the iconicized deity); *oṃ paṃ phaṃ baṃ bhaṃ maṃ auṃ vauṣaṭ:* to the three eyes (*netratrayāya vauṣaṭ*), *aṃ yaṃ raṃ laṃ vaṃ saṃ saṃ saṃ haṃ laṃ kṣaṃ aḥ phaṭ:* to the weapon (*astrāya phaṭ*).

In a similar fashion, *nyāsa* is made on the six 'lotuses' (*cakra*) in the yogic body; this is done in two parts, i.e. first the 'inner' section, where the *sādhaka* sits still and imagines the *cakras* one by one, then the 'outer' section (*bahirmātrikā-nyāsa*) where he places his fingers on his forehead, his throat, etc., i.e. on the regions behind which the *cakras* are imagined to be located.

[55] See chapter on Pilgrimage.

[56] *puṃ pūrṇaśailāya pīṭhāya namaḥ, kaṃ kāmarūpāya piṭhāya namaḥ*, etc.—notice that the *bījā* syllables are the initial syllables of each of the names of the 'seats'; this device goes through all tantric schools and incorporates all types of proper names used in tantrism, Hindu and Buddhist. cf. *praṃ* as the *bīja* of the *prajñāpārāmitā*-texts.

[57] *Vāmamārga*, 67. Note that the *bījas* used for the six limbs of the deity are different from those in note 54. Here *kavaca* means amulet, not armour or cuirass; because *hraiṃ* is the *bīja* connected with all sorts of amulets and charms.

[58] The *kalās* always refer, directly, to the *maṇḍala* representing the deity. Just as each deity has a number of auxiliary divinities to support him or her, the *kalās* support (*dhārayanti*) the *maṇḍala*. The ten *kalās* are the ten segments of the basic *maṇḍala* of the goddess, the *Śaḍāṅgi* (vd. above)—thus:

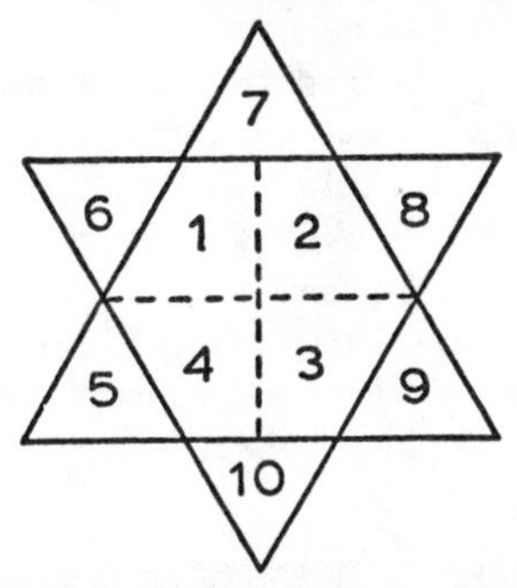

[59] *dhuṃ dhūmrāyai namaḥ, aṃ acciṣe namaḥ* (should probably read *arciṣe*, from *arcis* f, flame, bright light), *jvaṃ jvālinyai namaḥ, suṃ sūkṣmāyai namaḥ, viṃ visphulinginyai namaḥ . . . haṃ havyakavyavahāyai namaḥ . . . Vāmamārga*, 77.

[60] B. Bhattacharya, *Buddhist Iconography*, p. 93 ff.

[61] *Vāmamārga*, 78.

[62] According to this instruction the form would then be '*aṃ āṃ iṃ īṃ uṃ ūṃ*, etc . . . *kṣaṃ* xyz *kṣaṃ . . . aṃ āṃ*'. 'xyz' symbolizes the variables, i.e. the *bījas*, of the chosen deity, which differ between individual *sādhakas* according to their initiation.

[63] *māle māle mahāmāle sarvaśaktisvarupiṇi/ caturvargastvayi nyastastasmānme siddhidā bhava// Mantramahārṇava*, IV, 2; also *Vāmamārga*, 89.

[64] *guhyātiguhyāgoptrī tvaṃ gṛhāṇāsmatkṛtam japam/ siddhirbhavatu me devi tvatprasādānmaheśvari// Vāmamārga*, 89.

[65] *oṃ yaṃ yaṃ spṛśami pādena yaṃ yaṃ paṣyāmi cakṣuṣā/ sa eva dāsatāṃ yātu yadi śakrasamo bhavet// Vāmamārga*, 91.

> [66] *sādhakebhyaśca śaktibhyo dadyāt nirmalyacandanam/*
> *niveśeccakrarūpeṇa paṅktyākārena vā yathā//*
> *saktiyukto vasedvāpi yugma yugma vidhānataḥ/*
> *tataḥ puṣpam samādāya guroḥ pātre nivedayet//*
> *gurave canivedyātha . . .*
>
> (*Mahānirvāṇa Tantra*, 6th *Ullāsa*)

[67] *Vāmamārga*, 101.

[68] *aiṃ sapatnikaṃ guruṃ tarpayāmi namaḥ: Vāmamārga*, 102.

[69] The 'Wave of Beauty' (*Saundaryalaharī*), ascribed to Śaṃkarācārya by orthodox Brahmanical tradition, is in essence a poetical description or an elaborate paraphrase—or evasion, if you want—of the *mantra* called the *Śrīvidyā* (lit. technique of the goddess Lakṣmī); the text builds the *mantra*, as it were, without ever quoting it. On the common procedure of paraphrasing secret *mantras* which must not be written down see the chapter 'On Mantra'. On the text, see Norman Brown's edition of the *Saundaryalaharī* in the H.O.S., and my review article in *Quest*, Bombay 1960).

[70] The *Śrīvidyā-mantra* proper ends on . . . *yum*, before *ānandabhairava*.

[71] Both this and the previous *mantra* have only two semantically meaningful terms, viz. *ānandabhairavāya* (*ānandabhairavyai*) and *tarpayāmi*, i.e. 'I make *tarpana* to the "Bliss Śiva" and to the "Bliss Devi" ', Bhairava and Bhairavī being very frequent epithets of Śiva and the Devī.

[72] *sāyudhaṃ savāhanam saparivāraṃ tarpayāmi svāhā: Vāmamārga*, 103. The 'family' is her consort Śiva, and her sons Skanda (Kārtikeya, Kumāra—the war god) and Gaṇeśa (the 'Lord of Hosts', the remover of obstacles, Vighnāntaka—depicted with an elephant's head).

> [73] *samudre mathyamāne tu kṣīrābdhau sāgarottame/*
> *tatrotpannā surā devī kanyakārūpadhariṇī//*
> *gokṣīrasadṛsākāra kulāmṛtasamudbhavā/*
> *aṣṭadaśabhujair yuktā nirajāyatalocanā//*
> *anandaśikhare jātā ānandaśca maheśvaraḥ/*
> *tayoryoge bhavedbrahmā viṣṇuśca śiva eva ca//*
> *tasmādimāṃ surāṃ devīm pūrṇo'haṃ tāṃ pibāmyaham/*
> (*Kulārṇava Tantra*, III)

Although 'Maheśvara' is a synonym of Śiva, the phrase '*tayoryoge bhavedbrahmā viṣṇuśca śiva eva ca*'—i.e. 'Brahmā, Viṣṇu, and Śiva come forth from the union of Maheśvara (who is Śiva) and the Devī', tantric ideology and much of Hindu non-tantric mythology do not see a contradiction in such a statement, for these are pronouncements on two levels which do not conflict. For the tantric, the union of Śiva and Śakti is *paramārthika*, i.e. belonging to the realm of absolute, non-dual existence, whereas the great world gods belong to the *vyavahāra* (*saṃvṛti*), the phenomenal realm. In other words, the absolute Śiva-Śakti principle emanates, or projects, the totum of all phenomenal things and persons, and that includes the gods with Śiva; the first Śiva (Maheśvara in this verse) is a principle, the Śiva of the trinity in the same verse is a personal god.

[74] Although Buddhism denies any entity in the final analysis, the numinous *brahman* and the numinous *śūnyatā* (*stoṅ pa ñid*) are philosophical ultimates; the only difference is that the Brahmins stress this 'one' (*ekaṃ satyam, dvitīyo nāsti*, etc.) whereas the Buddhists—the *mādhyamikās* not excluded—suppress any statement that would create the notion of an existing entity. The Vajrayāṇa

yuganaddha (*sku 'grub, śes rab thabs, zuṅ 'jug* and other terms) is the symbol of the Void, and for the Buddhist tantric this complex is as central as is the Brahmin to the Hindu tantric who epitomizes it in the Śiva-Śakti union.

[75] *saśabdaṃ na pibed dravyaṃ na binduṃ patayedadhaḥ/*
vinā carvveṇa yatpānaṃ kevalaṃ viṣavardhanaṃ// . . .
ucciṣṭaṃ na spṛśeccakre . . .
saśabdaṃ noddharet pātraṃ tathaiva ca na pūrayet/
riktapātraṃ na kurvīta na pātraṃ bhramayet sadā/
(*Kaulāvali Nirṇaya*, II, 1–4)

sādhakānāṃ gṛhasthānāṃ pañcapātraṃ prakīrtitam/
atipānāt kulīnānāṃ siddhihāniḥ prajāyate//
yāvanna calayed dṛṣṭim yāvanna calayedmanaḥ/
tāvat pānaṃ prakurvīta paśupānam ataḥ param//
Mahānirvāṇa Tantra, 6th *Ullāsa*)

[76] *snehādbhayādanuraktyā paśuṃścakre praveśayan/*
kuladharmān paribhraṣṭo vīropi narakaṃ vrajet//
(*Mahānirvāṇa Tantra*, 8th *Ullāsa*)

[77] *varṇābhimānāccakre tu varṇabhedam karoti yaḥ/*
sa yāti ghoranirayaṃapi vedāntapāragaḥ//
(*Mahānirvāṇa Tantra*, 8th *Ullāsa*)

[78] *oṃ āḥ surekhe vajrarekhe hūṃ phaṭ svāhā.*
Vāmamārga, 110.

[79] *oṃ hrīṃ ādhāraśaktaye kamalāsanāya namaḥ.*
Vāmamārga, 110.

[80] *oṃ śayye tvaṃ mṛtarupāsi sādhanīyāsi sādhakaiḥ/*
ato'tra japyate mantro hyasmākaṃ siddhidā bhava.
Vāmamārga, 110.

[81] The bowl containing general, mixed ingredients which are more or less samples of the contents of the other bowls: flowers, paddy, rose-water, scent; however, to my knowledge, none of the four edible Ms is contained in this bowl.

[82] *aiṃ klīṃ sauḥ tripurāyai namaḥ imāṃ śaktiṃ pavitrīkuru mama śaktiṃ kuru kuru svāhā. Vāmamārga*, 110.

[83] *phir śakti ko gaurī kī aur apne ko śiv kī bhāvanā kar mūlamantra kā uccāraṇ kar mātṛmukh meṉ pitṛmukh arpit kare. Vāmamārga*, 111.

[84] *oṃ dharmādharmahavidīpte ātmāgnau manasā srucā/*
suṣumnāvartmanā nityamakṣavṛttirjuhomyaham//
Vāmamārga, 111.

akṣavṛttis is difficult; 'engaged in harnessing the sense-organs' is my own attempt, taking *akṣa* as sense-organ in general, which is permissible.

[85] *śiva śakti bhāvanāmay hokar akṣubdh aur sthir man rahe. Vāmamārga,* 111.

[86] *oṃ prakāśākāśahastābhyāmavalambyonmani srucā/*
dharmādharmakalāsnehapūrṇamagnau juhomyaham//
Ibid.

This is not the only possible translation of the *śloka* which is perhaps intentionally dark and ambiguous.

[87] Snellgrove, *The Hevajra Tantra*, passim.

[88] *caṇḍikāṃ pūjayed yastu vinā pañcamakārakaih/*
catvāri tasya naśyanti ayurvidyāyaśodhanam//
Kaulāvali Nirnaya, III

catvāri is rather elegantly placed at the beginning of the *śloka* just after *pañcamakārakaih*, so that with some non-grammatical imagination such as is quite acceptable to the Hindu, the extended meaning of the *śloka* would be: 'He who worships . . . without the five Ms, for him the four Ms (i.e. the first four, which are often called *catvāri*, *maithuna* being referred to as the fifth *pañcama*) perish, as do long life, knowledge, splendour, and wealth.'

[89] *madyaṃ māṃsaṃ tathā matsyaṃ mudrāmaithunameva ca/*
makārapañcakaṃ devi devatāprītidāyakam//
Ibid.

[90] *madyairmāṃsaistathā matsyairmudrābhirmaithunairapi/*
strībhiḥ sārddhaṃ mahāsādhurarcayed jagadambikām//
Kāmakhyā Tantra, 5th *Patala*)

[91] *yā surā sarvakāryeṣu kathitā bhuvi muktidā/*
tasyā nāma bhaveddevī tīrthaṃ pānaṃ sudurlabham//
(*Samayācāra*, quoted in *Vāmamārga*, 107)

10

THE TRADITION AND THE TARGET

SUMMARIZING and concluding this study, we must now place the tantric tradition into the cultural continuum that was and is India; and we must show what the tantric himself expects from his tradition, as well as what it may have to contribute to Asian culture—if Asia, in particular India, finds the time and the leisure to re-evaluate those elements of its past which are either extinct or dormant, but which will have to be resuscitated, to an extent, if Asia looks for a contribution to modern thought and culture, which has not grown in the West. This is, admittedly, difficult. All the things which Asian leaders want to incorporate into their various bodies politic are western imports: communism, democracy, nationalism, secularism, industrialism; in short, everything that counts in the 'building of modern nations'.

Cultural anthropology[1] deals with problems arising from highly specialized studies of this kind in a relatively recent subdiscipline called 'Culture and Personality'. Most anthropologists who have given thought to this new subject—I would mention the famous Margaret Mead, Cora du Bois, Douglas Haring, Melford E. Spiro, in the United States, Lévy-Strauss in France, Meyer-Fortes and Adrian Mayer in Britain—suffer from the great handicap of not being conversant with the classical traditions of some of the cultures with which they engage themselves. There is, particularly in American anthropology, an extreme aversion to philological procedures; structural and descriptive linguistics such as is in vogue in North America, and to an increasing extent in Britain and Europe, show a decided aversion which, I would add, is partly justified, again for reasons into which we cannot go here; but the investigation into as highly complex and sophisticated a pattern as tantrism does require textual knowledge, which again presupposes philological study in the classical sense, just as much as it requires the synchronic methodology of cultural anthropology. In this sense, this book was a first attempt to combine classical scholarship with modern cultural anthropology, and orientalist philology with sociological awareness.

Much modern anthropology also insists on quantifying methods, and I believe that this emphasis is irrelevant for our study. The only statistic that does seem important in winding up this investigation covers the frequency of themes within the tantric tradition. As we survey the frequency of themes within the body of tantric literature drawn into this study, we will see that elements which were pushed aside or played down by tantric teachers nevertheless take an important part within that literature. In other words, the fact that the absolutistic teaching of tantrism relating to the emancipation from the bonds of pain and birth and death is stressed as the key of tantric teaching by the masters does not imply that other elements are operationally less important to them. From the percentage of instructions not concerned with the supreme goal, inferences about the manner in which tantrism operates in fact, can and must be drawn against the absolutistic statements,however emphatic and vociferous, of the tantric teachers and their modern votaries. The modern Indian mind tends to confuse in a persistent fashion the 'ought' and the 'is'. When asked about religious practice, the answer given refers to the nuclear teaching, and not to the actual bulk of instruction and practice within the tradition. We can recognize a distinct pattern, which pervades all facets of cultural discourse: sophisticated Hindus in India and outside would deny that there is such a thing as a caste system, on the basis that caste has been 'abolished' by the constitution of independent India; or, that Hinduism is monistic or monotheistic, the variegated pantheon a sort of popular by-product, a step at best towards 'higher' things not to be taken too seriously by the earnest seeker. None of this is true; the caste system is as strong as, if not stronger than, it was before, and whatever modifications modern India stipulates is an 'ought', not an 'is'; Vivekananda, and the host of his monastic and lay followers who now constitute the Hindu renaissance, might themselves have believed that monism or some other form of Vedāntic speculation was the core of Hinduism, but this again is not the case. Whatever the Upaniṣadic and post-Vedāntic dictum about the essence of the canonical teaching, the polytheistic[2] element is so strong that no intelligent person could ignore it except for some sort of vested interest. Orthodox Hindus do not seem so worried about the existence of a strong basic polytheism, as modern, sophisticated, renaissance Indians are—Indians, that is, whose acquaintance with Hinduism is not much more than what Vivekananda and his younger contemporaries passed on in English.

Well over ninety-five per cent of Indian religious literature of all the three indigenous traditions deals with the polytheistic patterns, ritualistic elements, and themes which the Indian sophisticate has been relegating to *vyavahāra*, the phenomenal sphere. The not-so-sophisticated but learned traditionalist has been attaching equal importance to ritualistic instruction as he does to the philosophical five per cent which remain. And here is a point of contact, finally, between the orthodox Hindu and the tantric; both of them rely on the ritualistic observance, on the implied polytheistic structure, in other words on the *vyavahāra* framework, just as much as they do on the speculative residue. It is only the modern Indian, indoctrinated by the founding fathers of the Hindu renaissance—beginning with Rammohan Roy, Dayananda, Vivekananda up to our contemporary swamis like the late Shivananda, Chinmayananda, and the police saint Krishna Manon, etc.—who wax eloquent in defence of the 'pure philosophical' part of the tradition, playing down and denigrating the ritualistic part. This, however, I feel is spurious and has to be exposed as such: the Hindu renaissance is the outcome, on the religious side, of charismatic actions and teachers, who ignored Sanskrit, and who opposed traditionalism at a time when Indian nationalism came to the fore. And here is one of the chief errors of some of the best modern cultural anthropologists, both Indian and occidental: what they call Sanskritization is in reality a pattern of anti-Sanskritization. The modern swamis around whom throng thousands and thousands of Indians who know some English as well as an increasing number of guffawing occidentals who seek diversion in the mysterious East because they are bored or appalled by the unmysterious West represent the Hindu Renaissance which is largely spurious.

Tabulating twenty-five Hindu and ten Buddhist tantras of a median length of six hundred *ślokas* or other verses, the following averages for various themes emerged:

mantra notation and *mantra* instruction:	60%
maṇḍala construction and use:	10%
dhyānas for various deities:	10%
preparation of ritualistic ingredients:	5%
amulets, charms, etc.:	3%
the *mokṣa*-complex proper, including afferent and efferent *sandhābhāṣā*:	7%

The rest are tantric miscellanies; astrological indications, *phalaśruti*, 'accounts of the gains' with reference to various *sādhanās*, mutual eulogies between the male and the female deities who hold the didactic discourse. The latter are completely stereotype; at the beginning of almost every tantra, Hindu and Buddhist alike, the questioning deity beseeches the questioned one to let out the secret and it requires a considerable amount of pressing until the partner gives in and talks; then the god or the goddess would say that the secrets now to be divulged have never been divulged by anyone or to anyone, but that they were now going to be said due to the great love or admiration, etc., for the other divine partner.

This list does not really conflict with any of the patterns of topics which tantric commentators ascribe to tantric literature—

the topics listed as constituting an *āgama* are so standardized that each specific theme can be covered by any of these topics. No Indian commentator ever gave an estimate or a rule about the proportion which each topic should or did occupy in any given tantric text; this need has simply never been felt and the orthodox Hindu and Buddhist feeling about these things is strictly non-quantitative. Whether a topic occupies two verses in a book of one thousand verses or whether it occupies one-fourth of the whole text does not seem to be of conscious concern to the commentator. The Hindu commentator's terms *śruyate*, 'a canonical text says', and *smaryate*, 'the non-canonical scripture says', were diffusely applied: a single mention is as good as a hundred mentions. This is an important point to note: what has made the tantras famous in India and among students of Indica and esoterica in general are the erotocentric passages within the redemptive frame—in other words, the passages which utilize erotic imagery, either in *sandhābhāṣā* or otherwise, as indicators of an absolutistic, redemptivist teaching. The fact that these passages occupy less than seven per cent of the total bulk of tantric texts seen in diffusion is somewhat disappointing to the unwary philologist reading tantric literature; he has to search for the salient passages, interspersed as they are between awesome masses of other topics of questionable interest for the student of tantric thought proper. These topics are shared with all other genres of religious literature—the epic, the Purāṇas, the *śāstras*. To the tantric commentator, however, all these topics are equally important, at least in theory if not in homiletic practice. It would be both frustrating and misleading to direct any but a marginal interest of large tracts of material thematically shared with other kinds of religious literature in India. If tantrism has anything unique about it, which sets it into relief from other religious writing, the one aspect has to be singled out which is not shared with other texts. This aspect, clearly, is the one that made tantrism both famous and infamous through the ages. I have been trying to make up for the unpardonably antagonistic or apologetic tone of previous students of tantric literature. In so far as they were Indian, their hedging was understandable: anyone, scholar or poet alike, had to side with the puritan against the hedonist, with India's official culture against everything else. Arthur Avalon, Herbert Guenther, and a few others including myself have tried to state things without chips on our shoulders over a span of fifty years. But then, Avalon, Guenther, and this author were not Indian by birth, in spite of their varying commitments to the tantric tradition.

Whatever the distribution of topics in tantric literature, there can be no doubt, either to the practising tantric or to the analysing scholar, about the target of the tantric tradition. Opponents to tantrism, in India and elsewhere, have put forth as their chief argument the somewhat silly charge that tantrics pretend to be religious in order to indulge in drink and fornication. Silly, because drink and fornication can be relatively easily indulged in, even in India. The late Jay Shankar Prasād, the famous Hindi poet from Banaras, once wrote in a letter to his friend: 'why bother, is sexual intercourse ever unobtainable?' (*maithun durlahh kahān?*) No one has to undergo the excessive hardships, the degree of control, the tedium of initiation, of ritualistic perfection, and of minute detail in order to have fun, even in puritan India. No one in his senses would deny the fact that there has been a lot of misuse where pleasure was simply unobtainable; but there has been an equal amount of misuse in the non-tantric tradition. The late M. N. Roy, the keenest perhaps among Indian minds of this century, once told this author: 'The Marwāṛī (member of the Indian merchant caste) washes his abdomen and his body five times a day, following the minutest ritual; and he sucks the poor man's blood with equal vehemence.'

We must give all tantrics the benefit of doubt. This is precisely what India at large has neglected to do. Amongst South Indian Brahmins, particularly of the Śaivite tradition, there is a saying that no one can judge a *sādhu* except Śiva himself; the implication being that the possibility of misuse of the garment is known, but must be politely ignored. A secular government, admittedly, cannot share this attitude, but the tantric's concern here is not governmental or even secular.

What, then, is the final target of tantric *sādhanā* and of the tantric life? It is the same as that of all Hindu and Buddhist religion, namely the freedom from the misery of attachment. I deliberately avoid the term worldly existence (*saṃsāra*), because Vajrayāṇa Buddhism and for that matter all Mahāyāna Buddhism would then have to be counted out; for in it *saṃsāra* and *nirvāṇa* are inextricably one. And it does seem that Hindu tantra surreptitiously shares this sentiment with Mahāyāna and much of psychological analysis. I would go even so far as to say that this basic tenet of Mahāyāna Buddhism has been taken over consciously or otherwise by the Hindu tantrics who would have to continue making a speculative distinction between the worldly and the spiritual, *saṃsāra* and *mukti*, the phenomenal (*vyahāra*) and the absolute (*paramārtha*). The method of tantrism is more radical than that of any other system, and the immediate aim of the tantric ritual is to achieve enstasy. Following Professor M. Eliade, I used the term 'enstasy' instead of ecstasy. Enstasy connotes the various experiences described in the contemplative traditions of India and of the countries that were under Indian tutelage in matters of religion. Ecstasy was used as a generic term, subsuming about a dozen Indian terms and their Tibetan equivalents—like *samādhi*, *kaivalya*, and others, each of which branches off into more specific terms which were meant to describe more specific experiences. There is, however, no Indian or Tibetan word which could be called an exact equivalent of either enstasy or ecstasy, because these terms belong to a descriptive, critical universe of discourse meaningful to the sympathetic but critical outsider. The only Indian term which might justify lexicographical equivocation is *unmāda*, which has, however, a derogatory flavour, because words which use the root *mad* are pathological sememes in Sanskrit and in the vernaculars. Enstasy would perhaps correspond to such Indian terms as *bhāvanā* or *antarbhāvanā*; these are not pejorative, but they are almost totally colourless.[3]

The trouble is that the enstatic theme has been victimized in recent times by fraudulent esoterism of the sort that is rampant in the western world, and in some Indian circles which derive their stimulus from the lay appreciation of occidental mystery seekers, a process of progressive deterioration through reverse diffusion. Writing about tantrism, or any serious research in esoteric lore, tends to invite the charge of phoniness from the orientalist professional; but then one cannot really desist from important research for fear of this charge. Some of the best scholars are now working with tantric material: G. Tucci, the doyen of Tibetan research, in Rome, Hellmut Hoffman in Munich, deJong in Leiden, D. L. Snellgrove in London, H. V. Guenther in Canada, Alex Wayman and myself in the United States; apart from it, no scholar working in the Tibetan literary field can really avoid esoteric material in the long run, if he is at all interested in Buddhist matters.

Enstasy then is the ultimate target of all meditative disciplines in Asia, and the term applies equally to Christian mysticism and to sufism, from the comparativist viewpoint. Modern Hindu authors of pious popular literature use traditional terms to connote enstasy when they speak about Muslim or Christian saints. From the *sādhus*' and *paṇḍits*' platforms in India one often hears such statements as 'when Jesus had achieved *samādhi* . . .' or 'when Mohammed entered *kaivalya* . . .'

Enstasy, in all these traditions, is a non-discursive, quasi-permanent condition of the individual agent, and it is highly euphoric. In Indian theological parlance—Hindu, Buddhist, and Jain—it is tantamount with supreme insight or wisdom, and all other knowledge attained by discursive processes is thought to be vastly inferior; formal learning of any kind is, by implication, essentially opposed to enstasy, marring its voluntary repetition and intensification. I might add that modern pharmacology has produced some drugs which do indeed create an emotive approximation to enstasy; lysergic acid diathelymide (LSD 25) and certain other alcaloid drugs which cause a mental pattern that shows striking analogies to enstatic experiences, and which have achieved enormous, not-too-pleasant publicity in North America and parts of Western Europe during the past few years, could decidedly be classified as enstatic drugs.[4] Indian mystics have been using alcaloid drugs of simpler varieties since Vedic days; we do not yet know what exactly the *soma* of Vedic literature was, but studying the elaborate descriptions contained in the *soma*-hymns of the Ṛgveda, of the manner of which this potion was brewed, and its effects, I am tempted to think that the state of mind described in them comes much closer to alcaloid drug experiences than to alcoholic intoxication. In the previous chapter we have seen that the tantric adept uses hemp each time before he undergoes the main observance. The term for the drug, variously prepared, is *bhāṅg* in northern India, *siddhi* in Bengal—and we are aware that *siddhi* also means occult power—but the classical word used in the tantric manuals and in scholastic reference is *vijayā*, victory, or victory giver (feminine). *Cannabis Indica*, which has the same active ingredient as marijuana, creates a strongly euphoric mood, and the term *vijayā* might have been coined to signify it.[5]

The main difference between drug-induced experience and yogic enstasy is, however, that the latter yields enstatic information beyond the duration of the inebriated state, which the former does not.

There cannot be the slightest doubt that the Hindus and probably the Buddhists of earlier days did regard the taking of psychedelic drugs as part of the wide range of *sādhanās* which lead to enstasy, albeit perhaps only on the preliminary stages. The mythological and iconographical corollary to this feeling is, apart from the personification of *soma* as the quintessence of all mind-affecting beverages, the frequent epithet of Śiva as the Lord of herbs (*Auṣadhīśvara*). In Nepal, in the Gorakhpur district of eastern Uttar Pradesh, as well as in Mithila, Śiva is frequently depicted with a bowl filled with herbs under his arm, as one of the emblems of the mendicant.

Indian orthodox traditions teach asceticism as a prerequisite to contemplation leading to enstasy. It is certainly no overstatement to say that asceticism and orthodoxy are coextensive in most Indian notions of the religious life. Where such a life cannot be led, it is the pervasive ideal postulate. The ascetic remains the cynosure of the Indian people and India is even now referred to, from many of its pulpits, as *tapobhūmī* (earth of asceticism). However, there has always been a strong undercurrent, or counter-current if you will, of non- and even anti-ascetical teachings and these formed the core of the esoteric traditions of the subcontinent. Presumably, they are older than the Vedic tradition, and they are certainly older than either Brahmin or Buddhist systematic orthodoxy. Most indologists now agree that the ascetical trend was not due to the Indo-Aryan background of India's culture. The Vedas themselves, that is to say the *saṃhitā* portion, did not display much ascetical temperament. This must have emerged at some later stage, probably in the Upaniṣadic era, and we just do not know which section of indigenous speculation or folklore carried asceticism into the Vedic tradition. Many scholars in the field also agree that the non-ascetical, magical, occult, and what I have been calling the psycho-experimental propensity stem from some pre-Aryan strata of the Indian population, and that yoga in its earliest, non-systematized forms was a conglomerate of Vedic and pre-Vedic autochthonous elements. Somewhere along the way the Vedic element came to stand for the exoteric, institutionalized, sacerdotal aspects of Indian religion—what modern Americans would call the 'square' parts of it—and the non-Vedic, autonomous, psycho-experimental elements came to be regarded as dangerous and heretical. Orthodox Brahmins in the south often refer to the Veda as *trayī* (the collection of the three); they exclude the *atharvāṅgirasa* (the *Atharvaveda*) because this fourth Veda is full of magic and of hints of yogic experiment. The orthodox view, both in Hinduism and Buddhism, was that enstasy was to be reached through a long, tedious process of conformity to canonical instruction and discipline only; on the Hindu side, through rigid observance of the *nitya* and *naimittika* ritual and through the performance of the meditations laid down in the canonical texts.[6] Brahmanism seems to entertain a peculiar dislike for any supererogatory observance and tacitly denies that there could be much fruitful meditation outside the daily ritual incumbent on the *dvija*, the twice-born caste-Hindu. Yoga, even in the tradition of Patāñjali, but particularly of the kind propounded by such tantricizing teachers as

Matsyendranāth and Gorakhnāth, is felt to be inessential and harmful, or at least highly suspect, by the orthodox Brahmin or medieval and modern India.[7]

Yoga, brought to the most general denominator, simply means the concentration on a non-discursive internal object of a numinous kind, or the introjection of a conceptualized object usually of some mythological sort. Patañjali's classical definition which introduces the *sūtras* is *cittavṛtti nirodha*, the reversion of the object-directed tendency of the mind. It is not a blank, though it is ideally devoid of discursive ideas and concepts.

Now classical yoga fell in line with the Upaniṣadic tradition in the sense that it also stipulated the eradication of the sensuous personality—in other words, the ascetical life—as a prerequisite to meditative success. The opposing trends are what we must subsume under our caption, the tantric tradition. It defies orthodox Hinduism and Theravāda Buddhism and has a bad name in Hindu India and in Theravāda Buddhist Asia. The tantras—Hindu, Buddhist, and Jaina—amount to an enormous mass of didactic literature, regarded as canonical by their followers, and dangerous or downright heretical by the orthodox. The Indian tantras have little literary merit, however; their Sanskrit is crude—most of the extant Buddhist tantras are not even in Buddhist Hybrid Sanskrit, but just in plainly poor Sanskrit; there are frequent passages in both Hindu and Buddhist tantric literature which are not Sanskrit at all, but some sort of *apabhraṃśa* or early vernacular. The Brahmin's dislike for the tantras is very largely due to the fact of their poor language.[8]

One of the reasons why the modern teachers of the Hindu renaissance, beginning with the Swami Vivekananda, and continuing into our day with the great number of English-speaking and Sanskrit-quoting swamis, are not accepted by the orthodox and learned in India is this peculiar identification of Sanskrit-learning with the mastery of the *śāstra*. Learned Hindus, both monastic and lay, refuse to be impressed by the English and vernacular eloquence of the modern swami and his followers.

There is, on the other hand, quite a lot of pious admonition towards ascetical practices and a restrained way of life in all tantras, in line with orthodox scriptures. But these, I feel, are meant to make the teaching a bit more palatable to the Indian audience. Tantric method is radically opposed to the official climate. The tantras do not teach to subdue the senses, but to increase their power and then to harness them in the service of the achievement of lasting enstasy, the target of these methods thus being the same as that of the orthodox. To set the tenor of tantrism, I quote a passage from the *Advayavajvasaṃgraha*, an important Vajrayāṇa work; it says 'by the very acts by which an ordinary person suffers spiritual perdition, the initiate yogi obtains permanent emancipation from the fetters of birth and death'.[9]

The tantric teachers were exceedingly discreet about their teachings, and kept them secret for a long time. They developed a code language which was understood only by the tantric in-group. *Sandhā*-terminology consists largely in erotic simile and vocabulary, to be interpreted either literally (*mukhya*) or metaphorically (*gauṇa*) by the adepts according to their own light. The tantric commentators and some of their modern students aver that *sandhābhāṣā* intends to throw the minds of the aspirant into the peculiar frame of suspended contradiction which has been deemed essential for enstatic success. The pattern in which the thus trained minds work will seem pathological to many psychologists and psychiatrists, but tantric preceptors such as Jñānānanda and Sarāha deny that there is such a thing as mental disease en route to enstasy: 'do not think the mind is sick when there is *samādhi*—for this is only what appears to the ordinary people'[10] and if an adept seems to 'act mad' it is just because people around him do not see what it is all about, as they are lacking the adept's frame of reference. Ramakrishna, using a parable from his tantric days, said that sexual pleasure could not be explained to a child, nor narcotic experience to a person who has not taken the drug; the exalted state of the adept's mind is unintelligible to the non-adept. Also, the usually valid socio-ethical set of values is suspended for the adept, another reason why tantra has had a bad name in

India since its systematic inception around fifteen hundred years ago.

All yoga discipline postulates, on the theoretical side, the existence of a secondary somatic system consisting of centres, circles, or lotuses (*maṇḍala, cakra, kendra*) located along an imagined spinal column in that secondary body. It is important to know—a thing which both occidental critics and sympathetic Indian scholars alike have misunderstood—that this yogic body is not supposed to have any objective existence in the sense the physical body has. It is a heuristic device aiding meditation, not any objective structure; the physical and the yogic body belong to two different logical levels. Sympathetic psychologists under the inspiration of C. G. Jung have attempted to allocate the various nervous plexuses and ganglia to the centres of this yoga body.[11] They may be right, but the tantric texts never suggest that this body and its organs have physiological existence. It is for this reason that different schools within tantrism vary greatly in their description of the yogic body, being at the same time aware of there being differing descriptions; they never offer any apology about these differences, for each description fits a particular type of aspirant. The notion of *adhikārabheda*, the oft-mentioned difference of training and of meditational procedure, is as old as the Upaniṣads. It seems that the tantric teachers realized that different people are attracted by different configurational models, by virtue of their different psychophysical constitutions. In two of the most important Hindu tantric texts, the *Mahānirvāṇa* and the *Ṣaṭ-cakra-nirūpaṇa*, this yogic body model is taught to have six centres or lotuses beginning at the base of the spine; other texts speak of twelve centres, and the Buddhist tantric tradition usually assumes four. Common to all tantric and yogic traditions, however, is the notion of three ducts passing through the spinal column, the central one being closed in animals and ordinary human beings, which means yogically untrained people. Meditation opens the central duct, and a mystical force, called the coiled one (*kuṇḍalinī*) by the Hindus and the female ascetic, which also means the purified one (*avadhūtī*, Tibetan *kun 'dar ma* or *dbus ma*), ascends from its home base, which is the lowest centre thought to be located between the anal and the genital regions, and, piercing the centres one by one, is finally absorbed into the highest centre located in the brain. The other two ducts, called *īḍā* and *piṅgalā* by the Hindus and *lalanā* and *rasanā* (Tibetan *brkyang ma* and *ro ma*) by the Buddhists, function in all living creatures, and the yogi attempts to purify them at first by breath control or *prāṇāyāma*, an elaborate training which utilizes the notion of these two peripheral ducts, as a conceptual crutch as it were.

The force that moves from the base to the top of the yogic body in the process of successful meditation is always visualized as female, and it is the microcosmic representation of the *magna mater*, whom the Hindus conceive as Śakti, and the Buddhist Vajrayāṇis as wisdom (*prajñā*, Tibetan *śes rab*). The brain centre is identified with the supreme cosmic principle, the *brahman* for the Hindus, and the Great Void, *mahāśūnya* (Tibetan *stong pa chen*), for the tantric Buddhists. The merger or resorption of the dormant power conceived as female in the supreme principle is, of course, the esoteric pivot of all the erotic symbolism which pervades tantric thought and practice. The Buddhist tantras refer to the most complete *nirvāṇa* as *mahāsukha* (great bliss) and this is the term they use for enstasy reached through the threefold control which is the keynote of tantric *sādhanā*. All the code-language of the tantras, let us recall, refers to this process of enstasy *only*, and as emancipation from the cycle of birth and death is the eschatological sequel or concomitant of enstasy, the tantras are as much *dharma* as the orthodox, canonical scriptures. Hindu and Buddhist critics of tantric practices and teachings have constantly suggested that the tantric uses religion as a mantle for sexual desire and debauchery; the tantrics have constantly answered that the complicated, elaborate, and exceedingly difficult procedure followed by the tantrics would not at all be necessary to gratify sexual desire, whose objects are much easier to obtain without any yogic trappings.

Let me emphasize once more that the yogic or tantric body is a model, not a fact, that the centres or lotuses, and the three ducts, are systematic fictions; but neither are they, as many psychiatrists would hold, creations of the pathological fantasy of Indian esotericists.

Orthodox yoga, that is the system of Patāñjali and his protagonists, teaches the ascent of the dormant, coiled-up force as a process induced in the individual adept after due instruction by his *guru*, and as a procedure in which the adept practises in solitude. The tantric's practice, however, is undertaken in conjunction with a partner of the other sex. She is considered as the embodiment of Śakti, the active principle conceived as female, by the Hindus; and as *Mudrā* (Tibetan *phyag rgya*), or the passive principle of intuitive wisdom, also conceived as female, by the Buddhist tantrics.[12]

The method is diametrically opposed to that of the conservative on both sides, and enstasy is reached by utilizing precisely those mechanisms which the orthodox yogi seeks to suppress or eschew. Absolute, primitive celibacy is a *sine qua non* in most active yoga; in tantrism, there is indeed the injunction of celibacy, but it has a very specific meaning. The same term is used for continence, namely *brahmacaryam*, reverting to its original and literal meaning 'moving in the *brahman*', i.e. keeping one's mind directed towards the absolute.

Now the practical axiom of the tantrics, formulated much more precisely in Buddhist Vajrayāṇa than in Hindu tantrism, is this: enstasy is reached when we learn to immobilize mind, breath, and the seminal fluid. Tantric code-language (*sandhābhāṣā*) refers to these variously as the three jewels (*triratna, rin chen gsum*), the three nectars (*amṛtatraya, bdud rtsi gsum*), and by similar terms. Occasionally, *sandhābhāṣā* refers to the mind as 'the ape' due to its unsteady nature which is hard to control, to breath as 'the crocodile' (*makara*) due to its slow and tenacious motion, and to the sperm by a great number of chiffres, such as 'the sun' (*sūrya, aditi*), 'nectar' (*amṛta*); the most frequent Vajrayāṇa *sandhā*-term is the bodhi-mind, the mind of awakening or illumination, *bodhicitta* (*byaṅ chub kyi sems*), which is a philosophically loaded term, and which provided our efferent paradigm (Chapter 6). Anthropomorphically, the *bodhicitta* is the mind of each living Buddha, as of each enlightened person.

Breath control (*prāṇāyāma*) is common to all yogic disciplines, classical and later, and indeed it already forms part of the Vedic *sandhyā* ritual, though in a less elaborate form. The idea seems to be that by the control of the relatively most conscious somatic or vegetative function the adept begins to control other less conscious somatic events such as the heart-beat, which he also aims to arrest at will in pursuit of more intensive enstatic states. I am informed by Professor R. Leifer of the Psychiatry Department of New York Upstate Medical College that arrest of respiration in itself causes hallucinatory states under certain circumstances, and that aggregation of carbon dioxide is being used in psychiatry for the therapy of certain depressive states.

Control of the seminal fluid is thought to entail control of all passions and the achievement of desirelessness—and of course this notion stems from the common Indian ascetical heritage which postulates that passions jeopardize the advance towards enstasy. Loss of semen is a pervasive and ancient fear in Indian lore, and it is probably the core of the most powerful anxiety syndrome in Indian culture.

Finally, the control of the mind is almost tantamount with the various terms denoting the supreme achievement of the yogi, intuitive wisdom and freedom from rebirth. Control of mind, in the technical sense of the yogic and tantric traditions, means precisely what Patāñjali said in the opening verse of the *Yogasūtra*, *cittavṛtti nirodha*, witholding the mind from all discursive objects, or a total cessation of the cognitive, conative, and volitional functions of the mind.

This triple control is hierarchically conceived, control of breath being the first and easiest step, control of seminal ejaculation during sexual union the next higher, and preventing the mind from apprehending any external objects the final and highest step. These controls have to work simultaneously in the end, and the whole process of esoteric meditation converges towards the skill of arresting breath, seminal emission, and object apperception simultaneously. The successful retention of the three is *yuganaddha* (Tibetan *sku grub* or *zung 'jug*), 'binding together the opposed poles', Śiva and Śakti in Hindu tantra, *Prajñā* and *Upāya* in Vajrayāṇa, male and female adept in the human replica of the cosmic process of enstasy.

All the texts stress that these controls can be learnt only under the guidance of a personal teacher who has got to be an adept himself, a *siddha* who has succeeded in stabilizing these controls in himself or in herself as the case may be, and who must also be able to gauge and to classify any prospective disciple as to the latter's potential capacity for acquiring these controls. This takes us back to one of the oldest insights of the Indian tradition, the pervasive notion of *adhikārabheda*, which means 'difference in the individual's entitlement for a specific meditation'.

The prospective *guru* has to study his disciple for a considerable time in a close symbiosis. The *gurukula* of the Vedic period, the coenobite set-up of the Indian monastic tradition, conduces to this study, and the process is by no means unilateral. Both the teacher and the disciple have to test each other in order to effect a complete transference. The tantrics refer to this set-up simply as the *kula*, the family or clan, which is a real in-group. Then the *guru* judges which *mantra* or auditory instrument he will impart to the disciple, by using which the latter will learn the threefold control leading to enstasy.

Breath control is relatively easy to achieve. The process is roughly this; using the *mantra* as a time unit, the adept practises retention of breath by reducing his respiratory speed, keeping out and holding his breath for gradually increasing periods. This, when properly practised, brings about a certain euphoric effect, accompanied by mild hallucinations chiefly of a photic variety. Next, he learns to practise breath control together with his Śakti or Mudrā, his consecrated female partner. With her he enters into sexual union, the procedure being described somewhat perfunctorily in the tantric texts, but taught orally by the *guru* in great detail and variation according to the different somatic and psychological constitutions of the individual disciple and his *Śakti* or *Mudrā*. Most frequently, the female adept sits astride on the male yogi's lap who himself takes one of the traditional yogic postures which are slightly modified to adapt him to the situation. Buddhist iconography, especially Tibetan, shows a great variety of enstatic procedures at this stage. The *yab yum* (lit. honourable father and honourable mother) forms the centre of a large proportion of Tibetan icons.[13]

The model is, of course, purely Indian and I do not believe, as some Tibetologists hold, that the *yab yum* icon has indigenous Bon sources in Tibet. Śiva, the most sophisticated and complex deity of the Hindu pantheon, is symbolized and worshipped in the iconic form of the *liṅga* or phallus; in fact, anthromorphic representations such as are becoming more and more frequent in modern puritanical India are not permissible in formal Śaivite worship. Śiva is the tutelary deity of all monks and of all ascetic orders, he stands for complete control of the senses, and for supreme carnal renunciation. His phallic representation would seem to be an inane paradox unless we take into account the tantric ideological background of this symbolism, which is truly profound. And this is important as it is not known even to learned Hindus except those of a scholarly tantric background; the ithyphallic condition is not priapic, but represents precisely what the tantric aims to master, i.e. seminal retention in the laboratory setting of tantric ritualistic copulation. Let us remember the earlier quotation from the *Jñānasiddhi*, an important Vajrayāṇa text ascribed to Indrabhūti, *niṣpīḍya kamale vajraṃ bodhicittaṃ notsṛjet* (lit. having brought down the thunderbolt into the lotus, he should not let go the *bodhi*-mind), which is *sandhābhāṣā* (Chapter 6) for the central instruction of the second Vajrayāṇa control, referring to the retention of semen in the act.

Now the pervasive use of *bodhicitta* (mind of intuitive wisdom) as the efferent *sandhābhāṣā* term for semen, and the stress on its retention, show how closely retention and mind-control seem to be connected in the tantric's mind. The moment of suspense, effected by simultaneous breath and seminal control in conjunction with the *Śakti* or *Mudrā*, seems to effect suspension of the distracting mental functions—that is to say, of *all* the discursive functions of the mind, cognitive, conative, and volitional. The Hindu tantrics therefore represent these three functions of the mind in an equilinear triangle as the basic *maṇḍala* or mystogram; its apex points downwards symbolizing the female principle, its three sides are to represent *jñāna*, *icchā*, and *kriyā*, i.e. cognition, volition, and conation. Enstasy is reached when the adept succeeds in suspending, temporarily at first, but in increasing spans of time, all object-thought, and in concentrating on the non-discursive, interiorized object of his meditation, which is variously described in anthropomorphical terms as the *iṣṭam* (Tibetan *yid dam*), the chosen deity, or in absolutist, speculative terms as the case may be.

The paradoxical situation, then, is that the tantric appears to the orthodox Hindu and Buddhist as a libertine, whereas in reality he preserves a state of complete celibacy. The famous, or infamous, Fifth Dalai Lama had his problems *vis-à-vis* the orthodox reformed clergy, but I feel reasonably sure that they did not recognize the tantric disciplinary element in his case; he obviously knew of the said controls, when the majority of the people round him either did not remember or ignored the tantric heritage, which is strong even in the Gelugpa school.[14]

Of course, we admitted that there are many instances of abuse. Meditational subterfuge and ritualistic procedure may have been used as a pretext for sexual indulgence of a considerably more interesting sort than is either permissible or available in a progressively puritanical Indian society, which regards asceticism as the only socially acceptable way towards radical religious emancipation. In theory, most orthodox Hindus grant the possibility of these tantric controls, but thay are not ready to admit that the tantrics have achieved them in numbers which would justify condoning tantric ritual, and risking social disruption.

We are now at the end of our study. This chapter has been one of retrospect, but I hesitate to attempt a statement on the prospects of tantrism in India and elsewhere. Following my own *caveat*, to distinguish carefully between the 'is' and the 'ought', I would say that tantrism as a system of practice, as well as a method of thought, as an ideology, has little or no chances in India, but that it ought to be given a chance. Its actual chances are few, because

India wants to get ahead in the modernistic, technological, and economical domains. Every country that moved towards modernity has undergone a long period of puritanism. Britain, Germany, Russia, the United States: some of these countries have outgrown puritanism and have begun to enjoy the fruits of their former labours. Others haven't. I do not see, however, why a puritanical phase is necessary at all en route to modernity. A prediction, on the basis of an analogy, of the form 'all countries have so far undergone a phase of puritanism, therefore India has to . . .' rests on what Karl R. Popper has been castigating as historicism—the naive and dangerous notion that one can learn anything from history except history itself; that we can make predictions on the basis of historical precedence.[15] Speaking in terms of 'ought', I think that tantrism ought to be given a chance in India. I do not think it will.

Matters are different outside India. It is conceivable that the more affluent and more critical of the West, particularly Western Europe and North America, might espouse some form of tantrism, or some elements of the tantric tradition, properly translated and modified for western use, as one of its possible ideological, spiritual, or psychotherapeutical alternatives. Some steps have been made, but probably in the wrong direction: the frustrated middle-aged North American lusting for the mysterious has opened a door for tantrism to enter. However, I feel that this entry is dangerous, and that it would entail a misinterpretation, that it would make havoc out of tantrism. There are two kinds of audiences in the western world in whose hands any esoteric tradition would be bound to fail: the first, more numerous but less dangerous, are the truth seekers who feel frustrated with what their own religious traditions at home offer. Just as the Theosophical Society, the anthroposophists, the Ramakrishna-Vivekananda movement, the Divine Life Society, the Self-Realization League, Zen, etc., have found their way into the affluent West through these audiences, tantrism—in a watered-down, untutored form—may gain entrance in these countries. The other audience, small but more dangerous, is the one that looks for 'kicks', to use hardy American vocabulary once more. I'm not in principle against the use of drugs, against esotericism as an additional instrument for enriching individuals' lives, but I am decidedly against popularization, an unscholarly attempt at assimilation of imported systems. Let me put it this way: tantrism, like yoga and Vedānta and Zen, could be respectable even in the western world, provided that the tradition of solid scholarship, of learning and of intellectual effort which had been their base in the countries of their origin, did accompany their migration into the occidental world. Without these cultural efforts, I regard them as fraudulent. The expedient notion that yoga and esoteric practice are much more difficult to pursue than the knowledge of Sanskrit, Prakrit, and Tibetan, leaves me unimpressed. For if this were true, there would be fewer crackpots around the Atlantic, and many more orientalists. The oriental institutes, the anthropological and ethnographical departments at occidental universities would be filled with people who really want to learn. As it is, the pseudo-orientalized esoteric circles in the western world and the academicians *in Orientaliis* give each other a wide berth. This cannot be remedied, until the non-expert yields to the expert, and the expert, suffice it to say, is the sympathetic scholar. Facile claims to spiritual superiority on the side of enthusiastic esotericists leave the scholar who has studied the tradition by the sweat of his brow as cold as they do the initiate. And if the intelligent in modern India could view the tantric tradition with that warm empathy which the builders of Khajuraho and Konarak must have felt, tantrism in India may well be therapeutical for many cultural ills that beset her today.

As for the West, if the tantric camel is to enter at all and with profit it must enter through the eye of the needle that sews in Sanskrit and Tibetan, and that probes in terms of modern anthropology and analytical philosophy, and not through the offices of any non-intellectual, anti-academical, albeit spiritual eastern proselytization.

NOTES

[1] Cultural anthropology is virtually the same as social anthropology in Britain. The reasons why American anthropologists prefer the term 'cultural' to 'social' anthropology are somewhat intricate and not within the purview of this book. For the subject matter of our study however, the term 'social anthropology' just won't work. Tantrism has enormous cultural implications, but its social implications, at this time at least, are negligible. I dealt with this point in detail in an article, 'Die Geistigen Kraefte Asiens in der Krise der Gegenwart', in *Universitas* (see Bibliography).

[2] The first scholar who showed that Hinduism was basically polytheistic is a convert to Hinduism himself—Professor A. Danielou, *Polytheisme Hindu*, Paris 1959—proved that the monistic and absolutist philosophy is a sophisticated superstructure on Hinduism which by no means supercedes a healthy and intensive polytheism, of which all but the modernized Hindus seems to be aware; for its English version, see Bibliography.

[3] *Unmāda* 'mad', overly exulting, is one of the 1008 names of Śiva in the *Śivasahasranāma* which is chanted daily by all Śaivites throughout India as well as by almost all monastic sects. Here the term does indeed connote intensive enstasy; Indian mystical literature and hagiography frequently refer to the saint as behaving like a madman—thus Sri Ramakrishna Paramahamsa: '*ei je pāgaler mata byābahār kare*' (*Ramakṛṣṇakathāmṛta*, Bengali ed.), 'he (is a true saint) who acts as though he was a madman'.

Other terms for madness in a more or less clinical sense are derived from the same root, i.e. *unmattatā*, *sonmādatvam*, *pramādyam*, *unmādiṣṇu*; terms not derived from *mad* are compounds indicating loss of sense, etc., *naṣṭabuddhi*, *bhraṣṭabuddhi*, *hatajñāna*—all meaning simply loss of intelligence; *vikṣipta* (*-buddhi*) seems to indicate a particular sort of mental disorder, 'wandering' of the mind such as is the case with certain schizophrenics. Finally, there is an interesting term *vātula* which literally means 'inflated with wind'; this hails from the fact that Indian medicine (Ayurveda) holds the humour wind (*vāyu*, *vāta*), which is one of the three medical humours, responsible not only for rheumatism and gout, but also for mental derangements of all kinds.

[4] There is an ever-increasing amount of literature, partly serious, partly popular, and partly trash, on alcaloid drug experiences. Lysergic-acid-diathelymide experience seems closest to yogic enstatic states. R. H. Ward's *A Drugtaker's Notes*, Gollancz, London 1959 is a good statement; Constance C. Newland, *Myself and I*, Signet Paperback, New York 1963, is the most recent account of LSD experience. LSD 25 is the trade name of the drug; it has become a highly controversial subject in the United States, since two psychologists were removed

from the faculty of Harvard University on account of their having administered the drug to undergraduate students, in 1963.

[5] The drug is taken in two different forms in India: Brahmins in northern, central, and eastern India tend to take it as *bhāṅg*, prepared as a dessert in the shape of molasses; or as a beverage with sweet sherbet. In the north-west of India, especially among Sufi-Muslims, the hemp is dried and smoked; this of course is hashish, a term known to many Urdu speakers; however, the Urdu and Hindi term for smoked *Cannabis Indica* is *gāñjā*, and there is an overall notion that the taking of *gāñjā* is 'dirty', whereas the eating or drinking of *bhāṅg* is just a bit funny or out of date. There is some amount of government control; *bhāṅg* must not be exported from Bihar into Bengal.

[6] *Nitya* (eternal) refers to the rituals that have to be performed every day by the male members of the twice-born castes; *naimittika* (instrumental) refers to any ritual of a superoragory type, rituals for special purposes, on special occasions, with a specific object in mind.

[7] Professor V. Raghavan, Head of the Department of Sanskrit of Madras University and Chief Governmental Adviser on Sanskrit studies, who is an orthodox Brahmin, told me in 1954: 'None of your yoga and even less of your tantra is necessary to reach *mukti*. Any person who fulfils the religious duties of his class will achieve *mukti* when his body drops off. There is no shortcut, even through the methods of Patāñjali.'

[8] There is a notion among the tougher Brahmin traditionalists that a person who does not master Pāninian Sanskrit cannot understand *darśana*, or philosophical theology. This criticism extends to all Buddhists, including the Theravādins, for Pali (as all Prakrits) are thought to be just bad Sanskrit, as also to Jainism, whose main texts are in Ardhamāgadhī. Professor F. Edgerton, when Holkar Visiting Professor at Banaras Hindu University in 1953, found it impossible to convey to the paṇḍits of the Saṃskṛta Mahāvidyālaya that Buddhist Hybrid Sanskrit was *not* bad Sanskrit; for them, it was and remains just this, composed by people who had not studied the language properly.

[9] More literally 'by that act by which the beings boil in terrible hell for 100,000,000 *kalpas*, by that very deed the yogi is released', '*karmaṇā yena vai sattvāḥ kalpakoṭiśatānyapi pacyante narake ghore tena yogī vimucyate*'. (Also *Jñānasiddhi*, p. 31, 15).

[10] From Sarāhapādas *Dohākośa*, Hindi edition by the late Rahul Sāṃkṛtyāyana, Ch. III. It is interesting to note that a well-known American psychiatrist, considered as an avant-garde thinker by his colleagues, has voiced a convergent view in his book *The Myth of Mental Illness*, Basic Books, Inc., New York 1961. Professor Thomas S. Szasz had not been aware of this medieval Indian parallel before I communicatad it to him; this excludes the possibility of a guided premonition so frequent among psychologists of the Jungian type.

[11] See H. Jacobs, *Western Psychology and Hindu Sadhana*, Allen & Unwin, London 1961.

[12] '*Śakti*', as stated before, must never be used for the Buddhist '*Mudrā*', a point which was brought into relief by Lama Anagarika Govinda, *Foundations of Tibetan Mysticism*, Rider, London. *Śakti* is dynamic, the *mudrā* is quiescent. In Buddhist iconography, therefore, the female plays the passive part, in Hindu iconography the Devi usually asserts an active role. Thus, in the Bengali tradition, Śakti dances on Śiva who is prostrate 'like a corpse'; very frequently, there is a corpse of identical shape placed below the prostrate Śiva upon whose chest the Śakti dances; that latter figure's eyes are closed to indicate lifelessness, whereas the upper figure, though prostrate, has his eyes open. The Hindu tantric iconological thesis is '*śivaśaktivihīnaḥ śavāḥ*', Śiva without Śakti is a corpse', i.e. is inactive, non-existent. On the *Mudrā* the final word so far has been said by H. V. Guenther, in his *Naropa*, Oxford University Press, 1963, see Bibliography.

[13] See A. Gordon '*The Iconography of Tibetan Lamaism* and *Tibetan Religious Art*; G. Tucci, *Tibetan Painted Scrolls*, see Bibliography.

[14] For this explanation of the Fifth's wayward ways, I am indebted to Professor H. Wilhelm. The lovesongs composed by 'The Fifth' are highly popular in Tibet up to this day.

[15] K. R. Popper, *The Open Society and its Enemies* Princeton 1950.

BIBLIOGRAPHICAL SELECTION

This selection lists all the material used for the preparation of this volume; it also lists a large number of other primary and secondary tantric material. Though it does not claim to be exhaustive, it does claim to be the most representative tantric bibliography published in English so far. A complete tantric bibliography would make up a book of about seven hundred pages; and even such a work could not include all the titles contained in the tantra (*rgyud*) sections of the Tibetan canonical (*bkah 'gyur*) and commentary (*bstan 'gyur*) texts; nor could it include the secondary material published in Japanese and Chinese.

I hesitate to call this a descriptive bibliography, for I made short notes only for the titles which I have myself studied; over fifty per cent of the primary material listed below I have not even seen and it is left to other scholars to work with these titles, easily available on the basis of the indications given here.

As many of the works are difficult to obtain from their publishers, some of the latter being defunct, I have listed many titles in accordance with the 1963 catalogue of Messrs. Chowkhamba Sanskrit Series Office, Postbox 8, Varanasi 1, U.P., India, abbreviating them Ch.S.S. . . . /63. That firm is the most thorough agent for the type of literature required for indological study; all the texts so marked can be directly obtained from that house.

I have incorporated quite a bit of material previously published in the bibliographies of Prof. Mircea Eliade and Prof. Chintaharan Chakravarti, and I express my gratitude for their permission to use that material.

The following is the legend for the abbreviations of publishers used in the Bibliography itself:

AAS Ānandāśrama Sanskrit Series, Poona-Bombay (India).

ABORI Annals of the Bhandarkar Oriental Research Institute, Poona (India).

BEFEO Bulletin de l'Ecole française d'Extrême-Orient (Hanoi, North Vietnam—now Paris).

BSOAS Bulletin of the London School of Oriental and African Studies, London.

Ch.S.S. Chowkhamba Sanskrit Series Office, P.O. Box 8, Varanasi 1, U.P. (India), Catalogue 1963.

G.O.S. Gaekwad Oriental Series, Baroda (India).

HPS (Nepal) Catalogue of Nepalese Manuscripts by the late Pdt. Haraprasad Shastri, Calcutta.

IHQ Indian Historical Quarterly, 9 Panchanan Ghose Lane, Calcutta.

JAOS Journal of the American Oriental Society, Yale Station, New Haven, Conn., U.S.A., organ of the American Oriental Society.

JAS Journal of Asian Studies, formerly Far Eastern Quarterly, organ of the Association for Asian Studies, U.S.A.

JRAS Journal of the Royal Asiatic Society (London).

JRASB (now JASB) Journal of the (Royal) Asiatic Society of Bengal, Calcutta.

KSTS Kashmir Series of Texts and Studies, Government of Kashmir Publications, Srinagar, Kashmir (India).

RASB Catalogue of the Royal Asiatic Society of Bengal, Calcutta. All the items are found in Volume VIII, as this contains tantric and other esoteric entries.

S.Bh.S. Sarasvati Bhavan Series, Banaras U.P., India.

TSS Trivandrum Sanskrit Series, Trivandrum, Kerala (India).

Abhayakaragupta, *Niṣpannayogāvali*; G.O.S. CIX, Ed. B. Bhattacharya, Baroda 1949. One of the most important tantric Buddhist texts of medieval Vajrayāṇa.

Abhinavagupta, *Paramārthasāra*, with the commentary by 'Yogirāja' An important Kashmir Śaivite text, not as directly tantric as the same author's *Tantrāloka* and *Tantrasāra*, q.v.

Abhinavagupta, *Tantrāloka*, 12 volumes, KSTS Vols. 27–39, general editor Paṇḍit Madhusūdana Kaul Śāstrī, Kashmir Government

Publications, Srinagar 1921–38, with the complete commentary by Jayaratha. This large work is the classical treatise on Kashmiri tantric Śaivism.

Abhinavagupta, *Tantrasāra*, edited with notes by Paṇḍit Mukuṇḍa Rāma Śāstrī, KSTS Vl. 17, Srinagar 1918.

Advayavajra, *Advayavajrasaṃgraha*, ed. H. P. Shastri, G.O.S. XL, Baroda 1927. A collection of the aphorisms of Advayavajra, a famous Buddhist tantric teacher.

Aghorītantra, Sanskrit with Hindi translation and commentary by Paṇḍit Gauriśaṃkara Śarmā, publ. Gaṅgāviṣṇu Śrīkṛṣṇadās, Kalyan-Bombay 1951. A Hindu tantra centring on the Aghori-cult, an extremist tantric group; Aghori 'the-not-terrible-One' is an epithet of Śiva very frequent in Hindu tantric literature.

Agrawala, V. S., *India as Known to Pāṇīnī*, Lucknow 1953.

Aṃrtānandanātha, *Yoginī-hṛdaya-dīpikā*, an important commentary on the 'Heart of the Yoginī'-tantra. S.Bh.S. No. 7, Varanasi 1924.

Anand, M. R., *Kāmakalā—Some Notes on the Philosophical Basis of Hindu Erotic Sculpture*, Nagel, New York 1958.

Anand, M. R., 'The Great Delight—an Essay on the Spiritual Background of the Erotic Sculpture at Konarak', *MARG* No. 12, Bombay 1958.

Anand, M. R., with Stella Kramrisch, *Homage to Khajuraho*, *MARG* Monograph, Bombay 1960.

Auboyer, J., '*Moudrā* et *Hasta* ou le langage par signes', *Oriental Art*, III, Paris, 1950–1, 153–61.

Auboyer, J., *Khajuraho*, Mouton & Co., The Hague 1960. A magnificent work, with exquisite pictorial material and exhaustive historical commentary. The temple-complex of Khajuraho in central India is the most intensively tantric shrine extant.

Avalokiteśvara-guṇa-kāraṇḍa-vyūha (Sanskrit), ed. by Satyavrata Samasrami, Calcutta 1873.

Avalon, Arthur, nom-de-plume of Sir John Woodroffe, *Hymn to Kālī*, a translation and commentary of the *Karpurādistotra* (q.v.), with the Sanskrit text, 2nd. ed., Ganeshan & Co., Madras 1953.

Avalon, Arthur, *Principles of Tantra*, English translation and elaboration of a nineteenth-century Bengali treatise *Tantratattva*. 2nd. ed., Ganeshan & Co., Madras 1955.

Avalon, Arthur, *The Serpent Power*. Original, with complete translation and commentary, of the *Ṣaṭ-cakra-nirūpaṇam* 'description of the six centres' and the *Pañca-pādukā*, 'the five-legged stool (of Śiva)', two important Hindu tantric texts on the *kuṇḍalinī*, the 'coiled'-power in the postulated yogic body. 6th. ed., Ganeshan & Co., Madras 1958.

Avalon, Arthur, *Shakti and Shākta*, Ganeshan & Co., Madras 1956.

Avalon, Arthur, *Tantrarāja-tantra*—a short analysis; with a preface by Yogi Shuddhananda Bharati. Ganeshan & Co., Madras 1952.

Avalon, Arthur, *Hymns to the Goddess*, collection of hymns (*stotra*) ascribed to Śaṃkarācārya. 2nd. ed., Ganeshan & Co., Madras 1953.

Avalon, Arthur, *Garland of Letters* (*Varṇamālā*), 'Studies in Mantra-shastra', 3rd. ed., Ganeshan & Co., Madras 1955.

Avalon, Arthur, *The Great Liberation* (*The Mahānirvāṇatantra*), complete text, translation, commentary. The hitherto most thorough edition of this central Hindu tantric work. 5th. ed., Ganeshan & Co., Madras 1952.

Avalon, Arthur, *Introduction to Tantrashastra—a Key to Tantric Literature*, 3rd. ed., Ganeshan & Co., Madras 1956.

Bacot, J., *La Vie de Marpa, le 'traducteur'*, Paris 1937.

Bagalātantram; Bagalā is a rather uncanny Bengali and north-eastern Indian village goddess, identified with Durgā in the 'big tradition'. This tantra contains instructions in some bizarre sorcery. Ch.S.S. 3060/63.

Bagchi, Prabodh Ch., *Studies in the Tantras*, University Press, Calcutta 1939.

Bagchi, Prabodh Ch., 'On Foreign Elements in the Tantras', *IHQ*, VII, 1 (1931), 1–16.

Bagchi, Prabodh Ch. (ed.), *Kaulajñāna-nirṇaya and Some Minor Texts of the School of Matsyendranātha*, Calcutta Sanskrit Series III., Calcutta 1934.

Bagchi, Prabodh Ch., 'Further Notes on Tantrik Texts Studied in Ancient Kambuja', *IHQ*, VI., 1 (1930), 97–107.

Bagchi, Prabodh Ch., 'Decline of Buddhism in India and Its Causes', in *Sir Asutosh Mookerjee Silver Jubilee Volumes*. Vol. III, pt. 2., 405–21. Calcutta 1921–7.

Bagchi, Prabodh Ch., 'On the *Sādhanāmālā*', *IHQ*, 1934.

Bagchi, Prabodh Ch., 'Caryāgīti-kośa of the Buddhist Siddhas', in *Viśvabhāratī Quarterly*, 1956 (Santiniketan).

Banerjea, J. N., *The Development of Hindu Iconography*, University Publications, Calcutta 1956.

Bannerji, P. K., 'Sandhyābhāṣā', in *Viśvabhāratī Quarterly*, Santiniketan 1924.

Barret, Leroy C., *The Kashmirian Atharvaveda*, American Oriental Series, Vol. 18, Baltimore, Md., 1940.

Barrow, H. B., 'On Aghoris and Aghorapanthis', in *Proceedings of the Anthropological Society of Bombay*, III (1893), 197–251.

Baṭukabhairavopāsanādhyaya, a popular text emphasizing charms and cures. Baṭuka is a form of Śiva. Ch.S.S. 3061/62.

Bauddha-stotra-saṃgraha, Vol. I., Sarvajñamitra's *Sragdharā-stotra* 'hymn to the Goddess Sragdharā' ('she who wears a garland'); ed. S. C. Vidyabhushana, *Bibliotheca Indica*, Calcutta 1908.

Bendall, C., ed. 'Subhāṣitasaṃgraha', in *Le Muséon*, Nos. IV–V, Louvain 1903–4.

Bhairavānanda, *Saptadhātu-nirūpaṇam*, a commentary to the *Rudrayāmala* (q.v.)

Bharati, A., 'Die Geistigen Kraefte Asiens in der Krise der Gegenwart', in *Universitas*, Vol. XIII/6, Stuttgart 1958.

Bharati, A., *Aesthetical Norm and Value Modifications in Modern India*, Indian Renaissance Institute Monograph No. 1, Calcutta 1962.

Bharati, A., 'Metaphysics of Tantrism', *Quest* No. 25, Bombay 1960.

Bharati, A., 'The Hevajra Tantra'—review of D. L. Snellgrove's book; J.A.S., XX/2, 1961.

Bharati, A., 'Modern Hindu Exegesis of Mahāyāna Doctrine', in *Philosophy: East and West*, Univ. of Hawaii Press, Vol. XII/7, 1962.

Bharati, A., 'Pilgrimage in the Indian Tradition', in *History of Religious*, Univ. of Chicago Press, Summer 1963.

Bharati, A., 'Our Hindu Sculptures—are they obscene?' in *Radical Humanist*, Vol. XVII, Calcutta 1953.

Bharati, A., 'Was Śaṃkarācārya a Crypto-Buddhist?' in *Thought*, New Delhi 1954.

Bhāskararāya, commentary to the *Lalitāsahasranāma* (q.v.). Nirnaya Sagara Press, Bombay, Ch.S.S. 2775/63.

Bhāskararāya (here also called Bhāsurānandanātha), *Varivasyārahasyā*, ed. with an English translation by Pdt. S. Subbrahmanya Sastri, Theosophical Library Series, Adyar 1941, 1948.

Bhattacharya, Benoytosh, *An Introduction to Buddhist Esoterism*, Oxford University Press, London 1932.

Bhattacharya, Benoytosh, *Buddhist Iconography*, London 1924, reprint Fa. K. L. Mukhopadhyay, Calcutta 1959.

Bhattacharya, Benoytosh, 'Some Notes on the *Mithuna* in Indian Art', in *Rupam*, No. 1, Calcutta 1926.

Bhattacharya, Benoytosh, 'Tantric Cults among the Buddhists', in *Cultural Heritage of India*, ed. H. D. Bhattacharya, Vol. II, 208–21, Ramakrishna Mission Institute of Culture, Calcutta 1950–60.

Bhattacharya, Benoytosh, 'Glimpses of Vajrayāṇa', in *Proceedings and Transactions* of the Third Orientalist Conference, 1924, 129–41, Madras 1925.

Bhattacharya, Benoytosh, 'A Peep into Vajrayāṇa', in *Annals of the Bhandarkar Oriental Research Institute*, Vol X, Poona 1930.

Bhattacharya, Benoytosh, ed. Two Vajrayāṇa Works, G.O.S. XLIV, Baroda 1929 (*Prajñopāyaviniścaya* and *Jñānasiddhi*, q.v.).

Bhattacharya, Benoytosh, *Sādhanāmalā*, 2 volumes; Introduction, Text, Illustrations, Indices, G.O.S. XXVI & XLI, Baroda 1925–8.

Bhattacharya, Benoytosh, 'The Home of Tantric Buddhism', in *B.C. Law Commemoration*, Volume No. I., 254–61, 2 vols., Poona 1945–6.

Bhattacharya, Benoytosh, 'The Buddhists in Bengal', in *The Dacca Review*, II, 7, 91–104, Dacca (East Pakistan), 1921.

Bhattacharya, Benoytosh, ed., *Guhyasamājatantra* or *Tathāgataguhyaka* (q.v.). Baroda 1931.

Bhattacharya, Benoytosh, 'Origin and Development of Vajrayāṇa', *IHQ*, III, No. 4 (1927), 733–46.

Bhattacharya, Keshava Jagadvijayi, *Kramadīpikā*, with the commentary by Govinda Bhaṭṭa, and with further commentaries called *Gurubhaktimaṇḍākinī* and a laudatory hymn *Laghustavarājastotra*, Ch.S.S. 2962/63. One of the most highly literate and sophisticated statements of the Śākta doctrines.

Bhavānīsahasranāmam, 'the thousand names of Bhavānī' (Śakti), a litany popular in south India, in the style of the more famous *Lalitāsahasranāma* (q.v.), publ. Ramaswani Shastrulu & Sons, Madras 1960.

Bose, D. N., & Haldar, H. L., *Tantras—Their Philosophy and Occult Secrets*, third enlarged edition, Oriental Publishing House, Calcutta 1956.

Bose, Manindra Mohan, 'An Introduction to the Study of the Post-Chaitanya Sahajia Cult', in *Journal of the Department of Letters*, University of Calcutta, Vol. XVI, 1–162, Calcutta 1927.

Bose, Manindra Mohan, *The Post-Chaitanya Sahajia Cult of Bengal*, University Press, Calcutta 1930.

Brahmānanda, *Vāmācārasiddhāntasaṃgraha*, 'Survey of the Doctrines of Lefthanded tantrism'. The author, who appears to have come from the Andhra region in south-eastern India, challenges the negative criticism of Kāśīnātha of Banaras, particularly in the latter's *Vāmācāramatakhaṇḍanam* (see Kāśīnātha). Government Oriental Manuscripts Library of Madras, XII, 5720.

Brahmāyāmala, a manuscript dated 172 Nepalese Saṃvat Era, i.e. A.D. 1052, in H. H. Shastri, *Nepal Catalogue*, II, p. 60.

Bṛhatśavaratantram, 'Śavara' or 'Śabara' means 'a savage', or the member of a particular tribe; it is also an epithet of Śiva, probably reminiscent of his tribal origins. Ch.S.S. 3062/63.

Briggs, G. W., *Gorakhnāth and the Kānphaṭa Yogis*, Calcutta 1958.

Broad, C. D., *Mind and Its Place in Nature*, Harcourt, Brace & Co., New York 1925. By sheer convergence, this important book of the renowned British philosopher propounds a mind-matter view strikingly similar to that of tantrism.

Cakrapūjā (anonymous); the rules for the nocturnal observances of the Śāktas; Ch.S.S. 2983/63.

Caṇḍī, A Hindi monthly, the organ of the *Śākta-sammelana*, the informal, loosely organized 'Assembly of Sāktas', which consists of a number of learned followers of the tantric teachings. The journal was founded in 1940, and although its publication has been somewhat irregular during the past few years, it appears at more or less regular intervals, and it is a mine of information on tantric literature, discipline, and general speculations. It is the only periodical of its kind. Publ. and ed. by Rana Sri Parakram Jang Bahadur, Allahabad, U.P., India.

Candraśekhara, *Kulapūjācandrikā*, a manual of rituals to be performed by members of the initiate 'family' (*kula*). HPS II, 37.

Candraśekhara, *Puraścaraṇadīpikā*, a text dealing mainly with the *mantras* of expiation and atonement rituals. HPS II, 127. Compiled A.D. 1590, 1512 Śāka Era indicated in the colophon.

Carelli, Mario E., ed., *Sekoddeśatīkā of Nāḍapāda* (*Nāropa*), a commentary to the *Sekoddeśa* (anointment) section of the *Kālacakra Tantra* G.O.S. XC, Baroda 1941.

Carstairs, M., *The Twice Born*, Hogarth, London, and Indiana University Press, Bloomington 1959.

Chakravarti, Chintaharan, 'Antiquity of Tantricism', *IHQ*, VI, 1 (1930), 114–26.

Chakravarti, Chintaharan, 'The Cult of Bāro Bhaiyā of Eastern Bengal', *JRASB*, XXVI (1930), 379–88.

Chakravarti, Chintaharan, 'The Soma or Sauma Sect of the Śaivas', *IHQ*, VIII, 1 (1932), 221–3.

Chakravarti, Chintaharan, *The Tantras: Studies on Their Religion and Literature*, publ. Punthi Pustak, Calcutta, 1963.

Chandra, Lokesh, *Tibetan-Sanskrit Dictionary*, New Delhi, 1959–63. Though textually this dictionary does not contain anything that could not be found in the *Mahāvyutpatti*, it is extremely useful for the reading of Tibetan and Sanskrit tantric texts; in addition, it has over 200 drawings of tantric deities.

Chandra, P., 'The Kaula-Kapālika Cults at Khajuraho', in *Lalit-kalā*, No. 1–2, 1955–6, 98–107, New Delhi.

Charlesworth, M. J., *Philosophy and Linguistic Analysis*, Duquesne Studies, Philosophical Series No. 9, Duquesne University Press, Pittsburgh 1961.

Chatterji, R. M., ed., *Vividha-tantra-saṃgraha*, 'collection of various tantras', including the important *Śāktānandataraṅginī*, Bangabasi Press, Calcutta 1881–6.

Chattopadhyay, D. P., 'Tantra', in *Lokāyata—a Study in Ancient Indian Materialism*, People's Publishing House, New Delhi 1959, 269–358. An interesting survey of popular tantrism, with a strong Marxian slant.

Chou-yi-liang, 'Tantrism in China', in *Harvard Journal of Asiatic Studies*, Vol. VIII, 241–332, Harvard University Press 1945.

Clark, T. W., 'Evolution of Hinduism in Mediaeval Bengali Literature', *BSOAS*, Vol. XVIII, Pt. 3, London 1955.

Clark, W. E., *Two Lamaistic Pantheons*, 2 vols., Cambridge (Mass.) 1937.

Conze, E., *The Prajñāpāramitā Literature*, Mouton & Co., The Hague 1960.

Coomaraswamy, A. K., 'The Tantric Doctrine of Divine Biunity', ABORI, XIX (1938), 173–83.

Coomaraswamy, A. K., *Elements of Buddhist Iconography*, Cambridge (Mass.) 1935.

Coomaraswamy, A. K., *The Dance of Shiva*, Noonday Publ., New York 1957.

Dākārṇava-Tantra, 'the *Ḍāka*-Ocean Tantra'; on the *Ḍāka* and their female counterparts, the *Ḍākinī*—the latter are more important in Buddhist tantra where they are adepts of a higher order and identified with Prajñā rather than demoniacal and semidivine beings as in Hindu tantrism and folklore. Ch.S.S. 2991/63.

Daniélou, A., *Le polythéisme Hindou*, publ. Corréa, Paris 1960; English version *Hindu Polytheism*, Bollingen Series 1963, Pantheon Inc., New York 1963. An excellent analysis, showing that the official modern Hindu version denying the polytheistic element in Hinduism at the cost of monistically oriented speculation is not founded on the actual tradition.

Das, S. C., *A Tibetan-English Dictionary*, new print, Government of Bengal Publications Division, Calcutta 1962.

Dasgupta, N. Y., 'Doctrinal Changes—Tantrik Buddhism, Vajrayāṇa, Kālacakra-yāna, Sahajayāna', in *The Struggle for Empire*, Vol. V. of *The History and Culture of the Indian People*, 404–25 Bharatīya Vidyā Bhavan, Bombay 1959.

Dasgupta, Sh. B., *An Introduction to Tantrik Buddhism*, University Press, Calcutta 1950.

Dasgupta, Sh. B., *Obscure Religious Cults as Background of Bengali Literature*, University Press, Calcutta 1946.

Dasgupta, S. N., 'General Introduction to Tantra Philosophy', in *Philosophical Essays*, University Press, Calcutta 1951.

Datiya, Svami, *Tantrikapañcāṅga*, 'five limbs of tantric worship', a short treatise well known both in Bengal and the south. Ch.S.S. 3002/63.

Dattātrayatantram, with a Hindi commentary. Dattātraya is both a seer (*ṛṣi*) and a mythological combination of the three world gods

Brahmā, Śiva, and Viṣṇu. He is the tutelary deity of the royal house of Mysore; the present Governor of that State, the former Maharaja of Mysore, has written a book on the philosophy of Dattātraya (see Wadiyar, J.Ch.). Ch.S.S. 3013/63.

De, Sushil K., 'The Buddhist Tantric Sanskrit Literature of Bengal', in *New Indian Antiquary*, Vol. I., 1–23, Bombay 1938.

Deva, K. 'The Temples of Khajuraho in Central India', in *Ancient India* (Bulletin of the Archaeological Survey of India), No. 15, 43–65, New Delhi 1959.

Devi Prasad, *Śata-caṇḍī-yajña-vidhānam*, 'the injunctions of ritualistic procedure for the one hundred Caṇḍīs'. Caṇḍī is a wrathful aspect of Śakti; she is worshipped as Cāmuṇḍī in Mysore, a tutelary deity of the ruling house of the Wadiyar, worshipped by the ruler himself. Caṇḍī is also popular in Bengal, and her eulogy from the *Mārkaṇḍe-yapurāṇa* is chanted annually by the Brahmins in millions of Bengali households during the Durgā Pūjā festival in October, the most important festival of the Bengali calendar. Ch.S.S. 3118/63.

Devīkhaḍgamālā, 'the garland of the sword-emblems of the Goddess'; a litany of the *Lalitāsahasrānama*-type (*q.v.*), The Vavilla Press, Madras 1958.

Dhanvantarī-tantra-śikṣā with a Hindi commentary. Dhanvantarī is a medicinal, herb and therapy oriented aspect of Śakti; the text is popular with Vaidyas, i.e. indigenous medical practitioners and herbalists, and is worshipped by pious Hindu pharmacists all over India, Ch.S.S. 3035/63.

Diehl, K. G., *Instrument and Purpose Studies in Rites and Rituals in South India*, Gleerups Publ., Lund 1956.

Dikshitar, V. R., *The Lalitā Cult*. Monograph of the *Bulletin of the Dept. of Indian History and Archaeology*, University of Madras 1942.

Durgasaptaśatī, 'the sixty verses in praise of Durgā', complete with Harekānt Miśra's Hindi commentary 'Saralā' (the easy one); a popular hymnal to Durgā, Ch.S.S. 3026/63.

Durgopāsanakalpadruma, 'the wishfulfilling tree of Durgā-worship'; a recent Sanskrit compendium, Ch.S.S. 3030/63.

Edgerton, F., 'Prāṇa and Apāna', *JAOS* 78, 1958.

Edgerton, F., *Buddhist Hybrid Sanskrit Dictionary*, Yale University Press New Haven 1955.

Eliade, Mircea, *Le Yoga: Immortalité et Liberté*, Paris 1954. English version, trl. by W. R. Trask, *Yoga: Immortality and Freedom*, Bollingen Series, Pantheon Inc., New York 1958. The most outstanding critical survey of yogic and tantric traditions.

Erdmann, J. E., *History of Philosophy*, 3 vols., Harcourt, Brace & Co., New York 1925. This large work represents the attitude that there is no philosophy save in the West; more recent histories of philosophy have come away from this notion. On the positive side, this is the only history of philosophy in an English version that dealt with esoteric systems in the occidental religio-philosophical traditions which show amazing parallels to tantrism.

Evans-Wentz, W., ed., *Tibetan Yoga and Secret Doctrines—Seven Books of Wisdom of the Great Path;* trl. Lama Kazi Dawa-Samdup. Oxford University Press 1935.

Evans-Wentz, W., *Tibet's Great Yogi Milarepa: being the Jetsünkahbum*; trl. Lama Kazi Dawa-Samdup, Oxford University Press 1928.

Evans-Wentz, W., ed., *The Tibetan Book of the Dead* (*Bardo Thodöl*); trl. Lama Kazi Dawa-Samdup, London 1949.

These three volumes are standard translations of important Tibetan material—more important to the western lovers of the Asian mystique than to the Tibetans themselves. One of the greater merits of this collection, now available in paperback and well known all over the English-speaking world, is that the late C. G. Jung has made some of his most profound statements in the Preface which he wrote to these volumes.

Ewing, Arthur H., 'The Śāradā-tilaka Tantra', in *JAOS* VI, 23 (1902), 65–76.

Ferrand, J., *Relations des Voyages et Textes Geographiques Arabes Relatifs a l'Extrême Orient du VIIIe au XVIIIe Siècles.* Paris 1913–14.

Filliozat, J., *Étude de démonologie indienne: le Kumāratantra de Rāvana et les textes paralléles indiens, tibétains, chinois, cambodgiens et arabes*, Paris 1937.

Filliozat, J., 'Les Origines d'une technique mystique indienne', *Revue Philosophique* VI, 136, Paris 1946, 208–20.

Foucher, A. Ch., *Étude sur l'iconographie bouddhique de l'Inde.* 2 parts, Paris 1900–5.

Foucher, Max-Pôl, *The Erotic Sculpture of India*, Allen & Unwin, London 1959.

Frauwallner, E., *Geschichte der Indischen Philosophie*, Vienna-Saltzburg 1952.

Frauwallner, E., *Philosophie des Buddhismus*, Berlin 1955.

Ganguly, O. C., 'The Mithuna in Indian Art', *Rupam*, Nos. 22–3, Calcutta 1925.

Gaṇapatitattva, ed. Sudarshana Devi, Sanskrit with Hindi commentary. This is a tantric interpretation of Gaṇeśa, the son of Śiva and Śakti, who was absorbed as an important deity both into Hindu and Buddhist tantrism. Ch.S.S. 2966/63.

Gāyatrī Tantra, containing the 'removal of curses' (*gāyatrī-śāpoddhāra*), the '*Gāyatrī*-cuirass' (*-kavaca*) for protection, and the hymn to the ten 'Great Sciences', identified in the tantric contexts with ten representations of Śakti (*Mahāvidyā*). This is the central text on the tantric use of the Vedic arch-*mantra*. Ch.S.S. 2970/63.

Gāyatrīsahasranāmam, 'the thousand names of *Gāyatrī*', a litany of the *Lalitāsahasranāma*-type (q.v.). Vavilla Press, Madras 1954.

Geden, A. S., 'Tantras', entry in the *Encyclopaedia of Religion and Ethics*, ed. J. Hastings, Vol. XII, 129 f.

Getty, Alice, *The Gods of Northern Buddhism*, Oxford 1914.

Ghilḍayāl, Paṇḍit Devīprasād Kulasaṅghaśekhara, *Pañcamakāra tathā Bhāvatraya*, 'the five letters "m" and the three dispositions', an excellent treatise in Hindi with Sanskrit paradigms. publ. Kalyan Mandir, Katra-Allahabad 1954.

Ghosh, C. M. 'Prākṛta-paiṅgalam', in *Bibliotheca Indica*, Calcutta 1900–2.

Ghoshal, U. N., *Studies in Indian History and Culture*, University Press, Calcutta 1955.

Glasenapp, H. V., 'Die Entstehung des Vajrayāṇa', in *Zeitschrift der Deutschen Morgenlaendischen Gesellschaft*, Vol. 90, Leipzig 1936, 546–72.

Glasenapp, H. V., 'Tantrismus und Schaktismus', in *Ostasiatische Zeitschrift*, Vol. XII (new series), Berlin 1936, 120–33.

Glasenapp, H. V., *Buddhistische Mysterien*, Stuttgart 1940.

Glasenapp, H. V., *Heilige Staetten Indiens*, Diederich, Jena 1900.

Goetz, H., *The Historical Background of the Great Temples of Khajuraho*, *Arts Asiatiques*, fasc. 1., Paris 1958.

Goetz, H., 'Khajuraho', in *Maandblad vor Beeldende Kunsten*, Vol. XVI, 210–17, Leiden 1939.

Gopāla Pañcānana, *Tantradīpika*, RASB, VIII, 6230.

Gordon, Antoinette, *Tibetan Religious Art*, New York 1952.

Gordon, Antoinette, *The Iconography of Tibetan Lamaism*, New York 1939.

Govinda, Lama Anagarika, *Grundlagen Tibetischer Mystik*, Rascher, Zürich 1957. English version *Foundations of Tibetan Mysticism*, Rider & Co., London 1959.

Govinda, Lama Anagarika, 'Principles of Tantric Buddhism,' in *2500 Years of Buddhism*, Publications Division, Govt. of India, New Delhi 1956, 94–104.

Govinda, Lama Anagarika, 'The Psychological Attitude of Early Buddhist Philosophy' (according to the Abhidhamma Tradition); Readership Lectures, Patna University 1937–8, 68, 246: Rider & Co., London 1961.

Govinda, Lama Anagarika, 'The Significance of OM and the Foundations of Mantric Lore', in *Stepping Stones*, Kalimpong 1950–1, 17–47.

Gruenwedel, Albert, *Die Legenden des Naropa, des Hauptvertreters des Nekromanten-und Hexentums*, Leipzig 1933.

Gruenwedel, Albert, *Tārānātha's Edelsteinmiene*, Bibliotheca Buddhica, Vol. VIII, St. Petersburg (Petrograd) 1914.

Gruenwedel, Albert, '*Die Geschichten der vierundachtzig Zauberer (Mahāsiddhas)—aus dem Tibetischen ubersetzt*'. *Baessler Archiv*, Vol. V., 137–228, Leipzig 1916.

Guenther, H. V., *sGam.po.pa- The Jewel Ornament of Liberation*. The most scholarly and philosophically precise treatment of an important Tibetan text up to date, little known to the West. Rider & Co., London 1959.

Guenther, H. V., 'The Concept of Mind in Buddhist Tantrism', *Journal of Oriental Studies*, Hong Kong, July 1956.

Guenther, H. V., *Yuganaddha—the Tantric View of Life*, Chowkhamba Sanskrit Series, 2nd. edition, Varanasi 1964.

Guenther, H. V., *The Life and Teaching of Nāropa*—Translated from the Original Tibetan with Philosophical Commentary based on the Oral Transmission. Clarendon Press, Oxford 1963. The only authoritative work, so far, on the *Mahāmudrā*, *Karmamudrā*, and other focal themes of Tibetan tantrism.

Guenther, H. V., 'Levels of Understanding in Buddhism', *JAOS*, 78/1, 1960, 19 ff.

Guenther, H. V., *Philosophy and Psychology of Abhidhamma*, Buddha Vihara, Lucknow 1955.

For any advanced reading in Buddhist tantrism, the works of H. V. Guenther are indispensable, particularly his *Jewel Ornament of Liberation*, *Nāropa*, and *Yuganaddha*.

Guhyasamājatantra or *Tathāgataguhyaka*, ed. B. Bhattacharya, G.O.S. LIII, Baroda 1931. Probably the most important Buddhist tantra, second in age perhaps only to the *Mañjuśrīmūlakalpa* (q.v.) Prof. deJong at Leiden is at present working at the more elaborate Tibetan version and commentary of this tantra.

Guptasādhanātantra, 'the tantra of the secret *sādhanā*', Sanskrit with a Hindi commentary by Paṇḍit Baldevprasād Miśra, publ. Gaṅgāviṣṇu Śrīkrṣṇadās, at the Lakṣmīveṅkateśvara Press, Kalyan, Bombay 1953. Probably a very recent, and certainly an apocryphal, tantric text which contains, however, central information on the 'five Ms' and other salient themes.

Hadano, Hakuyu, 'Human Existence in Tantric Buddhism', in *Annual Reports of the Faculty of Arts and Letters*, Tohoku University, Sendai 1958. An enormous amount of excellent literature on tantrism is published every year in Japan, but unfortunately all of it in Japanese, with occasional English language abstracts attached to the publications. This is a matter of grave concern to Buddhologists all over the western world, but there is simply no remedy apparent save learning Japanese and Chinese so as to be able to handle Japanese sources; Japanese scholars will not write major works in any but their own language, not because they could not do it, but because the Japanese academical system does not acknowledge publications in other languages towards promotions, etc., of scholars in the liberal arts. On a cautious estimate, I believe that about as much is being published annually, in Japanese, on Buddhism, tantrism, Indian and Tibetan religious studies, as in all occidental languages put together. A great amount of scholarly duplication is regrettable, and inevitable, for the time being.

Haribhadra, *Saddarśanasamuccaya*, with Guṇaratna's commentary. Contains important references to the Kapālikas, the 'skull-carrying' sect of tantrism. Ch.S.S., 3089/63.

Harikṛṣṇa Veṅkaṭaramaṇa, *Durgopāsana-kalpadruma*, 'the wishfulfilling tree of Durgā-worship', being the eighth chapter of the *Bṛhajjyotiṣārṇava*, a tantric interpretation of astrological doctrines; publ. Khemraj Śrīkṛṣṇadās, Bombay 1953.

Hauer, J. W., *Die Dhāraṇī im Noerdlichen Buddhismus und ihre Parallelen in der sogenannten Mithrasliturgie*. Stuttgart 1927. This is one of the more serious attempts to trace some relationships between mid-eastern, Nestorian Christian, and Tibetan Buddhist tantric ritual.

Hazra, R. J., 'Influence of Tantra on the Tattvas of Raghunandana', *IHQ*, IX, 3 (1933), 678–704.

Hoffmann, H., *The Religions of Tibet*. Allen & Unwin, London 1961.

Hoffmann, H., *Quellen zur Geschichte der Bon-Religion*; publ. Verlag der Akademie der Wissenschaften, Berlin 1950. The most thorough analysis and description, so far, of systematized Bon.

Hummel, Siegbert, 'Die Lamaistischen Tempelfahnen und ihre Beziehung zu Yoga', in *Tribus*, I, Stuttgart 1952–3, 239–52.

Ingalls, D. H., *Materials for the Study of Navya Nyāya*, Harvard University Press, Cambridge, Mass. 1959.

Īśana-śiva-guru-deva-paddhati, Trivandrum Sanskrit Series, reprinted in *Proceedings and Transactions of the Fifth Indian Oriental Conference*, Lahore 1930.

Jacobs, H., *Western Psychology and Hindu Sādhanā*, Allen & Unwin, London 1961.

Jagannivāsa, *Śiva-siddhānta-sindhu*, RASB VIII, 6193.

Jaitra Siṃha, *Bhairāvarcana-parijāta*. The author is said to have been a ruling prince of the Vaghela dynasty of the Vindhya region. RASB VIII, 6468.

Janārdana, *Mantracandrikā*, RASB VIII, 6232.

Jayadratha-yāmala, with a preface by H. P. Shastri, H.P.S. (Nepal), I, p. 176 ff.

Jhaveri, M. B., *Comparative and Critical Study of Mantraśāstra*. Ahmedabad 1944. Though not too critical, this is the only extensive work written in English on Jaina tantrism. It also contains Apabhraṃśa and Sanskrit selections from the central Jaina tantric texts.

Jñānānanda Brahmacārin, *Tattvaprakāśa*, composed 1808 (colophon: 1730 Śāka Era), H.P.S., I., 137.

Jñānānanda Paramahaṃsa, *Kaulāvalinirṇaya*, with an English introduction by A. Avalon; *Tantric Texts*, Vol. XIV, Āgamanusandhāna Samiti, Sanskrit Press Depository, Calcutta 1928.
One of the most important Śākta treatises in the Hindu tantric tradition.

Jñānārṇava-tantra, ed. Paṇḍit R. R. Gokhale and Paṇḍit Gaṇeśa Śāstrī, Ānandāśrama Sanskrit Series, No. 69, Bombay 1952.

Jñānasaṃkalanī-tantra, a short apocryphal tantric text, Ch.S.S. 2989/63.

Jñānasiddhi by Indrabhūti, ed. B. Bhattacharya, G.O.S. LXIV, Baroda 1929. One of the few completely extant Sanskrit texts, focal in Vajrayāṇa writing. Printed in one volume together with the *Prajñopāyaviniścaya.*

Jung, C. G., 'On Maṇḍala Symbolism', in *Archetypes and the Collective Unconscious*, trl. R. F. C. Hull, London and New York 1955 (Collected Works of C. G. Jung).

Kaivalyakālikā-tantra, RASB VIII, 6383.

Kalhāṇa, *Rājataraṅginī*, ed. Durga Prasad, Bombay 1892. First trl. by M. A. Stein, London 1900. Trl. and publ. by R. S. Pandit, Allahabad 1935.

Kālikā-sahasranāma-stotram, 'the thousand names of Kālī-hymn', a litany of the *Lalitāsahasranāma* type (q.v.). Publ. Sri Rama Press, Madras 1957.

Kālīvilāsa-tantra, Ch.S.S. 2952/63.

Kāmakalā-vilāsa by Punyānanda Swāmī, a renowned Bengali tantric, with a Sanskrit commentary. Ch.S.S. 2950/63; also with text, English translation and notes ed. A. Avalon, Ganeshan & Co., Madras 1953.

Kāmya-Yantroddharā, probably the earliest treatise on *tantra* and *yantra* (mystical diagrams) authored in Bengal, ascribed to the Bengali tantric referred to as 'the doctor-mendicant' (Mahāmahopādhyaya Parivrājakācārya). H. P. Shastri described a manuscript of this text, dated Śāka 1297, i.e. A.D. 1375, in H.P.S. III, 53.

Kāraṇḍa-vyūha, see *Avalokiteśvara-guṇa-kāraṇḍa-vyūha.*

Karpurādistotram, with Vimalānanda's two commentaries 'Ānandadāyinī' and 'Subodhinī'. *Tantric Texts*, ed. A. Avalon, Ch.S.S. 2946/63.

Kāśīnātha Bhaṭṭa 'Bhada' (Śivānandanātha) lived at Banaras in the seventeenth century, taught right-handed tantrism and condemned the left-handed forms. *Durjana-mukha-capeṭikā* 'slap into the face of the wicked', i.e. the left-handed tantrics. This tract was translated by E. Burnouf as part of his preface to his *Le Bhāgavata Purāna*, p. LXXXV, Paris 1880.

Kāśīnatha Bhaṭṭa 'Bhada' (Śivānandanātha), *Vāmācara-mata-khaṇḍana*, 'refutation of the left-handed doctrine', JRASB, Vol. IV, p. 455 ff., Calcutta 1939.

Kāśīnāthānandanātha, *vulgo* Paramaniarañjana, *Śyāmāsaparyavidhi* colophon date Śāka Era 1699, i.e. A.D. 1717, RASB, VIII, 6303.

Kaula—and other Upaniṣads, with Bhāskararāya's commentaries, ed. A. Avalon and Paṇḍit Sītārām Śāstrī, Āgamānusandhāna Samiti, *Tantric Texts* Vol. XI, Luzac, London 1922.

Kaulajñānanirṇaya, 'adumbration of the wisdom of the Kaula (initiate group)', ed. P. C. Bagchi, University Press, Calcutta 1934.

Kaulāvalinirṇaya, *see* Jñānānanda Paramahaṃsa.

Kaulopaniṣad-Tripuropaniṣad-Bhāvopaniṣad, with Sanskrit and Hindi commentaries. Ch.S.S. 2691/63. These are apocryphal Upaniṣads, probably compiled within the last two hundred years. The title '*upaniṣad*' is often given to works whose authors want canonical status for them. Islamophiles created an 'Allāhupaniṣad', and recently a famous Indian writer wrote a Ramakrishna-Upaniṣad.

Kaviraj, Gopinath, *Tāntrik Vāṇmay men Śāktadṛṣṭi*, Bihār Rāṣṭrabhāṣā Parisat, Patna 1963. The author, often quoted in this book, has finally summarised his profound knowledge of Hindu tantrism in this Hindi work which is bound to be the most important survey in India's national language.

Kirfel, W., *Das Purāṅapañcalakṣaṇa*, Bonn 1947.

Kirfel, W. *Die Kosmographie der Inder*, Bonn 1940.

Kramrisch, St., and Anand, M. R., *Homage to Khajuraho*, Bombay 1960.

Kramrisch, St., and Anand, M. R., 'Chandella Sculptures in Khajuraho', *Journal of the Indian Society of Oriental Art*, Vol. 1/2, Calcutta 1939.

Kriyoḍḍīśatantra, with Hindi translation and commentary by Paṇḍit Lālmaṇi Śarma, publ. Gaṅgāviṣṇu Śrīkṛṣnadās, Lakṣmīveṅkateśvar Press, Kalyan-Bombay 1957.

Kṛṣṇamohana, *Āgamacandrikā*, a tantric digest mainly on the rites of the *Śrīvidyā* (q.v.) in its Bengali variant; the work was commissioned by him, and compiled by several paṇḍits. RASB VIII, 6365.

Kṛṣṇānanda 'Āgamavāgīśa', *Tantrasāra* 'the essence of tantra', not to be confused with the much more famous work on Kashmir Śaivism and tantrism by Abhinavagupta (q.v.); this is the most elaborate and popular tantric digest in Bengal. The author is said to have formulated the theological concept of the goddess Kālī ever since then prevalent in Bengal. ed. Rasikmohan Chatterji, Basumati Press, Calcutta 1929.

Kṛṣṇānanda 'Āgamavāgīśa', *Tarārahasyā*, not to be confused with the text ascribed to Saṃkarācārya. ed. J. Vidyasagar, Calcutta 1896.

Kṣemarāja, *Pratyābhijña-hṛdayam*, one of the central texts on the Kashmiri form of Śāktism and the *Pratyabhijña* 'intuitive recollection' school of the Śāktas and Śaivites of Kashmir. This edition includes a Hindi commentary and an auxiliary text *Parāpraveśikā*. Ch.S.S. 3075/63.

Kulacūḍāmaṇi-nigama, text with introduction by A. K. Maitra, 2nd. ed., Ganeshan & Co., Madras 1956.

Kulārṇava-tantra ed. A. Avalon, *Tantric Texts* V, with commentary by Tārānātha Vidyāratna, Luzac & Co., London 1917.

Kumāra-saṃhitā, a text dealing mainly with *ṣaṭkarma*, the six magical rites. It is probably of southern origin, as 'Kumāra' is the most frequent epithet of Skanda the war-god, the tutelary deity of many Tamilian groups, RASB, VIII, 6056.

Lakṣmītantram, a text of high status in the Pañcarātra School, the Vaiṣṇava tradition of formal worship, closest to tantrism. The text is classed as a *pañcarātra āgama*, a canonical work for the followers of the Pañcarātra. ed. V. Kṛṣṇamācārya, Ch.S.S. 3103/66.

Lakṣmaṇa Deśikendra, *Śāradātilakam*, with the commentary by Rāghava Bhaṭṭa. This is a famous Vedāntic treatise which gives a tantric interpretation to the monistic doctrine; Śāradā, here a synonym of Sarasvatī the goddess of music and learning, is contemplated as Śakti. Ch.S.S. 3123/63.

Lalitāsahasranāma (*-stotram*), 'the thousand names of Lalitā' (Śakti), one of the most important and pervasive litanies of a thousand names (about a thousand, to be exact—they are usually 1008 or more); these hymns are particularly popular in the Brahmanical South. Though used by orthodox, non-tantric Brahmins, it has strong tantric relevance. Publ. Vavillu Rāmasvāmī Śāstrulu & Sons, Madras 1955 (*see* also Bhāskararāya).

Lalleśvarī-vyākhyāni, 'the sayings of Lalleśvarī' vulgo Lallā, a medieval Kashmiri woman-saint of tantric propensity. With the commentary by Rajanakabhāskara. Ch.S.S. 3104/63.

Lalou, M., *Iconographie des étoffes paintes (paṭa) dans le Mañjuśrīmūlakalpa.* Buddhica Series, *Mémoires VI*, Paris 1930.

Laufer, Berthold, *Use of Human Skulls and Bones in Tibet.* Field Museum of Natural History, Department of Anthropology Publication X, Chicago 1923.

Leonard, G. S., 'Notes on the Kānphaṭa Yogis', in *Indian Antiquary*, Bombay 1878, Vol. VII, 298–300.

Lévi, Sylvain, 'On a Tantrik Fragment from Kucha (Central Asia)', *IHQ*, XII, 2, 197–214, Calcutta 1936.

Mahākālapañcarātra, RASB (Shastri) V., 4199 A.

Mahānirvāṇatantra with English translation and commentary, ed. A. Avalon, Ganeshan & Co., Madras 1953. The most important Hindu tantra.

Mahāyakṣiṇī-sādhanam, 'the *sādhanā* of the Great Yakṣiṇī'. The *yakṣiṇīs* (female counterpart of *yakṣa*) are powerful semi-divine female beings, similar—in the Hindu tradition at least—to forest-dwelling spirits. In Buddhist tantrism, however, they are highly evolved female adepts or goddesses, manifestations of the Prajña, and synonymous in most cases with the Ḍākinīs. Ch.S.S. 3080/63.

Maheśvara-tantram, Ch.S.S. Nos. 469–71, 1940.

Maheśvara-tantram, ed. Kṛṣṇapriyācārya. Maheśvara is one of the most frequent and ubiquitous epithets of Śiva known to all Hindus. This is an important text with all the truly tantric trimmings; this first edition was the first publication of the text. It is a scholarly edition and lists several variant readings. Ch.S.S. 3090/63.

Maheśvarānanda, *Mahārtha-mañjarī*, with the author's own commentary, ed. with notes by Paṇḍit Mukunḍa Rāma Shastri, *KSTS* No. XI, Srinagar 1918.

Maheśvarī-tantram. Maheśvarī 'the great goddess' is the correlate epithet of Śakti; this is an apocryphal text, complementary by ascription, to the *Maheśvara-tantram*—probably a composition for the sake of symmetry, with the perfectly genuine *Maheśvara-tantra*. Ch.S.S. 3091/63.

Majumdar, R. C., *An Advanced History of India*, Macmillan, London 1958.

Majumdar, R. C., 'Colonial and Cultural Expansion', in *The Age of Imperial Kanauj*, Ch. XIV, History and Culture of the Indian People, *see* Munshi, K.L.M., Bombay 1955.

Mālinī-vijayottara-tantram, ed. Paṇḍit Madhusūdan Kaul Sāstrī, with various commentaries. *KSTS* No. XXXVII, Srinagar 1922.

Mallik, Kalyani, *Nāth-sāṃpradāyer itihās* (*darśan o sādhanāpraṇāli*), 'the history, philosophy, and *sādhanā*-methodology of the Nāth Order'. This Bengali work by a brilliant woman-indologist of Calcutta University is the most exhaustive study up to date of the Matsyendranāth-Gorakhnāth tradition, germinal to *Haṭha-yoga*, Hindu and Buddhist tantrism alike. University Press, Calcutta 1950.

Mañjuśrīmūlakalpa (*Ārya-*), ed. Paṇḍit T. Gaṇapati Śāstrī, in three volumes. *Trivandrum Sanskrit Series*, Trivandrum 1920–5. This is probably the oldest extant Buddhist tantric text of the Vajrayāṇa.

Mantramahārṇava, Śrī Lakṣmīveṅkaṭeśvar Steam Press, Kalyan-Bombay 1940. These two are highly popular *mantra*-manuals, often quoted in the foregoing volume.

Mantramuktāvali, Śrī Lakṣmīveṅkaṭeśvar Steam Press, Kalyan-Bombay 1937.

Mantrasiddhi kā upāy (Hindi; anon.) This manual 'means of obtaining fruition in the use of *mantra*' is described, in its preface, as 'equivalent to a true *guru* for *mantra* practice'. Such auto-eulogies are frequent. Ch.S.S. 3071/63.

Marjarī-tantra, a text which centres on a highly popular, magically potent goddess of eastern India. RASB VIII, 5897.

Maspéro, Henri, 'Les Procédés de 'nourrir le principle vital dans la religion taoiste ancienne', *Journal Asiatique*, CCXXVIII, 177–252, 353–430, Paris 1937.

Masuda, Jiryo, *Der Individualistische Idealismus der Yogācāra-Schule*, 10. Heft, Materialien zur Kunde des Buddhismus, 84, 215, 264, Heidelberg 1926.

Mātrikābheda-tantra, a text concentrating on the meditational use of the *mātrikās* or syllable-letters of the alphabet. Ch.S.S. 3085/63.

Mātrikābheda-tantra, ed. Chintamani Bhattacharya, Calcutta Sanskrit Series No. VII.

Māyātantra, which has a detailed section on the preparation of several kinds of meat for the tantric Durgā-worship. RASB, VIII, 5985.

Merutantra; in part at least a very recent text as, of all places, the town of London is mentioned in it! Ed. Paṇḍit Raghunath Sastri, Lakṣmīveṅkaṭeśvar Steam Press, Bombay 1940.

Miśra, Paṇḍit Bhāgavataprasād Śāstrī, 'Vāgīśa', ed., *Mahā-mṛtyuñjaya-japa-vidhiḥ tathā mṛtyuñjaya stotram,* 'the manner of doing the *japa* of the Great Mṛtyuñjaya-*mantra,* and the Mṛtyuñjaya hymn'. This is one of the Vedic *mantras* which has been completely absorbed and assimilated into tantrism. Śrīkṛṣṇa Pustakālaya, Bombay and Kanpur 1950.

Mitra, Sarat Ch., 'On the Cult of Gorakṣanātha in Eastern Bengal', *Journal of the Department of Letters,* Calcutta University, Vol. XIV, 1927, 1–41.

Mitra, Sarat Ch., 'On the Cult of Gorakṣanātha in the District of Rangpur in Northern Bengal', *JASB* XIV, Calcutta 1927/28, 1–5.

Mṛgendra-tantram (*Srī-*) ed. Paṇḍit Madhusūdan Kaul Śāstrī; *Vidyāpāda* and *Yogapāda,* with the commentary by Nārāyaṇakaṇṭha, *KSTS,* Vol. 50, Srinagar 1930.

Munshi, K. L. M. general editor, *The History and Culture of the Indian People.* Planned for ten volumes, of which eight have been published so far. This is a veritable encyclopaedia of indological knowledge, its numerous contributors are exclusively Indian scholars. It is an indispensable reference work for tantric and all other themes. *Bharatīya Vidyā Bhavan,* Bombay 1950.

Nārāyaṇa, *Tantra-sāra-saṃgraha,* 'survey of the essential teachings of tantra', with commentary. One of the most comprehensive medieval tantric anthologies. Ch.S.S. 2998/63.

Navasiṃha (also called Ādyānanda), *Tantracintāmaṇi.* The author was supposed to be a minister of the Nepalese King Bhūpālendra or Mahindra Mallā and of his successor Bhāskaramallā in the late seventeenth century. RASB, VIII, 6217–8.

Navasiṃha, *Kulamukti-kallolinī,* RASB, VIII, 6308.

Navasiṃha, *Puṣpa-ratnākara-tantra,* a treatise mainly concerned with the enumeration and description of flowers to be used for the rituals of various deities. *HPS* (Nepal), II, p. 222.

Netra-tantram, 'the eye-tantra', with a commentary by Kṣemarāja, in two parts. This text, as the name implies, emphasized eye-cures and other healing magic centring on vision. Ch.S.S. 3040/63.

Newland, Constance C., *Myself and I*. This is an excellent, though popular, statement of experiments and experiences with the most powerful modern psychedelic drug Lysergic Acid Diathelymide (LSD 25); parallels with drug-induced tantric experiences are striking. Signet Paperback, New York 1963.

Nikhilananda, Swami, *The Gospel of Ramakrishna*, Ramakrishna Math, Madras-Mylapore 1950.

Nirvāṇatantra, RASB, VIII, 5888.

Niṣpannayogāvali by Mahapāṇḍita Abhayakaragupta (q.v.), ed. B. Bhattacharya, G.O.S. CIX, Baroda 1949.

Nitya-śoḍaśīkārṇava with Bhāskararāya's commentary, 'the ocean of the worship of the eternal sixteen-year-old virgin goddess'. The '*ṣoḍaśi*' as an object of formal worship is the focal living object of tantric hypostasization. The maiden 'installed' for the Kumāripūjā 'worship of the virgin', popular in Bengal up to this day, is a Brahmin girl of sixteen. *AAS*, Poona 1908.

Oman, J. C., *The Mystics, Ascetics, and Saints of India*, T. F. Unwin, London 1903.

Opler, Morris, review of M. Carstairs *The Twice Born* (q.v.). *American Anthropologist* VI, 61, 1959.

Pandey, K. C., *Abhinavagupta: an Historical and Philosophical Study*, Chowkhamba Sanskrit Series Vol. VI, Varanasi 1935, revised ed. 1959.

Panigrahi, K. C., 'Obscene Sculptures of Orissan Temples', in *Proceedings of the Hindain History Congress*, VIII, 94–7.

Paramasaṃhitā of the Pañcarātra. Ed. and trl. by S. Krishnaswami Aiyangar, G.O.S. LXXXVI, Baroda 1940.

Parānandasūtraṃ, an important scholium of medieval Śāktism. G.O.S. LVI.

Paraśurāmakalpasūtra with Rameśvara's commentary, ed. A. Mahādeva Śāstrī and Sakralāl Y. Dave, 2nd. ed., G.O.S. XXII, Baroda 1950.

Pāratriṃśikā, with the commentary of Abhinavagupta. These 'thirty verses in praise of the Supreme (fem.)' are classed as an *āgamaśāstra*, implying its canonical status in tantric literature. The fact that Abhinavagupta (q.v.) is said to have written the commentary would speak for its age and importance. Ch.S.S. 3046/7/63.

Pāśupatasūtra, TSS Vl. CXLIII, and *IHQ* Vol. XIX, 270 f.

Payne, E. A., *The Śāktas: An Introduction and Comparative Study*. Calcutta 1933.

Péri, Noel, 'Harītī, la mère-de-démons', *BEFEO*, XVII, 1–102, 1917.

Petech, L. *History of Medieval Nepal*, Serie Orientale Roma, Rome 1960.

Poleman, H., general editor, 'Tantra, Śaiva, and Spanda' in *A Census of Indic Manuscripts in the United States and Canada*, American Oriental Society Monograph Vol. 12, 1938. Over three hundred tantric manuscripts are listed in this obsolete edition. A long overdue edition would have to add some four hundred manuscripts acquired after the date of publication, not including Tibetan xylographs, of which roughly five thousand have been acquired by American libraries. The University of Washington Library at Seattle now owns the best collection of tantric material, both Indian and Tibetan, in the western hemisphere.

Popper, Karl. R., *The Open Society and Its Enemies*, Princeton 1950.

Pott, P. H., *Yoga en Yantra*, Leiden 1946.

Pott, P. H., *Introduction to the Tibetan Collection of the National Museum of Ethnology*, Leiden 1946.

Potter, K. H., *Presuppositions of Indian Philosophy*, Prentice Hall, Englewood-Cliffs, N.J., 1963. An excellent, important, and highly analytical statement of the salient features of Indian thought.

Prabodh, Chandra, 'Le Bouddhisme tantrique á Bali d'après une publication récente', *Journal Asiatique*, CCXVIII, Paris 1931, 159–67.

Prāṇamañjari (otherwise attributed to Premanidhi, second half of the eighteenth century), *Sudarśanā*, a commentary to the *Tantrarājatantra* (q.v.), RASB VIII, 6819; also an edition of the first chapter by J. B. Chaudhuri, Calcutta 1940.

Prāṇatoṣiṇī-tantram, 'the tantra that satisfies the vital force'; a very popular, oft-quoted Hindu tantric text (*see* also Rāmatoṣaṇa). Ch.S.S. 3059/63.

Prapañca-sāra-tantram, 'tantra of the essence of the phenomenal universe', ascribed to Śaṃkarācārya, but certainly not really composed by him, with a commentary (equally ascriptive) of Padmapāda, one of Śaṃkarācārya's four direct disciples. Ch.S.S. 3058/63.

Punyānanda, *Kāmakalāvilāsa*, with commentary and notes edited by Paṇḍit Mukunda Rāma Śāstrī, KSTS No. XII, Srinagar 1918.

Pūrṇānanda, *Śāktakrama*, a manual for Śākta worship; in Raja Rajendralal Mitra's *Notices on Sanskrit Manuscripts*, Vol. VI, 2067, Calcutta 1871/2.

Pūrṇānanda, *Ṣaṭkarmollāsa*, a text on the six magical rites, on *āsana* (the meditative postures), and on vessels (*kuṇḍa*) containing ritualistic ingredients. HPS (Nepal) IV, 308.

Pūrṇānanda, *Śrītattvacintāmaṇi*, a manual on the *Śrīvidyā* (q.v.) and other tantric observances. *Calcutta Sanskrit Series* No. 19.

Pūrṇānanda, *Śyāmārahasyā*, a text on rituals of the goddess Śyāmā, a synonym of Kālī or Durgā, especially in Bengal. Publ. P. C. Pal & Bros., Calcutta 1948.

Pūrṇānanda, *Tattvānanda-taraṅgiṇī*, a concise treatise on *mantras* and *bījas*, RASB VIII, 6200.

Pūtanāśānti, 'exorcism of demonesses', with a Hindi commentary *Śiśutoṣinī* 'peace-giver to children'. Pūtanā is a demoness particularly fond of taking homely guises, suckling and thereby poisoning infants; one of them tried this on the baby Kṛṣṇa and was killed by him—a famous episode in the Kṛṣṇa-lore. The Pūtanā is closest to the occidental vampire. Ch.S.S. 3053/63.

Rādhāmohana, *Tīkṣṇakalpa*, composed A.D. 1810 (colophon Śāka Era 1732), *HPS* II, 90.

Raghunātha Tarkavāgīśa, *Āgama-tattva-vilāsa*, abridged by his son Rāmakṛṣṇa into a much more famous digest called *Āgamacandrikā*; this was composed in A.D. 1687 (colophon Śāka Era 1609).

Raghuvīra and Lokesh Chandra, editors, *Vigalita-bauddha-granthāvali* 'a collection of lost Buddhist texts'; Sanskrit folios and xylographs of Buddhist tantric fragments preserved in the original. Ch.S.S. 2978/63.

Raghuvīra and Lokesh Chandra, editors, *Tibetan-Sanskrit Dictionary* of Buddhist terminology (Bhoṭapiṭaka Series), New Delhi 1957. Although there is hardly any material in this new work which was not contained in the *Mahāvyutpatti*, the standard traditional multilingual dictionary of Buddhist terms, this work has been arranged with an eye to Tibetan tantrism, with charts and drawn figures of the various tantric deities interspersed in its seven volumes. The late Dr. Raghuvīra was assisted by Mongolian and Tibetan Lamas at his Institute, in the production of this important dictionary, publ. Academy of Indian Studies, Hauz Khazi, New Delhi.

Rajanaka Utpala Deva, *Siddhitrayī* and *Pratyabhijña-kārikā-vṛtti* edited with notes by Paṇḍit Madhusūdana Kaul Śāstrī. KSTS No. XXXIV, Srinagar 1921.

Rājemiśra, *Tantrāhnikam*, 'tantric daily observances', a sort of tantric *brevier*. Ch.S.S. 3002/63.

Rāmagopala Śarmā, *Tantradīpanī*, composed A.D. 1704 (colophon Śāka Era 1626), *HPS* II, 79.

Rāmatoṣaṇa (Bhattacārya), *Prāṇatoṣiṇī* (q.v.), subtitled 'collected from the *tantra-śāstra*'; an anthology of tantric texts. Publ. Śrījīvānanda Vidyāsāgara Bhaṭṭācārya, Calcutta Press, Calcutta 1898.

Ramcharan, Sri, *Mātṛ-upāsana*, 'mother-worship', in Hindi, Kalyan Mandir, Katra-Allahabad 1949.

Rao, Gopinatha, T. A., *Elements of Hindu Iconography*, 4 vols., Madras 1914–16.

Ratna-gotra-vibhāga-mahāyānottara-tantra, a Buddhist tantra centring on the worship of the *dhyānī*-Buddhas in their tantric ramifications. Ch.S.S. 3099/63.

Riepe, D., *The Naturalistic Tradition in Indian Thought*, University of Washington Press, Seattle 1961.

Risch, Hubert, 'Le Haṭha-Yoga. Exposé sommaire de la méthode, quelques expériences physiologiques et applications thérapeutiques', Dissertation, Paris, Faculté de Médicine, 1951.

Roerich, George N., trl., *The Blue Annals*. One of the most important Tibetan 'histories', i.e. of the origin, development, and spread of Buddhism into Tibet. 2 parts. University Press, Calcutta 1949–53.

Roy, Samaren K., 'The Roots of Bengali Culture'. *Quest*, Bombay, May 1961.

Rudrayāmala, Anusandhāna Samiti, Calcutta 1895.

Rudrayāmalam-uttaratantram (improved edition of the above), ed. Śrī Jīvānanda Vidyāsāgara Bhaṭṭācārya, Vācaspati Press, Calcutta 1937

Ruegg, David-Seyffort, 'The Jo naṅ pas: a School of Buddhist Ontologists according to the *Grub mtha'i sel gyi me loṅ*'. *JAOS* 83/1, 1963, 73–92.

Sādhak kā saṃvād, 'the aspirant's discourse'. This anonymous Hindi booklet offers a practical introduction into the *dharma* of the Śāktas. Ch.S.S. 3165/63.

Sādhanāmālā see Bhattacharya, Benoytosh, ed.

Sahib Kaul, *Devināmavilāsa*, 'the delight of the names of the Goddess' ed. Paṇḍit Madhusūdana Kaul Śāstrī. 'Sahib Kaul'—a combination of an Arab-Muslim title with the Hindu designation 'Kaul', viz. a Kashmiri Brahmin belonging to the tantric *kula* or in-group (or just the caste-name Kaul, common in Kashmir—e.g. Pandit Nehru's actual caste-name was Kaul)—was probably the title of a high tantric religious dignitary in Kashmir, rather than the proper name of this prolific tantric teacher. *KSTS*, Vol. LXIII, Srinagar 1942.

Sahib Kaul, *Śrīvidyā-nitya-pūjā-paddhati*, the most important and largest Kashmiri work on the *Śrīvidyā* (q.v.). RASB VIII, 6354.

Śāktapramoda, an anthology of the 'ten great Sciences'—*daśamahāvidyā*, which refers to the *sādhanā* of ten aspects of Śakti; 'Vidyā', theomorphically seen, also simply means any specific goddess in the identification process. This is a very popular work of uncertain authorship. Ch.S.S. 3121/63.

Śaktisādhanā, ed. Pdt. B. Chaudhuri. A Hindi compendium on Śakti worship. Ch.S.S. 3117/63.

Śaktisaṅgama—tantra, ed. B. Bhattacharya, G.O.S. LXI, XCI, CIV, 3 vols., Baroda 1932, 1941, 1947. Together with the *Mahānirvāṇa*, this is the most important Hindu tantra.

Samatantra, ed. Paṇḍit Rāmanāth Dīkṣit. Ch.S.S. 3166/63.

Samayācāratantra, a Buddhist tantric work. RASB, VIII, 5920.

Śaṃkara Āgamācārya (not to be confused with Śaṃkarācārya, though the more conservative identify the two. This author was a Bengali tantric who lived around the mid-seventeenth century.) *Tārārahasyāvārttikā*, a commentary on the famous *Tārārahasyā* (q.v.), a manuscript is in the India Office Library in London (IV, 2603); published in part in the *Savitā Memorial Series*, Varendra Research Museum, Rajshahi, East Pakistan, 1961.

Sāmkṛtyāyana, Rahul, *Siddha Sarāhapāda kṛta dohākośa*, an excellent edition in Hindi, with the Tibetan texts transcribed into Nagari. Though based in part on Shahidullah's work (q.v.), it incorporates much more material. *Bihār Rāsṭrabhāṣā Pariṣad*, Patna 1957.

Santoshji, Sri, *Kaula-kīrtana*, 'litany of the Kaulas', a highly Sanskritized Hindi litany for lay followers of the tantric tradition, composed by a modern tantric. Ch.S.S. 2958/63.

Śarmā, Paṇḍit Caturlal, *Anuṣṭhāna-prakāśa-mahānibandha*, 'exhaustive essay on (tantric) ritualistic institutions', publ. Khemraj Śrīkṛṣṇadāss, Bombay 1951.

Śāstrī, Hīrānanda, 'Origin and Cult of Tārā', Archaeological Survey of India, *Memoir* No. 20.

Śāstrī, Jyotirbhūṣhaṇ V. V. R., 'The Doctrinal Culture and the Tradition of the Siddhas' in *Cultural Heritage of India* (3 vols.), general editor H. D. Bhattacharya. Publ. The Ramakrishna Mission Institute of Culture, Calcutta 1937–1950.

Sātvata-tantram; 'Sātvata' is a somewhat esoteric sectarian name of Viṣṇu. This is the only Vaiṣṇava text called a tantra quite literally. Its introduction says 'this tantra was taught to Śiva by Viṣṇu, and Śiva instructed Nārada (the chief among the divine seers) in it', *etat-tantraṃ nārāyaṇena śivāyopadiṣṭam śivena nāradāyeti granthato jñāyate.* Ch.S.S. 3164/63.

Saundaryallharī, 'the wave of beauty', ascribed to Śaṃkarācārya but, as Norman Brown has shown beyond doubt, certainly not actually written by the famous Śaṃkārācarya. It contains the 'wave of bliss' (*Ānandalaharī*) as its nuclear portion, and is no doubt the most revered classical text on the tantric *Śrīvidyā* q.v. There are many editions of this text, the best Indian one being that edited by Paṇḍit Subbramanyā Śāstrī at the Theosophical Society Library in Madras. However, the first critical edition, collating over forty manuscripts, is the one by W. Norman Brown, *Harvard Oriental Series*, Vol. 43, Cambridge, Mass., 1958.

Scherman, Lucian, 'Siddha; Sanskrit Letters as Mystical Symbols in Later Buddhism Outside India', in K. Bharatha Iyer, ed., *Art and Thought, Festschrift* in honour of Dr. Ananda K. Coomaraswamy on the Occasion of his 70th birthday, 55–62. London 1947.

Schiefner, F. A., *Tārānātha's Geschichte des Buddhismus in Indien*, Kaiserliche Akademie der Wissenschaften, St. Petersburg, Russia, 1869.

Sénart, Émile, 'Bouddhisme et Yoga', *Revue de l'histoire des religions*, Vol. XLII, 345–63, Paris 1900.

Shah, Priyabala, ed. *Mudrā-vicāra-prakaraṇam mudrā-vidhi.* An anthology, critically edited, on treatises and texts on *mudrā* in the (Hindu) sense of 'gestures' accompanying *sādhanā*. Ch.S.S. 3092/63.

Shah, U. P., 'A Peep into the Early History of Tantra in Jaina Literature', in *Bhārata Kaumudī*, Vol. II, Allahabad 1947.

Shahidullah, M., ed. and trl., *Les Chants Mystiques de Kaṇha et de Sarāha; les Dohā-kośa et les Caryā*. Paris 1928; reprinted and edited by L. Misch, Library of Congress, 1958.

Shastri, Dakshinaranjan, 'The Lokāyatikās and the Kāpālikās', *IHQ*, VII, i (1931), 152–37.

Śhāstrī, Hara Prasād (abbreviated H. P. Shastri in the text), *Bauddhagāṇ o Dohā*. An excellent, pioneering study of the early Bengali Buddhist chants, which happen to be the earliest preserved and recorded pieces of Bengali literature. Paṇḍit Hara Prasād Shastri, father of Prof. Benoytosh Bhattacharya, was the first Sanskrit scholar to turn to a serious study of tantric literature. Publ. *Vāṅgīya Śāhityā Pariṣad*, 2nd Ed., Calcutta 1959.

Śhāstrī, Hara Prasād, Catalogue of the Palm Leaf manuscripts in the Durbar Library of His Majesty the King of Nepal, at Khatmandu. Titles from this collection are marked *HPS* (Nepal) in this bibliography. Khatmandu, Nepal, 1906.

Shastri, Paṇḍit Madhusudan Kaul (spelt Śāstrī in two editions only), ed., *The Siddhitrayī and the Pratyabhijña-kārikā-vṛtti* of Rājanaka Utpala Deva, with notes. KSTS XXXIV, Srinagar 1921.

Shastri, Paṇḍit Madhusudan Kaul, *Śrī Mṛgendra Tantram, see Mṛgendra-tantram.*

Shastri, Vidushekhar, 'Sandhābhāṣā', *IHQ*, IV, 2 (1928), 287–96.

Shastry, V. V. Ramana, *see* Śāstrī, Jyotirbhūṣaṇ, V. V. R.

Shivapadasundaram, S., *The Shaiva School of Hinduism*, Madras 1934.

Singh, Mohan, *Gorakhnāth and Medieval Hindu Mysticism*, Lahore 1937.

Sircar, Dinesh C., 'The Śākta Pīṭhas', *JRSAB*, XIV, 1948, 1–108.

Sitikaṇṭha, *Mahānayaprakāśa*, an important text in the Kashmiri tantric tradition, ed. Pdt. Mukunda Rama Sastri, *KSTS*, Vol. XXI, Srinagar 1918.

Śivananda Gosvāmi, *Vidyārṇava*, a manual on the worship of Śakti, and a mystical interpretation of the construction of the city of Vijayanagara in south India; the map of that city is conceived as a *Śrīcakra*, a hypostasized circle of tantric adepts and deities. RASB VIII, 6206.

Śivananda Gosvāmi, *see* also Jagannivāsa.

Śivasūtra, one of the few tantric tracts in the terse *sūtra*-style. See also *Paśupatisūtra*, *Śrīvidyāratnasūtra*, and *Parānandasūtra*, *KSTS*, Vol., 1, Srinagar-Kashmir.

Snellgrove, David L., *The Hevajra Tantra*, 2 vols., London Oriental Series, Oxford University Press, London 1959.

Śrī Rājā Devānanda Siṃha, *Śāktapramodaḥ* (q.v.)

Śrī-cakra-saṃvara (also spelt *-saṃbara*), a Buddhist tantra, ed. by Lama Kazi Dawa-Sandup, *Tantric Texts*, Vol. VII.

Śrī-chinnamastā-nityārcanam, a manual of the worship of the goddess Chinnamastā, 'she with the split skulls'—a magically potent tantric goddess holding her two decapitated heads in her hands catching blood gushing from her trunk with the two mouths. She is worshipped both in Hindu tantrism and in Vajrayāṇa. Ch.S.S. 3134/63.

Śrī-kālī-nityārcanam; invocations, 'amulet'-*mantras*, 'nails' (viz. concluding *bījas*), and hymns for the complete daily worship of the goddess Kālī, the tutelary deity of Bengal in her non-Brahmanical form (Durgā being her high-caste counterpart). This is a sacerdotal manual much in use among tantric non-Brahmin Kālī-worshippers in Bengal, Mithila, and Assam. Ch.S.S. 3131/63.

Śrīnivasa Bhaṭṭa Gosvāmī, (also called Vidyānandanātha, his monastic name). *Caṇḍī-saparyā-krama-kalpāvali*, a detailed work on the formal worship of Caṇḍī (identical with Cāmuṇḍī), a Hindu tantric goddess close to some Bengali groups as well as to Kannaḍa-speaking Hindus in the southern state of Mysore. It is conceivable that the writings and teachings of this author might have formed some sort of liaison between Bengali and south Indian tantric proselytization. RASB VIII, 6404.

Śrīnivāsa Bhaṭṭa Gosvāmī, *Saubhāgya-ratnakara* or *Bhavānī-kara-ratna*, a detailed account of the worship and meditation on the goddess Tripurā, 'the lady of the three cities', a term mythologically loaded in Śaivite tantrism. RASB VIII, 6340–1.

Śrīnivāsa Bhaṭṭa Gosvāmī, *Śivārcana-candrikā*, 'the moonbeam of the worship of Śiva', one of the few purely tantric works of definitely south Indian origin. RASB VIII, 6231.

Śrīnivāsa, *Saubhāgyasubhagodaya*; only one manuscript is known, reported by Prof. Chintaharan Chakravarti, Library of the Maharaja of Alwar in Rajasthan, No. 2445.

Śrīvidyā. The South Indian tradition of tantrism centres almost totally on the *Śrīvidyā* which is the focus of the *Saundaryalaharī* (q.v.); it is perhaps also the only form of tantric thought and worship not suspect to Brahmin orthodoxy. The most important manuals on the *Śrīvidyā* used by the tantric *sādhakas* are the following:

Śrīvidyākhaḍgamālā, 'the garland of *Śrīvidyā* swords', Ch.S.S. 3145/63.

Śrīvidyā-nityārcanam, Ch.S.S. 3146/63.

Srīvidyā-nityāhnikam; this is a large anthology on the *Śrīvidyā* composed and compiled from other sources in part by Cidānandanātha Brahmāśrī Subramanya, a famous Tamilian Śākta. Ch.S.S. 3147/63.

Śrīvidyā-mantra-bhāṣyam, with a commentary *Trikāṇḍasārārthabodhinī*, Ch.S.S. 3150/63.

Śrīvidyāstavamañjarī, a collection of hymns of praise to the *Śrīvidyā*, Ch.S.S. 3150/63.

Śrīvidyāratnasūtra, a work in the terse *sūtra*-style. *Sarasvatī Bhavan Series* Vol. XI, Banaras.

Subramanyaśāstrī, K. S., ed., *Mantraśāstra-mātrikā-granthānām-vivaraṇātmikā sūcikā*, 'a descriptive index of the *mantra*-texts and of *mātrikā*-s (letter-arrangements)'.

This is an excellent, critical and modern catalogue of tantric material in Sanskrit, perhaps the only one of its type available to Indian scholars who do not read any western language. Ch.S.S. 3072/63.

Śukla, Ramādatt, *Hindi Tantrasār*, the Hindi rendition and interpretation of the *Tantrasāra* (q.v.). Kalyan Mandir, Katra-Allahabad 1958.

Sundarācārya (also called Saccidānandanātha, his monastic name), *Lalitārcana-candrikā* and *Laghu-candrikā*, RASB VIII, 6343.

Svacchanda-Tantra; a voluminous work of Kashmiri tantric Śaivism, about as large and important as Abhinavagupta's *Tantrāloka* (q.v.), which, in part at least, shows a close relationship to this work. With Kṣemarāja's commentary '*Uddyotā*', in seven volumes, ed. Paṇḍit Madhusūdan Kaul Śāstrī, *KSTS*, Vols. XXXI, XXXVIII, XLIV, XLVIII, LI, LIII, LVI, Srinagar 1921–35.

Śyāmā-rahasyā-tantram, 'the tantra of the secret of Śyāmā (i.e. Devī)'. Śyāmā is one of the most frequent Bengali epithets of the goddess. This, along with several other short tantric texts, is probably a very recent creation by some learned devotee; no text of this name is mentioned in the traditional lists of tantric texts. The impeccable Sanskrit of this particular text makes it even more suspect. Ch.S.S. 3129/63.

Szasz, Thomas S., *The Myth of Mental Illness*, Harper Bros., New York 1961.

Tajima, R., *Étude sur le Mahāvairocanasūtra*, Paris 1920.

Tantrādhikāri-nirṇayam, 'determination of those who are entitled to do tantric practices', Rājarājeśvarī Press, Varanasi 1945.

Tantrasamuccaya with an exposition by Śaṃkara (not *Śaṃkarācārya*) and a commentary by his disciple Narāyaṇa, 2 parts, Ch.S.S. 2995/63.

Tārārahasyā and *Tārārahasyāvārttikā*, *see* Śaṃkara Āgamācārya.

Tārātantram, collected and edited by Giriscandra Vedāntatīrtha. This text is Hindu-Śākta on the surface, but has strong Vajrayāṇa overtones of which the editor is probably not conscious. Tārā in the form here described is identical with the Tibetan Tārā (*sgrol ma*); 'Tārā' itself is an epithet both of the archetypal Buddhist goddesses (*Prajña*) and of the Hindu Śakti. Ch.S.S. 3004/63.

Tarkatīrtha, Pārvatī Caraṇa, ed. *Kālivilāsa Tantra* (q.v.), *Tantric Texts VI*, Luzac, London 1917.

Thākur, Devanāth, *Mantrakaumudī*; another *mantra*-manual, smaller in size and less popular than the *Mantramuktāvali* (q.v.). Ch.S.S. 3066/63.

Thomas, P., *Kāmakalā—The Indian Ritual of Love*. Taraporevala, Bombay 1956.

Thompson, E. J., and Spencer, A. M., trl. and ed., *Bengali Religious Lyrics: Śākta*. The Heritage of India Series, London, Oxford University Press, 1923.

Toḍalātantra, ed. Paṇḍit Bhadraśīla Śarmā. A work of the 'little tradition'; Toḍalā is the name of some village deity not even listed in the standard Sanskrit dictionaries. Like most of the little-deity tantras, it deals very largely with charms, spells, witchcraft, and projective magic. Ch.S.S. 3009/63.

Tripurā-sāra-samuccaya-tantram, a small text of the Tripurā group. Ch.S.S. 3012/64.

Tripurārahasyam; the 'mystery' (which is the common term for an intensive eulogistic treatment of any topic or deity) of the goddess Tripurā, a synonym of Śakti as Śiva's spouse, in her aspect as the destructress of the demon Tripura 'of the three cities', a loaded

Śākta mythologeme. With a partial Hindi translation and commentary. Ch.S.S. 3010–1/63.

Tucci, Giuseppe, '*Apropos* the Legend of Naropa', *JRAS*, 1935, 677–88.

Tucci, Giuseppe, *Indo-Tibetica*, 4 volumes, Rome, 1932–41.

Tucci, Giuseppe, 'Mcod rten' e 'tsha tsha' nel Tibet Indiano ed Occidentale; contributo allo studio dell' arte religiosa tibetana a del suo significatio' in the above, Vol. I, Pt. 1.

Tucci, Giuseppe, *Theory and Practice of Maṇḍala*, Rider & Co., London 1961.

Tucci, Giuseppe, *Tibetan Painted Scrolls*. Two very large, very beautiful, very expensive volumes. Rome, 1949.

Tucci, Giuseppe, 'Some Glosses upon the *Guhyasamāja*', *Mélanges Chinois et Bouddhiques*, Vol. III, 339–53, Brussels 1934–5.

Uḍḍamareśvara-tantra, ed. Paṇḍit Jagad Dhar; a text of magical rites *KSTS*, Vol. LXX, Srinagar 1947.

Uḍḍīśatantra, edited with a Hindi translation and commentary by Paṇḍit Śyāmsundarlāl Tripāṭhi of Muradabad, publ. Lakṣmīveṅkateśvar Press, Kalyan-Bombay 1954.

Ūmānandanātha, *Nityotsava*, a supplement to the *Paraśurāma Kalpasūtra* (q.v.), ed. Paṇḍit A. Mahadeva Śāstri, revised and enlarged by Swami Trivikrama Tīrtha, 3rd ed., re-issue, G.O.S. XXIII, Baroda 1948.

Upādhyay, B. S., 'Erotic Scenes on the Temples of Orissa', *Journal of Benares Hindu University*, Vol. V., 1940, 227–36.

Vaidyanātha, *Bhuvaneśvarīkalpalatā*, 'the wish-fulfilling creeper-plant of the "Lady of the Earth" '—Bhuvaneśvarī, the tutelary deity of Orissa; a tantric digest. RASB, VIII, 6383.

Vaidyarāj, Paṇḍit Vanshidhar Sukul 'Tantraśāstrī', *Vāmamārg*, 'the left-handed path', Hindi and Sanskrit, Kalyan Mandir, Katra-Allahabad 1951.

Vāmakeśvara-tantra, with *Nityaṣodaśīkārnava* (q.v.), and Bhāskararāya's commentary 'Setubandha' (bridge-maker); ed. Paṇḍit Kashinath Shastri Agashe, AAS No. 56, Bombay 1908.

Vāmakeśvarīmatam, with the commentary of Rājanaka Jayaratha, ed. Paṇḍit Madhusūdan Kaul Śāstri, *KSTS*, Vol. LXVI, Srinagar 1945.

Van Gulik, R.H., *Sexual Life in Ancient China*. With an appendix on Indian and Chinese Sexual Mysticism. E. J. Brill, Leiden 1964.

Van Manen, Johan, ed., *Minor Tibetan Texts*, No. 1: The Song of the Eastern Snow Mountain. *Bibliotheca Indica*, New Series No. 1426, Calcutta 1919.

Vandemātaram, 'the secret essence of the great *mantra* 'Vande Mātaram' (hail to thee, O Mother India). A modern tantric interpretation of Bankim Chatterji's famous national song which would have become the national anthem of independent India but for its difficult language and its unwieldy music. The *Vandemātaram* was composed in the late eighties of the last century, and proscribed by the British Government for a long time as 'incitive to violence'. Ch.S.S. 3107/63.

Varivasyārahasyam with the commentary by Bhāsurānandanātha. A large Hindu tantric text. Ch.S.S. 3108/63.

Varma, K. B. 'Khajuraho' (in Bengali), in *Prābāsi*, Vol. XXXI, Pt. II, Calcutta 1938, 89–95.

Vātulanātha-Sūtras with the *Vṛtti* of Ānandaśaktipāda, edited with an English translation, by Paṇḍit Madhusudan Kaul Śāstrī, *KSTS* No. 29, Srinagar 1923.

Vedāntatīrtha, Swami, *Sāvitrīprakāśa*, a tantric exegesis of the *Gāyatrimantra*. Ch.S.S. 3169/63.

Vidyāratna, Tārānātha, ed., *Tantrābhidhāna* with *Bījanighaṇṭu* and *Mudrānighanṭu*, *Tantric Texts* I, Calcutta 1913.

Vīratantra, RASB, VIII.

Viśvanath Singh, Maharaja of Rewa (Vindhya Pradesh), Central India (ruled until 1854). Though a devotee of the very un-tantric Rāma, he wrote some tantric treatises with a stress on *mantras* pertaining to Rāma, the seventh incarnation of Viṣṇu. The geographical proximity of the Khajuraho complex to Rewa may have something to do with this spiritual sideline of the ruler. *Mantrārthanirṇaya*, RASB VIII, 6494.

Waddell, L. A., 'The Dhāraṇī Cult in Buddhism. Its Origin, deified Literature and Images'. *Ostasiatische Zeitschrift* I, 155–95, Berlin 1921.

Waddell, L. A., 'The Indian Buddhist Cult of Avalokita and his Consort Tārā', *JRAS*, London 1894, 51–89.

Waddell, L. A., *The Buddhism of Tibet or Lamaism*. London 1895.

Wadiyar, Jayachamaraja, the present Governor, former Maharaja of Mysore. *Dattātreya*. Publ. G. Allen & Unwin, London 1960.

Ward, R. H., *A Drugtaker's Note*; a description of the author's experiences under L.S.D.-25. V. Gollancz, London 1959.

Watts, Alan W., general editor. *Patterns of Myth*, in three volumes. Vol. III, *The Two Hands of God—The Myths of Polarity* is highly relevant to tantrism. This is a popular, informative, and good presentation in the form of a well-selected anthology with critical commentary by such scholars as Charles A. Long, M. Oakes, a. o. Publ. G. Braziller, New York 1963.

Winternitz, M., 'Notes on the *Guhyasamāja-Tantra* and the Age of the Tantras', *IHQ*, IX/1, 1933, 1–10.

Woodroffe, Sir John, *see* Avalon, Arthur.

Yoginī-tantra, edited with a Hindi translation by Paṇḍit Kanhaiyalal Mishra. Publ. Gaṅgāviṣṇu Śrīkṛṣṇadas, Kalyan-Bombay 1957.

Zannas, E. and Auboyer, J. vd. Auboyer, J.

Zimmer, H., *The Art of Hindu Asia*, 2 volumes, Bollingen Series, New York 1955.

Zimmer, H., *Ewiges Indien*, Publ. Mueller & Kiepenhauer, Potsdam, and Orell Füssli Verlag, Zürich 1930 (19, 188, 219).

Zimmer, H., *The Philosophies of India*, Meridan G6, New York 1958.

Zimmer, H., 'Zur Bedeutung des Indischen Tantra-Yoga', *Eranos Jahrbuch*, Vol. I., Zürich 1933, 9–94.

INDEX

This index consists of three parts—Subjects and Modern Authors (A), Indian Terms and Names (B), and Tibetan Terms and Names (C). The bracketed cross-references in part A refer to the Indian Terms and Names section only. Titles and authors not listed in the Index may be found in the preceding Bibliographical Selection.

I have followed the Roman alphabetical arrangement advisedly, both in the Indian and the Tibetan indices, for the benefit of the majority of the readers who do not know Sanskrit or Tibetan. I use the term 'Indian', as it covers Sanskrit and several other Indian languages.

Risking the wrath of the more snobbish among the Tibetologists, again for the benefit of the lay reader, I have arranged the Tibetan terms in the Roman alphabet by their first grapheme, *not* by their first phoneme; thus, although *sku* is pronounced '*ku*' in Tibetan, it is listed under 's'; a procedure which, though not very elegant, will aid the majority of readers to trace the Indian and the English equivalents of the Tibetan terms.

Items which would have called for over one hundred entries are not listed at all (i.e. Hindu, Buddhist, tantra, etc.) and where there are over twenty occurrences, '*et passim*' has been added to the first few listings.

I believe pronunciation guides are redundant in books of this sort, as any guide to the correct pronunciation of Indian, and particularly of Tibetan, words would be long, necessarily technical, and totally beside the purpose of a study like ours.

A. *Index of Subjects and Modern Authors*

ABSOLUTE, *see brahman, paramārtha, vajra*
activity, 208 sq.
afferent terms, 173 sqq.
Aggrawala, V. S., 80, 153, 305
Ahmednagar, 88
Albiruni, 98
Allport, F. H., 57
Almora, 63 sq., 66, 96
analytical philosophy, 14, 151
Anand, Mulkraj, 305
anthropology, 279 sqq.
Apabhraṃśa, 289
Ardhamāgadhi, 301
Ārya Samāj, 104, 198
askesis, 197
Assam, 66, 196, 231, 249
asymmetrical classification, 128

Auboyer, J., 305
Avalon, Arthur, *see* Woodroff, Sir John
Ayer, A. J., 14, 42, 102

BAGCHI, P. C., 65, 70 sq., 167 sq.
Balkh, 71
Banaras, 90, 92
Banerjee, P. K., 166
Bengal, 66, 136
Bhagavadgitā, 9, 27, 232
Bhagavan Dass, 129
Bhārati, Swami Viśvānanda, 18, 31
Bhattacharya, Benoytosh, 21 sq., 24, 38, 65, 206 sq.
Bhattacharya, Vajraratna, 142 sqq.
Bhattacharya, Vidushekhara, 166 sq.
Bhils, 152
Bhojpur, 136
Bhuṭiyā, 64 sq.
Blue Annals, 38
Bodhisattva, 92, 177 sqq., 210, 266
Bon, 65, 100, 172, 221
Bose, D. N., 153, 182
Bradley, F. H., 13 sq., 36
brāhmaṇas, 160
Brindāvan, 90
Broad, C. D., 14, 35, 56
Brown, W. Norman, 210 sq., 225, 258, 276
Buddhist Hybrid Sanskrit, 70, 105, 140, 163, 194
Burma, 104
Burnouf, E., 167

CAMBODIA, 159
cannabis Indica, 301, and *see bhāṅg, gāñja, vijayā*
Carstairs, G. M. C., 251
Cārvākas, 114
Caryāpāda-s, 91
caste, *see jāti, varṇa*
causality, *see hetu*
celibacy, 162, 293
Chakravarti, Chintaharan, 10, 302
Chandella, 63
Charlesworth, M. J., 152
Chatterji, Suniti K., 158, 224
Chinmayananda, Swami, 281
Chittagong, 196
Christ, Jesus, 157, 286
circumambulation, 190, *see pradakṣiṇā*
classification of *mantras*, *see* formal, symmetrical, asymmetrical, isomorphemic, heteromorphemic, material
clerodendrum syphonantum, 91
cognition, *see manas, jñāna*
coitus, 72, 176 sqq., 203, 251 sq., 265, and *see maithuna, pañcamakāra*
Collingwood, R. G., 56
conation, 297
concentration, 155, and *see samādhi, dhyāna*
consciousness, *see vijñāna*
constituents, *see dhātu*
creatio ex nihilo, 212
'culture and personality', 21, 279

D'ALVIELLA, G., 100
Danielou, A., 301
Darjeeling, 71
Dasgupta, N. N., 108, 153
Dasgupta, S. B., 10, 15, 222
Dasgupta, S. N., 232
Dayānanda Sarasvatī, Swami, 153
demons, *see ḍakiṇī, yakṣa*
dependent origination, *see pratītya samutpāda*
Devanāgarī, 254 sqq.
Dhammapāda, 9, 181
dhāraṇi, 113 sqq., 255 sqq.
dhyāni-Buddhas, 23
dialectic reconciliation, *see samanvaya*
Diehl, K. G., 110, 140, 156

dispositions, 229 sqq., and *see bhāva*
Dravidian, 94, 202
dynamis, 200 sqq., 221 sq.

EDGERTON, F., 13, 176, 183 sq., 301
efferent terms, 173 sqq.
Ekajaṭā, 38, 134, 210 sq.
Eleadic, 28
eleocarpus ganitrus, 153 sq., 165 sqq., 180 sq., 210, 303, and *see rudrākṣa*
Eliade, Mercia, 10, 12, 90 sq. 108, 153 sq, 165 sqq, 180 sq., 210, 303
Ensinck, J., 57
enstasy, 165 sqq., 290, and *see samādhi*
Erdmann, J. E., 13, 55
erotic ritual, 24, 68 sqq., 72, 79, 292 sqq., and *see maithuna vāmācāra, pañcamakāra*
erotic sculpture, 213
eulogy, 232
exercitium, *see sādhanā*
existence, *see bhāva*

FORMAL classification, 128 sq.
Frauwallner, E., 48

GANDHI, M. K., 11
Ganges, 92, 196
Ganguly, D. C., 64
Garbiang, 64, 96
Gayā, 196
Ghilḍayāl, Paṇḍit, 232 sqq.
Ghoshal, U. N., 80
Glasenapp, H. v., 13, 19, 37 109, 154
Gorakhpur, 63, 287
Gordon, Antoinette, 302
Govinda, Lama Anagarika, 106, 133, 153, 167, 302
Guenther, Herbert V., 10, 16, 30, 35 sq., 54, 110, 154 sq., 286
Guha, B. S., 224
Gujarat, 148

HADANO, H., 218 sq.
Haldar, H. L., 153
haṭha-yoga, 240 sq.
Hauer, F. W., 152
Hegel, G. W. F., 13 sq.
Heidegger, M., 28
Hellenism, 28 sq.
hetaira, 236
heteromorphemic, 130, 137
Hindi, 116, 138, 145
Hindu Renaissance, 281 sqq.
Hoffmann, H., 37, 65, 183
human meat, 174
Hurvitz, L. N., 12
hypostasization, 90 sq.

IBN BATUTA, 64
iconography, 214 sqq., 249
illusion, *see pratibhāsa*
illumination, *see bodhi*
incense, 244 sqq.
incest, 171
Ingalls, Daniel H., 14
ingredients, 126, and *see padārtha*
initiation, *see dīkṣā*
intentional language, 164 sqq., and *see sandhābhāṣā*
intuition, *see jñāna*
isomorphemic, 130, 138

JACOBS, H., 302
Jainism, 13, 60, 95, 112, 121, 130, 139
Jhā, Paṇḍit Lakṣmināth, 24
Jung, C. G., 291

KANT, I., 13 sq., 36
Kanyā Kumāri, 99
Kashmir, 147
Kavirāj, Paṇḍit Gopināth, 101, 130, 250
Kerala, 89, 136, 231
Khajuraho, 63, 201, 299

Kolapur, 88
Konarak, 299
Koppers, W., 152
Kramrisch, St., 227
Kunga Labrang, Lama, 59

LANGER, Susan K., 36
lefthanded rites, *see* erotic ritual, *vāmācāra*
Leifer, Ronald, 294
Li, Fang-Kuei, 153
libation, *see tarpana, arghya*
Liṅgāyats, 187, and *see Vīraśivites*
liquor, *see mada, pañcamakāra*
logic, *see tarka, nyāya*
Lokāyatas, 114
Lokesh Chandra, 182
lysergic acid diathelymide (LSD-25), 286 sq., 300 sq.

Mādhyamikas, 17, 21, 23, 25, 29
Maharashtra, 231
Majumdar, R. C., 80 sq., 107, 153
malevolent rites, *see abhicāra, ṣaṭkarma*
Mānasarovar, 96
marijuana, *see vijayā, bhāṅg*
material classification, 128 sq.
matter, *see vastu*
meat, *see māṃsa*
menstrual fluid, *see rajas*
mind, *see citta, manas, vijñāna*
Mithila, 136, 287
Mohammed, 286
Mongolia, 61, 70
Monier Williams, Sir M., 86 sqq., 103 sqq.
monism, *see advaita*
Moore, G. E., 102
'motility', 155
Mount Abu, 95 sq.
Muhammad-bin-Tughlaq, 64
Muslim, 186
mystical cognition, *see samādhi, turīya*

NĀLANDĀ, 62, 159
Nebesky-Wojkowitz, R., 65, 220
Nepal, 60 sqq., 287
Newland, Constance C., 300
Nietzsche, F., 234
Nilgiris, 186
Norbu, Th., 224

OLDENBERG, H., 46
onomatopoeia, 138
Opler, Morris, 251 sq.

PĀLA dynasty, 63 sq.
Pāli, 9, 108, 123, 181, 301
Palni, 86
Pāṇini, 305
Passin, H. W., 12
passivity, 208 sq.
Patañjali, 239 sq., 293 sq.
penis, 173 sqq., 181, 210, and *see liṅga, vajra*
phenomenal existence, *see saṃvṛti, vyavahāra*
poetics, 206
polarity, male-female, 199 sqq.
Poppe, N. N., 227
Popper, K. R., 298
Potter, K., 14, 40, 42
Prior, A. N., 54, 57
Puri, 147

QALANDAR Shah, Baba, 152, 186

RADHAKRISHNAN, Dr. S., 11, 13
Raghavan, Dr. V., 239, 301
Raju, Dr. P. T., 13
Ramakrishna Paramahaṃsa, 191, 267, 290
Ramana Maharishi, 191

Rammohun Roy, 157
relativity, *see saṃvṛti*
Roerich, G. N., 36, 101, 227
rosary, *see rudrākṣa*
Rottleria tinctoria, 77
Roy, M. N., 284
Russell, Bertrand, 14, 34, 42, 153

SACRED cord, 150
St. Augustine, 28
salvation, *see mukti, nirvāṇa, kaivalya*
Sanskritization, 282 sq.
Santhals, 93
Śāstri, Paṇḍit Madhusūdan Kaul, 305
Saunders, Dale, 270
self, *see ātman*
semen virile, 174 sqq.
Shahidullah, M., 165 sqq., 212
Shastri, Paṇḍit Hara Prasad, 22, 166 sqq.
Shivananda, Swami, 281
Sholapur, 88
Shukla, Paṇḍit Ramādatt, 195
Sircar, D., 86 sqq., 98 sq.
Snellgrove, D. L., 10, 165 sqq., 182 sq., 278
Srinivas, M. N., 202
Stcherbatsky, Th., 13
Strawson, P. F., 14, 153
'substitutes', 228, and *see pratinidhi*
'suchness', *see tathatā*
Swat Valley, 88, 222
Śyāmānanda, Pañḍit Kaulakalpataru, 210
symmetrical classification, 128
Syrian Christians, 62
Szasz, Th. S., 301

TAGHLAKOT, 64, 96
Tamilnad, 136
Thailand, 104, 159
Theravāda, 289
Thomism, 28
Todas, 186
topography, 88 sqq.
Tripathi, R. P., 158
Tucci, G., 10, 58, 65, 222 sq., 286
Tukhāra, 63

ÜBERWEG, F., 13
Ullmann, St., 14
Upaniṣads, 9, 19, 97, 112, 117, 194, 243, 266, 288 sqq., *et passim*
urine, 174

VAIDYARĀJ, Paṇḍit, 250 sqq.
Vaiṣṇavas, 142, 145 sqq., 241
Vajrayāna Buddhism, 19, 27, 94, 143, 168, 201, 254 sqq., *et passim*
Veatch, H. B., 14
Veda, 94, 103, 140, 147, 153, 160, 243, 266 *et passim*
Vedānta, 11, 17, 24, 26, 29, 154, 281
Viraśivism, 187, 192, 198
Vivekananda, Swami, 10, 191, 270, 281, 289
volition, 297
vulva, 170 sqq., 210

WARD, R. H., 300
Wayman, Alexander, 286
Wilhelm, Hellmut, 11, 220 sq., 302
Wisdom, J., 14, 34, 102
Wittgenstein, L., 102
Woodroff, Sir John, 9, 109, 140, 154, 305 sq.
Wylie, T. V., 181

YAMUNĀ, 92, 176
yogi, 30, 36, *et passim*

ZAHOR, 222
Zen, 9, 299
Zia Barni, 64
Zimmer, H., 106, 153, 217, 217 sq.

B. *Indian Terms and Names*

ABHAYAKARAGUPTA, 304
abhicāra, 144
Abhidharmakośa, 47
Abhinavagupta, 193, 304 sq.
abisārikā, 206
ācāra, 65, 68
ācārya, 229
ādhāra, 249 sqq.
adhikāra, 189, 291
advaita, 21 sqq.
advaya, 200
Advayavajra, 22, 26, 37, 49, 305
Advayavajrasaṃgraha, 290, 305
Aghora, 162
Aghoritantra, 305
Akoracivacariyar, 192
Akṣobhya, 70, 74
ālayavijñāna, 48
Amoghasiddhi, 133
Amṛtānandanātha, 305
amṛtatraya, 293
Ānandalaharī, 137
anuttara, 244 sq.
Aparājitā, 203, 214, 224
apratiṣṭhita, 218 sq.
asparas, 125
Ardhanārīśvara, 24
arghya, 247 sqq..
āsana, 126, 144, 248 sqq.
Asaṅga, 26
Aśvaghoṣa, 209
Aśvins, 273
Atharvaveda, 67, 116
ātman, 19, 25
Auṣadhīśvara, 287
avadhūtī, 92, 291
āyatana, 30
Ayodhya, 90

BADARĪKAŚRAMA, 147
Bālāṃbikā, 99
Bhairavayāmala, 235
Bhairavī, *see* Śakti
bhāṅg, 253 sq., 301
bhāva, 54 sq., 211, 229 sqq.
Bhavāni, 88
Bhoṭa, 61 sqq.
Bhusukapāda, 29
bhūtaśuddhi, 112, 122, 246 sqq., 262
bīja, 111, 116, 131 sqq., 256 sq., 271
bodhi, 19, 164 sqq., *et passim*
bodhicitta, 174 sqq., 206 sq., 225, 265, 293
bola, 174 sq., 183
brahmacaryam, 162, 293
brahman, 17, 19, 23, 255, *et passim*
Bṛhaspati, 114

CĀMUṆḌĪ, 94
Caitanya, 188
cakreśvara, 260
Caṇḍālī, 175
Caṇḍī, 94, 267
Catuṣpīṭhatantra, 88
Causaṭṭhi Devi, 138
cīnācāra, 60 sqq., 241 sq.
Cīnadesa, 60 sqq.
citta, 30, 44 sqq.

ḍākiṇī, 133
Dakṣa, 86 sq.
dakṣiṇā, 189
dakṣiṇācāra, 179, 228, sqq.
daṇḍavat, 190
Dārada, 63
darśan(a), 188, 198

Daśāśvamedha Ghāṭ, 138
Dattātreyapīṭha, 186
deva, 43
dhāraṇa, 189
dharmakāya, 50 sq.
dhātu, 30
Ḍhūmrā, 255
dhvani, 109
dhyāna, 202
dīksā, 156 sq., 185 sqq.
divya, 229 sqq.
Ḍombī, 175
Durgā, 119, 195
Dvāraka, 147 sq.
dvārapālaka, 95

ekāgratā, 155
Ekajaṭā, 38, 134, 210 sq.

GAHAḌĀVALA, 64
gandharva, 215
Gandharvatantra, 249
Gaṇeśa, 127, 195, 203, *et passim*
gauṇa, 170, 290
Gautamītantra, 250
Gāyatrī, 113, 147, 162, 247, *et passim*
Gheraṇḍā-saṃitā, 250
Gorakhnāth, 66, 148 sqq., 239, 289, *et passim*
Guhyasamājatantra, 30, 52, 75, 136, 141, 177 sqq., 182 sq., 214
guru, 122, 187 sq., 240 sqq., *et passim*
gurukula, 195
Guhyasiddhi, 184

hādi-mantra, 128 sqq., *et passim*
Hariharānanda, 157
Harśa, 63
Hemāṃbikā, 99
hetu, 52
Hevajratantra, 88, 92, 174 sqq., 219
homa (*havana*), 126

icchā, 297
iḍā, 175 sqq., 247, 292
Indrabhūti, 183, 200
Īśāna, 23
iṣṭa (*devatā*), 214

JALANDHARĀ, 88 sqq.
Jaṃbudvīpaprajñapti, 60
japa, 76 sqq., 115, 129, 131 sqq., 156, 249 sqq., 256, *et passim*
jāti, 233
jñāna, 15, 19, 296, *et passim*
Jñānasiddhi, 183, 296
Jvālamukhī, 86

kādi-mantra, 218 sqq.
Kailāsa, 78, 96
kaivalya, 34
kakkola, 174 sqq., 183
kālacakra, 21, 37, 222 sq.
Kālacakrayāna, 153
Kalhāṇa, 63
Kāli, 210
Kālidāsa, 243
Kaliñjara, 174
Kālīvilāsatantra, 71, 231, 267
kāma, 158
Kāmakhyatantra, 278
Kāmaratnatantra, 131
Kāmarūpa, 87 sqq.
kāmaśāstra, 203
Kāmeśvarī, 89
kanchuli, 251
Kaṇha, 29
kaṇkanam, 192
kapāla, 172 sq.
kappu, 192
Kāraṇḍavyūha, 305
Karpurādistotram, 71 sqq., 136, 141, 157
karuṇa, 208 sq., 212 sq.
Kāśī, 64

Kāśīviṣālākṣi-tantra, 135 sq.
kaula, 71, 237
Kaulāvlinirṇaya, 141, 259, 277
kavaca, 102, 118
kāya, 222 sq.
Khuḍḍakapāṭha, 153
Kirātārjunīya, 163
krānta, 61, 71
kriyā, 297
Kṛṣṇa, 135, 146
Kubjikātantra, 66
kula, 194, 233 sqq.
Kulacūḍāmaṇitantra, 214 sq., 235, *et passim*
Kulārṇavantantra, 71, 269, *et passim*
Kumārasaṃbhava, 243
kumārīpūjā, 136, 160
kuṇḍalinī, 260 sqq., 291

LAKṢMĪ, 61, 117, 162, *et passim*
Lakṣmīṃkarā, 200
lalanā, 175 sq., 292
Lalitā, 61, 162
Lalitāditya, 63
Laṅkāvatārasūtra, 181
laya, 122
liṅga, 126, 192, 296, *et passim*
Locanā, 133
Lokeśvara, 134

mada, 240 sqq.
Mahabhārata, 86
Mahācīna, 60 sqq.
Mahākāla, 216
mahāmudrā, 194, 215 sq., *et passim*
Mahānirvāṇatantra, 66, 151, 171, 194, 244, 263
Mahāpīṭhapurāṇa, *see Pīṭhanirṇaya*
Mahāsanghikas, 104
mahāsukha, 206 sqq., 292
maithuna, 70, 203, 235, 244 sqq., 265 sq.
makāra, *see pañcamakāra*
māṃsa, 243 sqq.
manas, 47 sq.
maṇḍala, 118 sqq., 151, 254 sqq., *et passim*
Maṇipadmā, 134
Mañjuśrī, 219
Mañjuśrimūlakalpa, 141, 154
mantra, 9, 101 sqq., *et passim*
Mantramahārṇava, 123, 137
Mantramahodadhi, 90 sqq., 112, 123, 127, 244
Mantramuktāvali, 142 sqq.
māraṇa, 156
Marīcī, 255
māsaphalam, 143
mātrikā, 264, 273 sq.
Matsyendranāth, 149 sq., 224, 238, 289, *et passim*
māyā, 24, 225 sq.
Māyāvatī, 89 sqq., 99
Meru, 70, 79
mṛtyuñjaya, 132
mudrā, 112, 127, 142, 242 sqq., 293, *et passim*
mukhya, 170, 290
mukti, 34, 173, 256, *et passim*
Mukunda, 146
mūlādhāra, 17, 263
mūlamantra, 132

NĀDAPĀDA, 154 sq.
Nāgārjuna, 214
naimittika, 288
Nairātmyā, 25
Nārāyaṇa, 146
nirukta, 117
nirvāṇa, 34, 217, 292, *et passim*
Niṣpannayogāvali, 37, 304
nitya, 288
nyāsa, 91, 124, 264, 273 sq., *et passim*

ODDIYĀNA, 64, 88 sqq., 200, 222, 254, *et passim*
Oḍṛā, *see* Oḍḍiyāna

PADMAVAJRA, 184
Padmavatīkalpa (*sūtra*), 139
pañcamakāra, 24, 68 sqq., 232 sqq., 252 sqq.
paramahaṃsa, 147, 162
paramārtha, 18, 285 sq.
Paraśiva, 173, 215
Pārvatī, 66, 243
paśu, 68, 229 sqq., *et passim*
Paśupati, 230, and *see* Siva
pātra, 189, 253 sqq.
Periyapurāṇam, 213
phalaśruti, 282
Pheṭkāriṇī-tantra, 60
piṅgalā, 175 sqq., 247, 292
pīṭha, 69 sqq., 86 sqq., 124
pīṭhanirṇaya, 88 sqq.
prabhāsvara, 36
pradakṣiṇā, 93 sqq.
prajñā, 115, 170 sqq., 201 sqq., 206 sq., 292, *et passim*
Prajñāpārāmitā, 88, 202, 219
Prajñopāyaviniścayasiddhi, 184
prakṛti, 113, 204, 212
prāṇa, 155
prāṇāyāma, 189, 270, 274, 294
prasāda, 85 sq.
pratibhāsa, 22
pratinidhi, 229 sqq.
pratiṣtha, 160
pratītya-samutpāda, 22, 53
Pūrṇeśvari, 89
puruṣa, 204, 212

RĀGHAVABHAṬṬA, 249 sq.
rajas, 176 sqq.
Rājataraṅgiṇī, 63
Rāma (candra), 123, 146
Rāmānuja, 19, 142, 188
Rāmāyaṇa, 145
rasanā, 178 sqq., 292
Rāvaṇa, 123
Reṇukā, 88
Rudra, 135
rudrākṣa, 126, 196, 230, 256
Rudrayāmala, 227, 230 sq., 244, 271

Śabdakalpadruma, 98
sādhaka, 228 sqq., *et passim*
sādhanā, 18, 34, 68 sqq., 219 sq., 228 sqq., *et passim*
Sādhanāmālā, 73 sqq., 98, 132, 141
Sadyojāta, 23, 149
sahasranāma, 61
sajaha(*yāna*), 29, 88, 168, 213 sq.
Śākinī, 161
Śākta, 17, 41, 112, 142, 171, 194, 231, *et passim*
Śakti, 17, 66 sqq., 91, 109, 115, 124, 202, 210, *et passim*
Śaktisaṅgama-tantra, 75
samādhi, 110, 148, 171, 290
samanvaya, 18
samarasa, 176 sq., 212
samaya, 192
Śaṃbhalā, 222
Śaṃkarācārya, 17, 19, 26, 36, 75, 117, 211, 268
sāṃkhya, 176, 204 sq., 212
Sammohatantra, 70, 250
saṃsāra, 217
samvṛti, 18, 30
sandhābhāṣā, 92, 118, 137, 164 sqq., 209
sandhi, 161
sandhyā, 166 sq., 246, 271 sq.
Śāntideva, 255
Sarāha(pāda), 29, 35, 92, 200, 301
Sarasvatī, 61, 149, 230, 247
Saṭcakranipūraṇa, 291

Satī, 87 sqq.
ṣaṭkarma, 156
Saundaryalaharī, 36, 137, 211
Sekoddeśaṭīkā, 154
siddha, 28 sq., 127, 230, *et passim*
siddhi, 67, 71, 120, 124, 127, 196, 230, 256, 295
śīla, 233
Sitikaṇṭha, 24
Śiva, 17, 23, 61, 66, 70, 87 sqq., 93, 191 sqq., 230 sq., *et passim*
Śivasahasranāma, 300
spanda, 117
Śrihaṭṭa, 90 sqq.
Śrīnagar, 147
Śriṅgeri, 147
Śrīvidyā, 162, 258, 276, *et passim*
stambhana, 156
stava, 110
sthānalakṣaṇa, 126
Stiramati, 57
stūpa, 90
śukra, 174 sqq.
Sumaṅgalavilāsinī, 182
śūnya, 17, 22, 121, 208 sq., *et passim*
śūnyatā, 19, 24, 173, 213 sqq., *et passim*
sūrya, 293
suṣumnā, 175 sqq., 247
Suvarṇadvīpa, 62 sq.
svabhāva, 51 sq.

Tantrāloka, 158
Tantrarāja-tantra, 141
Tantrasāra, 98, 193, 272, 304 sq.
Tārā, 60 sq., 78, 126, 132, 210, *et passim*
Tārānātha, 63
Tārāsvarūpatattva, 210
Tārātantra, 66
tarka, 66
tarpana, 93 sqq., 248 sqq.
tathatā, 53, 217
Tathāgata, 49, 170
Tathāgataguhyaka, *see Guhyasamāja-tantra*
Tatpuruṣa, 23
tilaka, 126
tīrtha, 86 sqq.
trayi, *see Veda*
trikāya, 30
Tulsīdās, 145 sq.
turīya, 148

uccāṭana, 143, 156
upanayana, 193 sq.
upāya, 173 sqq., 208 sq., 212 sq., 295, *et passim*

VĀGDHARĀ, 136 sq.
Vahni, 127
Vairocana, 133, 177 sq., 255, *et passim*
Vājasaneyi-saṃhitā, 116
vajra, 76 sq., 173 sqq., *et passim*
Vajracchedikā, 181
Vajrasattva, 210
Vajravarāhī, 202, 209, 224
Vajrayoginī, 60, 201
Vāk, *see Sarasvatī*
Vakratuṇḍa, 128
vāmācāra, 179, 288 sqq., *et passim*
Vāmadeva, 23
Vāradātantra, 157
Varāhītantra, 195
varṇa-vicāra, 144
Varuṇa, 117
vaśīkaraṇa, 156
Vasiṣṭha, 69 sqq., 238 sqq.
vastu, 51 sq.
Vāyu, 155
vidveṣaṇa, 156
Vidyā, 210
vijayā, 235 sqq., 287, *et passim*
vijñāna, 47 sqq., *et passim*
Vijñānavāda, 29

Vikramaśīla, 62, 159
Vimalānanda, 128
Vindhyā, 61
vīra, 229 sqq.
virajāhoma, 162
Viṣṇu, 87, 93, 103, 127, 205, 243, *et passim*
Visphuliṅgiṇī, 255
Viśvasāratantra, 109, 154
vyavahāra, 18, 281, 285
yakṣa, 125
yāmala, 102, 118, 244
Yāska, 117
Yaśovarman, 63 sq.
yogācāra, 48
Yogasūtra, 294
Yogeśvarī, 88
Yoginī, 88, 125, 133
yuga, 143 sqq.
yuganaddha, 218, 241, 265, 294

C. *Tibetan Terms and Names*

bdgad med ma, 25, 175, 207 sq.
bdud rtsi gsum, 293
bka' rgyud pa, 65
'brel, see rten 'brel
brkyaṅ ma, 175 sq., 247, 292
Buston, 78
byaṅ chub kyi sems, 265, 293
bza' ba, 174

chaṅ ba, 174
chos kyi sku, 31, 50 sq.

dbus ma, 291
de bžin gśegs pa, 175
de bžin ñid, 53
dgoṅs pa, 168
dṅos po, 54 sq.
'dus kyi khor lo, 37, 155, 222 sq.

gci ba, 174
Gelugpa (*dge lugs pa*), 297
'gro ba, 174
gsal, 36
g'yun mo, 175
gzuṅs sṅags, 106

KANJUR (*bka' gyur*), 303
kha 'gro ma, 265
Kham luṅ po, 30
khu ba, 174 sqq.
kun 'dar ma, 175, 247, 291 sq.
kun gyi rnam par śes pa, 48

lha, 43
lha chen po, 216
Lui pa, 200

Na ro pa (*Nādapāda*), 154 sq.
ṅo bo, 51 sq.

'on ba, 174

Padma dkar po, 53
phyag rgyas chen po, 155 sq., 215 sq., 293

raṅ byuṅ, 46 sq.
raṅ bžin, 51 sqq.
raṅ 'tshed ma, 175
rdo rje, 173, *et passim*
rdo rje phag mo, 202, 209
rdo rje 'phren ba, 155

rgyu, 52
rgyud, 41 sqq., 65, 71, 215, 303, *et passim*
rin chen rigs, 175
rluṅ, 155
rnal byor, 30, 36
rnam par śes pa, 47 sqq.
ro ma, 175, 247, 292
ro mñam pa, 176
rten 'brel, 22, 53
rtse gcig, 155
rus pa'i rgyan, 174

śa, 174
śa chen, 174
sems, 30, 44 sqq., *et passim*
śes rab, 170 sqq., 201 sqq., 226, 292
sgam po pa (Gampopa), 50
si hlar, 174
skal ldan, 174
sku grub, 294
sku gsum, 30, 222 sq.
skyes gñis, 175
sṅags, 155
sprul sku, 31, 43, *et passim*
stoṅ pa ñid, 208 sq., 213 sqq., 226, 292

TANJUR (*bstan gyur*), 91 sq., 303
thabs, 175, 201, 208, 212 sq.
thaṅ ka, 133
thar wa, 34, 217, 292
thar wa'i bstan chos, 173
thod pa, 174
thugs, 45 sq.
Tsher mig, 221
tshod ma, 174

yab yum, 175, 207, 212 sq., 296
ye śes, 16, 19, 296, *et passim*
yid, 47 sq.
yid dam, 255

ZHI BA LHA, 255
zuṅ 'jug, 254 sq., 265, 294